Dissertations
in
American Economic History

This is a volume in the Arno Press collection

Dissertations

in

American Economic History

Advisory Editor
Stuart Bruchey

Research Associate
Eleanor Bruchey

*See last pages of this volume
for a complete list of titles.*

A STUDY
OF CAPITAL MOBILIZATION:
THE LIFE INSURANCE INDUSTRY
OF THE NINETEENTH CENTURY

Bruce Michael Pritchett

Revised Edition

ARNO PRESS

A New York Times Company

New York / 1977

Editorial Supervision: LUCILLE MAIORCA

————◦◦◦————

First publication in book form, Arno Press, 1977

DISSERTATIONS IN AMERICAN ECONOMIC HISTORY
ISBN for complete set: 0-405-09900-2
See last pages of this volume for titles.

Manufactured in the United States of America

————◦◦◦————

Library of Congress Cataloging in Publication Data

Pritchett, Bruce Michael.
   A study of capital mobilization.

   (Dissertations in American economic history)
   Originally presented as the author's thesis,
Purdue, 1970.
   Bibliography: p.
   1. Insurance, Life—United States—Finance—
History. 2. Insurance companies—United States—
Investments—History. I. Title. II. Series.
III. Title: Capital mobilization.
HG8957.P74 1977   338.4'3   76-45109
ISBN 0-405-09921-5

PREFACE

This book presents a revision of a dissertation
completed under the direction of Lance E. Davis in 1969.
The focus of the revision has not been to remove all the
foibles which characterize dissertations but rather to
update its empiric basis. This task seemed fundamental
since the hope that motivated completion of the original
was that of creating a complete and accurate record of the
activities of life insurance as a financial intermediary.
Such a hope was perhaps strange for one trained in the
"new" economic history. Perhaps it was strange by any
criterion since Raymond Goldsmith personally advised me
that he had "already done all that."

Nevertheless, it seemed strange to me in particular
then that the Institute of Life Insurance had funded so
many financial studies and had never gotten a satisfactory
one produced featuring its own industry. It also seemed
strange more generally to observe the many heroic efforts
to use advanced theory in ways inappropriate to the data
available rather than engage in the more homely pursuits
needed to generate a more complete basic record at the
outset.

The work which follows was produced to tell its own
story and as an attempt to raise the prevailing standard of

empiric thoroughness to see if, in fact, someone had
"already done all that--" in approaching studies of this
type in the way which was common then and now. Thus, it is
accordingly "revised" to include my latest results.

I appreciate those who have encouraged and helped me
to get this work into print. My wife, Patricia Sunderland
Pritchett, who typed and proofed much of the work and who
provides continuing support deserves particular mention in
this regard as do Lance E. Davis of California Institute of
Technology and Clayne Pope and Larry Wimmer of Brigham
Young University who's own work and friendship have been a
continuing inspiration.

Financial support for the original research was pro-
vided by fellowships from the Krannert School of Industrial
Administration, Purdue University, and through the National
Defense Education Act, Title IV. Continuing work has been
subsidized by the Research Division of Brigham Young
University.

September 1976   B. Michael Pritchett
                                  Brigham Young University
                                  Provo, Utah

A STUDY OF CAPITAL MOBILIZATION,

THE LIFE INSURANCE INDUSTRY OF THE NINETEENTH CENTURY

A Thesis

Submitted to the Faculty

of

Purdue University

by

Bruce Michael Pritchett

In Partial Fulfillment of the

Requirements for the Degree

of

Doctor of Philosophy

January 1970

Revised for Publication, 1976

TABLE OF CONTENTS

LIST OF TABLES

Table   Page

Table		Page

LIST OF FIGURES

ABSTRACT

Pritchett, Bruce Michael. Ph.D., Purdue University, January, 1970. A Study of Capital Mobilization, The Life Insurance Industry of the Nineteenth Century. Major Professor: Lance E. Davis.

This dissertation compiles and examines the financial history of the Life Insurance Industry as a case study of the capital mobilization activities of financial intermediaries in the last century. The Life Insurance Industry, for purposes of the study, is defined as consisting of companies authorized to contract policies on a "legal reserve" basis. The period 1843-1900 is emphasized, and the attempt is made to include the income and asset data of all companies for those years.

The figures for these companies are categorized by type and according to nine geographical regions, and presented as yearly series. The series are based upon company records and upon the reports of states then maintaining regulatory agencies. Previous studies by Professor Lester W. Zartman and the Institute of Life Insurance are also referenced and compared.

Premium income and real estate, mortgage, bond and stock holdings are given detailed presentation by region for the years 1874-1900. The percentage of premium income derived from each region, and the percentage of the four types of assets each contains, is contrasted for each year in the period. These comparisons are intended to give an estimation of the relative regional impact of the financial activies of life

insurance companies. The influx of funds to the insurance centers,

especially into New York City, at the expense of Southern and Far

Western areas is made particularly evident in this connection.

The study does present evidence supporting the traditional view

that the Life Insurance Industry gathered funds from a wide variety

of sources that might not have been as fully tapped otherwise. The

asset portfolios purchased with the accumulated funds, however, are

found to have been distorted, both as to the type of asset purchased

and as to the geographical areas represented. Further, little evidence

is given which would indicate that the life insurance companies

were able to make substantial, direct contributions to major industries

at critical periods in their early growth.

The study suggests that a major cause of distortion in the asset

holdings was the insurance regulation of the time. Further, the laws

which placed the most severe restrictions upon the asset holdings are

characterized as having produced little benefit that could be considered

as having offset their disruptive influence upon the process of capital

mobilization.

INTRODUCTION

A number of economic studies have sought to explain
the American growth experience. Some have sought to de-
scribe various phases of it, others to lend theoretic
rationale. Still others have attempted to generalize upon
the experience in such a way as to provide guidelines for
planners of the present day. One generalization that has
arisen from these efforts is that, as any economy grows and
specializes, a separation develops and enlarges between the
groups of individuals making the separate decisions to save
and to invest. It has been suggested that, over time, this
separation may widen and cause the imperfection with which
accumulated funds are utilized to become ever more acute.

The set of market institutions which an economy develops in this formative period has been said to be critical in providing it with the ability to answer the increasing demands for effective capital mobilization. The extent
to which the United States was able to accumulate and
mobilize large amounts of internal savings has been cited
as one of the reasons it was able to mount and sustain
early industrial growth. The rise of various financial
intermediaries has been given much attention in this connection, often to the extent of citing the intermediaries'
contributions to the development of one or more of America's
basic industries.

It is the writer's opinion that some of the conclusions
that have arisen from the various studies have an inadequate
basis because most of them share at least one common flaw.
While attempting to make assertions about an early and
critical time in American development they have exhibited a
dearth of evidence concerning the period. It matters little
whether one wishes to subscribe to the notion of a "take-
off" period as Rostow does, or to allow that the foundations
of industrialization were laid in a more general time such
as the 1790-1865 interval spoken of by North; it seems that
one must at least conclude that certain vital preconditions
of advanced growth took place prior to 1900. And, having
granted that minimal assertion, anyone wishing to speak of
the role of financial intermediaries in growth must admit to
planting in shallow soil as far as reliable data is con-
cerned. Raymond Goldsmith has suggested: "The second half
of the nineteenth century is the decisive period in the
development of financial intermediaries in the United
States..."[1]

That much effort has been directed toward the history
of financial intermediaries is obvious; nevertheless, one
need not look very hard at even the most impressive studies
to discover the point that is to be made. Consider even the
monumental studies in savings and wealth which have been

---

[1]Raymond W. Goldsmith. Financial Intermediaries in the
American Economy Since 1900. (Princeton, N.J.: Princeton
University Press, 1958), p. 59.

carried out by various scholars associated with the National
Bureau of Economic Research. Table 1, given below, summarizes part of the work that has been done in this connection
for the period prior to 1900, and serves, as much as anything else, to point out the holes in our present understanding. For example, one would be in particular trouble if he
were to attempt to talk about trends in life insurance or
savings and loan institutions from the data to be found
therein.

Purpose of the Study

If the rather substantial resources of the National
Bureau have left some holes in the story of financial intermediation prior to 1900 considerable fortitude would be
needed for one paper to undertake to fill very many of them.
This study has chosen the rather more modest task of choosing one intermediary and attempting to document its history
for the last century as fully as possible with regard to its
role in capital mobilization.

The Life Insurance Industry, as characterized by the
"legal reserve" companies of this country, has been chosen
for detailed examination as a case study in the general
problem of documenting the history of intermediation. This
choice was made partly because level-premium insurance
generates an abundance of the long-term investment funds
essential to growth, and partly because of the need for
empirical justification of several generalizations that have

Table 1 .   Percentage distribution of resources of four main intermediaries by region.[a]

Region	Commercial Bank Deposits		Mutual Savings Bank Deposits		Savings and Loan Assets		Life Insurance Reserves		Combined	
	1850	1900	1850	1900	1850	1900	1850	1900	1850	1900
New England	27.2	9.1	49.6	43.7	-	6.6	-	12.2	29.7	16.1
Middle Atlantic	32.6	43.9	50.4	50.6		33.7		37.1	34.6	43.8
East North Central	7.3	19.4		2.2		34.5		20.5	6.5	17.1
West North Central	1.1	10.7		0.5		4.5		8.7	0.9	8.1
South Atlantic	18.7	5.0		2.9		6.8		8.0	16.6	5.0
East South Atlantic	7.8	2.5				2.5		4.7	6.9	2.3
West South Atlantic	5.3	1.9				4.7		3.8	4.7	2.0
Mountain		2.2				1.6		2.0		1.7
Pacific		5.3				5.1		3.0		4.0
United States	100.0	100.0	100.0	100.0		100.0		100.0	100.0	100.0

[a]Compiled from: Raymond W. Goldsmith, Financial Intermediaries in the American Economy Since 1900 (Princeton, N.J.:Princeton University Press, 1958), pp. 114-115.

arisen from the spate of early insurance biography and folklore concerning the industry's role in the nation's growth.

The financial activities of life insurance companies in the United States have been well documented in original records since the beginning of effective state regulation in 1854 and detailed corporate reports exist even earlier. However, little effort has been made toward organizing the data available and employing it in the context of the capital mobilization problem. The efforts which have been made toward discussing the role of this now imposing intermediary in financing the nation's industrialization and in promoting capital mobility have consisted of conjecture and intuition in much larger part than necessary.

With the foregoing in mind, then, the writer has sought to peruse the rather substantial financial documentation of the insurance industry and compile it as completely as possible as it pertained to capital mobilization. The presentation of the compilation and the manner in which it was accomplished constituted a major goal of this paper. Specific attention was also turned to the legal framework within which the industry was constrained to operate and to various effects that the laws may have had upon the industry's actions. The regional characteristics of the capital flows connected with the collection and investment of insurance funds was also examined. The latter examination, of necessity, took place within a complex legal climate inasmuch as insurance has historically been regulated by the individual states.

Necessity of the Study

A purely practical matter of necessity entered into this particular study. It seemed that, if it was to be undertaken at all, it had to be undertaken quickly. Each additional year of delay would compound the difficulty of the job. For the most part, insurance records have been collected to facilitate regulation, to examine marketing, or for simple business accounting. Items necessary for regulation, and which have been thought valuable by insurance departments, have been compiled and are available from official publications. Those deemed unimportant are not. Industry organizations have compiled many figures. Many of these compilations have emphasized the marketing aspects of the industry. All other records, the uncompiled, the outdated, etc., were rapidly going up in smoke. Many modern insurance departments, companies, and organizations, caught up in the "paper glut" of current business, have instituted systematic records disposal programs. Such a system programs the destruction of all but specified documents over a certain age, into the routine of the institution and is usually very thorough. The Massachusetts and Connecticut Insurance Departments, for example, have instituted such programs.

Other items indicating the necessity of this type of

study have and will be mentioned, but it appears that some
might well question them. The Institute of Life Insurance,
for example, in its compilation of statistics suggests:

> "It was not the objective in pre-
> paring this summary of these historical
> statistics of life insurance to compile
> original statistics for this purpose.
> Rather, the objective was one of evalu-
> ating the available information and
> developing from the known body of mate-
> rial the most consistent and representa-
> tive series of figures. Some of the
> figures presented here are original in
> the sense that they represent adjustments
> of existing figures for errors in addi-
> tion or for omissions. These adjustments
> have been noted beneath each table.
> It might be worthwhile to point out
> some of the improvements that might be
> achieved if one were to compile original
> statistics in this field..."
> "It is felt that while such research
> would represent a valuable contribution
> to the historical statistics of life in-
> surance, the resulting statistics would
> not greatly alter the picture of the
> trend and development of life insurance
> illustrated by the statistics here
> presented."[2]

The Institute's compilation represents most of the
reliable data that is currently available and it will remain
for the reader to determine the accuracy of the above opinion of it, and of any further work in the area.

---

[2]Institute of Life Insurance, The Historical Statistics
of the United States, 1759 to 1958 (New York: Institute of
Life Insurance; 1960), p. 21.

The Institute recognized that in addition to the series which they did choose to compile a fuller accounting could have been made but was not, for reasons which they enumerated.

> "The general procedure in preparing the statistics was to examine the various sources and compare the series available as to bases of reporting, completeness of coverage and so on. In those cases where alternative series were available, the selection was determined by completeness of coverage in terms of the number of companies for which data were obtainable, and basis of reporting most consistent with current practice - on two conditions:
>
> 1. that the series be available for a sufficiently long period to preserve the trend.
>
> 2. that component items could be obtained on the same basis or level of coverage as the totals.
>
> An illustration might make this more clear:
>
> For the period 1879-1887, total assets can be obtained for all the companies operating in New York State. For the same period, totals for a larger group of companies can be obtained from the 1888 Spectator Insurance Year Book. The distribution of assets, by type, however, is available only for the companies operating in New York State. Rather than estimate a distribution for the larger asset totals or report a distribution which would not add to the total shown, the New York State figures were used for the total and for the distribution by type."[3]

The writers of the Institute's report also pointed out various difficulties in insurance data in general as well as

---

[3]Institute of Life Insurance, Historical Statistics..., p. 21.

making other exclusions which they determined desirable.
They suggested that the annual statements filed by the companies were not consistent in form over the entire period.
Further, the reports of some companies known to have been
operating were missing. The companies were not consistent
among themselves in their definitions of the various items
they supplied in their reports.

The writers explained:

> "It is extremely difficult to obtain
> data for any given period on the operations
> of all the life insurance companies operating
> in the United States. Theoretically one
> should be able to compile complete statistics
> by consulting the insurance reports of each
> state and the District of Columbia, but in
> practice this is not feasible. State insurance
> reports began in the 1850s and it was not
> until 1919 (business for the year 1919) that
> all the states (and the District of Columbia)
> were issuing reports.... Until 1919, there-
> fore, there would be no way of obtaining data,
> from the state reports, for companies which
> operated in only those states for which re-
> ports were not available. Subsequent to 1919,
> the difficulties in compiling statistics arise
> from the lack of uniformity in the various
> reports with regard to the selection of items
> to be presented and the basis of reporting and
> from the failure of some states to issue reports
> on a regular annual basis.
> Fortunately the unavailability of complete
> statistics for all companies does not appear
> to be a serious problem. The life insurance
> companies omitted from the sources utilized
> are very small relative to those for which data
> are available, so that even when a fairly large
> number of these very small companies are omit-
> ted they account for a very small percentage
> of the total business."

---

[4] Ibid. p. 18-19.

It may certainly be agreed that the interpretation of a large total based upon a smaller sample introduces the probability of an error in interpretation. One might be inclined to comment, however, that in choosing to present only a partial set of data (as for the 1879-1887 period), the writers of the Institute paper have encouraged an even greater, and unmeasurable, error of interpretation. In ignorance or lacking a better series, their data is often taken to be a complete representation of the total.

For many purposes this probably presents no great problem, but if one wishes to discuss the regional impact of the industry, for example, the very companies that are excluded from the New York figures or even those of the Spectator may well be the ones from specific regions of the country. Further, it does not seem adequate to cite the percentage that the New York data comprises of the Spectator data (as the Institute writers do), nor to extrapolate the fact that, in 1958 the 913 reporting companies constituted 99.7% of the business of all 1362 companies operating that year, back to the earlier period (as they also do). The latter example is obviously not particularly useful and the former gives the impression that the Spectator data represents a full accounting, which it does not. The fact is that, because a more full accounting was "extremely difficult to obtain," the Institute has taken the most available data and assumed that the unknown portion was both small and not significantly different from the known.

The section on methodology outlines this study's approach
to that portion which the Institute deemed, "not feasible."

Preliminary Explanations

It has been found desirable to include a section hereafter which places the whole study in general historical
context, and which deals with a few of its elements more
specifically at the same time. For this reason a few explanations are in order at this point which might otherwise
have been more appropriate in the general discussion of
methodology.

Life Insurance Industry: In tables original to this
paper the industry was treated as though it consisted only
of "Legal Reserve" companies contracting only "Ordinary
Life", and "Endowment" policies, and "Industrial" and "Annuity" business. This concept of the industry excluded "Fraternal", "Co-operative", "Assessment" and other types of
companies. Further, every attempt was made to eliminate the
values attributable to the branches of multiple-line firms
which dealt in insurance of the latter types. In some cases
this principle was used in reverse to include values in the
data which may have been attributable to branches of a
company offering the accepted lines of insurance, even
though the company may have been known principally for
another line of insurance or even for another function
entirely (as in the case of a bank authorized to insure
lives). This process was not difficult, in general, since

regulatory reporting often required separate records to be
kept.

Regulatory Agencies: Regulation of the insurance
industry has historically taken place at the state level.
In some states taxation privileges have been granted to
political subdivisions upon occasion. Such cases generally
included no other privileges, however. In recent years,
each state has had a regularly constituted Insurance Department headed by a Commissioner or Superintendent. Before the
formation of such departments most were still subject to
some general office of the state, such as the Comptroller,
under the provisions of whatever general laws the state may
have had governing financial institutions, or under general
corporate law.

Regions: The concept of a geographical region was
useful in some of the discussions. One of the more difficult parts of the study was the regionalization of railroad
investments. In that connection it was convenient to use
the regions defined in many of the issues of Poor's Manual
of Railroads.[5] These were found to have rather general
application and were used consistently throughout the computations original to this study. The regions are as
follows:

---

[5]H. V. Poor and H. W. Poor, Poor's Manual of the Railroads of the United States (New York: American Bank Note
Company, 1901), p. VI.

Region 1, New England: Maine, New Hampshire, Vermont, Massachusetts, Rhode Island, Connecticut.

Region 2, Middle Atlantic: New York, New Jersey, Pennsylvania, Delaware, Maryland, District of Columbia.

Region 3, Central Northern: Ohio, Michigan, Indiana, Illinois, Wisconsin.

Region 4, South Atlantic: Virginia, West Virginia, North Carolina, South Carolina, Georgia, Florida.

Region 5, Gulf and Mississippi Valley: Alabama, Mississippi, Tennessee, Kentucky, Louisiana.

Region 6, Southwestern: Missouri, Arkansas, Texas, Kansas, Colorado, New Mexico, Oklahoma (Oklahoma Territory, Indian Country).

Region 7, Northwestern: Iowa, Minnesota, Nebraska, North Dakota, South Dakota, Wyoming, Montana.

Region 8, Pacific: Washington, Oregon, California, Nevada, Idaho, Arizona, Utah.

Region 9, Foreign: All areas not otherwise specified.

These subdivisions obviously did not exist in the 1900 configuration throughout the entire period. Luckily, railroad rails and other investment items are not as given to change as the political winds. Any use of the regions was made as though the boundaries existed throughout the period as they did in 1940.

HISTORICAL CONTEXT

The more biographical parts of life insurance history
are probably among the best chronicled in business and financial history. The following material is not included with
the intent of contributing greatly to this body of history.
Rather, this section presents a brief historical account,
together with those specific events and conditions, which
serve to provide to other portions of the study with a more
meaningful context. Items which may be more conveniently
presented in the form of historical narrative will also
appear, as will other items the sort thought to be useful
in interpreting other parts of the presentation.

The Early Years

The earliest policies issued in the United States insuring the lives of persons were written by the American
branches of foreign companies, principally from England.
These policies were most often issued against the possibility of accidental death in the course of travel by sea and
often were written upon the human cargo of slave ships.

The Corporation for the Relief of Poor and Distressed
Presbyterian Ministers and of the Poor and Distressed Widows
and Children of Presbyterian Ministers (now called, Presbyterian Minister's Fund) was the first domestic company to

issue policies. It is still operating from its office on
Rittenhouse Square in Philadelphia. The fund was founded
for pious purposes and issued its first policy May 22, 1761.
Its initial capital came from the contributions of people
sharing the purposes of the founding religious organization.
This did not, however, prevent the organization from obtaining a sound basis in investment assets. As the company's
biography puts it, "One of the immediate concerns of the
Corporation was the profitable investment of its capital as
fast as it was paid in.... These, up until the time of the
revolution, were exclusively in Bonds or in Bonds and
Mortgages."[1]

The size of the fund's assets was never such to make it
of major importance from the standpoint of capital mobilization, but its basic investment policies were characteristic
of the early period. By 1840 several other companies had
been formed. These included:

The Episcopal Corporation (1769), the Insurance Company
of North America (1794), The Pennsylvania Company for Insurance on Lives and Annuities (1812), Massachusetts Hospital
Life Insurance Company (1818), the Baltimore Life Insurance
Company (1830), The New York Life Insurance and Trust Company
(1831), New England Mutual Life Insurance Company (1835),

---

[1] Alexander Mackie. _Facile Princeps_ (Lancaster, Pa.:
Lancaster Press, 1956), p. 143.

Girard Life Insurance Annuity and Trust Company (1836).
The author has prepared estimates of the character of the
business of these companies based upon fragmentary accounts,
the more complete portions of their reports as submitted to the pre-insurance-department regulatory agencies,
and the estimates of other writers of their actions. These
estimates are not included here, however, because of their
tentative nature as compared with the rest of the data presented herein. For purposes of this study the early actions
of these companies were not significant for the most part.[2]
Most either failed outright or did not pursue the life insurance provisions of their charters.

It is not until the formation of companies based on the
mutual principle that the industry really began to flourish.

---

[2]For some exceptions see: Lance E. Davis. "The New England
Textile Mills and the Capital Markets," The Journal of Economic
History, XX (March, 1960), pp. 1-30, and Lance E. Davis,
"Stock ownership in the early New England textile Industry,"
Business History Review, XXXII (1958), pp. 204-22.

Table 2. Growth of American Life Insurance, 1759-1900[3]

Year	Number of Companies	Year	Insurance in Force (Millions)
1759	1	--	--
1769	2	--	--
1800	4	--	--
1820	5	1815	.037
		1820	.092
		1825	.161
1830	9	1830	.600
		1835	2.75
1840	15	1840	4.69
		1845	14.
1850	45	1850	96.
		1855	125.
1860	43	1860	205.
		1865	622.
1870	129	1870	2,013.
		1875	1,875.
1880	59	1880	1,536.
		1885	2,058.
1890	60	1890	3,522.
		1895	5,002.
1900	84	1900	7,656.

The Mutuals

The coming of mutual life insurance marks the beginning
of life insurance as a viable engine for promoting savings
and investment. The idea of participating in the ownership
and profits of the insuring company had great appeal to the
public and seemed to raise insurance from the class of a
simple wager against one's own longevity to the standing of
a secure investment in their minds. The table above reveals

----

[3]J. Owen Stalson. Marketing Life Insurance (Cambridge,
Mass.: Harvard University Press, 1942), pp. 748-52, 816-17.

the great growth, both in insurance in force and in the
number of operating companies, which the mutual principle
initiated in the decade of the forties. The Mutual Life
Insurance Company of New York, New York Life, New England
Life, Connecticut Mutual, Penn Mutual, Mutual Benefit Life
and other major companies began their rise to prominence
during this period.[4]

Though several companies had failed prior to the great
success of the so-called "Mutual Era," the small number of
companies and insured persons involved had not yet provided
a spectacular contraction of the sort which followed in
later years. Even what has been referred to as the "first
bubble era" did not involve major companies. "The first
'bubble era' in our Life Insurance history may be said to
have ended with the close of the year of 1850. From then to
1857 only about a dozen new companies were started. More
than half of them failed after a brief experience but the
failures were due to efforts to start companies in Southern
and Western states where business was not yet sufficient to
sustain them."[5]

---

[4] See Appendix B for a listing of the incorporation
dates of all companies of the period.
[5] Charles Kelley Knight. "The History of Life Insurance
in the United States to 1870, With an Introduction to Its
Development Abroad." A thesis presented to the faculty of
the Graduate School in partial fulfillment of the requirements for the degree of Doctor of Philosophy (Philadelphia,
Pa., The University of Pennsylvania, 1920) p. 115.

Sales Promotion

The appeal of the mutual policies themselves ought not
to be overrated. The mutual companies brought with them a
dynamic leadership which launched many of the principles of
sales promotion which persist today. Principles which seem
to have greatly encouraged savings among lower income families and to have effectively made these previously untapped
savings available for investment, at least this is an idea
that has enjoyed a great deal of space in the insurance
press over the years.

> "One important reason for the great
> capital accumulation in this country has
> been the highly efficient machinery for
> collecting and investing savings. In this
> regard, life insurance has been a truly
> effective instrument. It has tended to
> stimulate saving through the selling efforts
> of a large agency force; it has gathered
> together and loosed the individual small
> savings of millions which would otherwise
> have been of limited productive use. In
> the countries of the Far East, savings
> take place but there is little or no effec-
> tive mechanism for collecting these savings,
> loosing them, and directing them into pro-
> ductive investment. Instead, they find
> their way into sterile use--i.e., hoards
> under mattresses, gold and silver, precious
> stones, etc. Life insurance has also
> notably increased the mobility of savings,
> from one section of the country to another,
> from one industry to another..."[1]

The specific citation just used is of fairly recent
origin but is not unlike many others from all periods of

---

[1]George T. Conklin, Jr. "A Century of Life Insurance
Management," Investment of Life Insurance Funds, David
McCahan, Ed. (Philadelphia: The University of Pennsylvania
Press, 1953). p. 247.

insurance history. It represents a notion worthy of more
detailed notice. If this intermediary did, in fact, garner
savings that would have otherwise been unavailable for
investment, it would seem that its importance as a mobilizer
of funds would be largely established on those grounds
alone. Further, objections which have or might be raised to
the appropriateness of the various uses of these funds would
be blunted to the extent that the industry had performed a
unique function.

Various items that may help in assessing the plausibil-
ity of this notion will be discussed in the next several
pages.

With the rise of person-to-person solicitation, and the
innovations which accompanied it, the number of policies
contracted increased dramatically. Life insurance agents
were not unique to the "Mutual Era". William Bard, president of New York Life Insurance and Trust Company, had used
agents in 1831. But, since the firm did many things other
than sell insurance, these early agents seemed to have
mainly become involved in arranging and buying mortgages in
behalf of the company. The early agents of other companies
seem to have been content to transact their business by the
more "respectable" method of waiting at their agencies for
customers.

Active solicitation, in the sense we think of it today,
seems to have gotten its start with the mutual companies of
the early forties. As this highly successful technique

evolved in the few ensuing years the agents began to receive advice and training on how to handle customers and overcome objections. Sales manuals were introduced and many of the techniques currently intended to encourage sales, competition, and "team spirit" became common. Agents were often assigned specific areas to work; other times they moved freely about the state. By 1859 agents had become sufficiently common that Northwestern included in its "Instructions for the Government of Agents and Positions" a section answering the already common complaint of their men, "there are so many agents for Life Assurance in the place."[2]

Table 3. Number of Agents Employed, 1860-1865.[3]

Year	New York	Elsewhere	Total
1860	647	1243	1890
1861	690	1303	1912
1862	701	1745	2446
1863	832	2119	2951
1864	881	2631	3512
1865	1049	3146	4195

[2]Harold F. Williamson and Orange A. Smalley, Northwestern Mutual Life (Evanston, Ill.: Northwestern University Press, 1957), p. 37.

[3]New York Insurance Department, Annual Report of the Superintendent of the Insurance Department of the State of New York (New York: Charles Van Benthuysen, printer, 1860-66). The table is a digest of all agents reported by companies in their individual filings with the New York department during these years.

The flourish caused in the industry by the new mutual policies in the forties and by the Tontine policies (to be discussed hereafter) of the sixties brought great demands for agents.

"...Successful agents of a company were made attractive offers of double the commission rates and substantial money advances by other companies and frequently a general agent would go over to another company with his entire field force. [A general agent was semiautonomous, hired his own agents, and contracted to sell the parent firm's insurance] thus, the New York Life received notice one morning that their entire Manhattan office consisting of a general agent and over two hundred agents had gone over to Equitable."[4]

The situation of the agent was not quite as bright as first appears, however. The ever-increasing competition for new customers caused agents to make common use of the practice of offering substantial premium rebates. Often the higher commission rates were largely offset in this way.

The missionary zeal which company officials tried to instill was not directed only at their employees. In a real burst of fervor the president of Berkshire Life declared to his policyholders, "Every policyholder should be a missionary of Life Insurance to aid in extending its benefits to others

---

[4]Douglass C. North, "The Large Life Insurance Companies Before 1906," Doctoral Dissertation (Berkeley, Calif: University of California at Berkeley, 1952), p. 20.

whose families need the protection. It is earnestly desired
that each one will use his exertions to promote the interests and extend the business of the Company. If every mem-
ber will secure but one other, the business of the Company
would be rapidly increased, and the benefits of Life Insurance become widely spread."[5]

The business of the companies did become widely spread.
The extent of this dispersion may be seen for the later
years in the section on regional income and investment.
Even many smaller companies achieved a wide field of opera-
tion relatively early. Note, for example, the experience of
Union Mutual Life Insurance Company in Table 4 given below.

"The Tontine Revolution"

A discussion of the rise of active solicitation and
competition should probably not be left without mention of
Henry B. Hyde, who has been called, "the prime mover and best
embodiment of the post Civil War Life Insurance business."[1]
Henry worked for the Mutual of New York until he reached the
position of cashier at age twenty-five. At that time he asked
advice of the Company's president in forming a new company to
write policies for those customers then being turned away by
Mutual's $10,000 per person limit. His resignation was

---

[5]Berkshire Life Insurance Company, Annual Report.
(Worchester, Mass: Berkshire Life Insurance Company, 1867),
Introductory Statement by Thomas F. Plunkett, President.
[1]Morton Keller, The Life Insurance Enterprise (Cambridge,
Mass: Harvard University Press, 1963), p. 16.

Table 4 . Claims paid by Union Mutual Life Insurance Company[a].

Year	Region 1	Region 2	Region 3	Region 4	Region 5	Region 6	Region 7	Region 8	Region 9
1851	$17,450	$12,000	$9,500		$ 1,000	$1,200	$1,000	$400	$2,500
1852	30,466	24,442	2,180		600	2,500			1,600
1853	25,800	17,600	4,426		500	1,000			500
1854	26,025	17,700	3,800			1,600			
1855	22,056	9,300	8,700		12,000				
1856	24,822	35,000	7,000			8,200			
1857	13,605	8,681	5,560		9,650	8,900	1,150		2,000
1858	13,600	2,000	4,000		9,580	963			2,791
1859	4,100	11,500	10,146		5,000	5,000	1,500		8,344
1860	36,000	9,000	2,600		1,000	2,800			
1861	23,800	14,560	6,350		2,800	7,500			3,300
1862	49,425	14,100	4,000		3,000	8,000			6,000

[a]Union Mutual Life Insurance Company, Annual Statement (Boston:Union Mutual Life Insurance Company, 1851-1862.) These values were computed from the reportings of claims paid by state.

promptly accepted. Undaunted, Hyde took rooms on the floor above the Mutual and immediately hung a sign larger than his former employer's. Within a week Equitable Life Assurance Company was launched. In the ten years following its inception in 1859, it moved to first place in annual sales. In the early years Hyde devoted all his energy and money to the development of an elaborate field force. He increased the pay of his agents by raising their commission rates, circularized them with suggestions for more aggressive methods of reaching every insurable person, and continuously traveled throughout the country to improve and expand agency organization."[2]

Hyde's innovations no doubt stimulated his sales force at least as much as his admonitions. In 1868 Henry B. Hyde rediscovered Lorenzo Tonti and came out with what was then announced as "the greatest reform thus far promulgated by any life-insurance company;"[3] - Tontine insurance. The new policies essentially reversed the traditional Life insurance "bet" in that the insured person wagered that he would not meet an untimely end. The policies generally provided that any person who died would receive the face value of his policy. Any person who's insurance lapsed would forfeit his payments. Those who lived beyond the termination of the

---

[2]See: Douglass C. North, "Capital Accumulation in Life Insurance Between the Civil War and the Investigation of 1905," Men in Business, William Miller, Ed. (Cambridge, Mass.: Harvard University Press, 1952), p. 245.
[3]Carlyle Buley, Vol. I of The American Life Convention (New York: Appleton-Century-Crofts, Inc., 1953), p. 93.

policy would receive, in addition to the bargained for
insurance, their share of accrued dividends and lapsed policies. In this way the "new" insurance combined with traditional coverage many benefits of mutual policies plus the
promise of extra dividends and the spice of a wager. The
agents and policies were backed by newspaper advertisements
and articles, by posters and sales booklets. The competition
for sales and agents flourished. By 1905, the four largest
companies using Tontine policies had contracted $5,774,000,000
in new business, whereas, the five largest companies using
traditional annual dividend insurance had only $998,000,000,
total, in force.

"The rank of "The Equitable" among all
American companies, as to new business done
since its organization, stands as follows:

In 1860 it was the ninth
In 1861 it was eighth
In 1862 and 1863 the seventh
In 1864 and 1865 the sixth
In 1866 the fourth
In 1867 the third
In 1868 the second.

The cash premium income of the Equitable
Life, for the year ending December 31, 1868,
its ninth year, ($4,479,196.61) exceeds that
of any company organized during the past
twenty years.
It is a very simple matter to account
for this surprising growth of the Equitable
as compared with that of a large majority of
other companies. It is emphatically "The
People's Company." All of its profits go
to the assured. Its cash plan-its annual
dividends of profits-its plan of returning
to each policy-holder precisely the sum
that belongs to him-are all easily understood by the public and fully appreciated.

> While the "Stock" companies pay all
> profits to stockholders, and the "Mixed"
> companies pay enormous sums to stockholders
> -the Equitable pays all profits to policy-
> holders."[4]

When the "Tontine Revolution" is viewed in the context
in which it has just been presented (and this seems to be
the traditional approach), a distorted impression may be left
with the reader. Reference to a table covering a longer
period, like Table 2 rather than to the more commonly used
Table 5, will disclose that the "Mutual Era" produced results
at least as impressive. Note especially the relative
growth in the number of companies in the decade of the forties
and the relatively stable period following, as compared with
the decade of the sixties and the disasterous seventies. A
similar comparison may be made using the data for insurance
in force. Even such a brief examination should suggest a
closer look at the traditional interpretation of the "Tontine
Revolution".

Referring back to the illustration of the vast amount
of insurance placed by the four largest Tontine companies as
contrasted with the five largest traditional companies, one
might look at "the hole as well as the doughnut". Connecticut Mutual Life, Mutual Benefit Life, and other mutual com-

---

[4]Equitable Life Insurance Company, Annual Report (New
York:Equitable Life Insurance Company, 1869).

Table 5 . Ordinary insurance in force with American Life Companies (All plans
combined)[a].

Years	Number Companies	Number of Policies	Amount of Insurance	Average Policy
1870	59	653,023	$1,752,950,105	$2,684
1871	58	726,496	1,903,050,035	2,619
1782	59	754,675	1,996,653,057	2,646
1873	56	801,598	2,060,147,923	2,570
1874	50	763,201	1,912,991,814	2.507
1875	45	774,625	1,922,043,146	2,481
1876	38	706,179	1,735,995,190	2,458
1877	34	633,096	1,556,105,323	2,458
1878	34	612,843	1,480,921,223	2,416
1879	31	595,486	1,439,961,165	2,418
1880	30	608,681	1,475,994,672	2,425
1881	29	627,265	1,539,848,581	2,455
1882	29	661,458	1,637,648,872	2,476
1883	29	705,659	1,763,730,015	2,499
1884	29	750,567	1,870,728,059	2,492
1885	29	814,691	2,023,517,487	2,483
1886	29	848,481	2,222,413,051	2,619
1887	29	929,853	2,474,507,120	2,661
1888	29	1,021,631	2,761,577,128	2,703
1889	30	1,139,894	3,144,677,311	2,759
1890	46	1,311,253	3,610,603,933	2,754
1891	48	1,452,234	3,954,587,616	2,723
1392	51	1,595,965	4,306,528,303	2,698
1893	51	1,739,947	4,625,202,612	2,658
1894	50	1,829,527	4,748,456,084	2,595
1895	52	1,940,908	4,917,688,210	2,534
1896	53	2,032,567	5,055,949,508	2,487
1897	53	2,204,601	5,330,478,062	2,418
1898	54	2,419,818	5,714,959,068	2,362
1899	63	2,822,854	6,481,523,963	2,296
1900	69	3,170,208	7,090,141,189	2,236

[a]Frederich L. Hoffman, "Fifty Years of American Life Insurance Progress,"
Publications of the American Statistical Association, XII (September, 1911),
722.

panies were among the very largest when the revolution
began, but slipped badly in relative status thereafter. The
steadfast position of such men as Mr. Greene, President of
Connecticut Mutual Life, in denouncing the new insurance as
immoral and unsound did not change the realities of the
tastes of the public.

The trends in assets and income in the two decades
after the introduction of the Tontine policies, as revealed
in Table 14 and Table 61 suggest the same sorts of trends
that appeared in the number of companies and insurance in
force. The serious retrenchment that took place in the
industry is muted in the asset series because of inclusion
of companies from all parts of the country, and by a convention of construction which includes assets held by inactive
corporations until such are disposed of by sale (Refer to
the section on methodology).

The competition between companies handling various
types of policies accounts for only part of the problem
encountered in the seventies, of course. One of the most
protracted depressions in the nation's history occurred
during most of the decade. This will be discussed further
in another connection; as will the state of the insurance
regulations and the large number of new companies of the
period. Suffice it to say that the combined effects of hard
times and various innovations produced a revolution like
many others - many dead, many wounded, and a "victory" for
some survivors.

The success of the agents in placing their policies was largely a result of the large, future rewards that they were able to promise their clients. The passage of time proved many of these promises to have been inflated and the predictable public outcry arose when they were not realized. This was compounded by the failure of many smaller "assessment," and "co-operative," companies. These had been largely unregulated in many states. Together, these conditions brought a legacy of distrust and indignation that was reflected in a great many publications of the day. Almost every insurance superintendent wrote a version of the following denunciation. The Kentucky version makes the most colorful reading.

> "The nefarious system of speculative insurance, which has grown up so rapidly in some of our neighboring States and spread its baleful influence over the whole Union, has lately met with more than one severe check, notably in Pennsylvania, the home and birth-place of the most infamous of the foul brood.
> Kentucky has not escaped unharmed from the depredations of these defiant lawbreakers and swindlers, especially in certain of the mountain counties. The Commissioner trusts to do something, with the assistance of the Attorney General and Commonwealth's Attorneys, toward hunting down and driving out of our borders these unprincipled and shameless violators of the law."[5]

---

[5]Insurance Bureau of Kentucky, Annual Report of the Commissioner of the Insurance Bureau of Kentucky to the Auditor of Public Accounts (Frankfort, Ky.: Kentucky Yeoman, 1881), p. VIII.

The Policyholders

A direct test of the hypothesis that, the Life Insurance Industry mobilized the funds of large numbers of small or reluctant savers that would not have been reached otherwise, seems difficult to devise. In the absence of such a test it seems that something must at least be said about the persons who bought the policies, about the cost of the policies, and about the policies themselves. The facts concerning these minimal items, at least, ought not to contradict the hypothesis.

In its early Annual Reports the New England Mutual Life Insurance Company expressed continuing pride over the high quality of the risks covered by its policies. To substantiate its claim the company consistently recorded the vocations of its policy holders. If we may accept the company's appraisal of its business, then we may assume that a sample of the policyholders of all companies would yield a group no more elite than that found in Table 6.

Ideally, one would hope to be able to draw a sample of the original policies from the earlier years to compare with the figures in Table 6. Since no satisfactory sample was obtainable the table must largely be taken at face value, except for a few comparisons offered by fragments of data from other companies. See Table 7 for a comparison based upon the

Table   6 .   Occupaions of New Policyholders, New England Mutual Life Insurance Company.[a]

	1846	1847	1848	1849	1850	1851	1852	1853	1854	1855	1855
Clerks	100	25	40	30	20	22	49	43	48	53	63
Merchants, traders and brokers	403	135	154	122	90	136	118	154	187	221	289
Agents and superintendents		5	16	12	7	11	9	11	16	21	29
Bank, Insurance and Railroad Officers	14	15	14	14	14	5	6	12	12	13	27
Farmers	49	22	23	18	13	4	23	16	13	9	5
Miners											
Manufacturers	87	29	34	26	17	28	33	29	32	35	29
Lawyers	87	16	28	22	16	7	11	24	22	19	19
Physicians	53	20	13	13	13	5	13	11	11	12	19
Engineers and Machinists	31	18	12	11	9	6	16	16	11	6	12
Mechanics	157	38	77	55	33	47	94	38	30	21	51
Females	22	8	21	15	9	9	19	15	16	17	22
Teachers	59	16	12	9	5	9	8	10	10	9	21
Government Officers	31	7	8	10	13	6	12	4	7	10	6
Clergymen	69	21	17	15	13	14	14	16	15	15	17
Editors and Publishers	53	11	16	12	7	1	6	5	4	4	3
Students	89	30	19	16	15	7	4	11	13	16	11
No Occupation	6	3									7
Expressmen and Conductors	5	4									
Mariners	27	15	20	24	27	14	29	24	27	19	9
Miscellaneous	21	28	33	24	14	12	24	17	17	16	22
Total	1363	466	557	448	335	343	488	456	491	516	666

Table 6 . (Continued)

	1857	1858	1859	1860	1861	1862	1863	1864	1865	1866	1867
Clerks	56	83	110	156	145	190	233	277	329	332	335
Merchants, traders and brokers	205	309	414	557	323	431	461	497	680	724	969
Agents and superintendents	15	24	32	48	29	36	45	55	59	105	152
Bank, insurance and Railroad Officers	19	19	19	30	26	38	50	62	70	61	53
Farmers	10	18	27	35	24	26	31	35	139	217	290
Miners											
Manufacturers	46	44	42	64	46	43	68	92	171	181	192
Lawyers	22	36	49	37	34	59	54	49	53	69	85
Physicians	18	16	13	33	20	42	43	44	61	66	71
Engineers and Machinists	9	14	19	28	25	23	32	40	42	48	54
Mechanics	31	56	88	125	79	240	277	313	435	596	856
Females	12	14	16	22	12	15	17	20	50	103	155
Teachers	11	16	22	29	22	43	36	30	29	45	62
Government Officers	9	9	8	11	83	23	24	25	27	57	87
Clergymen	12	19	26	24	21	22	35	48	51	68	85
Editors and Publishers	2	5	7	18	10	12	10	7	7	19	30
Students.	11	15	18	35	22	23	15	7	17	38	43
No Occupation			4	17	13	12	6		23	30	36
Expressmen and Conductors	5	5	5	16	9	12	13	14	19	23	26
Mariners	10	15	20	29	15	39	36	32	28	55	82
Miscellaneous	29	48	68	74	42	35	53	71	109	141	176
Total	532	765	1007	1388	1003	1364	1539	1718	2399	2978	3839

Table 6 . (Continued)

	1868	1869	1870	1871	1872	1873	1874	1875	1876	1877	1878
Clerks	521	453	359	283	269	255	286	289	274	241	203
Merchants, Traders and Brokers	1373	1065	741	741	586	573	545	581	581	580	456
Agents and Superintendents	266	255	166	167	150	107	118	94	106	103	82
Bank, Insurance and Railroad Officers	75	94	75	47	64	31	37	31	62	75	41
Farmers	624	573	519	341	336	196	118	94	80	76	57
Miners						21	48	21	17		
Manufacturers	393	178	115	220	191	143	132	96	122	152	136
Lawyers	105	106	68	65	48	39	48	60	46	50	66
Physicians	146	101	76	53	76	49	35	39	46	60	44
Engineers and Machinists	98	147	143	88	106	45	52	39	30	39	40
Mechanics	1083	1182	884	594	552	344	268	190	176	223	107
Females	159	52	34	64	37	42	41	39	39	40	44
Teachers	83	64	43	43	22	19	11	19	16	25	10
Government Officers	79	57	50	28	42	16	32	16	32	30	20
Clergymen	115	51	50	17	42	26	26	23	29	21	28
Editors and Publishers	41	34	28	28	22	12	16	22	26	19	24
Students	30	34	11	22	17	9	12	14	13	15	7
No Occupation	50	51	55	51	26	21	11	5	12	23	13
Expressmen and Conductors	51	62	40	54	51	9	33	21	25	16	8
Mariners	117	81	91	55	51	36	26	34	22	34	16
Miscellaneous	282	123	15	12	109	63	64	52	37	49	51
Total	5691	4763	3563	2979	2761	2056	1959	1780	1791	1871	1453

Table   6   .   (Continued)

	1879	1880	1881	1882	1883	1884	1885	1886	1887	1888	1889
Clerks	226	282	289	336	383	398	413	396	442	587	730
Merchants, Traders and Brokers	483	589	637	603	726	722	717	731	720	954	1090
Agents and Superintendents	99	141	121	150	252	261	270	245	256	269	298
Bank, Insurance and Railroad Officers	74	59	98	137	87	100	113	121	117	128	127
Farmers	33	47	73	83	82	85	88	134	124	135	145
Miners											
Manufacturers	121	165	155	87	158	153	147	181	168	162	192
Lawyers	69	74	91	86	103	97	91	97	101	104	161
Physicians	33	44	50	55	98	89	81	70	99	117	113
Engineers and Machinists	28	42	61	35	48	54	61	43	52	58	62
Mechanics	106	131	103	130	188	173	158	142	179	193	285
Females	42	63	51	67	77	82	86	73	64	98	149
Teachers	9	11	10	27	34	37	41	28	52	38	60
Government Officers	18	26	29	6	12	18	25	26	33	53	22
Clergymen	17	22	28	37	42	38	35	50	49	69	66
Editors and Publishers	22	15	29	27	35	38	42	46	41	32	40
Students	11	10	12	18	24	17	11	11	24	26	21
No Occupation	16	7	10	8	14	10	5	8	7	4	8
Expressmen and Conductors	2	10	20	6	15	18	23	20	20	31	40
Mariners	11	10	7	8	9	12	14	5	7	9	1
Miscellaneous	66	52	135	140	125	116	107	92	154	203	87
Total	1486	1800	2009	2046	2512	2518	2528	2519	2699	3570	3697

Table 6 . (Continued)

	1890	1891	1892	1893	1894	1895	1896	1897	1898	1899	1900
Clerks	769	891	817	788	888	989	963	1181	1264	1442	1550
Merchants, Traders and Brokers	1019	1013	994	827	870	911	859	1057	936	1127	1163
Agents and Superintendents	336	329	339	329	352	374	375	616	467	392	374
Bank, Insurance and Railroad Officers	122	29	79	84	94	104	102	247	199	306	371
Farmers	150	214	206	211	236	161	126	179	217	219	227
Miners									191	217	209
Manufacturers	194	193	179	135	174	213	140	221	281	206	205
Lawyers	123	135	113	111	128	143	130	139	178	184	198
Physicians	122	125	136	118	138	158	157	202	184	165	189
Engineers and Machinists	82	88	103	65	82	119	103	120	179	156	180
Mechanics	349	92	318	434	435	436	398	496	397	248	180
Females	122	104	111	88	81	75	72	141	101	105	103
Teachers	60	74	71	66	72	78	96	91	78	96	83
Government Officers	26	8	27	17	19	21	20	44	53	66	71
Clergymen	71	65	81	64	67	71	60	81	97	56	50
Editors and Publishers	30	21	38	32	37	41	33	40	46	33	39
Students	28	34	20	18	33	48	39	37	42	39	36
No Occupation	8	7	11	7	8	9	6	14	19	16	34
Expressmen and Conductors	34	1	30	26	31	37	21	23	26	17	24
Mariners	2	12	16	18	22	9	10	22	35	33	11
Miscellaneous	80	173	27	39	45	51	54	145	146	73	29
Total	3727	3608	3716	3477	3812	4048	3764	5096	5136	5196	5326

a Compiled from: New England Mutual Life Insurance Company, Annual Statement (Boston:New England Life Insurance Company, 1846-1900).

Table 7 . Occupations of New Policyholders[a].

_____

Merchants & Traders[b]	1,213
Mechanics	369
Lawyers	194
Clerks	263
Clergymen	93
Physicians	105
Druggists & Apothecaries	22
Ladies	95
Gentlemen	32
Cashiers of Banks	29
Brokers	84
Booksellers	41
Manufacturers	151
Professors in Colleges	14
Teachers	54
Secretaries of Companies	14
Engineers	14
Agents	50
Editors	13
Cartmen	7
Presidents of Companies	6
Students	52
Hotel Keepers	20
Farmers	72
Officers, U.S. Army & Navy	54
Shipmasters	20
Laborers	7
Millers	10
Bank Tellers	13
Other Occupations	109
Total	3,220

[a]The Mutual Life Insurance Company of New York, Annual Report (New York: The New York Life Insurance Company, 1848), p. 5.

[b]The categories represent the policies contracted from The Company's Commencement, February, 1843, to the close of its fourth year, January 31, 1847.

policies issued by the Mutual Life Insurance Company of New
York during the first five years of its business.

Both of the tables represent the business of Eastern
companies but each did substantial business in much of the
rest of the country. The compilations do not seem to reveal
the great differences in composition that the early New
England Mutual officials might have liked to have seen, suggesting
that Table 6 might be quite representative. On the other
hand, some of the less established companies, in their fight
to obtain sales, may have taken significantly poorer risks.
Table 6 and Table 7 seem to reflect some bias in favor of the
more monied classes; classes who would presumably be know-
ledgable enough to engage in some form of saving, other than
hoarding, if insurance had not been available. On the other
hand, for even the earliest periods, these tables also suggest
a surprisingly broad, popular base. One would likely not
want to take issue with life insurance as a popular intermediary
on the basis of these lists of policyholders.

Popular Insurance Expenditures

Another approach to disconfirming the possibility of
a large popular base in the early Life Insurance Industry
would be to show that the policies that were purchased were
too expensive to have been generally held. At this point,
recall that the policies of "industrial", "assessment", "fraternal",
and "co-operative" companies were generally much smaller and

much less expensive in absolute terms. Such policies did not
constitute a significant part of the insurance picture until
after 1875 (Table 8); but to the extent that they were held
in any year, the size of the average policy and payment would
be reduced. Also, the term of the payment might be much less.
For example, many industrial policies had weekly premiums
collected by officers of the policyholder's employer; whereas,
many traditional policies had yearly premiums which were to
be sent in regularly by the policyholder, without notification
by the insuring company.

Table 9 presents the average payment due upon all
policies of legal-reserve companies (except industrial). Of
course, the mortality table yields various premium rates
according to the age of the insured. Rather than compute the
table for a range of ages an attempt was made to arrive at the
age of the average policy holder in the early period. Several
computations were made based upon the fragmentary data
available. Each of these indicated a mean and median age of
about thirty-five for the most common policyholder. As representative of these computations, consider the following.
The average policholder of New England Mutual Life Insurance
in the period 1847-60 was 30-35 years.[1] The First Annual

---

[1]Lance E. Davis, "United States Financial Intermediaries
in the Early Nineteenth Century: Four Case Studies, "Doctoral
Dissertation (Baltimore:John Hopkins University, 1956), computed
from data on p. 308.

Table 8 . Life Insurance in Force in the United States Types as Percentages of Total.[a]

Year	U.S. Business of Regular U.S. Life Companies	U.S. Business of European Companies	Fraternal	Assessment	U.S. Business of Canadian Companies	War Risk and U.S. Government Insurance
1815	100.000					
1820	100.000					
1825	100.000					
1830	100.000					
1835	100.000					
1840	100.000					
1845	97.90	2.10				
1850	98.97	1.03				
1855	92.59	7.41				
1860	95.35	4.65				
1865	98.73	1.27				
1870	99.85	0.15				
1875	99.89	0.11				
1880	78.16	0.06	21.78			
1885	55.64	0.00	44.36		0.01	
1890	53.59	0.00	46.40		0.04	
1895	47.57	0.17	52.22		0.10	
1900	54.71	0.05	42.43	2.71		

[a] J. Owen Stalson, Marketing Life Insurance, Its History in America (Cambridge, Massachusetts: Harvard University Press, 1942), p. 818.

Table 9 . Average premiums and policy size.

Year	No. of policies	Average policy size	Premium[g] partici- pating	Premium non-part- cipitating	Changed by	Ave. yearly premium	N.N.P. per capita
1843[a]	114	$4,348	$27.50		Mut. of N.Y.[c]	$120-	$107[e]
1844	214	3,714	26.60		N. Eng. Mut.	99-	
1845	580	3,506					
1846	1,193	2,978	24.00		State Mut.	71-	
1847	1,516	2,882	27.50		Conn. Mut.	79-	
1848	1,861	2,616					
1849	2,797	2,576	27.50		Hope Mut.	71-	
1850	3,032	2,449	27.50	$18.40	Hart. L.&T.	67-45	135
1851	2,739	2,396	27.50	21.30	Chart. Oak	66-51	
1852	1,867	2,665					
1853	2,259	2,622					
1854	2,753	2,780					
1855	2,614	2,992					
1856	3,476	2,853					
1857	4,135	2,804					
1858	5,254	2,930					
1859[b]	49,608	2,852					
1860	56,046	2,921	26.73	23.54	N.Y. companies[d]	67-59	158
1861	57,202	2,889	27.50	22.20	N.Y. Life	79-64	
1862	65,252	2,819					
1863	98,015	2,729					
1864	146,729	2,697					
1865	209,392	2,774	26.87		Mut. of N.Y.	75-	
1866	305,390	2,833					
1867	401,140	2,896					
1868	537,594	2,844	26.38		Mut. of N.Y.	75-	147[f]
1869	656,572	2,797					147
1870	747,807	2,707	26.22	20.44	N.Y. companies	71-55	147
1871	785,360	2,678					147
1872	804,444	2,629	26.26		Conn. Mut.	69-	147
1873	817,081	2,552					147
1874	799,534	2,498					147-169
1875	774,625	2,481					147-169
1876	706,179	2,458					147-169
1877	633,096	2,458					147-169
1878	612,843	2,417					147-169
1879	595,486	2,418					169-179
1880	608,681	2,425	26.21	20.81	All companies	64-50	169-179
1881	627,265	2,455					169-179
1882	661,458	2,476					169-179
1883	705,659	2,499					179-175
1884	750,567	2,493					179-175
1885	814,691	2,484	26.21	20.27	AETNA	65-50	179-175
1886	848,481	2,619					179-175
1887	929,853	2,661					179-175
1888	1,021,631	2,703					175-168
1889	1,339,894	2,347	27.10		Mut. of N.Y.	64-	175-168
1890	1,272,895	2,783	26.53	21.30	All companies	74-59	175-168
1891	1,400,007	2,758	26.35		Conn. Mut.	73-	175-168
1892	1,532,812	2,740					175-168
1893	1,671,039	2,700					175-168
1894	1,780,307	2,616	26.21	21.84	AETNA	69-57	168-195
1895	1,877,808	2,566					168-195
1896	1,975,747	2,514					168-195
1897	2,155,241	2,439	27.10	21.70	Mut. of N.Y.	66-53	168-195
1898	2,397,863	2,378					168-195
1899	2,741,423	2,318	28.11		N.Y. Life	65-	196-244
1900	3,071,253	2,262	26.93	21.88	All companies	61-49	195-244

Table 9 . Average Premiums and Policy Size.

Footnotes

[a] The Insurance Commissioners, Massachusetts Reports on
Life Insurance: 1859-1865 (Boston: Wright and Potter, 1865),
pp. 55-317. Columns 1-3 for 1843-58 were adapted or calculated from this source and represent the whole life
policies of all companies doing business in Massachusetts.

[b] Superintendent of the Insurance Department of the State
of New York, Forty-Second Annual Report of the Superintendent
of the Insurance Department of the State of New York (Albany:
State Printer, 1901), pp. xxix-xxx. Columns 1-3 for 1859-
1900 were adopted or calculated from this source and represent the total of all policies (except industrial) put into
force by legal reserve Life companies authorized to do
business in New York.

[c] J. Owen Stalson, Marketing Life Insurance (Cambridge,
Mass.:Harvard University Press, 1942), pp. 321-322. Premium
rates identified by the name of a particular company were
extracted from Table 13.

[d] Frederick L. Hoffman, "Fifty Years of American Life
Insurance Progress," Publications of the American Statistical
Association, XII (September, 1911), pp. 746-7. Premiums
identified as representing "N.Y. companies" or "All companies"
represent the compilations of the New York Insurance
Department and The Spectator Year Book for the given years.

[e] Robert F. Martin, National Income in the United States,
1799-1938 (New York:National Industrial Conference Board,
1939), p. 6. The figures for 1843-68 were calculated from
Martin's estimates as deflated by the Warren abd Pearson
general price index adjusted to a 1926 base: see: U.S.
Department of Commerce, Historical Statistics of the United
States, 1789-1945 (Washington: U.S. Department of Commerce,
1949), pp. 231-2.

[f] Simon Kuznets and Raymond Goldsmith, Income and Wealth
of the United States (Baltimore:The John Hopkins Press, 1952),
pp. 30, 55. The data is presented in current dollars according
to the price index of page 30.

[g] The "Average Yearly Premium Paid" gives a range based
upon whether the "Participating" or "Non-participating" rates
are used. These terms refer to the status of the policy
holder's participation in company interest, dividend, etc.
accruals.

Report of the company, December 2, 1844, gives the age
distribution of the policyholders at that time as: under
twenty, 9; twenty to thirty, 95; thirty to forty, 127; forty
to fifty, 80; fifty to sixty, 25; sixty and over, 4.

Perhaps the point of Table 9 could have been more
graphic if the N.N.P. per capita figures had been adjusted
by a factor based upon family size and unemployment so as to
yield the income of the average worker. As it stands, it
seems that we ought to conclude that the policies being sold
were within reach of a large part of the population.

Reinforced Savings

The Life Insurance Industry is generally rather fond of
pointing to the contractual, systematic nature of premium
payments as an inducement to the saver to reach the savings
goals he had in mind at the time the policy was contracted.
As one goes back into the period under discussion, this "inducement" was much more pronounced. Indeed, before the passage of nonforfeiture laws, if the insured neglected to have
his premium in the hands of the agent by the due date his
contract was terminated forthwith. Any cash values which the
policy may have accrued reverted totally to the company, regardless of the number of premiums paid. At first it was not
even required that the company notify the insured of the approaching premium payment nor to take account of contingencies
which may have delayed prompt payment. Recall, in this connection that one of the selling features of the Tontine policy

was that the amassed values of policies and dividends
forfeited by others would be divided among those who successfully completed their contracts. The forfeiture provisions
may sound severe from a humanitarian standpoint, but if they
did, in fact, make faithful, regular savers of those who
would otherwise have been given to thrift only sporadically,
or not at all, then the system must be given a plus in that
respect, if in no other. The traditional assertion has been
that the harsh incentives did promote thrift.

One problem with this assertion is that many contracts
did not endure long enough for the insured to obtain much
experience with the virtue.

Table 10.   The Duration of Forfeited Policies in Massachusetts[1]

Policies forfeited	No. Premiums paid	Amount insured	Net value at forfeiture
758	1	$1,728,650	$21,059
391	2	844,900	20,362
243	3	537,013	20,095
132	4	337,450	17,697
178	5	427,500	27,462
107	6	227,200	16,867
82	7	173,950	16,369
117	8	250,550	26,545
74	9	148,800	19,335
33	10	89,600	12,125
19	11	32,700	4,534
19	12	51,000	8,761
24	13	57,500	9,597
3	14	5,500	1,345
2,180	–	$4,912,313	$222,153
266 Bonuses,............		30,028	11,986
Totals			
2,180	–	$4,942,341	$234,139

[1]Elizur Wright, Massachusetts Reports on Life Insurance
(Boston: Wright and Potter, State Printers, 1865), p. 128.

Table 10 represents the total of whole life policies
and bonuses forfeited in 1859, and not restored in 1860, in
companies doing business and reporting in Massachusetts.

The reactions of those policyholders having their
contracts terminated by the forfeiture provisions of the
early policies soon attracted the attention of the regulatory officials. As the various insurance departments came
into existence, effective agitation for reform was begun in
most states. Elizur Wright, of the Massachusetts department,
was in the forefront of the movement. His message in the
Fourth Massachusetts Insurance Report included the following:

> "The absurdity of having the forfeiture
> of an annual premium insurance work the for-
> feiture of one on which the premium has all
> been paid down, is too flagrant to need dwell-
> ing on.... The excuse offered for this palp-
> able injustice, is, that every insuree is
> made aware, before taking his policy, that
> such is the condition of forfeiture, both of
> it and of all the additions that may be made
> to it. If a person in such circumstances,
> commencing a life-long experiment, does not
> misunderstand the conditions of the policy,
> he may misunderstand his own strength, and
> may be very unwise in piling up penalties
> to be visited years hence on his want of
> punctuality. Why should the Company invite
> him to do it?"[2]

Mr. Wright suggested remedial legal provisions to the
legislature, but his efforts were strongly opposed in the

---

[2]Julius L. Clarke, History of the Massachusetts Insurance Department (Boston: Wright and Potter, State Printers,
1876), p. 42.

sessions of 1859-60. A law was passed in 1861, the first
of its kind. It read, in part, as follows.

> "No policy of insurance on life, issued
> on or after the tenth day of May, in the year
> eighteen hundred and sixty-one, by any com-
> pany chartered by the authority of this
> Commonwealth, shall be forfeited or become
> void by the non-payment of premium thereon,
> any further than regards the right of the
> party insured therein to have it continued
> in force beyond a certain period, to be
> determined as follows...."[3]

The intent of the bill was to see that in the case of
the termination of a contract nothing should be forfeited
except the policyholder's share of accrued divisible surplus
and any expectation of being insured beyond the term already
fully paid for in cash. Underlying the legal provisions was
the basic notion that the insured or his representatives
should be entitled to all the insurance paid for, regardless
of the specifics of his contract.

Within the industry it was thought that the law went
much further than it should have.

> "This law was inequitable for several
> reasons, prominent among which are the
> following: It made the same percent of the
> reserve as a surrender charge against all
> policies, while in equity this charge should
> have not only have been a less percent,
> but also a smaller number of dollars upon
> the older policies, as the prospective con-
> tributions to death claims were greater in

---

[3] The Commonwealth of Massachusetts, Supplement to the
General Statutes of the Commonwealth of Massachusetts (Boston:
Wright and Potter, State Printers, 1862), Chapt. 186, Sec. 1.

the later than in the earlier contracts.
This law applied to policies upon which the
premiums for a year, or even a less time,
had been paid; thus no allowances were made
for the large initial expenses. The company
would sometimes be compelled to continue a
bad risk for the full amount. It forced
the office to carry insurance at a price for
which it could not afford to issue new policies
on healthy lives; that it did not leave a
sufficient margin for fluctuations in the
death rate among the members...."[4]

In spite of continuing objections from the industry,

the original law of 1861 continued in Massachusetts for

twenty years; whereupon, it was repealed and replaced by a

negotiated version.

Over the years various companies had included as selling

points provisions softening the forfeiture clauses. Some began

to permit reinstatement of a lapsed policy within a prescribed

time. Others allowed partial vesting after a stated number of

premiums had been paid. Not long after the Massachusetts law

many companies claimed that all their policies were protected

against forfeit (though, in fact, this type of statement meant

much less than the insured believed).

In spite of continuing industry opposition to non-for-

feiture as set forth in the 1861 law of Massachusetts, other

states began to pass similar regulations. Often the companies

were able to keep the provisions most objectionable to them

out of the laws. Other times serious confrontations developed

---

[4]The Spectator Company, Insurance Yearbook, 1884-85
(New York:The Spectator Company, 1885), p. 259.

between the Insurance Departments and the large companies
acting in concert. The 1877 law of Maine and the 1879 law
of New York each specified non-forfeiture after the policy
had been in force for three full years. These were generally acceptable to the companies of the day. However, other
states who had less to offer as a market and, perhaps, less
desire to compromise with the companies, experienced great
difficulties in obtaining compliance with the laws they had
framed. For example, many companies found Section 451 of
the Political Code of California (1874) unacceptable. They
withdrew from the state. California was left with four
companies authorized to transact business in the state (a
fact causing no little difficulty in obtaining data on
premium receipts for those years in California since the
withdrawn companies ceased to report on insurance previously
placed in force). But the Insurance Commissioner, J. W.
Foard, was able to obtain a measure of satisfaction when the
courts upheld certain principles of his law. He wrote in
his report of 1876:

> "Remembering the air of injured
> innocence assumed by certain life insurance
> companies composing the Chamber of Life
> Insurance, and that withdrew from legitimate
> business in this State on the passage of the
> Act adding Section 451 to our Civil Code,
> March 30th, 1874 - as also, the coarse abuse
> of our Legislature and the Insurance Com-
> missioner, indulged in by a portion of the
> so-called insurance press because of said
> enactment - it affords me great pleasure
> to cite a recent decision of the Supreme
> Court of the United States, more than
> affirming the justice of our law.
>   In the case referred to, "New York Life
> Insurance Company, Appellants, v. Statham
> and two other like cases - appeals from the

Table 11 . Termination of Policies[a].

Years	Number of Companies	By Death Percent	By Maturity Percent	By Expiry Percent	By Surrender Percent	By Lapse Percent	By Change and Decrease Percent
1864	27	14.7[b]	...	2.5	12.8	67.2	2.7
1865	30	10.6	...	1.9	11.5	69.9	6.1
1866	39	8.0	...	1.1	10.4	70.0	10.5
1867	43	7.3	...	.9	10.7	69.1	12.0
1868	55	6.2	...	1.0	15.6	65.5	11.6
1869	71	6.4	...	2.2	17.1	63.2	11.1
1870	71	7.0	...	1.1	18.7	61.1	12.1
1871	68	6.4	...	1.0	22.1	60.6	9.9
1872	59	7.9	...	.7	22.9	58.8	9.7
1873	56	7.9	...	.7	25.0	53.9	12.5
1874	50	7.1	...	1.6	28.0	54.0	9.3
1875	45	9.0	...	2.6	28.9	51.7	7.7
1876	38	9.0	...	2.7	33.3	48.8	6.2
1877	34	8.5	...	4.0	37.3	41.4	8.8
1878	34	9.9	4.4	4.2	34.2	34.3	10.0
1879	31	12.9	5.7	4.7	34.4	34.3	7.9
1880	30	17.1	6.4	4.3	29.9	34.2	8.0
1881	30	19.0	6.5	4.9	27.9	35.3	6.4
1882	30	17.3	5.9	4.4	29.4	37.5	5.5
1883	29	17.4	7.5	2.7	25.8	40.3	6.2
1884	29	14.9	5.1	5.0	25.2	46.6	3.1
1885	29	16.2	4.5	5.2	25.2	45.5	3.3
1886	29	16.3	3.9	5.8	25.2	45.2	3.5
1887	29	16.6	3.6	5.3	24.5	46.4	3.6
1888	29	15.4	3.6	5.7	22.3	49.8	3.2
1889	31	14.5	3.1	6.1	21.1	51.5	3.7
1890	55	10.4	1.7	4.2	13.6	67.7	2.4
1891	58	9.4	1.5	5.4	15.4	65.4	2.9
1892	63	10.3	1.3	3.6	14.8	66.4	3.5
1893	65	8.6	1.3	3.4	14.3	67.9	4.6
1894	64	6.7	1.8	3.1	13.4	71.4	4.6
1895	64	8.1	1.1	3.6	15.1	68.1	4.0
1896	64	9.1	1.5	3.6	16.6	64.2	5.0
1897	66	9.4	1.5	3.9	17.3	63.3	4.6
1898	70	9.6	1.6	3.7	13.8	66.2	5.0
1899	78	10.6	1.7	3.9	13.2	65.4	5.2
1900	89	9.8	1.8	7.1	10.5	66.5	4.3

[a]Frederick I. Hoffman, "Fifty Years of American Life Insurance Progress," Publications of the American Statistical Association, XII (September, 1911), 741.

[b]The percentages are based on the amounts of ordinary life insurance terminated as a result of specific causes relative to total terminations from all causes in a year.

> Circuit Court for the Southern District
> of Mississippi," the Court decrees "that
> the money paid by the purchaser, subject to
> the value of any possession which he may
> have enjoyed, should ex aequo bono be
> returned to him."[5]

While the laws were being formed, however, the terminations
continued apace, with varying degrees of injury to one of
the parties to the contract or the other. Nothing of substance may be said about any effect which the laws may have
had upon the number of terminations.

Summary

In this section some exception has been taken to the
usual interpretation given the events surrounding the "Tontine Revolution". On the other hand, it seems that additional
credibility has been lent to the generally accepted notion
of the insurance industry as a mobilizer of popular funds.
Attention has been called to the rapid growth rate of the
business. Table 12 will help to place the concept of life
insurance growth in a broader national context.

Many other interesting facets of insurance history could
have been discussed; some will be in other connections. But,
as was mentioned, many histories have been written which treat
the marketing and biographical aspects of the industry most

---

[5] Insurance Commissioner of the State of California,
Annual Report of the Insurance Commissioner for the State of
California (Sacramento:D.W. Gelwicks, State Printer, 1874),
p. 9.

Table 12 . Life Insurance and the National Economy.

Year	Total Income of Life Insurance Companies (millions)	United States National[a] Income (millions)	Life Insurance Income as a % of National Income
1843	$ .393	$1,868	.02%
1850	4.293	2,420	.18%
1860	8.896	4,311	.21%
1870	117.101	6,827	1.72%
1880	81.556	7,227	1.13%
1890	204.728	11,700	1.75%
1900	419.295	14,500	2.89%

[a]Robert F. Martin, National Income in the United States, 1799-1938 (New York:National Industrial Conference Board, 1939), p. 6. The value for 1843 represents a linear interpolation at Martin's estimates in current prices. The 1850-80 values are directly from those estimates. The values for 1890, 1900 are from Kuznets' estimates in current prices. See: Simon Kuznets and Raymond Goldsmith, Income and Wealth of the United States (Baltimore:The John Hopkins Press, 1952), p. 30.

admirably. Several of these may be found in the bibliographic
section of this paper. Rather than pursue these items further
here, let us turn from the more general elements of the history
to examine several more specific parts of the financial
record of the industry.

METHODOLOGY

The Principal compilation of data original to this
study is found in Table Al. This section deals mainly with
the definitions and methods used in deriving the various
entries of that table. The reader might also refer to the
section, Preliminary Explanations, for a further discussion
of some related items.

Acknowledgments

Because of the great lengths to which many companies,
institutions, and agencies were willing and able to go in
locating and making available the documents used in this
study at least some mention should be made of them at this
point.

Many of the older companies in the industry seem to be
very aware of their historical beginnings and were, on the
whole, very willing to make whatever remained of their early
records available for proper use. Most helpful in this regard
were the Connecticut Mutual Life Insurance Company, and
Massachusetts Mutual Life Insurance Company, to whom I am
very grateful. Other companies who were of substantial help
in supplying access to, and information from, their company
records include: Aetna, Berkshire, Equitable, Home, John
Hancock, Manhattan, Metropolitan, Mutual Benefit, Mutual of

New York, National, New England Mutual, New York Life, North-
wester, Presbyterian Ministers Fund, Prudential, Penn Mutual,
State Mutual, Union Mutual, and U.S. Life.

The directors of research at the several state insurance
departments and their departmental staffs were also of great
aid, more especially those of the New York and Massachusetts
Departments. The personal help of these gentlemen was of great
aid.

The resources and personnel of several great libraries
were invaluable, principally: The New York State Library,
Archives Division, Legislative Reference Section, and Law
Library; The University of Illinois, Inter-library Loan
Division; Purdue University, Inter-library Loan Division;
Harvard University Libraries and The New York City Library.
Other libraries of assistance included: the company collections
of the various companies mentioned above, the Library of the
American Life Convention, and the Library of the College of
Life Insurance.

In a few instances sufficient material was obtainable
from the institutions named by mail. For the most part, how-
everm it was necessary to examine the records on the site.
In general, institutions such as the Institute of Life Insurance try to spare the companies this rather disruptive process
by providing researchers the material they need. In this
case, much of the inquiry required original information. I
am greatly indebted that the institutions involved were most

gracious and helpful and expressed no undue concern over the conclusions to which their information might lead.

The General Method of Compilation

The exception taken to a study of all legal-reserve life insurance companies by the Institute of Life Insurance has been mentioned previously. It appears that only the work of J. Owen Stalson has made a serious attempt at gathering the data of all companies. Since Mr. Stalson concentrated his effort principally upon the amount of insurance in force and other data more closely related to his central topic of marketing, the general compilation of those series more relevant to the industry's role as intermediary has remained to be completed.

This study has attempted to identify every company that has been authorized to transact insurance upon lives (legal-reserve) whether the authorization was given to the company as a principal business or to one of a company's divisions. Every company so identified appears in Appendix B. The years for which income and asset data were identified for a given company has been noted in Appendix B and such data included in Table A1. If no such years appear it may simply not have been located; the company may have been inactive; the company may have failed to report or to report on time; or, the company may have ceased to transact legal-reserve life business under the listed name. Many of these circumstances were noted in the column "Comments" of Appendix B.

A strict order of priority was observed in the compilation of the data. The order was determined as follows: Every official company report was given primacy. These items were mainly drawn from company reports viewed on the site. These appear in the Bibliography (the only company records so appearing) and represent reports of most of the companies listed just above. A general exception to this rule was made whenever official reports of the regulatory agency of the home state of the company were also found, and such reports disallowed some item (usually some assets) on legal grounds. In these cases the legal version of the value of the asset was accepted.

Second in priority were the official reports of the regulatory agency of the home state of the company, followed, according to geographical proximity, by the official reports of the other states' regulatory agencies. If all the items needed for a company were not at hand by this time appeal was made to biographical works which the company may have authorized, then to the Spectator Insurance Yearbook for the year. Next, the Spectator compilation Life Insurance History was referenced and, in a few instances, other financial publications of the day or biographies of the companies which were not company authorized.

All entries appearing in Table A1 were compiled by individual company for each year. The rule of priority was observed in each company's data. For those items in which the

concept of region is used, the items were first allocated by
state. Thus, any given number in Table A1 represents the aggregation of the data of many companies and, as appropriate, many
states.

At this point the reason for this detailed outline of
the rule of priority should be clear. It did not seem appropriate to identify the substantial list of references that
pertained to each individual number in Table A1. It did seem
appropriate that the reader should be sufficiently informed
of these references to be able to reproduce any given number
should he desire to do so. All sources referenced in Table A1
appear in the Bibliography; these were employed according
to the rule of priority.

Volumes of the official reports of the various insurance
departments were used according to the years indicated below.
The states are listed according to the first year of life
insurance data used.

Massachusetts, 1856[1]	Minnesota, 1871
New York, 1859[2]	Pennsylvania, 1873
New Hampshire, 1860	Tennessee, 1873
Connecticut, 1866	Texas, 1875
Rhode Island, 1866	New Jersey, 1876
Ohio, 1867	Delaware, 1880
California, 1868	Colorado, 1882
Illinois, 1868	Louisiana, 1886
Maine, 1868	Indiana, 1887
Vermont, 1868	Georgia, 1887

---

[1]For such Life data as was reported for the years 1837-
55 see: Elizur Wright, Massachusetts Reports on Life Insurance
(Boston:Wright and Potter, State Printers, 1865).
[2]For such Life data as was reported for the years 1830-
1859 see: William Barnes, New York Insurance Reports (Albany,
N.Y.:Weed, Parsons and Company, 1873), Vol. I, II.

Missouri, 1869	Nebraska, 1888
Wisconsin, 1869	No. Dakota, 1890
Iowa, 1870	Washington, 1890
Kentucky, 1870[3]	Virginia, 1893
Michigan, 1870	So. Dakota, 1897
Kansas, 1871	Alabama, 1897[4]
Maryland, 1871	No. Carolina, 1900

Each subsequent volume of the reports mentioned was used in the compilation of the data for each succeeding year. Regular reporting was not begun in the unlisted states before 1900, with the exception of Idaho, Nevada, and West Virginia. The three states named are known to have reported the business of 1900 but their reports were not located.

In New York additional official reporting was obtained from the annual reports of the Comptroller, from the "Letter Books" of the Comptroller, and from the unified (boxed) letters to the Comptroller. This was strictly a matter of gleaning for unaccounted bits of information and not a productive enterprise to be recommended in general. The unfiled letters are correspondences on all subjects (including personal) received by the Comptroller's office and not indexed in any way. The official Comptroller's reports have been rather well researched by Barnes.

> "...He (Barnes) decided to go back with his undertaking (of gathering insurance reports)

---

[3]See also: Secretary of State of the State of Michigan, First Annual Report of the Secretary of State of the State of Michigan, Relating to Insurance, (Lansing, Mich.: W. S. George and Company, Printers to the State, 1870).
[4]See also: Board of Commissioners, Abstract of the Returns of the Insurance Companies Doing Business in the State of Rhode Island (Providence, R.I.: Printer to the State, 1861).

to the earliest official statements ever
made by insurance companies in the State of
New York. The records of the Insurance
Department and the musty archives of the
Comptroller's office were repeatedly and
thoroughly searched for the purpose of
finding all reports and documents relating
to insurance companies which had ever been
filed in the State Hall, at Albany. Reports in divers forms, more or less perfect, were, with great labor and persis-
tence found, from time to time, going back
to the year 1831, shortly after the epoch
of the enactment of the original Revised
Statutes, under the provisions of which
these annual statements had been first
made and filed."[5]

There was also some earlier reporting in Massachusetts

that might have gone beyond the Wright compilation cited,

but these records were not obtained. Julius Clarke comments,

"For a period of nineteen years, ending
with 1855, the returns of Insurance Companies
doing business in Massachusetts were made
to the Secretaries of the Commonwealth,
by whom they were annually reported to the
Legislature in the form of Abstracts, substantially in conformity with that for 1837,
already cited. The last of the series of
Abstracts prepared under this regime was
published in January, 1856, and covered the
returns for the year ending Dec. 1, 1855,
that relating to the business of outside Companies being rendered by Secretary Wright,
Jan. 1, and that relating to Home Companies
by his successor, Secretary DeWitt, Jan. 31,
1856.
As the business of insurance in Massachusetts
was thenceforth to be supervised by the State
Insurance Department, a few of the more
important statistical items given in these
closing Abstracts may have interest here.

---

[5]Barnes, Vol. I, New York Insurance Reports, p. IX.

> There were 171 Companies transacting
> business in the State at the close of
> 1855. Of these, 118 were Home Companies,
> including five Life Companies, and fifty-
> three were incorporated elsewhere, the
> latter including twelve Life Companies;
> also five Companies from foreign countries.
> The five Life Companies, including
> the Massachusetts Hospital Life, were at
> that date in possession of assets amounting
> to $1,863,095, with $742,081 of liabilities.
> Their total outstanding insurance on lives
> amounted to only a little more than twelve
> millions of dollars, the premium reserve
> on which was estimated by themselves at
> $693,961."[6]

Among the more valuable secondary sources consulted were

the Spectator Life Insurance Yearbooks for the years 1873-1911;

and the excellent works, cited elsewhere, of Stalson and of

Knight.

The idea behind compiling as complete a record as

possible for the industry was to represent all regions and

types of companies as fully as possible. This was thought

necessary to avoid bias in the regional analysis and in the

distribution of assets by type, as well as in the assessment

of the overall financial impact of the industry. So, while

the companies with only fragmentary records were not included

in Table A1, it was found advisable to estimate values for

others. The records of some of the very largest companies

were found to have frequent omissions, particularly in the

earliest years. The omissions of the earliest years were

frequent among the relatively inactive companies. These

---

[6]Clarke, History of the Mass. Ins. Dept., pp. 26-27.

sometimes occurred because of special charter provisions the
large companies had obtained (a situation discussed more
fully later), sometimes because of partial reporting, and
often from broken data series. Since the companies were
relatively inactive, it was thought appropriate to estimate
the missing values by simple linear interpolation. Thus,
while the company might have been missing a year or two of
data between each observed year, the values between the
observed years changed by a very small percentage and specific purchases were generally identifiable.

The estimates of the missing years were thought to be
fairly good for this reason. On the other hand, such a
situation caused the estimation of a large percentage of the
total value of some series in the earliest years. This is
illustrated by Table 13.

Within a few years the size of the relatively dormant
holdings and income streams of the large companies was
offset by those of the new, growing enterprises of the
Mutual Era.

The question may arise as to the wisdom of including
inactive companies in the data. It might be noted that,
since the question at hand is centered upon the mobilization
of capital, the deletion of the portfolio of a large company
from the record the moment it ceased to contract new policies would have had some highly distorting effects upon the
account of total insurance holdings obtained. The question
of when to make such a deletion would also be a difficult

Table 13. Income and Asset Observations as a Percent of the Estimated Total.

Year	Total Income	Total Assets	Year	Total Income	Total Assets
1843	45.84	35.54	1872	94.03	93.39
1844	48.28	40.40	1873	96.81	96.02
1845	51.55	43.87	1874	98.56	96.93
1846	49.59	50.28	1875	96.24	94.13
1847	56.48	69.06	1876	96.64	93.55
1848	73.29	75.86	1877	95.50	92.30
1849	54.42	57.49	1878	98.29	94.50
1850	63.15	67.38	1879	97.92	91.45
1851	64.09	62.86	1880	99.58	96.08
1852	67.54	69.23	1881	96.85	92.58
1853	69.10	70.39	1882	99.60	98.05
1854	70.64	68.54	1883	97.27	94.01
1855	70.02	75.25	1884	98.64	97.49
1856	72.17	72.91	1885	99.48	97.13
1857	73.91	71.08	1886	97.64	96.12
1858	71.65	73.14	1887	86.41	97.85
1859	76.14	73.91	1888	96.61	97.39
1860	74.81	72.33	1889	99.71	98.66
1861	75.49	72.68	1890	98.49	95.79
1862	94.13	83.75	1891	99.94	99.34
1863	79.50	78.61	1892	99.94	99.10
1864	81.90	80.45	1893	97.63	97.38
1865	83.63	81.47	1894	99.94	99.27
1866	87.23	82.21	1895	98.90	99.04
1867	89.44	91.73	1896	97.94	99.12
1868	90.87	88.33	1897	98.84	99.59
1869	91.32	84.23	1898	99.99	98.06
1870	91.31	97.39	1899	99.93	99.42
1871	93.07	91.38	1900	96.70	99.08

one since some of the companies continued to contract occasional new policies. There were also a few cases of companies becoming reactivated. There was little question about
removing a portfolio from the list when the company had been
liquidated and the assets sold, or in the case of the amalgamation of one company with another.

Some omissions of the type mentioned also occurred in
the records of the more dynamic companies at intervals
throughout the period of the study. If the series involving
an omission was thought to have a rate of change which
varied significantly from the linear, then the omission was
filled by averaging the growth rates between the previous
two years and the succeeding two years and adding that
percentage to the value preceding the omission. If such an
omission was for more than one year or if the series was too
short to determine rates of change, then the rate of change
calculated for the observed values of the series for the
industry as a whole was imputed to that part of the company's
series having the omission.

Toward the end of Table 13, the values approach 100%.
This indicates the increased reporting which resulted from
the multiplied number of regulatory agencies and industry
organizations, and the improvement in communications general
to the country. By way of emphasis, let it be noted that
the number of companies included in Table 13 is a much
higher percentage of the total number of companies than the
percentage (based upon the values involved) which was

recorded in that table, especially in the earliest years.

The appearance of an asterisk (*) in any table of this study indicates that a small positive value has been lost in rounding.

Estimation of Assets

That the categories and definitions used by the companies and institutions were subject to change has already been noted. This paper has formed a single set of categories and definitions and used them consistently in compiling all series original to this study. They have also been used as consistently as feasible in presenting and contrasting the series compiled by others.

The New York Insurance Department has been a dominant figure in insurance reporting because of its early origin and the large number of companies which prepared data according to its dictates. The major classes of assets have been prepared in essential agreement with the definitions of New York in order to make them as widely comparable as possible, and to minimize the number of series to be redefined.

Total Assets

This total was the summation of all admitted assets, observed or estimated to have been held as reserves against level-premium (including Tontine) and industrial policies by any division of a domestic company authorized to transact legal-reserve life insurance in the period 1843-1900.

Domestic holdings of foreign companies were not included.
Foreign holdings of domestic companies were included but
were listed as a separate category. The dollar amounts of
this class, and all other dollar amounts in the paper, were
presented in the dollar values current to the year of record
(unless specific note to the contrary was made).

Real Estate

The total amount given in any year in this category was
the sum of the cost values of all real properties owned by
the company, less the encumberances thereon. Items such as
office furniture, safes, etc., were not included here. The
market value of the properties would have been more desirable for certain parts of the analysis, such as, in examin-
ing the great losses from such investments in the 1870s.
However, so many of the companies and departments were
sporadic in their use or reporting of this information (as
well as in their definitions of market value), particularly
in the early years, that cost value was chosen for use
uniformly throughout the study.

It should be noted that these investments usually
consisted only of such real property as was legally obtained
through the foreclosure of mortgages, and of the companies'
offices and adjacent properties. The conditions of such
ownership were generally rather carefully specified by the
statutes of the various states in an effort to control
possible tendencies toward land speculation.

The regionalization of real estate holdings was not a complicated procedure since records of the property were always specific as to location. The only problem was to obtain detailed lists of these holdings. Connecticut was one of several states that required detailed schedules of the various items presented as totals in the annual report to the department. These were not unlike the supporting schedules currently filed by the companies. Schedule "A" usually contained a complete list of all real properties, "B" was the list of all mortgages, "C" listed all collateral loans, and "D" or "E" was a list of the securities held. The exact format varied a little from state to state. Connecticut is mentioned especially in this connection since the annual report of that state's Insurance Department included full details of the real estate schedules for each company doing business there.

New York also required such schedules to be submitted. These were not included in the published report of the department. A large number of the submitted reports were placed on file in the archives of the New York State Library, Albany. These were mostly handwritten, often carbon copies, and were bound into huge volumes (about 30), titled, "Schedules, Mortgages, Real Estate, Etc." Schedules of this sort also appeared randomly in the annual reports of various insurance departments in connection with periodic investigations and for other special purposes.

The Armstrong Report[1] also contained a few exhibits which
seem to have been taken from schedules of the sort mentioned.

The years and companies for which regionalization of the
real estate holdings was accomplished were detailed in
Appendix B. The allocation was made on the basis of the
aggregated schedules of real estate which were obtained from
the sources outlined. The properties of the companies for
which schedules had been obtained were allocated by state
for each year. The state data was then collected into
regions. The percentage of total real estate that each region
represented was then calculated. These percentages were used
to allocate the real estate holdings of all companies. It
should be noted that many of the companies in Appendix B were
not active in the period of the regionalization, or were not
included in the reports because they held no mortgages in
the period.

United States Bonds

This category included all the financial instruments
issued by the federal government and held by the insurance
companies under discussion. Some of these instruments were
referred to at various times as "stocks" or by other names.

---

[1] New York State, Testimony Taken Before the Joint Committee
of The Senate and Assembly of the State of New York to Investigate and Examine into the Business and Affairs of Life Insurance
Companies doing Business in the State of New York, Vol. I-VII
(Albany, N.Y.:Brandow Printing Co., 1905). Volumes I and II
of this edition contain, "Exhibits in Connection with the
Testimony...." Cited hereafter as "Armstrong Report".

United States Bonds and all other bonds and stocks in the
study were presented according to their market values.
The reporting of U.S. Bonds was probably more correct than
that of any other category because virtually every form of
report called for them to be listed separately, and because
the companies liked to feature their holdings of such
securities prominently in their records.

Other Stocks and Bonds

The market value of every stock and bond in the companies'
portfolios, not appearing in "United States Bonds", was
aggregated to obtain the items of this series. See the
section "Portfolio Classification" for a discussion of the
detail of this category.

Mortgages

The items of this series contained the totals of all
debt obligations issued on real estate collateral. The
category was overstated slightly because of the practice of a
few companies of issuing loans on mixed collateral. One
example of this was a loan extended upon a home, lot and small
portfolio of assorted securities with a lump sum valuation.
This was a problem of small, relative magnitude.

Mortgages were viewed as having value to the company
equal to the amount of the loan left outstanding in any
given year.

Regionalization of the mortgages was accomplished in
the same manner as that explained above for real estate.
The sources involved in the two calculations differed only
slightly. No state recorded the mortgage schedules with the
faithfulness that the Connecticut department had exercised
in recording those of real estate. A much larger part of
this data was taken directly from the original documents.
However, the incidence of occasional mortgage records appearing in printed documents was much higher than for real
estate. Again, Appendix B details the companies and years
included in the original observations.

Collateral Loans

This classification contained a variety of loans.
Loans with securities as collateral were included here.
Some reports included a separate classification for "Security Loans," this practice was not followed. In the earliest reports unsecured loans to persons were fairly common.
Often these loans were made to company officials or to
persons or enterprises in which an official had an interest.
Some of the earliest report forms of the regulatory agencies
made specific provision to detect this type of loan. Many
of these agencies disallowed any such loan for purposes of
official reporting. The same fate often befell some of the
miscellaneous receivables and other loans that formed the
remainder of this category.

Loans of this type were almost always aggregated in any report. This allowed easy tabulation of a total but did not permit much to be said about the detail by type or by region. This effect may not have been totally unintentional because of some of the loans involved. The schedules mentioned earlier detailed the items submitted as collateral but such listing could not yield knowledge of the ultimate purpose of the loan; neither could it disclose the location of such use. In the cases where company records were complete enough the collateral items were referred to their respective accounts, but these were usually kept by number or by name. Further cross-referencing was usually not possible and was not undertaken.

Premium Notes

These notes were interest bearing notes given by the policyholders in lieu of cash premiums. A large percentage of the early business was contracted on the basis of this type of note which was often given on the assurance that the dividends from the insurance would offset its rate of interest. It has been widely claimed that many of the early lapses were attributable to this type of solicitation. In the reports prior to 1870, the distinction between the notes of this class and the "Deferred and Uncollected Premiums" was not consistently kept or defined. This problem was given particular attention during collection of the data but no claim can be made for the early entries in these two series beyond that.

The same problems discussed in connection with collateral loans also accounted for the lack of detail in reporting premium notes.

It should also be mentioned the gross amount of premium notes outstanding was often much larger than the figure reported here. These additional notes were disallowed as assets by the insurance departments on the grounds that they were not received for premiums due in the current year.

Cash

This series might well have been given the widely used heading, "Cash in Office and Bank." Most companies understood this term to include cash in the hands of agents, general agents, or in branch offices, or income in transit between any of the above. Other forms of receivables were not included.

Few problems were encountered with this series since most reports called for, and defined it, consistently.

Deferred and Uncollected Premiums

This category was referred to in some of the tables by the shorter title "Premiums Due" and contained items of many forms. Particularly in the days of early competition, agents would allow various periods of grace in order to obtain a contract. Premiums due, but payable on an other than yearly basis, or otherwise receivable, were also included here.

Again, regulatory agencies were increasingly strict regarding what was permitted to be officially admitted here and the items disallowed by such agencies are not included.

All Other Assets

The values placed in this series were residuals. Assets not allocated to other categories were grouped here. These included, in general, only furniture and other equipment and supplies. Miscellaneous receivables and other items deemed admissible on the reports to the regulatory agencies were also included from time to time.

Each of the categories given above occurred with regularity in both company records and those of various institutions and agencies. Unusual series were adjusted to the more common ones used here as necessary. Omissions were estimated according to the general procedure previously outlined.

Portfolio Classification

Assets which have appeared in some compilations only as "Other Bonds and Stocks," have been classified in this study according to type and to region. This was done for the purpose of disclosing, with some precision, the various enterprises that could be said to have been financed by funds mobilized by life insurance companies, and to determine where these enterprises were located.

Each security of every company for each year was examined

for this purpose. The allocations were then made according
to state and subsequently regionalized. Finally, the data
of each firm was aggregated and the total for the industry
obtained. As before, any omissions were estimated at the
most atomic level, according to the method given and then the
process of classification and aggregation begun. This process was simple enough in the early years. Each company
held only a few securities. Over time the number of companies
and securities multiplied dramatically.

A large number of companies included detailed lists of
their securities in their Annual Reports. Many insurance
departments included the report schedules listing the securities
in their official publications. Among states following this
practice were New York, Massachusetts, and Connecticut. The
substantial list of references used in classification was the
same as that explained in the general methodology and included
all the available annual reports, all the reports of
regulatory agencies, etc.

State and Local Bonds

These consisted of the finanacial instruments of all
political subdivisions, excluding those of foreign countries.
Some securities that might have appeared here do not because
of the intent of their issuance. Issues which were made
by a political subdivision to specifically fund a railroad,
canal, or utility project do not appear, but were listed as

a part of those categories to which they corresponded by reason
of the purpose of their issuance. This type of classification
obviously decreased the size of "State and Local Bonds" but
it was hoped that the convention would identify more clearly
the source of the money used to fund various types of projects - the more direct aim of this study.

Regionalization of this series was simply a matter of
allocating a large number of well-identified entries into the
well-defined regions named.

Railroad Securities

These classifications (as bonds and as stocks) included
only investment in domestic lines or domestic branches of international lines. Railroad securities of lines all or partly
in other countries were also categorized but do not appear
separately in this paper; rather, they were listed as
"Foreign Bonds". As mentioned, bonds issued by any political
body specifically for funding any railroad project appeared
here.

The regionalization of rail investment was accomplished
with the aid of Poor's Manuel of Railroads[1] and copies taken
from various maps and forwarded by The Association of American
Railroads.[2]

---

[1] Poor, 1868-1901, various pages.
[2] These copies were not completely identified but aided in
locating some of the lines prior to the information of Poor's
Manuel. They appear to have been prepared from Railway Age, and
from: Atlas of Railway Progress (New York:Engineering News and
American Railway Journal, 1889), Various years and pages.

Surprisingly, the earliest years were not difficult to
work with since only a few of the best known lines were involved.
These were often located only in one state. As the number
of different rail securities grew to the five hundred or so
held by some of the large insurance companies in 1900, a
more systematic approach was needed.

For each succeeding year each rail security of each company was examined. Money invested in a specific security was
allocated to the particular branch of the line for which the
issue was intended (this identification was often given). If
the rail line involved extended into more than one state the
investment was allocated according to the percentage of the
line's total track mileage lying within each state. The
lists of securities and mileage figures were updated for each
year.

Aside from its tedium, no particular disadvantage was
found in this system as long as the line was included within
one state or if the branch was specified. No great problem
was found in allocating lines that expanded rather uniformly
along existing routes. However, purchases of the securities
of a line such as Union Pacific in 1868 may not have been
accurately allocated. To the extent that heavy construction
at the head of the line was not offset by branch development
along the line allocation by total mileage placed too large
a percentage of the investment in the area of the established
line, and too little at the head of the line, where the expendi-

tures were actually taking place.

Much of this latter problem was removed when the data was regionalized, since much expansion of this type involved only one region. The company data was subsequently aggregated, after necessary estimations, and the industry data presented.

The remaining classes of securities were allocated to regions according to the same general principles employed in the instance of the railroads. Most of these securities represented companies whose investment, expenses, and service were localized. These offered no unusual problems. Interstate canals or utilities were allocated on the basis of mileage percentages, as in the case of railroads. Lists containing the securities of interstate corporations, such as American Cotton Oil Company, usually indicated the division for which the bonds were issued (Georgia, in this case). If they did not, and no other basis was found for reasoned allocation, then the investment was divided according to the values of the facilities reported in each state, or simply divided among the states in which the company was known to be active. Allocations of this type involved a small total value.

Utility Securities

These classifications included all securities issues of any public or private utility project. This was interpreted broadly to include not only water-works, gas-light and electric companies but also telephone, telegraph, irrigation, sewerage and other related projects.

Industrial Securities

Industrial securities included the securities issues of factories, mills and other institutions producing tangible products. Enterprises which might be considered "Commercial," such as retail establishments and even hotels, were listed as "Other Bonds." This distinction was not always easy to make. The "Industrial" classification was interpreted very broadly as the following list indicates. This list includes every security in this class which was identified by name in the 1895-1900 period, i.e., it contains most of the industrial securities ever owned by Life insurance companies.

Abstract Safety Vault
Adams Express
Adams Nickle Plating
Agawam Mfg.
Am. Bicycle
Am. Bridge Co.
Am. Cotton Oil
Am. Lithographic
Am. Mail Steamship
Am. Waltham Watch
Am. Woolen
Am. Writing Paper
Arlington Mills
Arnold Print Works
Asphalt Block
Asphalt Co. of Am.
Bath Iron Works
Bayridge Co.
Boott Cotton
Boston Steamship
Bridesburg Mfg.

Brooklyn Wharf
Campbell Co.
Cambria Iron Co.
Central Foundry
Central Iron
Chicago Cons.
   Brewing & Malting
Cocheco Mfg.
Collier, G. W.
Cons. Coal
Crane Iron Works
Crompton and Knowles
   Loom Works
Crowfoot Cattle
DeBarbleben Coal & Iron
Des Moines Stock Yd.
Dix Field and Peru
   Bridge Co.
Duluth Union Depot
Dwight Mfg.
Eastern Illinois Coal

Ellicott Square Co.
Freeman Mfg.
Freihofer Vienna Baking
Galveston Wharf
Gansevort Freezing
Geisendorf, J. C.
General Electric
Ginn and Co.
Gloucester Ferry
Good, John; Machines
Goshen Foundry & Gas
Hamilton Mfg.
Hartford and N.J. Transport
Hartford Carpet
Hoboken Ferry
Indianhead Mills (Ala.)
International Navigation
International Pulp
Jefferson & Clearfield Iron
Kellog & Buckley
Keystone Lumber & Salt
Knickerbocker Ice
Lackwanna Iron & Steel
Lehigh & Wilkesbarre Coal
Lehigh Coal & Navigation
Lehigh Valley Coal
Ludlow Mfg.
McKey-Nesbit
Manchaung
Manhattan Refrig.
Maryland Brewing
Mass. Building Co.
Mass. Cotton Mills
Mass. Fireproof Storage
    and Warehouse
Massillion & Cleveland
    Coal
Merrimac Mfg.
National Oar
National Folding Voc
National Tube
N. Eng. Cotton Yarn
N. Eng. Gas & Coke
N.J. Steamboat
N.J. Zinc
Ninchill & Schulkill
Ocean Steamship
Old Colony Steamboat

Otis Fall Pulp
Pacific Coast Co.
Pa. & Va. Iron & Coal
Pontoosuc Woolen Mfg.
Portland Elevator Co.
Portland Port Auth.
Pratt Reed & Co.
Providence, Fall River
    & Newport Steamboat
Pullman Palace Car
Qualif. Cotton Mills
Quinnemont Coal & Iron
Reading Iron Works
Retsof Mining
Richardson Silk
Richmond Stove Co.
Rockland Rockport Line
St. Joseph Stock Ys.
Scranton Silk
Seville Packing
Sheldon Marble
Shenandoah Iron
Slater, Wm. A., Corp.
Smith & Richardson
Standard Harrow
Standard Mfg.
Sutton, Wm., Mills
Swift and Co.
Talbot Mills
Thorndike Co.
Torrington Co.
Tremont & Suffolk, Mills
Umbagog Paper Co.
U.S. Envelope
Utica Cement
Utica Knitting
Vt. Marble
Va. Coal
Vulcan Iron Works
Washington Mills
Wells Fargo
Westinghouse
Westmorland Coal
Whittenton Mfg.
Williamantic Linen
Woodbury Cotton Duck
York Mfg.

Canal Securities

Securities entered in these categories were the stocks
and bonds of actual canals, and of companies providing transit through both canals and other inland waterways. Navigation companies and other branches of canal companies (such
as an associated railroad) were placed elsewhere.

Other Securities

With the exception of three years in which stock entries
appear, this diverse class is composed of debt issues. They
are mostly those of non-profit organizations (such as the
construction bonds of schools, churches, etc.), of commercial enterprises, and of financial institutions.

Financial Stocks

Financial bonds were evident only for the last few years
of the century. Financial stocks, on the other hand, included a significant portion of all stocks throughout the
period. These were mostly bank stocks. Some companies also
purchased the stocks of other insurance companies, and those
of other types of financial institutions. Possible reasons
for this will be discussed later.

Foreign Assets

All foreign securities were bonds, principally those of
governments or of railroads. These were largely held in
response to the deposit laws of the respective countries.

These securities were first divided into categories identical
with those of domestic securities. Since their number was
relatively small no useful purpose was found in preserving
these distinctions. All types of foreign bonds were lumped
into the "foreign bonds" category.

In the regional analysis foreign assets and income were
designated, "Region 9."

Income

The sources and methodology used to determine total income and total premium income were the same as those outlined for total assets. Total income included premium
income and the returns from all asset holdings, including
related interest, rents, dividends, etc. Also included were
any returns from subsidiaries and other minor items. No
meaningful way was determined to regionalize total income.
The task of trying to locate the various assets generating
the income was no small matter, but, beyond that, income of
this type was generated mostly by funds that were being held
in trust for the policyholders.

By contrast, premium income represented a rather clear-
cut withdrawal of funds from the geographic area of the policyholder. This type of income was regionalized, but additional
data was needed to accomplish that task. Most companies did
not keep early records of the geographic origin of their income.
The only satisfactory way discovered for obtaining the needed

data was based upon the tax laws of the various states. The section on insurance law references many of the early regulations requiring premiums taxes. These laws were compiled to determine the period they included and the office to which the payment they required was to be made. The records of these offices were then obtained. Most often these were included in the published report of the insurance department of the state, if such had been formed.

Most of the annual reports giving such data recorded the premiums received for business contracted within the states, as well as the taxes paid or other items. The degree to which various expense items were allowed to be extracted from the reported tax base varied from state to state, but the law was usually written with sufficient clarity to permit any needed adjustments to be clearly determined.

In the exceptional cases, where the tax record did not include the premiums involved, they could often be calculated from the tax rate and a published list of tax receipts or from other reports. For the latter part of the period the Spectator Insurance Yearbook also provided a rather comprehensive listing of premium receipts by company and by state. For the latter years, these were used as supplementary sources and were particularly useful for those states where insurance departments had not yet been formed or for states not requiring the needed reporting. Some additional omissions were obvious in the series of some of the states. These occurred

when an established company would withdraw temporarily from
a state. In such cases the company would usually not file a
tax return; however, the premiums from all policies remaining
in force in the state obviously continued to come in. This
fact was indicated by unaccounted residuals in the company's
premiums receipts and by the similar size of its income upon
reactivation within the state. Such omissions were filled
by the method previously outlined.

Regional Capital Flows

Mention has been made of the fact that certain items of
income and of investment were not allocated geographically.
Nevertheless, an attempt was made to examine possible geographical distortions that may have existed in the flows of
life insurance funds on the basis of partial data. For
this purpose regional investments were defined as including
real estate, mortgages, stocks, and all but federal bonds.
Other funds that might have gone into an area because of
expenses, return premiums, rebates, dividends, or death
claims were excluded. The expense items obviously added to
the figures of the insurance centers. The other items were
excluded on the assumption that they were consistent among
the regions. This exclusion reduced the amounts involved
but probably did not change the percentages.

In the case of death claims this assumption may have been
unfortunate. One might be inclined to think that the mortality

table would have held rather consistently across the country. This was the rationale of the exclusion. There was some evidence to the contrary; however, especially for the earlier years. In 1851, for example, the Mutual Life Insurance Company of New York stated in its Annual Report,

> "During the past year, the Trustees have had a careful investigation made by their Actuary, with a view to ascertain how far the actual experience of the Company, during the eight years of its existence, corresponded with the Tables upon which their rates of premium are based. And they have the satisfaction of stating, that, notwithstanding the mortality occasioned by the cholera, and the frightful ratio of deaths in California, even among the few lives in that country insured in this Company, the aggregate losses are decidedly within the Tabular expectation, giving assurance of the soundness of the Company. From the same investigation, the Trustees have also been confirmed in the wisdom of discontinuing to insure California risks, which they did in January, 1849; and also that the extra charges for a residence in our Southern States, have thus far been inadequate to cover the extra hazards of that portion of the Union."[1]

In spite of the problems involved, the regional analysis was conducted with premium income as a proxy of outflows of funds, and the sum of regional investments as a proxy of inflows of funds to a region. Besides presenting the dollar values involved in these measures, additional series were

---

[1] Mutual Life Insurance Company of New York, Annual Report (New York:Mutual Life Insurance Company of New York, 1851), p. 9.

INTERPRETATION AND COMPARISON

The following sections present many of the series which have resulted from employing the procedures described. Interpretations that might be given some of the results appear as well as some comparisons with the works of others.

Major Asset Categories

Table 14 presents the dollar value of total assets, and the major categories therof, for the period 1843-1900. This table and each of the others remaining in the paper, was calculated or compiled from the information of Table A1, unless specific note to the contrary is given.

Table 15 has been prepared from census reports and purports to be a complete listing of legal reserve companies. By comparing Tables 14 and 15 an estimation of the relative completeness of the listings may be made. In 1880 the census figure for total assets was 95.67% and in 1890, 93.11% of the corresponding values from Table 14. The census compilers admitted to the possibility of some omissions and to having relied only upon official compilations for some of their data. It appears that some of the census omissions have been filled by the present study.

INTERPRETATION AND COMPARISON

The following sections will present many of the series which have resulted from employing the procedures described. Interpretations that might be given some of the results appears as well as some comparisons with the works of others.

Major Asset Categories

Table 14 presents the dollar value of total assets, and the major categories thereof, for the period 1843-1900. This table and each of the others remaining in the paper, was calculated or compiled from the information of Table A1, unless specific note to the contrary is given.

Table 15 has been prepared from census reports and purports to be a complete listing of legal reserve companies. By comparing Tables 14 and 15 an estimation of the relative completeness of the listings may be made. In 1880 the census figure for total assets was 95.67% and in 1890, 93.11% of the corresponding values from Table 14. The census compilers admitted to the possibility of some omissions and to having relied only upon official compilations for some of their data. It appears that some of the census omissions have been filled by the present study.

TABLE 14. TOTAL LIFE INSURANCE ASSETS, BY CLASS (THOUSANDS OF DOLLARS)

YEAR	REAL ESTATE	U.S. BONDS	OTHER STOCK, BONDS	MORT-GAGES	COLLAT-ERAL LOANS	PREM-IUM NOTES	PREM-IUMS DUE	PREM-CASH	ALL OTHER	TOTAL
1843	349.	14.	98.	636.	650.	17.	53.	73.	70.	1961.
1844	361.	12.	255.	750.	602.	37.	57.	64.	69.	2208.
1845	387.	11.	280.	1026.	558.	82.	62.	96.	75.	2578.
1846	342.	24.	318.	1241.	634.	410.	60.	91.	82.	3202.
1847	266.	129.	352.	1193.	707.	511.	42.	107.	80.	3387.
1848	258.	241.	427.	1455.	769.	825.	46.	127.	131.	4283.
1849	362.	395.	894.	2688.	1096.	1727.	80.	273.	212.	7727.
1850	327.	367.	747.	3911.	1261.	1995.	71.	610.	232.	9519.
1851	369.	437.	927.	4901.	1635.	2806.	95.	555.	280.	12007.
1852	352.	428.	1057.	6434.	1726.	3329.	188.	543.	282.	14339.
1853	364.	434.	1281.	7774.	1544.	3802.	212.	468.	311.	16189.
1854	391.	471.	1644.	9183.	1102.	4111.	222.	556.	340.	18020.
1855	372.	473.	1607.	9758.	1087.	4167.	256.	476.	332.	18529.
1856	401.	529.	1772.	11660.	1163.	4675.	303.	624.	422.	21550.
1857	428.	591.	1836.	13413.	1387.	5487.	377.	585.	570.	24674.
1858	675.	630.	1954.	15741.	1445.	5371.	252.	983.	577.	27628.
1859	705.	681.	2120.	17318.	1463.	5879.	253.	840.	649.	29908.
1860	1087.	1134.	2348.	19887.	1612.	6893.	657.	1258.	722.	35597.
1861	1119.	3049.	2497.	20528.	1713.	7016.	783.	1449.	919.	39073.
1862	1124.	6826.	2334.	18637.	1599.	6751.	785.	2338.	831.	41194.
1863	1272.	14664.	3526.	19987.	1707.	7780.	1146.	2515.	988.	53586.
1864	2301.	20705.	4458.	20618.	1924.	11619.	2606.	2562.	1140.	67933.
1865	2330.	20832.	8115.	20700.	1980.	17717.	5780.	3428.	1310.	82192.
1866	2934.	22479.	12245.	29512.	2036.	21367.	9139.	5540.	2005.	107257.
1867	4212.	24619.	13865.	40502.	2515.	37212.	12575.	5101.	4660.	145261.
1868	5609.	26139.	17372.	67410.	4402.	51755.	21291.	5374.	3937.	203288.
1869	8823.	29116.	21959.	97402.	4991.	54532.	24431.	7428.	5699.	254380.
1870	10302.	24086.	24739.	113205.	5534.	64044.	24828.	11354.	5971.	284063.
1871	12129.	24855.	28631.	149298.	7778.	69031.	20228.	14353.	6339.	332642.

TABLE 14 (CONTINUED)

YEAR	REAL ESTATE	U.S. BONDS	OTHER STOCK. BONDS	MORT- GAGES	COLLAT- ERAL LOANS	PREM- IUM NOTES	PREM- IUMS DUE	CASH	ALL OTHER	TOTAL
1872	14659.	24196.	33660.	177430.	7763.	67971.	17782.	14373.	7042.	364876.
1873	15582.	22317.	34630.	197982.	7468.	61345.	13930.	19847.	6433.	379534.
1874	21583.	23535.	51301.	222570.	6631.	59267.	13255.	18978.	8797.	425918.
1875	25423.	24800.	54505.	234433.	6252.	54618.	9559.	15994.	9202.	434787.
1876	32460.	32465.	59233.	233531.	6666.	42984.	7473.	13635.	9553.	438000.
1877	35687.	41814.	68365.	222657.	7286.	37529.	5194.	11246.	10100.	439878.
1878	51218.	44471.	75272.	203995.	7317.	34036.	4556.	13494.	9184.	443544.
1879	55731.	46752.	80865.	192557.	13869.	29400.	4400.	15203.	8366.	447144.
1880	54623.	40025.	94430.	178583.	32336.	28759.	4551.	21902.	7082.	462291.
1881	56843.	32050.	108363.	177749.	44351.	26688.	4876.	18585.	6629.	476135.
1882	54419.	16109.	117281.	180559.	62067.	22911.	5185.	15584.	5600.	479715.
1883	58139.	14206.	132981.	202607.	43079.	22478.	6210.	17907.	6213.	508822.
1884	59561.	12686.	153709.	213458.	35419.	20349.	6612.	21314.	6325.	529634.
1885	65571.	16159.	178381.	222193.	18581.	21092.	7372.	26790.	6225.	562365.
1886	68349.	14341.	193070.	239027.	23558.	19805.	8054.	22912.	6490.	595608.
1887	67849.	12559.	205687.	252984.	33028.	18814.	9073.	25286.	6669.	631949.
1888	71338.	11462.	223835.	263588.	32496.	18587.	12131.	30859.	7696.	671992.
1889	78691.	9180.	250342.	288420.	36968.	19577.	12389.	34792.	7501.	737860.
1890	84899.	6501.	263524.	328022.	39257.	20349.	13345.	32599.	7435.	796326.
1891	88879.	6721.	300860.	341807.	49171.	20444.	15228.	35273.	7340.	865720.
1892	100967.	6840.	349515.	355042.	45256.	23628.	18228.	42807.	7981.	950266.
1893	112234.	7957.	372608.	386452.	34636.	27198.	21940.	45617.	10089.	1018732.
1894	122506.	15849.	415124.	403862.	40399.	29972.	21680.	52155.	10412.	1111959.
1895	128058.	17036.	472057.	417030.	41726.	34564.	21806.	51265.	12517.	1196060.
1896	139684.	21644.	486825.	449601.	50099.	43651.	23929.	50595.	13940.	1279669.
1897	142069.	14797.	556217.	456095.	93720.	14196.	24016.	71174.	13683.	1385968.
1898	150984.	13322.	641197.	467416.	103792.	14522.	26415.	77672.	14175.	1509495.
1899	156052.	8558.	740894.	472585.	129334.	15231.	28868.	74156.	16076.	1641755.
1900	159537.	7460.	847561.	502272.	147637.	16566.	33261.	77528.	17837.	1809659.

Table 15. Census Reports of Total Assets of Class A Companies (Thousands).

Kind of Asset	1880[a]	1890[b]
Real Estate	$63,821 $64,207[c]	$80,306 $80,733[c]
Mortgages	$184,753	$288,131
Stocks and Bonds	$115,826 $120,733[c]	$242,697 $258,543[c]
Collateral Loans	$ 14,107	$ 41,954
Premium Notes	$ 30,527	$ 15,020
Cash	$ 14,792	$ 35,310
Total	$442,272	$741,426

[a]U.S., Bureau of the Census, Eleventh Census of the United States:1880. Compendium, 1444-1449.
[b]U.S., Bureau of the Census, Twelfth Census of the United States:1890 Compendium, Part II, 592-595.
[c]Adjusted to market value.

The compilation of life insurance statistics presented
by the Institute of Life Insurance has been mentioned
previously. It was that compilation which also formed the
basis of the presentation in the Commerce Department's
Historical Statistics..., cited earlier. Table 16 has
been prepared from the Institute version of the study and
is given here for comparison.

An examination of Table 16 and Table 14 will reveal the
broader total coverage offered by the latter. The period of
the total asset series is extended by eleven years, and
that of the major categories by twenty-two years. In each
case, the values of Table 14 are considerably more complete.
Note should also be taken of the current knowledge of the
details of stock and bond holdings as revealed in Table 16.
This knowledge may be extended somewhat by the various
tables appearing later in the paper.

Another of the most respected studies of life insurance
assets should be discussed at this point, even though some
of the figures discussed will not be given in detail until
later. Lester W. Zartman compiled a percentage distribution
of life insurance assets for each decade from 1860-1900.
These percentages were first published in 1906, though they
may have been the result of a dissertation presented to the
Faculty of the Department of Political Economy in Yale
University earlier. The percentages were based upon the
reports of twenty-nine large life insurance companies. The

Table 16 . Assets of U.S. Life Insurance Companies (Millions of dollars).[a]

Year-End	ASSETS					
	Total	Bonds	Stocks	Mortgages	Real Estate	Others[b]
1900	1,742	707	95	501	158	281
1899	1,595	654	83	468	154	236
1898	1,463	581	72	455	145	210
1897	1,345	503	56	452	138	196
1896	1,244	445	54	442	135	168
1895	1,160	423	53	412	125	147
1894	1,073	369	50	394	117	143
1893	988	323	47	374	105	139
1892	919	306	39	351	97	126
1891	841	270	31	334	86	120
1890	771	241	30	310	81	109
1889	714.5	251.7	"b	283.3	75.7	103.8
1888	657.1	231.6	"	262.5	68.6	94.4
1887	597.6	207.8	"	244.9	63.4	81.5
1886	561.6	197.7	"	227.5	59.9	76.5
1885	524.7	182.6	"	212.9	58.0	71.2
1884	492.2	152.1	"	205.7	54.6	79.8
1883	472.4	137.6	"	187.6	51.7	95.5
1882	450.0	124.0	"	172.7	51.4	101.9
1881	429.6	129.2	"	160.2	51.1	89.1
1880	418.1	124.8	"	164.8	51.6	76.9
1879	401.7	116.2	"	173.8	49.2	62.5
1878	404.1	112.8	"	189.1	42.8	59.4
1877	396.4	100.8	"	201.1	31.6	62.9
1876	407.4	85.7	"	217.9	29.2	74.6
1875	403.1	73.9	"	219.7	22.6	86.9
1874	387.3	65.3	"	210.1	18.3	93.6
1873	360.1	56.6	"	189.8	15.0	98.7
1872	335.2	54.7	"	164.3	12.5	103.7
1871	302.6	52.4	"	134.9	10.8	104.5
1870	269.5	48.1	"	108.0	9.0	104.4
1869	229.1	45.1	"	83.6	7.0	93.4
1868	176.8	40.9	"	58.0	4.8	73.1
1867	125.6	33.2	"	37.0	3.6	51.8
1866	91.6	28.3	"	23.7	2.3	37.3
1865	64.2	22.4	"	16.5	1.7	23.6
1864	49.0					
1863	37.8					
1862	30.1					
1861	26.7					
1860	24.1					
1859	20.5					
1858	15.9					
1857	14.0					
1856	15.0					
1855	12.7					
1854	11.4					

[a]Institute of Life Insurance, The Historical Statistics of the United States, 1759 to 1958 (New York: Institute of Life Insurance, 1960), pp 9-10.
[b]Included with "Bonds."

TABLE 17 (CONTINUED)

YEAR	REAL ESTATE	UNITED STATES BONDS	OTHER STOCK, BONDS	MORT-GAGES	COLLAT-ERAL LOANS	PREM-IUM NOTES	PREM-IUMS DUE	CASH	ALL OTHER
1872	4.018	6.631	9.225	48.627	2.122	18.628	4.873	3.939	1.930
1873	4.105	5.880	9.124	52.165	1.968	16.163	3.670	5.229	1.655
1874	5.067	5.526	12.045	52.256	1.557	13.915	3.112	4.456	2.065
1875	5.847	5.704	12.536	53.919	1.438	12.562	2.199	3.675	2.117
1876	7.411	7.412	13.524	53.318	1.522	9.814	1.706	3.113	2.181
1877	8.113	9.506	15.542	50.618	1.656	8.532	1.181	2.557	2.256
1878	11.547	10.026	16.971	45.992	1.650	7.674	1.027	3.042	2.071
1879	12.464	10.456	18.085	43.064	3.102	6.575	0.934	3.430	1.671
1880	11.816	8.658	20.427	38.630	6.995	6.221	0.985	4.738	1.532
1881	11.938	6.731	22.759	37.332	9.315	5.605	1.024	3.963	1.392
1882	11.344	3.358	24.448	37.639	12.936	4.776	1.081	3.245	1.167
1883	11.426	2.792	26.135	39.819	9.449	4.418	1.220	3.519	1.221
1884	11.246	2.433	29.022	40.303	6.687	3.842	1.248	4.024	1.194
1885	11.660	2.873	31.720	39.510	3.304	3.751	1.311	4.764	1.107
1886	11.476	2.408	32.416	40.132	3.955	3.325	1.352	3.847	1.090
1887	10.736	1.987	32.548	40.032	5.226	2.977	1.436	4.001	1.055
1888	10.616	1.706	33.309	39.225	4.836	2.766	1.805	4.592	1.145
1889	10.665	1.244	33.928	39.089	5.010	2.653	1.679	4.715	1.017
1890	10.661	0.816	33.092	41.192	4.936	2.555	1.676	4.144	0.934
1891	10.266	0.776	34.753	39.482	5.680	2.361	1.759	4.074	0.848
1892	10.625	0.720	36.781	37.362	4.762	2.486	1.918	4.505	0.840
1893	11.017	0.781	36.576	37.935	3.400	2.670	2.154	4.478	0.590
1894	11.017	1.425	37.333	36.320	3.633	2.695	1.950	4.690	0.936
1895	10.707	1.424	37.333	34.367	3.489	2.890	1.823	4.266	0.647
1896	10.913	1.691	39.468	35.126	3.914	3.410	1.869	3.953	0.689
1897	10.251	1.068	38.034	32.908	6.762	1.024	1.733	5.135	0.987
1898	10.002	0.883	40.132	30.965	6.876	0.962	1.750	5.146	0.939
1899	9.505	0.521	42.478	28.785	7.878	0.928	1.758	4.517	0.979
1900	8.816	0.412	46.835	27.755	8.158	0.915	1.838	4.264	0.986

TABLE 17. TOTAL LIFE INSURANCE ASSETS, BY CLASS (PERCENTAGES)

YEAR	REAL ESTATE	UNITED STATES BONDS	OTHER STOCK, BONDS	MORT-GAGES	COLLAT-ERAL LOANS	PREM-IUM NOTES	PREM-IUMS DUE	CASH	ALL OTHER
1843	17.791	0.717	5.022	32.425	33.142	0.861	2.726	3.730	3.887
1844	16.368	0.561	11.547	33.969	27.242	1.682	2.578	2.915	3.139
1845	15.031	0.442	10.875	39.788	21.662	3.183	2.387	3.714	2.918
1846	10.683	0.745	9.938	38.758	19.814	12.795	1.863	2.857	2.547
1847	7.867	3.305	10.389	35.229	20.864	15.092	1.240	3.164	2.351
1848	6.033	5.633	9.972	33.980	17.944	19.360	1.077	2.958	3.047
1849	4.683	5.110	11.571	34.782	14.183	22.355	1.036	3.534	2.747
1850	3.439	3.851	7.842	41.082	13.252	20.954	0.748	6.408	2.432
1851	3.074	3.643	7.724	40.819	13.619	23.370	0.795	4.624	2.332
1852	2.458	2.982	7.913	44.867	12.038	23.219	1.310	3.788	1.964
1853	2.248	2.678	7.913	48.020	9.537	23.483	1.309	2.885	1.923
1854	2.170	2.615	9.125	50.959	6.113	22.616	1.231	3.085	1.686
1855	2.008	2.553	8.671	52.664	5.867	22.492	1.384	2.568	1.793
1856	1.859	2.457	8.224	54.109	5.397	21.692	1.407	2.896	1.960
1857	1.733	2.366	7.441	54.362	5.622	22.237	1.528	2.372	2.309
1858	2.445	2.281	7.072	56.975	5.231	19.439	0.911	3.558	2.088
1859	2.357	2.276	7.089	57.904	4.891	19.657	0.846	2.809	2.172
1860	3.053	3.185	6.595	55.868	4.529	19.365	1.845	3.534	2.027
1861	2.863	7.804	6.392	52.537	4.384	17.956	2.004	3.708	2.352
1862	2.727	16.571	5.666	45.242	3.881	16.388	1.832	5.675	2.017
1863	2.374	27.364	6.581	37.299	3.186	14.519	2.139	4.693	1.845
1864	3.387	30.478	6.563	30.350	2.832	17.104	3.837	3.771	1.678
1865	2.834	25.346	9.874	25.185	2.429	21.556	7.032	4.171	1.593
1866	2.736	23.958	11.416	27.516	1.899	19.921	8.521	5.165	1.869
1867	2.900	16.948	9.545	27.882	1.731	25.617	8.667	3.512	3.208
1868	2.759	12.858	8.545	33.160	2.165	25.459	10.473	2.644	1.936
1869	3.468	11.446	8.632	38.290	1.962	21.437	9.634	2.920	2.240
1870	3.627	8.479	8.709	39.852	1.948	22.546	8.740	3.597	2.102
1871	3.646	7.472	8.507	44.892	2.338	20.752	6.081	4.315	1.906

Table 18. Percentage Distribution of Total Assets, Zartman's Study[a] Compared[b].

Type of Asset	1860	1970	1880	1890	1900
Cash Items	2.4%	4.3%	4.5%	4.2%	4.3%
	3.5	4.0	4.7	4.1	4.3
	2.4	3.5	3.4	4.7	4.2
Deferred Premiums	3.1	5.4	1.1	3.3	5.4
	1.8	8.7	1.0	1.7	1.8
	c	9.4	1.0	1.7	1.8
Premium Notes	20.5	21.5	5.2	1.2	.9
	19.4	22.5	6.2	2.6	.9
	16.0	24.2	6.1	2.7	.9
All Other	1.4	1.2	1.5	.9	.9
	2.0	2.1	1.5	.9	1.0
	2.1	2.1	1.8	1.0	.9
Mortgage Loans	59.2	44.4	38.6	41.0	28.8
	55.9	39.9	38.6	41.2	27.8
	61.8	36.5	43.3	39.1	29.3
Real Estate	2.7	3.5	12.2	10.4	9.6
	3.1	3.6	11.8	10.6	8.8
	2.5	3.1	12.2	10.7	9.6
Collateral Loans	1.6	1.2	5.7	4.6	4.3
	4.5	1.9	7.0	4.9	8.2
	9.0	1.6	3.1	4.4	6.8
U.S. Bonds	3.1	9.1	8.7	.9	.4
	3.2	8.5	8.7	.8	.4
	2.5	11.1	10.6	1.2	.6
Foreign Public Bonds	---	---	.0	1.2	3.4
	---	.04	.02	1.6	4.2
	---	---	---	.5	2.4

Table 18. (Continued).

Type of Asset	1860	1870	1880	1890	1900
State & Local Bonds	8.1	21.6	37.7	15.8	12.8
	2.4	5.8	14.0	6.6	5.1
	1.9	6.6	14.7	5.9	6.0
Railroad Bonds	.8	1.2	4.7	21.2	28.8
	2.2	1.1	4.3	21.2	32.7
	.2	.32	2.0	17.5	29.0
Utility Bonds	---	.0	.0	.6	1.7
	---	.28	.37	1.2	2.2
	---	.0	.0	1.1	1.6
Miscellaneous Bonds	.1	.2	.0	.4	1.7
	.08	.3	.3	.3	1.3
	.0	.0	.2	.5	.4
Railroad Stocks	.5	.4	.4	2.3	2.5
	.34	.38	.33	2.35	3.18
	.2	.4	.2	2.8	2.6
Financial Stocks	1.6	1.1	1.0	1.2	2.7
	1.3	.8	1.1	1.3	2.1
	1.3	1.0	1.3	.8	2.8
Utility Stocks	.1	.0	.1	.1	.1
	.27	.03	.02	.19	.28
	.1	.0	.0	.0	.0

[a]Lester W. Zartman, The Investments of Life Insurance Companies (New York:Henry
Holt and Company, 1906), p. 14.
[b]The first row of figures in each class has been drawn from Zartman's study; the
second row from tables in the current study; the third row from decade estimates using
only New York Insurance Department data (see text).
[c]These are not segregated in the early New York reports, usually being listed
with "other assets" or, occasionally, with "Premium Notes."

names of these companies were not detailed in the book, nor
were the amounts serving as basis for the percentages. The
lack of these details and of any precise description of
methodology have made a strict comparison with the present
study impossible. It may be that these needed details were
disclosed in the original dissertation, but substantial effort
was not sufficient to obtain a copy of this document from
Yale University.

Table 17 represents the percentage that each element
categorized in Table 14 represents of the total asset figure
for the corresponding year. Table 18 is a comparison of these
percentages, and of some drawn from later in this study,
with those presented by Zartman. Some adjustment of the
classifications has taken place to make the two studies
more comparable. Table 18 also includes a third set of
estimates. These are based on decade estimates by the author.
The decade estimates were made using only the information
available in the New York insurance reports. This was done
in the belief that the large companies consistently reported
in the New York reports would approximate the unnamed large
companies of the Zartman study. Some variations in method
were also used in the decade estimates to examine their
effects upon the results.

Table 18 indicates loose agreement among many of the
estimates. The largest difference occurs in the instance
of state and local bond allocation. The consistently larger

percentages of the Zartman study for this class of
securities provide some measure of the degree to which
the convention of allocating specialized bond issues to
other categories has diminished the values given for that
category in this paper. (Recall that if a state funded a
railroad expansion, etc., the bonds issued were allocated
to railroads.)

Real Estate

Figure 1 is presented to help convey a general feel
for the major trends that occurred in the holding of real
estate. Table 19 lists the dollar amounts of real estate
involved and subdivides these by region. Table 20 gives
the percentage of total assets accounted for by each of
these dollar amounts.

The marked decline in the percentage of assets
held as real estate in the early years was the compound
effect of several factors. Note that there was no cor-
respondingly sharp decline in the dollar amounts of
real estate held. This harmonizes with previous
statements that there were large stagnant portfolios,
dominant in the series, which were being rapidly over-
taken by the values of the portfolios of the expanding
mutual companies. Real estate was a large part of the
assets of the older companies. Recall that some of these

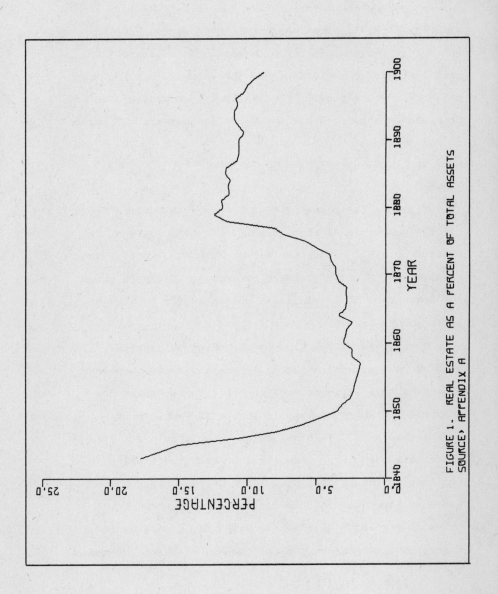

FIGURE 1. REAL ESTATE AS A PERCENT OF TOTAL ASSETS
SOURCE: APPENDIX A

TABLE 19. REAL ESTATE OWNED (THOUSANDS OF DOLLARS)

| | REGIONS | | | | | | | | | |
YEAR	1	2	3	4	5	6	7	8	9	TOTAL
1843	0.	0.	0.	0.	0.	0.	0.	0.	0.	349.
1844	0.	0.	0.	0.	0.	0.	0.	0.	0.	361.
1845	0.	0.	0.	0.	0.	0.	0.	0.	0.	387.
1846	0.	0.	0.	0.	0.	0.	0.	0.	0.	342.
1847	0.	0.	0.	0.	0.	0.	0.	0.	0.	266.
1848	0.	0.	0.	0.	0.	0.	0.	0.	0.	258.
1849	0.	0.	0.	0.	0.	0.	0.	0.	0.	362.
1850	0.	0.	0.	0.	0.	0.	0.	0.	0.	327.
1851	0.	0.	0.	0.	0.	0.	0.	0.	0.	369.
1852	0.	0.	0.	0.	0.	0.	0.	0.	0.	352.
1853	0.	0.	0.	0.	0.	0.	0.	0.	0.	364.
1854	0.	0.	0.	0.	0.	0.	0.	0.	0.	391.
1855	0.	0.	0.	0.	0.	0.	0.	0.	0.	372.
1856	0.	0.	0.	0.	0.	0.	0.	0.	0.	401.
1857	0.	0.	0.	0.	0.	0.	0.	0.	0.	428.
1858	0.	0.	0.	0.	0.	0.	0.	0.	0.	675.
1859	0.	0.	0.	0.	0.	0.	0.	0.	0.	705.
1860	0.	0.	0.	0.	0.	0.	0.	0.	0.	1087.
1861	0.	0.	0.	0.	0.	0.	0.	0.	0.	1119.
1862	0.	0.	0.	0.	0.	0.	0.	0.	0.	1124.
1863	0.	0.	0.	0.	0.	0.	0.	0.	0.	1272.
1864	0.	0.	0.	0.	0.	0.	0.	0.	0.	2301.
1865	0.	0.	0.	0.	0.	0.	0.	0.	0.	2330.
1866	0.	0.	0.	0.	0.	0.	0.	0.	0.	2934.
1867	0.	0.	0.	0.	0.	0.	0.	0.	0.	4212.
1868	0.	0.	0.	0.	0.	0.	0.	0.	0.	5609.
1869	0.	0.	0.	0.	0.	0.	0.	0.	0.	8823.
1870	0.	0.	0.	0.	0.	0.	0.	0.	0.	10302.
1871	0.	0.	0.	0.	0.	0.	0.	0.	0.	12129.

TABLE 19 (CONTINUED)

100

					REGIONS					
YEAR	1	2	3	4	5	6	7	8	9	TOTAL
1872	0.	0.	0.	0.	0.	0.	0.	0.	0.	14659.
1873	0.	0.	0.	0.	0.	0.	0.	0.	0.	15582.
1874	6863.	12176.	843.	78.	4.	1326.	31.	0.	263.	21583.
1875	6856.	14258.	2153.	86.	5.	1763.	47.	0.	254.	25423.
1876	7869.	18112.	3566.	145.	10.	2402.	84.	0.	271.	32460.
1877	6810.	19692.	5728.	220.	58.	2668.	252.	0.	258.	35687.
1878	7977.	26364.	10547.	701.	162.	4696.	486.	0.	285.	51218.
1879	7975.	27902.	13199.	649.	159.	4835.	455.	0.	512.	55731.
1880	7216.	26622.	14311.	541.	141.	4495.	464.	0.	828.	54623.
1881	7004.	27157.	16060.	481.	134.	4469.	462.	0.	1076.	56843.
1882	6722.	26688.	14817.	303.	116.	4169.	381.	0.	1225.	54419.
1883	7193.	29288.	15221.	149.	110.	4325.	340.	0.	1514.	58139.
1884	7059.	30877.	14315.	235.	85.	4138.	328.	0.	2524.	59561.
1885	7477.	34924.	14383.	341.	65.	4268.	342.	0.	3770.	65571.
1886	7425.	37015.	13768.	78.	28.	4444.	441.	0.	5150.	68349.
1887	7025.	37873.	11472.	52.	8.	4735.	858.	0.	6126.	67849.
1888	7057.	39799.	9362.	31.	3.	5554.	1993.	0.	7538.	71238.
1889	7323.	43366.	9707.	83.	13.	6111.	3427.	10.	8651.	78691.
1890	7467.	45528.	8250.	107.	2.	6162.	4466.	706.	12211.	84899.
1891	8104.	50431.	7774.	169.	1.	6820.	4349.	719.	10511.	88879.
1892	8235.	60911.	7016.	324.	1.	7094.	4719.	706.	11961.	100967.
1893	8878.	66910.	7563.	385.	1.	8408.	5447.	862.	13780.	112234.
1894	9055.	73542.	7112.	410.	82.	9491.	5951.	760.	16103.	122506.
1895	8825.	75566.	6580.	391.	302.	10538.	9125.	917.	15814.	128058.
1896	9537.	82702.	6950.	383.	320.	11721.	9615.	1452.	17004.	139684.
1897	8986.	80396.	6674.	480.	445.	15171.	11554.	1813.	16549.	142069.
1898	9049.	83599.	8134.	735.	430.	15707.	13942.	2141.	17246.	150984.
1899	9307.	85214.	8495.	728.	394.	15345.	16646.	2330.	17593.	156052.
1900	9209.	88558.	8321.	531.	247.	15425.	16934.	2448.	17863.	159537.

TABLE 20. REAL ESTATE OWNED (PERCENT OF TOTAL ASSETS)

YEAR	REGIONS 1	2	3	4	5	6	7	8	9	TOTAL
1843	0.0	0.0	0.0	0.0	0.0	0.0	0.0	0.0	0.0	17.791
1844	0.0	0.0	0.0	0.0	0.0	0.0	0.0	0.0	0.0	16.368
1845	0.0	0.0	0.0	0.0	0.0	0.0	0.0	0.0	0.0	15.031
1846	0.0	0.0	0.0	0.0	0.0	0.0	0.0	0.0	0.0	10.683
1847	0.0	0.0	0.0	0.0	0.0	0.0	0.0	0.0	0.0	7.867
1848	0.0	0.0	0.0	0.0	0.0	0.0	0.0	0.0	0.0	6.033
1849	0.0	0.0	0.0	0.0	0.0	0.0	0.0	0.0	0.0	4.683
1850	0.0	0.0	0.0	0.0	0.0	0.0	0.0	0.0	0.0	3.430
1851	0.0	0.0	0.0	0.0	0.0	0.0	0.0	0.0	0.0	3.074
1852	0.0	0.0	0.0	0.0	0.0	0.0	0.0	0.0	0.0	2.458
1853	0.0	0.0	0.0	0.0	0.0	0.0	0.0	0.0	0.0	2.246
1854	0.0	0.0	0.0	0.0	0.0	0.0	0.0	0.0	0.0	2.170
1855	0.0	0.0	0.0	0.0	0.0	0.0	0.0	0.0	0.0	2.008
1856	0.0	0.0	0.0	0.0	0.0	0.0	0.0	0.0	0.0	1.859
1857	0.0	0.0	0.0	0.0	0.0	0.0	0.0	0.0	0.0	1.733
1858	0.0	0.0	0.0	0.0	0.0	0.0	0.0	0.0	0.0	2.445
1859	0.0	0.0	0.0	0.0	0.0	0.0	0.0	0.0	0.0	2.357
1860	0.0	0.0	0.0	0.0	0.0	0.0	0.0	0.0	0.0	3.053
1861	0.0	0.0	0.0	0.0	0.0	0.0	0.0	0.0	0.0	2.863
1862	0.0	0.0	0.0	0.0	0.0	0.0	0.0	0.0	0.0	2.727
1863	0.0	0.0	0.0	0.0	0.0	0.0	0.0	0.0	0.0	2.374
1864	0.0	0.0	0.0	0.0	0.0	0.0	0.0	0.0	0.0	3.387
1865	0.0	0.0	0.0	0.0	0.0	0.0	0.0	0.0	0.0	2.834
1866	0.0	0.0	0.0	0.0	0.0	0.0	0.0	0.0	0.0	2.736
1867	0.0	0.0	0.0	0.0	0.0	0.0	0.0	0.0	0.0	2.900
1868	0.0	0.0	0.0	0.0	0.0	0.0	0.0	0.0	0.0	2.759
1869	0.0	0.0	0.0	0.0	0.0	0.0	0.0	0.0	0.0	3.468
1870	0.0	0.0	0.0	0.0	0.0	0.0	0.0	0.0	0.0	3.627
1871	0.0	0.0	0.0	0.0	0.0	0.0	0.0	0.0	0.0	3.646

TABLE 20 (CONTINUED)

YEAR	REGIONS									TOTAL
	1	2	3	4	5	6	7	8	9	
1872	0.0	0.0	0.0	0.0	0.0	0.0	0.0	0.0	0.0	4.018
1873	0.0	0.0	0.0	0.0	0.0	0.0	0.0	0.0	0.0	4.105
1874	1.611	2.859	0.198	0.018	0.001	0.311	0.007	0.0	0.062	5.067
1875	1.577	3.279	0.495	0.020	0.001	0.405	0.011	0.0	0.058	5.847
1876	1.797	4.135	0.814	0.033	0.002	0.548	0.019	0.0	0.062	7.411
1877	1.548	4.477	1.302	0.050	0.013	0.607	0.057	0.0	0.059	8.113
1878	1.799	5.944	2.378	0.158	0.037	1.059	0.109	0.0	0.064	11.547
1879	1.784	6.240	2.952	0.145	0.036	1.081	0.112	0.0	0.115	12.464
1880	1.561	5.759	3.096	0.117	0.030	0.973	0.100	0.0	0.179	11.816
1881	1.471	5.704	3.373	0.101	0.028	0.939	0.097	0.0	0.226	11.938
1882	1.401	5.563	3.089	0.063	0.024	0.869	0.079	0.0	0.255	11.344
1883	1.414	5.756	2.991	0.029	0.022	0.850	0.067	0.0	0.297	11.426
1884	1.333	5.830	2.703	0.044	0.016	0.781	0.062	0.0	0.477	11.246
1885	1.329	6.210	2.558	0.061	0.011	0.759	0.061	0.0	0.670	11.660
1886	1.247	6.215	2.312	0.013	0.005	0.746	0.074	0.0	0.865	11.476
1887	1.112	5.593	1.815	0.008	0.001	0.749	0.088	0.0	0.969	10.736
1888	1.050	5.922	1.393	0.005	0.000	0.827	0.297	0.001	1.122	10.616
1889	0.993	5.877	1.315	0.011	0.002	0.828	0.464	0.001	1.172	10.665
1890	0.938	5.717	1.036	0.013	0.000	0.774	0.561	0.089	1.533	10.661
1891	0.936	5.825	0.898	0.020	0.000	0.788	0.502	0.083	1.214	10.266
1892	0.867	6.410	0.738	0.034	0.000	0.747	0.497	0.074	1.259	10.625
1893	0.871	6.568	0.742	0.038	0.000	0.825	0.535	0.085	1.353	11.017
1894	0.814	6.614	0.640	0.037	0.007	0.854	0.535	0.068	1.448	11.017
1895	0.738	6.318	0.550	0.033	0.025	0.881	0.763	0.077	1.322	10.707
1896	0.745	6.461	0.543	0.030	0.025	0.916	0.751	0.113	1.328	10.913
1897	0.648	5.801	0.482	0.035	0.032	1.095	0.834	0.131	1.194	10.251
1898	0.599	5.538	0.539	0.049	0.028	1.041	0.924	0.142	1.142	10.002
1899	0.567	5.190	0.517	0.044	0.024	0.935	1.014	0.142	1.072	9.505
1900	0.509	4.894	0.460	0.029	0.014	0.852	0.936	0.135	0.987	8.816

pre-mutual companies were very active in the mortgage markets. Many foreclosed properties, as well as their substantial office properties, were on their records.

By contrast the expanding mutual companies were coming under increasing regulation. Many of the investment laws strictly prescribed the reasons for which real estate could be acquired.

The dramatic increase in the percentage of real estate holdings that occurred in the period 1874-79 was accompanied by increases in the dollar amounts as well. This large shift was probably accounted for by the increased foreclosures that accompanied the protracted depression of the period. This interpretation is given support by Figure 4 and the tables adjacent to it, which suggest roughly corresponding declines occurred in both the percent and amount of mortgages held. On the level of the individual companies this pheno- menon was quite evident. The schedules of real estate holdings listed mainly home office property in 1874. By 1880, the schedules are filled with entries identifying foreclosed homes and farmland.

United States Bonds

As noted, many new, mutual companies were chartered in the early and mid 1840's. Many of the charters written con- tained provisions that the company should hold certain parts of its assets in specific types of investments which the

104

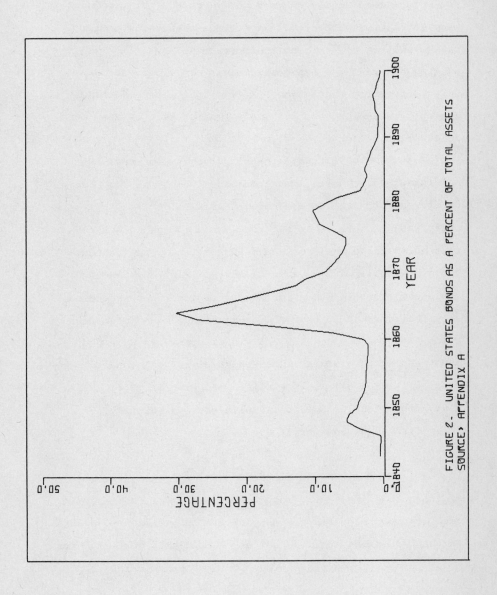

FIGURE 2. UNITED STATES BONDS AS A PERCENT OF TOTAL ASSETS
SOURCE, APPENDIX A

legislators hoped would protect the investment of the policyholder. Most often these assets were to be United States
Bonds, state and local bonds, or mortgages. In 1859, the New
York Insurance Department was formed. This department, and
others rising afterward, inforced the newly passed laws and
required all companies operating within their states to
either purchase, or purchase and deposit with the department,
the specified assets. These laws often specified minimal
amounts that were to be deposited before business could be
transacted. Once these assets were obtained by the companies
their relative importance in the portfolios fell as other
assets were accumulated.

The adverse effects of the seventies upon many of the
other insurance holdings also led to increased purchases
of safer securities during that period.

All of these matters seem to be in relatively good
accord with the record of United States Bond holdings as
revealed in Figure 2, Table 14 and Table 17.

Other Bonds and Stocks

The broad definition of this group of securities included
both those that were thought to be most speculative and those
thought to be among the safest. Together, these securities
revealed little other than their relative scarcity in the
portfolios in the early years and their increasing importance
after 1872. Bond holdings of all types increased rapidly

after that year as liberalized laws permitted them to be
held. The increases were the result of the increasing number
of such issues being made, the higher return to be had, and
the improving reputations of the various issuing institutions.

Each of these classes of securities was analyzed
separately and more detailed discussion is presented in
connection with each class later. Tables 21-24 present the
total figures for each class of bonds and stocks, both according
to the percentage of total assets. This permits comparison
of the relative positions of the classes that will be discussed
only separately hereafter.

Mortgages

Figure 4 illustrates the history of mortgages as a
percent of total asset holdings. By now the reader has
noticed that the various Figures have been scaled according
to the range of the data presented therein. With that in
mind, the changes in Figure 4 should not appear to be quite
so precipitous as at first glance. Table 25 reveals the
dollar amounts of mortgages to have been generally increasing
over most of the period.

As suggested, the earliest companies were heavily invested
in mortgages. Apparently these assets were also attractive
to the newly developing mutual companies. The additional
purchases of United States bonds necessitated by regulation
in the early sixties has been discussed. This alternative

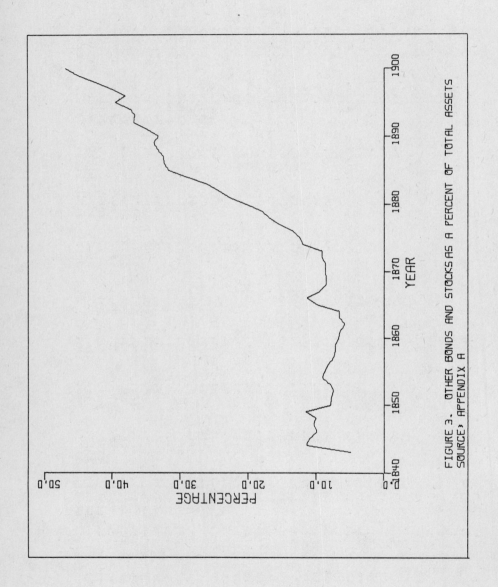

FIGURE 3. OTHER BONDS AND STOCKS AS A PERCENT OF TOTAL ASSETS
SOURCE: APPENDIX A

TABLE 21. TOTAL BONDS OWNED (THOUSANDS OF DOLLARS)

| YEAR | REGIONS | | | | | | | | | U.S. BONDS | TOTAL BONDS |
	1	2	3	4	5	6	7	8	9		
1843	47.	16.	0.	0.	0.	0.	0.	0.	0.	14.	77.
1844	109.	53.	0.	0.	0.	0.	0.	0.	0.	12.	174.
1845	86.	101.	0.	0.	0.	0.	0.	0.	0.	11.	199.
1846	79.	144.	0.	0.	0.	0.	0.	0.	0.	24.	247.
1847	70.	146.	0.	0.	0.	0.	0.	0.	0.	129.	345.
1848	65.	135.	2.	0.	0.	0.	0.	0.	0.	241.	444.
1849	116.	269.	4.	35.	0.	0.	0.	0.	0.	395.	819.
1850	119.	225.	2.	22.	0.	0.	0.	0.	0.	367.	735.
1851	159.	297.	2.	23.	0.	0.	0.	0.	0.	437.	918.
1852	183.	377.	2.	0.	0.	0.	0.	0.	0.	428.	990.
1853	218.	451.	3.	0.	0.	0.	0.	0.	0.	434.	1105.
1854	276.	552.	5.	0.	0.	0.	0.	0.	0.	471.	1305.
1855	349.	475.	25.	0.	0.	0.	0.	0.	0.	473.	1322.
1856	375.	507.	58.	1.	0.	0.	0.	0.	0.	529.	1471.
1857	331.	457.	256.	0.	0.	0.	6.	0.	0.	591.	1640.
1858	376.	593.	285.	0.	4.	0.	0.	0.	0.	630.	1889.
1859	408.	741.	293.	0.	7.	0.	0.	0.	0.	681.	2129.
1860	486.	774.	377.	0.	7.	0.	0.	0.	0.	1134.	2777.
1861	525.	831.	411.	0.	7.	0.	0.	0.	0.	3049.	4823.
1862	403.	1200.	282.	0.	7.	0.	0.	0.	0.	6826.	8719.
1863	802.	1451.	293.	4.	24.	0.	0.	0.	0.	14664.	17239.
1864	1335.	1791.	387.	5.	30.	23.	0.	22.	0.	20705.	24298.
1865	1925.	4207.	531.	6.	41.	68.	0.	28.	0.	20832.	27699.
1866	3555.	5470.	668.	101.	70.	83.	0.	147.	0.	22479.	32574.
1867	3510.	6327.	686.	89.	99.	204.	119.	218.	0.	24619.	36673.
1868	3973.	7621.	997.	203.	230.	229.	189.	304.	0.	26139.	40083.
1869	4224.	11421.	1180.	283.	257.	289.	237.	308.	83.	29116.	47399.
1870	5379.	11811.	2207.	548.	376.	274.	244.	297.	100.	24086.	45321.
1871	5641.	14662.	2203.	794.	853.	337.	255.	340.	164.	24855.	50154.

TABLE 21 (CONTINUED)

YEAR	REGIONS									U.S. BONDS	TOTAL BONDS
	1	2	3	4	5	6	7	8	9		
1872	6144.	16768.	4077.	738.	904.	433.	328.	393.	178.	24198.	54188.
1873	6006.	17344.	4243.	714.	766.	580.	425.	463.	162.	22317.	53019.
1874	6251.	23684.	7488.	1006.	1139.	821.	659.	887.	347.	23535.	68069.
1875	8179.	28398.	7989.	934.	1127.	1181.	657.	928.	317.	24800.	74510.
1876	9951.	30281.	7611.	947.	1194.	1680.	583.	1005.	310.	32465.	86027.
1877	11188.	36430.	8548.	701.	1743.	2545.	548.	936.	207.	41814.	104661.
1878	12315.	40797.	9344.	743.	1216.	3359.	573.	994.	110.	44471.	113926.
1879	11706.	46951.	9337.	596.	1057.	3592.	690.	962.	77.	46752.	121720.
1880	13641.	52214.	12772.	650.	1213.	5431.	787.	997.	87.	40025.	127816.
1881	14038.	59343.	15378.	858.	1392.	6237.	1880.	997.	89.	32050.	132265.
1882	11857.	57021.	22028.	2292.	1606.	6227.	4649.	1001.	87.	16109.	123476.
1883	10384.	58231.	26864.	2667.	2206.	7279.	8053.	1941.	100.	14206.	131932.
1884	11828.	60570.	35212.	3306.	2909.	8016.	10871.	2475.	975.	12886.	149048.
1885	11173.	67210.	37033.	3272.	4765.	14364.	18034.	3072.	1374.	16159.	176458.
1886	11195.	66147.	39917.	5147.	6375.	17633.	22602.	3323.	3517.	14341.	189897.
1887	11806.	66730.	41280.	6007.	6183.	20708.	27357.	3442.	4126.	12559.	200198.
1888	13504.	66658.	41662.	10690.	8294.	23423.	33177.	3773.	4334.	11462.	216867.
1889	13778.	67240.	47673.	12560.	13488.	25616.	38207.	4717.	5887.	9180.	238546.
1890	14046.	66927.	51108.	12040.	11974.	27884.	43525.	5457.	12621.	6501.	252022.
1891	14801.	77095.	57880.	9900.	14059.	32934.	48682.	8648.	16457.	6721.	287178.
1892	18675.	89573.	66590.	11810.	16810.	34495.	53664.	13335.	19731.	6840.	331724.
1893	18781.	103165.	66139.	13209.	17560.	35377.	52871.	13411.	20225.	7957.	348656.
1894	25388.	111456.	72647.	14570.	19221.	36680.	63411.	16379.	21178.	15849.	396779.
1895	31074.	124769.	87501.	18877.	25715.	39698.	67515.	17540.	25579.	17036.	455305.
1896	33417.	126826.	91905.	18442.	26882.	42506.	68634.	18616.	25827.	21644.	474699.
1897	41848.	145327.	96563.	22206.	30600.	58759.	75180.	19901.	30796.	14797.	535978.
1898	43959.	162410.	107525.	26162.	29308.	70493.	93155.	29217.	32906.	13322.	608458.
1899	49474.	180648.	127465.	31584.	29344.	98968.	95338.	40175.	49965.	8558.	711517.
1900	56509.	211530.	143559.	38656.	34942.	112024.	106024.	43218.	76615.	7460.	830550.

TABLE 22. TOTAL BONDS OWNED (PERCENT OF TOTAL ASSETS)

| YEAR | | | | | REGIONS | | | | | U.S. BONDS | TOTAL BONDS |
	1	2	3	4	5	6	7	8	9		
1843	2.371	0.837	0.0	0.0	0.0	0.0	0.0	0.0	0.0	0.717	3.926
1844	4.929	2.394	0.0	0.0	0.0	0.0	0.0	0.0	0.0	0.561	7.883
1845	3.346	3.932	0.0	0.0	0.0	0.0	0.0	0.0	0.0	0.442	7.720
1846	2.459	4.508	0.0	0.0	0.0	0.0	0.0	0.0	0.0	0.745	7.712
1847	2.078	4.307	0.0	0.0	0.0	0.0	0.0	0.0	0.0	3.805	10.190
1848	1.527	3.152	0.049	0.0	0.0	0.0	0.0	0.0	0.0	5.633	10.360
1849	1.503	3.485	0.046	0.456	0.0	0.0	0.0	0.0	0.0	5.110	10.600
1850	1.255	2.361	0.023	0.230	0.0	0.0	0.0	0.0	0.0	3.851	7.720
1851	1.321	2.470	0.019	0.190	0.0	0.0	0.0	0.0	0.0	3.643	7.643
1852	1.277	2.632	0.017	0.0	0.0	0.0	0.0	0.0	0.0	2.982	6.908
1853	1.346	2.784	0.017	0.0	0.0	0.0	0.0	0.0	0.0	2.678	6.825
1854	1.533	3.066	0.027	0.0	0.0	0.0	0.0	0.0	0.0	2.615	7.241
1855	1.881	2.563	0.135	0.0	0.0	0.0	0.0	0.0	0.0	2.553	7.132
1856	1.740	2.351	0.269	0.007	0.0	0.0	0.0	0.0	0.0	2.457	6.824
1857	1.341	1.852	1.036	0.0	0.0	0.0	0.023	0.0	0.0	2.395	6.647
1858	1.362	2.148	1.032	0.0	0.014	0.0	0.0	0.0	0.0	2.281	6.838
1859	1.365	2.476	0.981	0.0	0.022	0.0	0.0	0.0	0.0	2.276	7.119
1860	1.365	2.176	1.058	0.0	0.019	0.0	0.0	0.0	0.0	3.185	7.802
1861	1.343	2.127	1.053	0.0	0.018	0.0	0.0	0.0	0.0	7.804	12.344
1862	0.979	2.913	0.686	0.0	0.017	0.0	0.0	0.0	0.0	16.571	21.165
1863	1.497	2.708	0.547	0.008	0.045	0.0	0.0	0.0	0.0	27.364	32.170
1864	1.964	2.637	0.570	0.008	0.044	0.034	0.0	0.032	0.0	30.478	35.768
1865	2.415	5.119	0.647	0.008	0.050	0.083	0.0	0.034	0.0	25.346	33.701
1866	3.314	5.100	0.623	0.094	0.066	0.078	0.0	0.137	0.0	20.958	30.370
1867	2.417	4.356	0.610	0.061	0.068	0.141	0.082	0.150	0.0	16.948	24.833
1868	1.954	3.847	0.491	0.100	0.113	0.112	0.093	0.149	0.0	12.658	19.717
1869	1.661	4.490	0.464	0.111	0.101	0.114	0.093	0.121	0.033	11.446	18.633
1870	1.894	4.158	0.777	0.193	0.132	0.097	0.086	0.104	0.035	8.479	15.925
1871	1.696	4.408	0.662	0.239	0.256	0.101	0.077	0.102	0.049	7.472	15.063

TABLE 22 (CONTINUED)

YEAR	REGIONS									U.S. BONDS	TOTAL BONDS
	1	2	3	4	5	6	7	8	9		
1872	1.684	4.596	1.117	0.202	0.248	0.119	0.090	0.108	0.049	6.631	14.843
1873	1.582	4.570	1.118	0.188	0.202	0.153	0.112	0.122	0.043	5.280	13.970
1874	1.937	5.608	1.758	0.236	0.268	0.193	0.164	0.208	0.082	5.526	15.979
1875	1.881	6.531	1.838	0.215	0.259	0.272	0.151	0.213	0.073	5.704	17.137
1876	2.272	6.913	1.738	0.216	0.273	0.384	0.133	0.229	0.071	7.412	19.641
1877	2.544	8.282	1.943	0.159	0.396	0.579	0.125	0.213	0.047	9.506	23.793
1878	2.776	9.198	2.107	0.167	0.274	0.757	0.130	0.224	0.025	10.026	25.685
1879	2.618	10.500	2.088	0.133	0.236	0.803	0.154	0.215	0.017	10.456	27.222
1880	2.951	11.295	2.763	0.141	0.262	1.175	0.170	0.216	0.019	8.658	27.648
1881	2.948	12.464	3.230	0.180	0.292	1.310	0.395	0.209	0.019	6.731	27.779
1882	2.472	11.886	4.592	0.478	0.335	1.423	0.569	0.209	0.018	3.358	25.739
1883	2.041	11.444	5.280	0.524	0.434	1.431	1.583	0.381	0.020	2.792	25.929
1884	2.233	11.436	6.648	0.624	0.549	1.514	2.053	0.467	0.184	2.433	28.142
1885	1.987	11.951	6.585	0.582	0.847	2.554	3.207	0.546	0.244	2.673	31.378
1886	1.880	11.106	6.702	0.864	1.020	2.960	3.795	0.558	0.591	2.408	31.863
1887	1.868	10.559	6.532	0.951	0.978	3.277	4.329	0.648	0.653	1.987	31.679
1888	2.010	9.519	6.183	1.591	1.234	3.486	4.937	0.562	0.645	1.706	32.272
1889	1.867	9.113	6.488	1.702	1.828	3.472	5.178	0.639	0.798	1.244	32.329
1890	1.764	8.404	6.418	1.512	1.504	3.502	5.466	0.685	1.585	0.816	31.656
1891	1.710	8.905	6.686	1.144	1.624	3.804	5.623	0.999	1.901	0.776	33.172
1892	1.986	9.426	7.008	1.243	1.769	3.630	5.647	1.403	2.076	0.720	34.909
1893	1.844	10.127	6.492	1.297	1.724	3.473	5.190	1.316	1.985	0.781	34.228
1894	2.283	10.023	6.533	1.310	1.729	3.299	5.703	1.473	1.905	1.425	35.683
1895	2.598	10.432	7.316	1.578	2.150	3.319	5.645	1.467	2.139	1.424	38.067
1896	2.611	9.909	7.180	1.441	2.100	3.321	5.362	1.454	2.018	1.691	37.087
1897	3.019	10.486	6.967	1.602	2.208	4.240	5.424	1.436	2.222	1.068	38.672
1898	2.912	10.759	7.123	1.733	1.942	4.670	6.171	1.936	2.180	0.883	40.309
1899	3.013	11.003	7.764	1.924	1.787	6.028	5.807	2.447	3.043	0.521	43.339
1900	3.123	11.689	7.933	2.136	1.931	6.190	5.659	2.388	4.234	0.412	45.895

TABLE 23. TOTAL STOCK OWNED (THOUSANDS OF DOLLARS)

YEAR	REGIONS								TOTAL STOCK	TOTAL STOCK BONDS
	1	2	3	4	5	6	7	8	STOCK	BONDS
1843	30.	5.	0.	0.	0.	0.	0.	0.	36.	113.
1844	81.	12.	0.	0.	0.	0.	0.	0.	93.	267.
1845	84.	9.	0.	0.	0.	0.	0.	0.	93.	292.
1846	87.	8.	0.	0.	0.	0.	0.	0.	95.	342.
1847	129.	6.	0.	0.	0.	0.	0.	0.	136.	481.
1848	214.	11.	0.	0.	0.	0.	0.	0.	225.	668.
1849	364.	106.	0.	0.	0.	0.	0.	0.	470.	1289.
1850	332.	46.	0.	0.	0.	0.	0.	0.	378.	1113.
1851	420.	27.	0.	0.	0.	0.	0.	0.	447.	1365.
1852	460.	35.	0.	0.	0.	0.	0.	0.	494.	1485.
1853	536.	74.	0.	0.	0.	0.	0.	0.	610.	1715.
1854	669.	141.	0.	0.	0.	0.	0.	0.	811.	2116.
1855	633.	125.	0.	0.	0.	0.	0.	0.	758.	2080.
1856	608.	198.	25.	0.	0.	0.	0.	0.	831.	2302.
1857	532.	221.	13.	0.	21.	0.	0.	0.	787.	2427.
1858	452.	230.	13.	0.	0.	0.	0.	0.	695.	2584.
1859	399.	259.	13.	0.	0.	0.	0.	0.	672.	2801.
1860	390.	276.	37.	0.	0.	0.	0.	0.	704.	3481.
1861	390.	294.	40.	0.	0.	0.	0.	0.	723.	5546.
1862	239.	178.	24.	0.	0.	0.	0.	0.	442.	9160.
1863	509.	395.	23.	1.	0.	22.	0.	0.	951.	18190.
1864	628.	164.	42.	0.	0.	31.	0.	0.	865.	25163.
1865	918.	195.	97.	0.	0.	39.	0.	0.	1249.	28948.
1866	1746.	255.	108.	0.	0.	41.	0.	0.	2149.	34724.
1867	1904.	377.	125.	0.	0.	4.	0.	0.	2411.	38484.
1868	2464.	605.	352.	0.	0.	7.	0.	0.	3428.	43511.
1869	2805.	574.	260.	13.	7.	54.	46.	0.	3759.	51158.
1870	2794.	544.	259.	0.	0.	7.	0.	0.	3603.	48924.
1871	2594.	709.	191.	44.	0.	7.	0.	0.	3545.	53650.

T. LE 23 (CONTINUED)

YEAR	REGIONS								TOTAL STOCK	STOCK BONDS
	1	2	3	4	5	6	7	8		
1872	2721.	957.	195.	0.	0.	2.	0.	0.	3875.	58034.
1873	2624.	1285.	135.	0.	0.	11.	0.	34.	4090.	57109.
1874	3478.	1679.	1619.	19.	0.	24.	307.	0.	7125.	75184.
1875	3127.	1843.	122.	0.	0.	19.	0.	0.	5112.	79622.
1876	3507.	2317.	146.	0.	0.	10.	0.	0.	5981.	92008.
1877	3323.	2111.	179.	0.	0.	98.	12.	0.	5725.	110386.
1878	3518.	2213.	192.	0.	0.	3.	0.	0.	5926.	119853.
1879	3520.	2256.	187.	0.	0.	12.	0.	0.	5974.	127694.
1880	3450.	2915.	323.	31.	0.	7.	1.	0.	6727.	134542.
1881	3245.	4542.	336.	0.	0.	7.	81.	26.	8237.	140502.
1882	3327.	5971.	531.	0.	0.	7.	105.	60.	10000.	133477.
1883	4553.	7091.	2512.	4.	3.	199.	914.	78.	15355.	147287.
1884	5079.	8121.	3113.	5.	4.	252.	1839.	110.	16522.	167570.
1885	5726.	7846.	3187.	4.	5.	325.	2197.	165.	19457.	195915.
1886	5727.	8494.	3642.	5.	61.	715.	2194.	191.	21031.	210928.
1887	5967.	9060.	3739.	35.	7.	690.	2476.	200.	22174.	222372.
1888	5908.	9027.	3888.	414.	9.	820.	2495.	203.	22763.	239631.
1889	6620.	11576.	4649.	175.	20.	1026.	2555.	241.	26863.	265409.
1890	6647.	12399.	4694.	169.	342.	1472.	4452.	387.	30563.	282645.
1891	6999.	17024.	4967.	111.	367.	2385.	4540.	467.	36860.	324038.
1892	7457.	21324.	6679.	250.	391.	2933.	4871.	456.	44362.	376086.
1893	6980.	24668.	7326.	425.	392.	2822.	8055.	1426.	52095.	400790.
1894	8157.	26923.	9159.	442.	747.	2171.	6548.	1225.	55372.	452150.
1895	9459.	30100.	9190.	674.	746.	2240.	5805.	1153.	59367.	514671.
1896	9385.	31476.	10717.	708.	772.	1866.	3783.	890.	59597.	534295.
1897	10525.	35232.	11094.	734.	813.	2234.	4103.	1095.	65831.	601809.
1898	13113.	44020.	11641.	848.	811.	2205.	5335.	992.	78966.	687424.
1899	15702.	48563.	12780.	914.	907.	2208.	5723.	1101.	87898.	799415.
1900	18408.	55776.	14060.	1003.	1085.	2713.	6558.	1483.	101086.	931635.

TABLE 24. TOTAL STOCK OWNED (PERCENT OF TOTAL ASSETS)

YEAR	REGIONS								TOTAL STOCK	TOTAL STOCK, BONDS
	1	2	3	4	5	6	7	8		
1843	1.534	0.279	0.0	0.0	0.0	0.0	0.0	0.0	1.813	5.739
1844	3.661	0.563	0.0	0.0	0.0	0.0	0.0	0.0	4.225	12.108
1845	3.263	0.335	0.0	0.0	0.0	0.0	0.0	0.0	3.597	11.317
1846	2.715	0.256	0.0	0.0	0.0	0.0	0.0	0.0	2.971	10.683
1847	3.816	0.189	0.0	0.0	0.0	0.0	0.0	0.0	4.005	14.194
1848	4.998	0.246	0.0	0.0	0.0	0.0	0.0	0.0	5.245	15.605
1849	4.715	1.367	0.0	0.0	0.0	0.0	0.0	0.0	6.082	16.682
1850	3.489	0.484	0.0	0.0	0.0	0.0	0.0	0.0	3.973	11.693
1851	3.496	0.228	0.0	0.0	0.0	0.0	0.0	0.0	3.724	11.367
1852	3.205	0.243	0.0	0.0	0.0	0.0	0.0	0.0	3.448	10.356
1853	3.309	0.457	0.0	0.0	0.0	0.0	0.0	0.0	3.766	10.591
1854	3.714	0.785	0.0	0.0	0.0	0.0	0.0	0.0	4.499	11.740
1855	3.417	0.674	0.0	0.0	0.0	0.0	0.0	0.0	4.092	11.224
1856	2.822	0.920	0.114	0.0	0.0	0.0	0.0	0.0	3.856	10.680
1857	2.157	0.896	0.052	0.0	0.084	0.0	0.0	0.0	3.188	9.836
1858	1.637	0.832	0.046	0.0	0.0	0.0	0.0	0.0	2.515	9.353
1859	1.334	0.868	0.044	0.0	0.0	0.0	0.0	0.0	2.245	9.365
1860	1.095	0.777	0.105	0.0	0.0	0.0	0.0	0.0	1.977	9.779
1861	0.998	0.751	0.102	0.0	0.0	0.0	0.0	0.0	1.851	14.195
1862	0.580	0.433	0.043	0.002	0.0	0.042	0.0	0.0	1.072	22.237
1863	0.950	0.738	0.061	0.0	0.0	0.046	0.0	0.0	1.775	33.945
1864	0.924	0.242	0.061	0.0	0.0	0.047	0.0	0.0	1.273	37.041
1865	1.117	0.237	0.118	0.0	0.0	0.047	0.0	0.0	1.519	35.220
1866	1.628	0.238	0.100	0.0	0.0	0.038	0.0	0.0	2.004	32.374
1867	1.311	0.260	0.086	0.0	0.0	0.003	0.0	0.0	1.660	26.493
1868	1.212	0.297	0.173	0.0	0.0	0.003	0.0	0.0	1.686	21.403
1869	1.103	0.226	0.102	0.005	0.003	0.021	0.018	0.0	1.478	20.111
1870	0.983	0.191	0.091	0.0	0.0	0.003	0.0	0.0	1.268	17.223
1871	0.780	0.213	0.057	0.013	0.0	0.002	0.0	0.0	1.066	16.128

TABLE 24 (CONTINUED)

YEAR	REGIONS								TOTAL STOCK	STOCK BONDS
	1	2	3	4	5	6	7	8		
1872	0.746	0.262	0.053	0.0	0.0	0.001	0.0	0.0	1.062	15.905
1873	0.691	0.339	0.036	0.0	0.0	0.003	0.0	0.009	1.078	15.047
1874	0.817	0.394	0.380	0.005	0.0	0.006	0.072	0.0	1.673	17.652
1875	0.719	0.424	0.028	0.0	0.0	0.004	0.0	0.0	1.176	18.313
1876	0.801	0.529	0.033	0.0	0.0	0.002	0.0	0.0	1.366	21.006
1877	0.755	0.480	0.041	0.0	0.0	0.022	0.003	0.0	1.301	25.095
1878	0.793	0.499	0.043	0.0	0.0	0.001	0.0	0.0	1.336	27.022
1879	0.787	0.505	0.042	0.0	0.0	0.003	0.0	0.0	1.336	28.558
1880	0.746	0.631	0.070	0.007	0.0	0.001	0.000	0.0	1.455	29.103
1881	0.682	0.954	0.070	0.0	0.0	0.001	0.017	0.006	1.730	29.509
1882	0.693	1.245	0.111	0.0	0.0	0.001	0.022	0.013	2.085	27.824
1883	0.895	1.394	0.494	0.001	0.001	0.039	0.180	0.015	3.018	28.947
1884	0.959	1.533	0.588	0.001	0.001	0.048	0.347	0.021	3.497	31.639
1885	1.018	1.395	0.567	0.001	0.001	0.058	0.391	0.029	3.460	34.838
1886	0.962	1.426	0.612	0.001	0.010	0.120	0.368	0.032	3.631	35.414
1887	0.944	1.434	0.592	0.006	0.001	0.109	0.392	0.032	3.509	35.188
1888	0.879	1.343	0.579	0.062	0.001	0.122	0.371	0.030	3.387	35.660
1889	0.897	1.569	0.630	0.024	0.003	0.139	0.346	0.033	3.641	35.970
1890	0.835	1.557	0.589	0.021	0.043	0.165	0.559	0.049	3.838	35.494
1891	0.808	1.967	0.574	0.013	0.042	0.275	0.524	0.054	4.258	37.430
1892	0.785	2.244	0.703	0.026	0.041	0.309	0.513	0.048	4.668	39.577
1893	0.685	2.421	0.719	0.042	0.038	0.277	0.791	0.140	5.114	39.342
1894	0.734	2.421	0.824	0.040	0.067	0.195	0.589	0.110	4.980	40.662
1895	0.791	2.517	0.768	0.056	0.062	0.187	0.485	0.096	4.964	43.031
1896	0.733	2.459	0.837	0.055	0.060	0.146	0.296	0.070	4.656	41.743
1897	0.759	2.542	0.800	0.053	0.059	0.161	0.296	0.079	4.750	43.422
1898	0.869	2.916	0.771	0.056	0.054	0.146	0.353	0.066	5.231	45.540
1899	0.956	2.958	0.778	0.056	0.055	0.135	0.349	0.067	5.354	48.693
1900	1.017	3.082	0.777	0.055	0.060	0.150	0.362	0.082	5.586	51.481

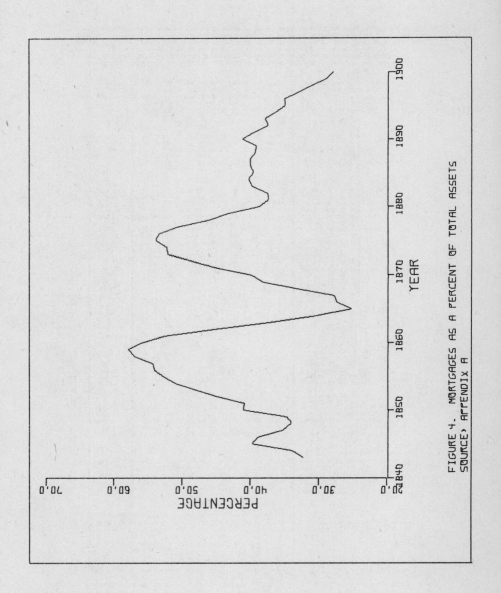

FIGURE 4. MORTGAGES AS A PERCENT OF TOTAL ASSETS

SOURCE, APPENDIX A

TABLE 25. MORTGAGES HELD (THOUSANDS CF DCLLARS)

	REGIONS									
YEAR	1	2	3	4	5	6	7	8	9	TCTAL
1843	0.	0.	0.	0.	0.	0.	0.	0.	0.	636.
1844	0.	0.	0.	0.	0.	0.	0.	0.	0.	750.
1845	C.	0.	0.	0.	0.	0.	0.	0.	0.	1026.
1846	0.	0.	0.	0.	0.	0.	0.	0.	0.	1241.
1847	0.	0.	0.	0.	0.	0.	0.	0.	0.	1193.
1848	0.	0.	0.	0.	0.	C.	0.	0.	0.	1455.
1849	0.	0.	0.	0.	0.	0.	C.	0.	0.	2688.
1850	0.	0.	0.	0.	0.	0.	0.	0.	0.	3911.
1851	0.	0.	0.	0.	0.	0.	0.	0.	0.	4901.
1852	0.	0.	0.	0.	0.	0.	0.	0.	0.	6434.
1853	0.	0.	0.	0.	C.	0.	0.	0.	0.	7774.
1854	0.	0.	0.	0.	0.	C.	0.	0.	C.	9183.
1855	0.	0.	0.	0.	0.	0.	0.	0.	0.	9758.
1856	0.	0.	0.	0.	0.	0.	0.	0.	0.	11660.
1857	0.	0.	0.	0.	0.	0.	0.	0.	0.	13413.
1858	0.	0.	0.	0.	0.	0.	0.	0.	0.	15741.
1859	0.	0.	0.	0.	0.	C.	0.	0.	0.	17318.
1860	0.	0.	0.	0.	0.	0.	0.	0.	0.	19887.
1861	0.	0.	0.	0.	0.	C.	0.	0.	0.	20528.
1862	0.	0.	0.	0.	0.	0.	0.	0.	0.	18637.
1863	0.	0.	0.	0.	0.	0.	0.	0.	0.	19987.
1864	0.	0.	0.	0.	0.	C.	0.	0.	0.	20618.
1865	0.	0.	0.	0.	0.	0.	0.	0.	0.	20700.
1866	0.	0.	0.	0.	0.	0.	0.	0.	0.	29512.
1867	0.	0.	0.	0.	0.	0.	0.	0.	0.	40562.
1868	0.	0.	0.	0.	0.	0.	0.	0.	0.	67410.
1869	0.	0.	0.	0.	0.	0.	0.	0.	0.	97402.
1870	0.	0.	0.	0.	0.	0.	0.	0.	0.	113205.
1871	0.	C.	0.	0.	0.	C.	0.	0.	0.	149298.

TABLE 25 (CONTINUED)

YEAR	1	2	3	4	5	REGIONS 6	7	8	9	TOTAL
1872	0.	0.	0.	0.	0.	0.	0.	0.	0.	177430.
1873	0.	0.	0.	0.	0.	0.	0.	0.	0.	197982.
1874	28118.	132152.	34747.	61.	86.	3291.	24042.	73.	0.	222570.
1875	29288.	136925.	39756.	56.	110.	3404.	24820.	73.	0.	234433.
1876	29070.	135847.	42633.	50.	123.	3352.	22383.	73.	0.	233531.
1877	27032.	118959.	51634.	35.	151.	3066.	21714.	67.	0.	222657.
1878	23932.	102432.	51070.	20.	154.	2903.	23424.	60.	0.	203995.
1879	17915.	90770.	58741.	17.	149.	3404.	21508.	53.	0.	192557.
1880	15197.	83551.	55650.	12.	152.	3616.	20357.	45.	0.	178583.
1881	13513.	87013.	53676.	8.	153.	4191.	19154.	39.	0.	177749.
1882	12825.	87507.	55886.	19.	210.	4560.	19517.	35.	0.	180559.
1883	12778.	92538.	68371.	30.	340.	4830.	23688.	33.	0.	202607.
1884	12273.	93251.	76169.	41.	452.	4708.	26534.	29.	0.	213458.
1885	12209.	93977.	81736.	67.	576.	5662.	27937.	26.	4.	221193.
1886	11471.	93824.	94939.	220.	680.	8743.	29121.	23.	6.	239027.
1887	11373.	104952.	94578.	256.	854.	11141.	29799.	20.	10.	252984.
1888	9945.	118637.	82823.	353.	1052.	21907.	28843.	17.	12.	263588.
1889	11306.	127168.	91491.	417.	1418.	25596.	30728.	234.	61.	288420.
1890	12284.	140124.	101771.	530.	1871.	31079.	39364.	869.	131.	328022.
1891	12458.	140879.	104363.	631.	2184.	31722.	47215.	2030.	325.	341807.
1892	12277.	146910.	103439.	718.	3021.	31322.	53780.	3077.	499.	355042.
1893	14545.	150107.	116684.	1103.	3325.	43752.	58585.	3515.	837.	386452.
1894	15096.	153976.	116455.	1418.	3283.	48118.	60888.	3811.	817.	403862.
1895	17441.	158408.	122764.	1770.	3693.	47164.	60284.	4524.	982.	417030.
1896	18070.	170500.	129315.	2221.	4268.	48680.	70510.	4776.	1261.	449601.
1897	17617.	173013.	131949.	3024.	5125.	48245.	69725.	5621.	1576.	456095.
1898	18758.	178941.	129209.	3685.	6584.	51958.	70875.	5566.	1840.	467416.
1899	21339.	179337.	130449.	3690.	7265.	52936.	70734.	5033.	1802.	472585.
1900	22815.	171679.	145828.	4311.	9714.	59177.	81588.	5270.	1890.	502272.

use of incoming funds appears to have cut deeply into the
number of new mortgages that were contracted until the
needed bonds were acquired. The temporary reduction in
the dollar value of total mortgages was not particularly
large. However, the expanding size of total asset holdings
caused the percentage of mortgages to drop precipitously
by comparison.

The large number of foreclosures that was discussed in
connection with the large transfer of properties from active
mortgages into wholly owned items of real estate, seems to
have set the stage for the downward trend that persisted.
After the hard lessons learned during the deflated mortgage
markets of the seventies the increasing opportunities to
buy securities were found to be increasingly attractive.

The author would like to have presented a complete
categorization of mortgages by type, inasmuch as many of the
schedules were at hand. This task was, in fact, only
accomplished for Penn Mutual Life. After examination of that
single company's complete mortgage record the magnitude of
the task was apparent. The more modest alternative of
presenting a few examples along these lines was chosen. The
excellent biograpy of Northwestern Mutual Life[1] contains a
rather complete analysis of the character of the mortgages
held by that company. Table 26 and 27 contain Urban/rural
breakdowns for Mutual Benefit Life and Aetna Life respectively.

-----

[1]See: Harold F. Williamson and Orange A. Smalley, Northwestern Mutual Life (Evanston, Ill.:Northwestern University
Press, 1957).

Table 26. Mutual Benefit Life, Mortgage Experience (Thousands)[2]

Year	Farm	City
1882	$ 12	$ 6,644
1883	1,061	6,667
1884	5,863	7,322
1885	10,978	6,359
1886	11,918	7,931
1887	13,405	6,555
1888	12,679	7,875
1889	13,009	9,609
1890	14,122	11,389
1891	14,927	12,713
1892	16,973	12,370
1893	16,973	12,670
1894	18,592	11,864
1895	20,286	11,788
1896	22,090	11,456
1897	22,372	10,824
1898	20,966	11,390
1899	21,499	11,199
1900	24,195	11,854

[2] Mutual Benefit Life Insurance Company, Company Records.

Table 27 . Urban, rural mortgages of AETNA Life Insurance Company (thousands)[a].

Year	Urban		Rural		Total Loans[b]	
	No.	Amount	No.	Amount	No.	Amount
1862	1	$ 9,000			1	$ 9,000
1863	3	19,000			3	19,000
1864	1	12,000			1	12,000
1865	1	2,000			1	2,000
1866	1	10,000			1	10,000
1867	6	120,000	7	$ 101	13	321,000
1868	13	141,000	85	758	96	899,000
1869	9	61,000	365	1,067	374	1,122,000
1870	12	98,000	540	1,836	532	1,434,000
1871	6	82,000	598	1,067	606	1,149,000
1872	9	58,000	653	1,310	662	1,368,000
1873	10	86,000	733	1,191	743	1,277,000
1874	46	338,000	650	1,926	896	1,363,000
1875	48	251,000	1566	1,491	1614	1,742,000
1876	19	43,000	1967	1,981	1986	2,034,000
1877	7	23,000	1519	1,950	1586	1,973,000
1878	5	12,000	1230	1,487	1255	1,499,000
1879	6	33,000	515	567	521	600,000
1880	24	63,000	721	990	745	1,053,000
1881	22	838,000	1441	2,819	1463	2,634,000
1882	24	119,000	2689	3,434	2653	3,553,000
1883	14	121,000	3035	2,363	3049	3,978,000
1884	7	21,000	3033	2,363	3069	2,394,000
1885	4	36,000	1064	1,942	1068	1,078,000
1886	8	35,000	1681	2,099	1659	2,134,000
1887	4	23,000	1880	2,447	1834	2,470,000
1888	2	6,000	2055	2,747	2037	2,733,000
1889	10	55,000	2057	2,633	2067	2,878,000
1890	3	8,000	2893	3,360	2596	3,368,000
1891	1	3,000	2478	3,369	2479	3,372,000
1892	6	7,000	1894	2,880	1900	2,807,000
1893	21	136,000	3324	3,172	3345	5,388,000
1894	5	11,000	2938	3,997	2928	4,006,000
1895	6	40,000	2654	3,690	2660	3,736,000
1896	7	560,000	2592	3,888	2599	4,383,000
1897	17	98,000	1836	2,807	1853	2,908,000
1898	28	128,000	1579	2,493	1604	2,621,000
1899	74	458,000	3068	5,463	3080	5,916,000
1900	22	316,000	3382	6,654	3409	6,970,000

[a]Compiled from: R.H. Pierce, A Record of Mortgage Loan Experience (Hartford, Conn.:Aetna Life Insurance Company, 1948(, pp. 11-17.
[b]This table summarizes all types of loans on Real Estate Collateral.

The example provided by the mortgage record of Penn
Mutual Life Insurance Company is more complete. Ledger
records containing the original entries of all mortgages
contracted by this company from its origin to the late
1890's are intact at the home office and were allocated by
type and by region to obtain Table 28 and Table 29, respectively. Note that no record was obtained for 1900.
Initial contact with the mortgage records of the various
companies through the official mortgage schedules, mentioned
earlier, had suggested that this company's mortgage record
should offer a sort of boundary example.

The company's later schedules were unusual both by reason
of the high percentage of mortgages from outside the home
region and because of the large amount of loans to industrial
and commercial concerns; more especially the latter.

In retrospect, the tables suggest that some specific
policy change must have occurred in 1890. The record varies
significantly as of that date with regard to both type and
region. The company's record prior to that date is probably
much more typical of the entire industry, though still
among the more diversified in both respects.

The types identified in Table 28 are as follows: 1, Rural;
2, Urban Residential; 3, Urban Land; 4, Industrial; 5, Com-
merical. The high concentration in urban properties in the
earliest years seems to be quite typical, judging from those
records of other companies which have been examined. The Penn

TABLE 2x. PENN MUTUAL MORTGAGE EXPERIENCE, BY TYPE

YEAR	1	2	3	4	5
1945	0.00	71.43	28.57	0.00	0.00
1946	0.00	71.43	28.57	0.00	0.00
1947	0.00	71.43	28.57	0.00	0.00
1948	0.00	71.43	28.57	0.00	0.00
1949	0.00	60.00	40.00	0.00	0.00
1950	0.00	77.78	22.22	0.00	0.00
1951	0.00	68.67	23.33	0.00	0.00
1952	0.00	69.67	24.24	30.30	0.00
1953	0.00	54.41	13.33	26.67	0.00
1954	0.00	54.41	22.06	23.53	0.00
1955	0.00	31.04	22.06	23.53	0.00
1956	0.29	42.07	18.52	44.44	12.36
1957	6.41	32.10	16.55	41.34	18.94
1958	4.75	24.92	20.59	24.69	17.99
1959	4.36	28.06	19.32	22.73	14.06
1960	2.44	20.82	23.39	21.58	14.47
1961	18.02	32.53	24.41	20.07	12.53
1962	20.61	37.20	24.62	15.23	7.21
1963	17.17	31.20	23.74	13.19	7.04
1964	12.44	34.75	21.39	13.46	0.00
1965	12.48	44.62	22.54	18.69	1.94
1966	10.82	44.99	25.??	17.02	2.42
1967	6.04	41.99	26.21	16.28	1.83
1968	10.82	45.08	21.32	12.07	2.24
1969	10.16	45.08	28.62	14.06	1.93
1970	12.44	46.90	24.13	14.36	1.71
1971	5.51	45.24	25.14	13.00	3.01
1972	6.51	46.24	23.14	16.96	
1973			22.39		

TABLE 28 (CONTINUED)

TYPE

YEAR	1	2	3	4	5
1874	14.23	34.43	24.15	18.73	8.47
1875	13.93	39.71	22.33	16.24	7.76
1876	16.83	38.71	21.01	15.16	8.29
1877	16.42	37.70	21.35	15.86	8.67
1878	15.97	52.97	0.00	23.42	8.52
1879	15.14	50.49	0.96	24.07	10.30
1880	16.37	43.65	1.12	24.34	15.57
1881	11.55	43.37	1.20	26.45	17.51
1882	12.40	44.80	1.37	23.60	11.00
1883	14.12	46.27	1.04	21.87	11.38
1884	12.53	50.56	1.97	21.25	13.71
1885	13.91	47.38	2.01	22.97	13.41
1886	13.90	48.26	2.02	21.79	14.04
1887	14.00	47.91	2.11	21.94	14.13
1888	14.01	45.65	0.00	21.87	14.75
1889	17.38	40.74	0.00	23.76	14.07
1890	7.29	13.09	0.00	13.30	44.33
1891	4.01	13.94	0.00	7.47	74.54
1892	3.86	13.60	0.00	7.60	74.88
1893	3.26	5.03	0.00	7.85	72.35
1894	3.44	3.65	0.00	9.35	73.25
1895	3.50	3.73	0.00	8.52	77.47
1896	4.74	4.16	0.00	12.02	78.47
1897	3.80	3.69	0.00	12.53	73.94
1898	3.97	1.40	0.00	13.07	71.56
1899	5.16	2.81	0.00	17.00	76.02
1900	0.00	0.00	0.00	0.00	0.00

TABLE 24. PENN MUTUAL MORTGAGE EXPERIENCE, BY REGION

REGIONS

YEAR	1	2	3	4	5	6	7	8
1845	0.00	100.00	0.00	0.00	0.00	0.00	0.00	0.00
1846	0.00	100.00	0.00	0.00	0.00	0.00	0.00	0.00
1847	0.00	100.00	0.00	0.00	0.00	0.00	0.00	0.00
1848	0.00	100.00	0.00	0.00	0.00	0.00	0.00	0.00
1849	0.00	100.00	0.00	0.00	0.00	0.00	0.00	0.00
1850	0.00	100.00	0.00	0.00	0.00	0.00	0.00	0.00
1851	0.00	100.00	0.00	0.00	0.00	0.00	0.00	0.00
1852	0.00	100.00	0.00	0.00	0.00	0.00	0.00	0.00
1853	0.00	100.00	0.00	0.00	0.00	0.00	0.00	0.00
1854	0.00	100.00	0.00	0.00	0.00	0.00	0.00	0.00
1855	0.00	99.30	3.70	0.00	0.00	0.00	0.00	0.00
1856	0.00	97.24	2.76	0.00	0.00	0.00	0.00	0.00
1857	0.00	68.72	31.28	0.00	0.00	0.00	0.00	0.00
1858	0.00	71.21	28.79	0.00	0.00	0.00	0.00	0.00
1859	0.00	69.78	30.22	0.00	0.00	0.00	0.00	0.00
1860	0.00	71.91	28.09	0.00	0.00	0.00	0.00	0.00
1861	0.00	78.68	21.32	0.00	0.00	0.00	0.00	0.00
1862	0.00	85.04	14.95	0.00	0.00	0.00	0.00	0.00
1863	0.00	91.16	8.49	0.00	0.00	0.00	0.00	0.00
1864	0.00	92.56	7.44	0.00	0.00	0.00	0.00	0.00
1865	0.00	100.00	0.00	0.00	0.00	0.00	0.00	0.00
1866	0.00	100.00	0.00	0.00	0.00	0.00	0.00	0.00
1867	0.00	100.00	0.00	0.00	0.00	0.00	0.00	0.00
1868	0.00	100.00	0.00	0.00	0.00	0.00	0.00	0.00
1869	0.00	97.40	1.46	0.00	0.00	0.00	0.00	0.00
1870	0.00	97.08	1.80	0.00	0.00	1.15	0.00	0.00
1871	.13	97.08	1.80	0.00	0.00	.99	0.00	0.00
1872	.36	95.35	3.02	.40	0.00	.87	0.00	0.00
1873	.30	93.57	5.06	.33	0.00	.73	0.00	0.00

TABLE 24 (CONTINUED)

PERIODS

YEAR	1	2	3	4	5	6	7	8
1874	.22	74.77	4.62	.24	0.00	.14	0.00	0.00
1875	.19	74.26	5.23	.21	0.00	.12	0.00	0.00
1876	.18	72.40	7.17	.20	0.00	.20	0.00	0.00
1877	.18	72.11	7.50	.21	0.00	0.00	0.00	0.00
1878	0.00	74.56	0.45	0.00	0.00	0.00	0.00	0.00
1879	0.00	73.73	6.21	0.00	0.00	0.00	0.00	0.00
1880	0.00	73.85	6.15	0.00	0.00	0.00	0.00	0.00
1881	0.00	76.64	3.35	0.00	0.00	0.00	0.00	0.00
1882	0.00	76.17	3.36	0.00	0.00	0.00	0.00	0.00
1883	0.00	77.43	2.57	0.00	0.00	0.00	0.00	0.00
1884	0.00	76.74	2.02	0.00	0.00	0.00	0.00	0.00
1885	0.00	74.19	2.43	0.00	0.00	0.00	0.00	0.00
1886	0.00	71.05	2.95	0.00	0.00	17.02	22.22	0.00
1887	0.00	71.39	1.97	5.95	9.46	19.14	25.06	0.00
1888	0.00	43.24	4.89	4.94	7.84	14.91	25.67	0.00
1889	0.00	36.14	5.50	7.87	9.35	14.43	27.70	0.00
1890	0.00	34.74	5.51	7.45	151	19.03	30.57	0.00
1891	0.00	22.06	0.78	7.53	11.40	14.42	30.44	0.00
1892	0.00	27.09	6.09	6.33	12.05	15.11	28.00	0.00
1893	0.00	27.03	3.95	6.69	12.44	13.42	29.19	0.00
1894	0.00	35.73	3.36	5.02	16.99	12.14	30.44	0.00
1895	0.00	36.36	3.50	6.53	0.00	0.00	27.01	0.00
1896	0.00	33.45	4.55	0.00	0.00	0.00	0.00	0.00
1897	0.00	34.77	0.00	0.00	0.00	0.00	0.00	0.00
1898	0.00	33.08	0.00	0.00	0.00	0.00	0.00	0.00
1899	0.00	0.00	0.00	0.00	0.00	0.00	0.00	0.00
1900	0.00	0.00	0.00	0.00	0.00	0.00	0.00	0.00

Mutual mortgages are more representative in this respect
than the record of Aetna, for example, which became one of
the most abundant in Midwestern farm mortgages; or Northwestern
which maintained a similar abundance.

The commercial mortgages that became so much in evidence
in the nineties included a large number of retail establishments and hotels. For lack of an appropriate category, some
lodge buildings, Y.M.C.A.'s, and church buildings were
also placed in this class.

The Penn Mutual percentages of Table 29 may be contrasted with those of Table 30, which is the regional table
for the insurance industry as a whole. Notice that the basis
of the percentages in the latter case is total assets
rather than mortgages alone. The heavy concentration of
mortgages near the home office evident in the early Penn
Mutual record is a much more typical pattern than its late
diversification and interest in Southern loans. The industry pattern shows a generally low percentage of loans
in both the Southern regions and in the Pacific region, as
well as in foreign mortgages.

Collateral Loans

Inability to allocate this class of assets by type
or region in any justifiable fashion has made it of less
interest in this study than it might otherwise have been.
A large number of the schedules of these items were compared

TABLE 30. MORTGAGES HELD (PERCENT OF TOTAL ASSETS)

YEAR	1	2	3	4	5	6	7	8	9	TOTAL
1843	0.0	0.0	0.0	0.0	0.0	0.0	0.0	0.0	0.0	32.425
1844	0.0	0.0	0.0	0.0	0.0	0.0	0.0	0.0	0.0	33.969
1845	0.0	0.0	0.0	0.0	0.0	0.0	0.0	0.0	0.0	39.788
1846	0.0	0.0	0.0	0.0	0.0	0.0	0.0	0.0	0.0	38.758
1847	0.0	0.0	0.0	0.0	0.0	0.0	0.0	0.0	0.0	35.229
1848	0.0	0.0	0.0	0.0	0.0	0.0	0.0	0.0	0.0	33.980
1849	0.0	0.0	0.0	0.0	0.0	0.0	0.0	0.0	0.0	34.782
1850	0.0	0.0	0.0	0.0	0.0	0.0	0.0	0.0	0.0	41.082
1851	0.0	0.0	0.0	0.0	0.0	0.0	0.0	0.0	0.0	40.819
1852	0.0	0.0	0.0	0.0	0.0	0.0	0.0	0.0	0.0	44.867
1853	0.0	0.0	0.0	0.0	0.0	0.0	0.0	0.0	0.0	48.020
1854	0.0	0.0	0.0	0.0	0.0	0.0	0.0	0.0	0.0	50.959
1855	0.0	0.0	0.0	0.0	0.0	0.0	0.0	0.0	0.0	52.664
1856	0.0	0.0	0.0	0.0	0.0	0.0	0.0	0.0	0.0	54.109
1857	0.0	0.0	0.0	0.0	0.0	0.0	0.0	0.0	0.0	54.362
1858	0.0	0.0	0.0	0.0	0.0	0.0	0.0	0.0	0.0	56.975
1859	0.0	0.0	0.0	0.0	0.0	0.0	0.0	0.0	0.0	57.904
1860	0.0	0.0	0.0	0.0	0.0	0.0	0.0	0.0	0.0	55.868
1861	0.0	0.0	0.0	0.0	0.0	0.0	0.0	0.0	0.0	52.537
1862	0.0	0.0	0.0	0.0	0.0	0.0	0.0	0.0	0.0	45.242
1863	0.0	0.0	0.0	0.0	0.0	0.0	0.0	0.0	0.0	37.299
1864	0.0	0.0	0.0	0.0	0.0	0.0	0.0	0.0	0.0	30.350
1865	0.0	0.0	0.0	0.0	0.0	0.0	0.0	0.0	0.0	25.185
1866	0.0	0.0	0.0	0.0	0.0	0.0	0.0	0.0	0.0	27.516
1867	0.0	0.0	0.0	0.0	0.0	0.0	0.0	0.0	0.0	27.882
1868	0.0	0.0	0.0	0.0	0.0	0.0	0.0	0.0	0.0	33.160
1869	0.0	0.0	0.0	0.0	0.0	0.0	0.0	0.0	0.0	38.290
1870	0.0	0.0	0.0	0.0	0.0	0.0	0.0	0.0	0.0	39.852
1871	0.0	0.0	0.0	0.0	0.0	0.0	0.0	0.0	0.0	44.682

TABLE 30 (CONTINUED)

REGIONS

YEAR	1	2	3	4	5	6	7	8	9	TOTAL
1872	0.0	0.0	0.0	0.0	0.0	0.0	0.0	0.0	0.0	48.627
1873	0.0	0.0	0.0	0.0	0.0	0.0	0.0	0.0	0.0	52.165
1874	6.602	31.028	8.158	0.014	0.020	0.773	5.645	0.017	0.0	52.256
1875	6.736	31.492	9.144	0.013	0.025	0.783	5.709	0.017	0.0	53.919
1876	6.637	31.015	9.734	0.012	0.028	0.765	5.110	0.017	0.0	53.318
1877	6.145	27.044	11.738	0.008	0.034	0.697	4.936	0.015	0.0	50.618
1878	5.396	23.094	11.614	0.005	0.035	0.655	5.281	0.013	0.0	45.992
1879	4.006	20.300	13.137	0.004	0.035	0.761	4.810	0.012	0.0	43.064
1880	3.287	18.073	12.038	0.003	0.033	0.783	4.404	0.010	0.0	38.630
1881	2.838	18.275	11.273	0.002	0.032	0.860	4.023	0.008	0.0	37.332
1882	2.673	18.241	11.650	0.004	0.044	0.951	4.068	0.007	0.0	37.636
1883	2.511	18.187	13.437	0.006	0.067	0.949	4.656	0.006	0.0	39.819
1884	2.317	17.607	14.381	0.008	0.085	0.889	5.010	0.005	0.0	40.303
1885	2.171	16.711	14.534	0.012	0.102	1.007	4.968	0.005	0.001	39.510
1886	1.926	15.753	15.940	0.037	0.114	1.468	4.889	0.004	0.001	40.132
1887	1.800	16.608	14.966	0.041	0.135	1.763	4.715	0.003	0.002	40.032
1888	1.480	17.655	12.325	0.053	0.156	3.260	4.292	0.002	0.002	39.225
1889	1.532	17.235	12.400	0.057	0.192	3.469	4.165	0.032	0.008	39.089
1890	1.543	17.596	12.780	0.067	0.235	3.903	4.943	0.109	0.016	41.192
1891	1.439	16.273	12.055	0.073	0.252	3.664	5.454	0.235	0.038	39.482
1892	1.292	15.460	10.685	0.076	0.318	3.296	5.659	0.324	0.052	37.362
1893	1.426	14.735	10.665	0.108	0.326	4.295	5.751	0.345	0.082	37.935
1894	1.358	13.847	10.473	0.127	0.295	4.327	5.476	0.343	0.073	36.320
1895	1.458	13.244	10.264	0.148	0.309	3.943	5.040	0.378	0.082	34.867
1896	1.412	13.321	10.103	0.174	0.333	3.803	5.509	0.373	0.099	35.126
1897	1.286	12.483	9.520	0.218	0.370	3.461	5.031	0.406	0.114	32.908
1898	1.243	11.854	8.560	0.244	0.436	3.442	4.695	0.369	0.122	30.965
1899	1.300	10.923	7.946	0.225	0.454	3.224	4.308	0.307	0.110	28.785
1900	1.261	9.487	8.058	0.238	0.537	3.270	4.508	0.291	0.104	27.755

with the corresponding schedules for the other classes of
assets. The securities hypothecated as collateral for most
of these loans were of the same general types as those owned
by the companies. These included many rail securities and
a larger proportion of industrials, utilities, and financials;
though fewer large companies were represented among the hypothecated securities.

Figure 5 indicates a trend similar to the one described
in connection with the real estate holdings of the early
years. As collateral loans came under increasing legal
inspection and regulation, incoming funds were put into
other assets. Some loans were disposed of, but for the most
part, the decrease in percentage was simply a matter of the
increasing relative size of other asset holdings.

The unusual situation indicated in the 1879-82 period
was the result of an influx of nearly fifty million dollars
worth of collateral loans. This influx was reflected mostly
in the holdings of Equitable, Mutual of New York and Mutual
Benefit Life. The sharp change was not as evident in other
companies. What must have been a rather specific cause for
the influx of these companies was not determined.

This class of assets has produced some of the more lurid
incidents in life insurance history. Many writers have
detailed such matters. Only two instances will be cited here.
These are cited to indicate certain conditions that did
exist upon occasion and were important causes of weakness in

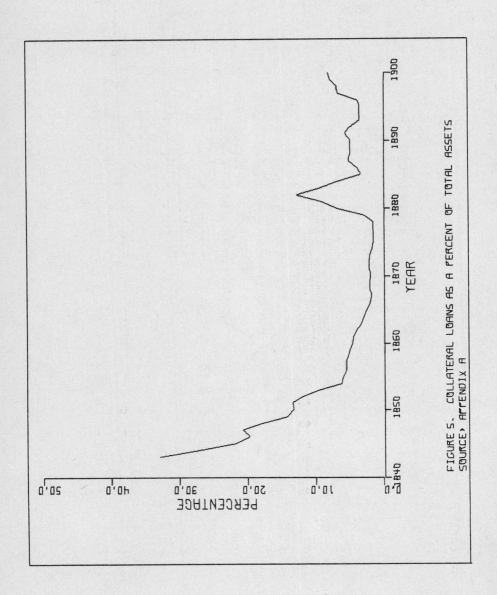

FIGURE 5. COLLATERAL LOANS AS A PERCENT OF TOTAL ASSETS
SOURCE, APPENDIX A

some companies and in some regulation attempts.

In connection with the financial difficulties of the Continental Life Insurance Company (Hartford), Henry Woodward reports,

> "In the summer of 1887, a local firm of brokers with which the president of the Continental had had extensive dealings failed. Within a few days the affairs of the concern were published in detail. Among the securities hypothecated to the firm to reinforce speculative margins, and in several cases re-hypothecated elsewhere, the Parties who had filled the gap of $125,000, recognized some of their own stocks. [Woodward had accounted that certain "Parties" had previously put up funds and securities to assist the Continental in another crisis.] Others had vanished. Stocks and bonds... supposed... to be securely stored in the vaults of the company [Continental], turned up, to their surprise, in the same place [i.e. at the brokerage house]."[1]

There had been some early attempts to correct various irregularities in the practices of some of the companies. Part of the lack of success of these early efforts was due to some rather clever maneuvers by the firms involved. The report of the Armstrong Investigation (1906), revealed the example of one individual associated with such activities over the previous thirty years.

---

[1]P. Henry Woodward, _Insurance in Connecticut_ (Boston: D.H. Hurd and Co., 1897), p. 101.

"Testimony of William S. Manning,
cont'd... Q. "Do you remember the (Senate)
investigation of 1877? A. Yes, very
distinctly. Q. Do you remember getting out
a report of that investigation? A. Yes,
sir, very distinctly... Q. How many did
you publish? A. Well, I suppose about
three or four hundred books... Q. And this
book was copyrighted by you... A. Yes sir,
and I will give you my reason for copyrighting
it, if you would like to have it. When the
Miller examination of the Mutual Life and
other companies was given out publicly, I
believe you will find it in the testimony
there by Mr. McCurdy, that that evidence was
copyrighted by some one connected with Mutual
Life or in their interest, in order that
they might not have that distributed. Q. You
mean that the Mutual Life copyrighted Mr.
McCurdy's evidence? A. That is the evidence....
Q. You copyrighted the evidence on that
occasion? A. Yes, we did. Q. Has it ever
been published?.... A. I don't know how I
can answer....I did not copyright it
(personally)..."[2]

Premium Notes

The general trends of Figure 6 reflect the history of
the use of premium notes in sales promotion that was given
previously. The expanded use of premium notes in the early
growth of the mutual companies and in the competitive period
of the Tontine policies is clearly in evidence in the forties
and mid-sixties. Premium notes were a feature of insurance
in the early years that seemed to please many companies and
policyholders. The major test which the problems of the seven-

---

[2]New York State, Armstrong Report..., IV, 3698.

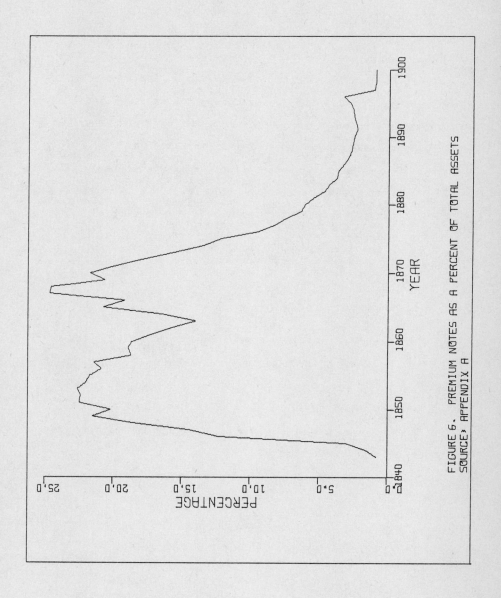

FIGURE 6. PREMIUM NOTES AS A PERCENT OF TOTAL ASSETS
SOURCE: APPENDIX A

ties provided the system revealed its shortcomings. The large number of early terminations in this period offered little return to the companies to offset the heavy starting costs of the policies, especially when the early premiums were paid largely in notes, later defaulted. The lower dividends of the period also fell behind policyholders' expectations in offsetting the interest required by the note. Woodward's history mentions another problem;

> "The Premium note...proved an unexcelled device for canvassing purposes. Under this system fifty percent of the first four premiums were payable in a note, bearing six percent interest, which was made a policy lien and was deducted from the death claim by the terms of the contract. Limited to the first four years, the method made it easy to take large amounts of insurance at small cost. These were extinguished by dividends with a rapidity dependent upon rates of interest.... These were unsatisfactory, however, to claimants who wanted the face of their claims in cash. This was one reason for giving up the system."[1]

Woodward's comments were related specifically to the practices of Connecticut Mutual Life Insurance Company.

---

[1] Woodward, p. 64.

Deferred and Uncollected Premiums

This category is represented in Figure 7 and in some
of the tables as "Premiums Due". In general, this series
only reflected the relatively small, constant percentage of
the total asset structure that might be expected in many
forms of business. The various receivables and accruals seem
only to have kept general pace with the size of the operations
they represented. The one principal exception to this
generalization occurred in connection with the strong competition of the Tontine period. In the general history of
that period mention was made of the deferrals, rebates, and
other devices that were used by many agents and companies to
lessen initial premium payments and promote the expansion
of their business. These practices seem to be reflected in
the temporary rise in the prominence of this class of assets
during that period.

Cash

The early records of the companies and departments
regularly listed the location of cash accumulations. The
amounts deposited at specific banks or on hand were listed
religiously. These early records were compiled by the author
from 1843 through the sixties. At that point in time the
records began to fail as the number of accounts and offices
multiplied and the official demand for the enumeration lessened.

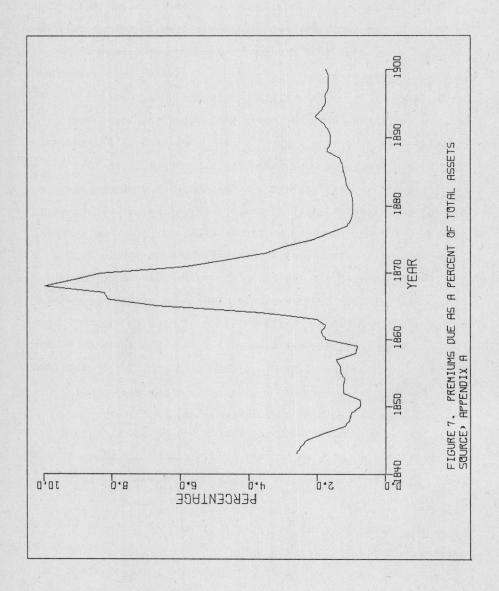

FIGURE 7. PREMIUMS DUE AS A PERCENT OF TOTAL ASSETS

SOURCE: APPENDIX A

The incomplete series is not included here but the
regularities it revealed were seldom violated in the period
examined. For this reason one might conclude that they
persisted somewhat longer. Virtually all cash on hand was
accumulated at the home office. General agents and branch
offices regularly forwarded their uninvested surplus. Bank
deposits were virtually always in one or more banks in the
city of the home office. Branch offices had occasional
small acounts in the principal cities where they were located.
Some of the Eastern companies , not in New York City or Boston,
sometimes had additional accounts in these financial
centers; mostly in New York.

These general proactices, then, placed the preponderance
of cash in New York City, with smaller accumulations in Boston
and Hartford. A few other large cities such as Chicago,
Philadelphia, St. Louis and New Orleans had some deposits,
but they were infinitesimal by comparison.

The frequent, sharp fluctuations in the percentage of
cash held was the result of the relatively small size of such
holdings and the residual position that cash holdings generally
held in the operations of the companies. Whenever any other
series experienced a dramatic change , cash holdings were
also effected.

The number of companies with their transitional cash
holdings still on hand at the end of the accounting period
accounted for the sharp influx of cash. Often a significant

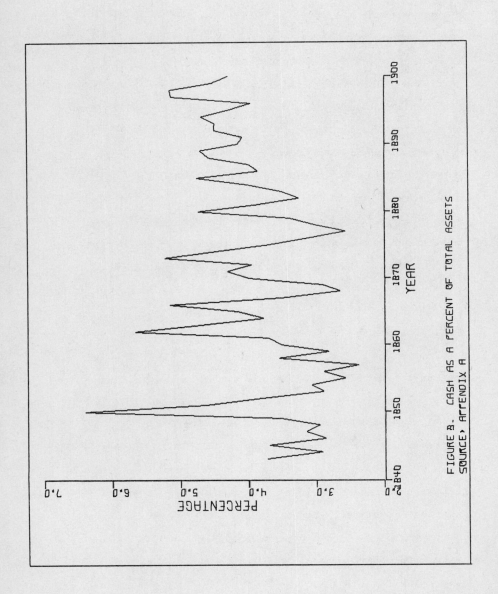

FIGURE 3. CASH AS A PERCENT OF TOTAL ASSETS

SOURCE, APPENDIX A

change in total industry cash holdings was the result of a
single large firm holding the cash from the recently completed
sale of a large block of some other asset.

The general rise in cash holdings during the latter
part of the century was a phenomenon that came under serious
question during the Armstrong Investigation. If cash were
simply being held to meet normal business contingencies one
might expect its percentage importance to decrease as the
total asset portfolio increased in value. They did not,
however, The Armstrong Investigation revealed that some of
these funds were being channeled into other types of financial
institutions. These institutions invested the funds in
higher risk assets, forbidden to the life companies by law.
This avoidance of the law often yielded higher returns to
the life company; it also set the stage for profits to be
accumulated by life company officers who, coincidentally, had
substantial personal interest in the other institutions
involved.

In its more legitimate form, the profits of the manipulation went to the life company by virtue of the fact that
the other intermediaries were owned or controlled by it,
rather than by an individual. In his testimony before the
Armstrong Committee, Edmund D. Randolph, Treasurer of New
York Life Insurance Company, gave evidence of how higher returns were obtained through the placement of funds with subsidiaries.

"...Q. What was the reason of putting up
$13,000,000 with the New York Security and
Trust Company? [A subsidiary]. A. It would
arise from the loans that have been the subject
of inquiry, money that they would put there
by reason of reaping a higher rate of interest.
Q. The New York Security and Trust Company
loaned its money on collateral? A. Yes....
Q. And by its arrangement with you in account
4 you get the benefit of interest within one-
half of one percent of the amount the Trust
Company was getting. A. Yes sir...."[1]

Subsidiary institutions became important to the life

companies for other reasons as well as those mentioned. It

was partly a logical integration based upon the increasing

need of the life companies for banking, brokerage, and other

services. In some cases, for example, the life companies had

been forbidden by law to make direct purchases of new securities;

rather they were to purchase them on the open market. Such

legal acts were strong incentive to the larger companies to

move toward holding increased numbers of subsidiaries.

---

[1]New York State, Armstrong Report..., I. 452-453

Table 31.   Subsidiaries and Affiliates of Selected Life Insurance
            Companies (January 1, 1905).[2]

Mutual Life	Equitable Life
Guarantee Trust Co.	Mercantile Trust Co.
U.S. Mortgage & Trust	Equitable Trust Co.
Morristown Trust Co.	Commercial Trust Co.
National Bank of Commerce	National Bank of Commerce
Fifth Avenue Trust Co.	Fifth Avenue Trust Co.
Morton Trust Co.	Fidelity Trust Co.
American Exchange National Bank	Hibernia Bank and Trust
First National Bank	Franklin National Bank
Central Trust Co.	Lawyers Mortgage Company
Bank of California	Lawyers Title Insurance &
Title Guarantee & Trust Co.	Trust Co.
Chemical National Bank	Missouri Safe Deposit Co.
Girard Trust Co.	Cafe Savarin Co.
Metropolitan Trust Co.	
Lawyer's Title Insurance &	New York Life
Trust Co.	New York Security & Trust Co.
Mutual Alliance Trust Co.	Central National Bank
Commercial Trust Co.	National City Bank
Brooklyn Trust Co.	First National Bank
Industrial Trust Co.	National Bank of Commerce
Calletin National Bank	First National Bank of Chicago
Aston National Bank	Hanover National Bank
Central Realty Bond & Trust Co.	City Trust Company

---

[2]North, 20.

The use of subsidiaries and affiliates was useful in
other manipulations that allowed some companies to hold
higher returns securities than those specified by law. One
of these was to sell or trade such securities to the subsidiaries permanently (of to purchase and hold them in the name
of the subsidiary company). Another was to make such transfers
on a temporary basis for the period during which accounting
for report purposes was being made and then have them returned.

Much of the testimony of the Armstrong Committee deals
with the various aspects of this manipulation. One instance
is given here.

"Testimony of William S. Manning....
Q. Now, this argument was an argument before
the State Senate Committee on Insurance on behalf of the Anti-Monopoly League resolution
in 1883? A. Yes, Sir, in 1883.... Q. In this
argument you devote yourself largely to the
character of the investment? A. Yes sir.
Q. Being made by insurance companies? A.
Mostly sir. Q. And you criticize those
investments quite severely? A. Yes sir, as
the present Committee have done also....
Q. To illustrate your attitude at that time
I find this statement in your argument:
'Is it any wonder that in the struggle to
make large profits the spirit of speculation
enters into their operations, thereby placing
in jeopardy the principal, the safety of
which is the foundation of the fabric of
life insurance.' A. I say that to-day.....
I will state this. At that time the insurance companies had invested, as that
[the exhibit] will show, about eighty-
three million dollars upon stock collaterals
--speculative stock collaterals or speculative
stocks. The following year after that argument came out they did not invest any, but
they managed to get around it by using trust
funds which they organized, and through those

trust funds made their dealings, as is
shown by this Committee...."[2]

Other Assets

Figure 9 suggest that this category behaved much
more predictably than did cash in its role as a small,
residual classification. Company equipment and the other
items would normally be expected to become a generally
decreasing percentage of the rapidly expanding asset portfolios as the figure indicates. Further, the miscellany of
items lumped into this category would hardly be expected
to produce a smooth series.

Additional Bond Categories

Inasmuch as most of the categories of stocks are identical in character with those of the bonds, the features
common to the two categories will be discussed only in
connection with the bonds. This procedure has its obvious
limitations but will, hopefully, reduce the tendency to
repetition.

State and Local Bonds

Two general movements into bonds of the United States
were discussed earlier. The same movements are generally

[2]New York State, Armstrong Report...., IV. 3696-3697

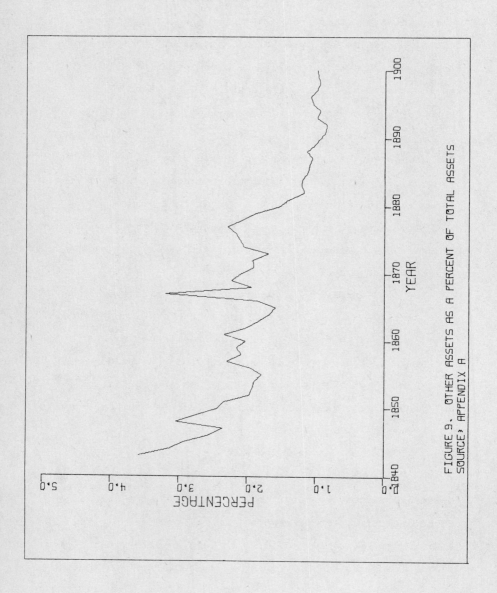

FIGURE 9. OTHER ASSETS AS A PERCENT OF TOTAL ASSETS
SOURCE, APPENDIX A

evident in Figure 10, and for much the same reasons. The early, legal provisions discussed in connection with the federal bonds included provision that part of the required service could be alternatively held in specified state and local securities. These were usually to be those issued by the state involved or by incorporated cities or towns of that state. These provisions were evident earliest in the laws of New York and some of the surrounding states. Thus, the early interest in the securities of New England and the Middle Atlantic States was probably not only because of the proximity of those states to the insurance centers but also because these companies had substantial, legal encouragement to purchase them.

The movement of funds toward safer securities during the seventies was even more evident in the state and local securities than in the federal. The legal requirements leading to purchases of unusual amounts of U.S. Bonds were mostly fulfilled by that time and the bonds of political subdivisions were yielding preferable interest rates.

Railroad Bonds

Table 34 showing the expansion of railroad mileage in the United States, has been included to give some indication of the opportunity for investment in railroad securities. It will also be referenced later to help in determining important periods of rail expansion. The indication is that

when an established company would withdraw temporarily from a state. In such cases the company would usually not file a tax return. However, the premiums from all policies remaining in force in the state obviously continued to come in. This fact was indicated by unaccounted residuals in the company's premiums receipts and by the similar size of its income upon reactivation within the state. Such omissions were filled by the method previously outlined.

Regional Capital Flows

Mention has been made of the fact that certain items of income and of investment were not allocated geographically. Nevertheless, an attempt was made to examine possible geographical distortions that may have existed in the flows of life insurance funds on the basis of partial data. For this purpose regional investments were defined as including real estate, mortgages, stocks, and all but federal bonds. Other funds that might have gone into an area because of expenses, return premiums, rebates, dividends, or death claims were excluded. The expense items obviously added to the figures of the insurance centers. The other items were excluded on the assumption that they were consistent among the regions. This exclusion reduced the amounts involved but probably did not change the percentages.

In the case of death claims this assumption may have been unfortunate. One might be inclined to think that the mortality

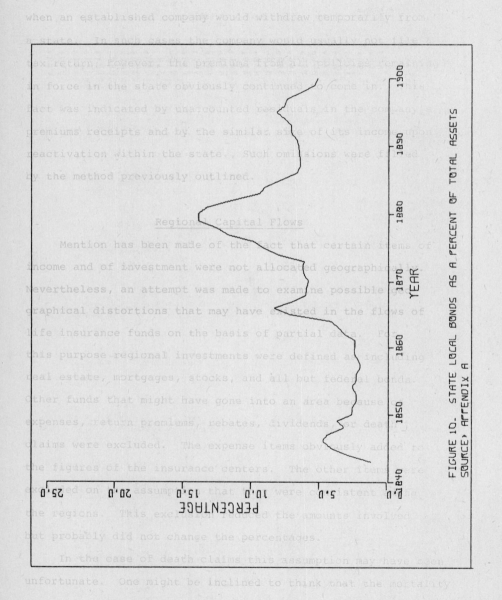

FIGURE 10. STATE LOCAL BONDS AS A PERCENT OF TOTAL ASSETS
SOURCE, APPENDIX A

TABLE 32. STATE, LOCAL BONDS OWNED (THOUSANDS OF DOLLARS)

YEAR	1	2	3	4	5	6	7	8	TOTAL
					REGIONS				
1843	14.	11.	0.	0.	0.	0.	0.	0.	25.
1844	31.	34.	0.	0.	0.	0.	0.	0.	65.
1845	24.	84.	0.	0.	0.	0.	0.	0.	108.
1846	25.	130.	0.	0.	0.	0.	0.	0.	154.
1847	23.	127.	0.	0.	0.	0.	0.	0.	150.
1848	22.	113.	2.	0.	0.	0.	0.	0.	137.
1849	39.	213.	4.	35.	0.	0.	0.	0.	290.
1850	36.	189.	2.	22.	0.	0.	0.	0.	249.
1851	66.	217.	2.	23.	0.	0.	0.	0.	308.
1852	82.	240.	2.	0.	0.	0.	0.	0.	325.
1853	103.	274.	3.	0.	0.	0.	0.	0.	379.
1854	138.	332.	5.	0.	0.	0.	0.	0.	475.
1855	132.	282.	4.	0.	0.	0.	0.	0.	418.
1856	171.	304.	4.	1.	0.	0.	0.	0.	481.
1857	147.	264.	67.	0.	0.	0.	0.	0.	484.
1858	167.	366.	76.	0.	0.	0.	0.	0.	609.
1859	175.	496.	81.	0.	0.	0.	0.	0.	751.
1860	239.	518.	87.	0.	0.	0.	0.	0.	844.
1861	257.	557.	99.	0.	0.	0.	0.	0.	913.
1862	234.	1009.	72.	0.	3.	0.	0.	0.	1318.
1863	596.	1250.	74.	4.	20.	0.	0.	0.	1945.
1864	1093.	1553.	132.	5.	24.	23.	0.	22.	2852.
1865	1685.	3892.	219.	6.	31.	68.	0.	28.	5928.
1866	3220.	5117.	282.	101.	58.	83.	0.	147.	9007.
1867	3210.	5938.	549.	89.	78.	75.	0.	143.	10081.
1868	3616.	7361.	614.	203.	195.	82.	0.	161.	12231.
1869	3830.	9862.	682.	252.	211.	92.	41.	162.	15131.
1870	4020.	9732.	1621.	519.	322.	90.	48.	154.	16508.
1871	4389.	12737.	1584.	733.	806.	172.	71.	142.	20634.

TABLE 32 (CONTINUED)

YEAR	REGIONS								TOTAL
	1	2	3	4	5	6	7	8	
1872	4766.	13245.	3215.	490.	685.	266.	136.	188.	22991.
1873	4720.	13563.	3077.	487.	566.	290.	151.	257.	23113.
1874	6298.	19377.	5600.	696.	877.	614.	311.	616.	34389.
1875	6260.	23975.	6279.	641.	853.	967.	258.	649.	39882.
1876	7996.	24982.	6618.	497.	890.	1393.	193.	711.	43280.
1877	8234.	31162.	7665.	421.	1440.	2172.	163.	654.	51910.
1878	9405.	33686.	8162.	436.	895.	2448.	123.	685.	55842.
1879	9649.	40114.	7994.	295.	747.	2588.	251.	654.	62292.
1880	10607.	38603.	9416.	234.	682.	4010.	272.	669.	64493.
1881	9743.	37933.	9446.	369.	766.	3529.	539.	667.	62992.
1882	5930.	31371.	12024.	482.	866.	3338.	353.	636.	55001.
1883	6044.	25595.	10741.	655.	919.	2459.	832.	567.	47812.
1884	6941.	25772.	8359.	902.	1084.	2770.	990.	610.	47429.
1885	6517.	22689.	7215.	459.	1343.	3032.	2056.	550.	43860.
1886	6460.	16541.	8024.	382.	1813.	3071.	2771.	422.	39484.
1887	6640.	15372.	8356.	565.	1901.	3486.	3689.	414.	40423.
1888	6544.	12299.	9628.	1776.	2054.	6163.	4900.	410.	43774.
1889	6808.	12373.	9784.	2791.	4396.	6332.	5290.	420.	48195.
1890	6911.	11684.	12337.	2376.	5111.	6805.	6520.	655.	52398.
1891	7276.	12608.	14897.	2274.	5658.	7793.	7074.	745.	58325.
1892	7710.	14039.	16074.	2371.	6256.	8231.	8748.	4348.	67778.
1893	7407.	15743.	15803.	3970.	6324.	9250.	9152.	4677.	72327.
1894	11615.	17798.	16768.	4227.	7410.	9737.	9645.	7326.	84526.
1895	12838.	25038.	18370.	4651.	8875.	10087.	10789.	7306.	97954.
1896	12595.	24395.	16764.	4065.	9605.	12660.	9544.	7220.	96848.
1897	14797.	26224.	17276.	4193.	10744.	11837.	9444.	7027.	101545.
1898	15487.	23026.	16017.	4078.	9058.	10778.	9297.	6703.	94445.
1899	19487.	17550.	15851.	4165.	7273.	9407.	7306.	6769.	87810.
1900	22336.	19039.	15441.	4088.	6309.	10727.	7496.	6413.	91850.

150

TABLE 33. STATE AND LOCAL BONDS OWNED (PERCENT OF TOTAL ASSETS)

YEAR	REGIONS								TOTAL
	1	2	3	4	5	6	7	8	
1843	0.697	0.558	0.0	0.0	0.0	0.0	0.0	0.0	1.255
1844	1.408	1.549	0.0	0.0	0.0	0.0	0.0	0.0	2.957
1845	0.920	3.263	0.0	0.0	0.0	0.0	0.0	0.0	4.183
1846	0.768	4.047	0.0	0.0	0.0	0.0	0.0	0.0	4.815
1847	0.680	3.740	0.0	0.0	0.0	0.0	0.0	0.0	4.420
1848	0.517	2.635	0.049	0.0	0.0	0.0	0.0	0.0	3.201
1849	0.501	2.756	0.046	0.456	0.0	0.0	0.0	0.0	3.758
1850	0.380	1.981	0.023	0.230	0.0	0.0	0.0	0.0	2.614
1851	0.551	1.805	0.019	0.190	0.0	0.0	0.0	0.0	2.565
1852	0.573	1.676	0.017	0.0	0.0	0.0	0.0	0.0	2.267
1853	0.635	1.693	0.017	0.0	0.0	0.0	0.0	0.0	2.344
1854	0.766	1.843	0.027	0.0	0.0	0.0	0.0	0.0	2.637
1855	0.712	1.521	0.022	0.0	0.0	0.0	0.0	0.0	2.256
1856	0.793	1.411	0.020	0.007	0.0	0.0	0.0	0.0	2.231
1857	0.595	1.069	0.272	0.0	0.0	0.0	0.023	0.0	1.960
1858	0.604	1.325	0.274	0.0	0.0	0.0	0.0	0.0	2.204
1859	0.584	1.657	0.270	0.0	0.0	0.0	0.0	0.0	2.511
1860	0.671	1.455	0.244	0.0	0.0	0.0	0.0	0.0	2.371
1861	0.657	1.426	0.254	0.0	0.0	0.0	0.0	0.0	2.337
1862	0.569	2.450	0.174	0.0	0.006	0.0	0.0	0.0	3.199
1863	1.112	2.333	0.139	0.008	0.037	0.0	0.0	0.0	3.630
1864	1.609	2.286	0.195	0.008	0.035	0.034	0.0	0.032	4.199
1865	2.050	4.735	0.266	0.008	0.038	0.083	0.0	0.034	7.213
1866	3.032	4.771	0.263	0.094	0.054	0.078	0.0	0.137	8.398
1867	2.210	4.088	0.378	0.061	0.054	0.051	0.0	0.098	6.940
1868	1.779	3.621	0.302	0.100	0.096	0.040	0.0	0.079	6.017
1869	1.506	3.877	0.268	0.099	0.083	0.036	0.016	0.064	5.948
1870	1.415	3.426	0.571	0.183	0.113	0.032	0.017	0.054	5.811
1871	1.319	3.829	0.476	0.220	0.242	0.052	0.021	0.043	6.203

The following sections will present many of the series which have resulted from employing the procedures described. Interpretations will be offered concerning the several series as well as some comparisons with the works of others.

Table presents the dollar value of total assets . . .

. . . able to reach all the others remaining in the panel . . . would rather compute from the information . . .

Table has been obtained from census reports and sur-

. . . to be able to make a . . . single region . . . particular . . . ive . . . consistency of the findings may be made. In 1880 the census . . .

. . . corresponding values from Table 14. The census compilers . . . used . . . among . . . the . . . company . . . data. . . . appears that some of the census omissions have been filled . . .

TABLE 33 (CONTINUED) INSURANCE ASSETS, BY CLASS (THOUSANDS OF DOLLARS)

YEAR	1	2	3	4	5	6	7	8	TOTAL
1872	1.306	3.630	0.881	0.134	0.188	0.073	0.037	0.051	6.301
1873	1.244	3.574	0.811	0.128	0.149	0.077	0.040	0.068	6.090
1874	1.479	4.550	1.315	0.163	0.206	0.144	0.073	0.145	8.074
1875	1.440	5.514	1.444	0.147	0.196	0.222	0.059	0.149	9.173
1876	1.826	5.704	1.511	0.113	0.203	0.318	0.044	0.162	9.881
1877	1.872	7.084	1.743	0.096	0.327	0.494	0.037	0.149	11.801
1878	2.120	7.595	1.840	0.098	0.202	0.552	0.028	0.154	12.590
1879	2.158	8.971	1.788	0.066	0.167	0.579	0.056	0.146	13.931
1880	2.294	8.350	2.037	0.051	0.148	0.867	0.069	0.145	13.951
1881	2.046	7.967	1.984	0.078	0.161	0.741	0.113	0.140	13.230
1882	1.236	6.539	2.507	0.101	0.181	0.696	0.074	0.133	11.465
1883	1.188	5.030	2.111	0.129	0.181	0.483	0.164	0.111	9.397
1884	1.311	4.866	1.578	0.170	0.205	0.523	0.187	0.115	8.955
1885	1.159	4.034	1.283	0.082	0.239	0.539	0.366	0.098	7.799
1886	1.085	2.777	1.347	0.064	0.304	0.516	0.465	0.071	6.629
1887	1.051	2.433	1.322	0.089	0.301	0.552	0.584	0.065	6.397
1888	0.974	1.830	1.433	0.264	0.306	0.917	0.729	0.061	6.514
1889	0.923	1.677	1.326	0.378	0.596	0.858	0.717	0.057	6.532
1890	0.868	1.467	1.549	0.298	0.642	0.855	0.819	0.082	6.580
1891	0.840	1.456	1.721	0.263	0.654	0.900	0.817	0.086	6.737
1892	0.811	1.477	1.692	0.250	0.658	0.866	0.921	0.458	7.132
1893	0.727	1.545	1.551	0.390	0.621	0.908	0.898	0.459	7.100
1894	1.045	1.601	1.508	0.380	0.666	0.876	0.867	0.659	7.602
1895	1.073	2.093	1.536	0.389	0.742	0.843	0.902	0.611	8.190
1896	0.984	1.906	1.310	0.318	0.750	0.989	0.746	0.564	7.566
1897	1.068	1.892	1.246	0.303	0.775	0.854	0.681	0.507	7.327
1898	1.026	1.525	1.061	0.270	0.600	0.714	0.616	0.444	6.257
1899	1.187	1.069	0.965	0.254	0.443	0.573	0.445	0.412	5.349
1900	1.234	1.052	0.853	0.226	0.349	0.593	0.414	0.354	5.076

Table 34 . Total Miles of Track Operated by U.S. Railroads[a].

Year	Mileage	Year	Mileage	Year	Mileage
1830	23	1854	16,720	1878	81,747
1831	95	1855	18,374	1879	86,556
1832	229	1856	22,076	1880	93,262
1833	380	1857	24,503	1881	103,108
1834	633	1858	26,989	1882	114,677
1835	1,098	1859	28,789	1883	121,422
1836	1,273	1860	30,626	1884	125,345
1837	1,493	1861	31,286	1885	128,320
1838	1,913	1862	32,120	1886	136,338
1839	2,302	1863	33,170	1887	149,214
1840	2,818	1864	33,908	1888	156,114
1841	3,535	1865	35,085	1889	161,276
1842	4,026	1866	36,801	1890	199,876
1843	4,185	1867	39,050	1891	207,446
1844	4,377	1868	42,229	1892	211,051
1845	4,633	1869	46,844	1893	221,864
1846	4,930	1870	52,922	1894	229,796
1847	5,598	1871	60,301	1895	233,276
1848	5,996	1872	66,171	1896	239,140
1849	7,365	1873	70,268	1897	242,013
1850	9,021	1874	72,385	1898	245,334
1851	10,982	1875	74,096	1899	250,143
1852	12,908	1876	76,808	1900	258,784
1853	15,360	1877	79,082		

a   U.S. Department of Commerce, Historical Statistics of the United States, Colonial Times to 1957 (Washington:U.S. Department of Commerce, 1961), pp. 427-29. Mileage for 1900-1890 was taken from Series Q48 and for 1889-1830 from Series Q15.

large amounts of capital were needed by the rail system
throughout the entire period of this study.

The securities were certainly available. As early as
1837[1] there were eight different rail securities listed on
the New York Stock Exchange. These were not always held in
the highest esteem, however. Several years later the supposedly
sophisticated markets of Europe were still balking at even
the bonds of American rail companies. A German banker is
quoted as stating that an American railroad bond could not
be sold, "...even if signed by an angel."[2]

The total amount of rail securities held by life companies grew quite consistently, except for the interruption
of the civil war years as shown by Table 35. Since the
amounts given in the table are at market values, it is not
certain that the number of securities held declined even
then. Notice, however, that few such investments involved
sections of lines in regions other than New England (Region 1)
and the Middle Atlantic States (Region 2) in the early years.
Such purchases occurred particularly late in the cases of
Southern and Western regions. Obviously, some of this is
because of the lack of lines in parts of those regions, but,
each of the regions contained substantial mileage much earlier

---

[1]The New York Stock Exchange, Understanding the New York
Stock Exchange (New York:The New York Stock Exchange, 1967),
p.7.
[2]North, 93.

TABLE 35. RAILROAD BONDS OWNED (THOUSANDS OF DOLLARS)

YEAR	__	__	__	REGIONS	__	__	__	__	TOTAL
	1	2	3	4	5	6	7	8	
1843	16.	5.	0.	0.	0.	0.	0.	0.	22.
1844	40.	19.	0.	0.	0.	0.	0.	0.	59.
1845	37.	17.	0.	0.	0.	0.	0.	0.	54.
1846	34.	15.	0.	0.	0.	0.	0.	0.	49.
1847	32.	19.	0.	0.	0.	0.	0.	0.	51.
1848	31.	22.	0.	0.	0.	0.	0.	0.	53.
1849	56.	56.	0.	0.	0.	0.	0.	0.	113.
1850	70.	36.	0.	0.	0.	0.	0.	0.	106.
1851	79.	80.	0.	0.	0.	0.	0.	0.	159.
1852	86.	137.	0.	0.	0.	0.	0.	0.	223.
1853	99.	177.	0.	0.	0.	0.	0.	0.	275.
1854	118.	220.	21.	0.	0.	0.	0.	0.	339.
1855	182.	193.	54.	0.	0.	0.	0.	0.	396.
1856	187.	203.	189.	0.	0.	0.	0.	0.	443.
1857	170.	178.	209.	0.	4.	0.	0.	0.	537.
1858	194.	211.	213.	0.	7.	0.	0.	0.	619.
1859	218.	228.	290.	0.	7.	0.	0.	0.	665.
1860	231.	239.	312.	0.	7.	0.	0.	0.	766.
1861	251.	255.	211.	0.	4.	0.	0.	0.	825.
1862	158.	175.	219.	0.	4.	0.	0.	0.	848.
1863	195.	185.	255.	0.	10.	0.	0.	0.	603.
1864	229.	291.	313.	0.	13.	0.	0.	0.	709.
1865	285.	291.	323.	0.	22.	0.	0.	0.	555.
1866	301.	329.	283.	0.	35.	0.	0.	0.	965.
1867	260.	369.	325.	0.	46.	130.	115.	76.	1258.
1868	301.	411.	344.	31.	53.	146.	189.	143.	1550.
1869	322.	526.	412.	29.	47.	174.	196.	146.	1787.
1870	1214.	938.	407.	57.		162.	196.	143.	3146.
1871	1123.	882.				145.	184.	159.	3043.

TABLE 35 (CCNTINUED)

				REGIONS					
YEAR	1	2	3	4	5	6	7	8	TCTAL
1872	1179.	915.	459.	244.	47.	144.	192.	205.	3386.
1873	1115.	889.	439.	224.	43.	138.	227.	206.	3279.
1874	1483.	2807.	590.	299.	56.	184.	328.	271.	6016.
1875	1425.	2781.	581.	289.	76.	192.	345.	279.	5968.
1876	1494.	4082.	634.	299.	100.	287.	390.	294.	7581.
1877	1437.	4282.	593.	280.	114.	373.	386.	282.	7746.
1878	1626.	6100.	872.	307.	121.	912.	456.	309.	10702.
1879	1654.	5927.	1043.	300.	117.	977.	440.	309.	10766.
1880	2617.	11895.	3047.	332.	164.	1179.	515.	328.	20077.
1881	3632.	19107.	5641.	489.	253.	2106.	1166.	330.	32725.
1882	5326.	22517.	9652.	1810.	351.	2677.	4185.	342.	46859.
1883	3853.	27837.	15408.	2012.	993.	3966.	6778.	1273.	62119.
1884	4267.	30126.	26027.	2404.	1343.	3671.	8913.	1745.	78496.
1885	4023.	40133.	27361.	2813.	2891.	9891.	14810.	2164.	104085.
1886	4084.	45209.	29635.	4765.	3491.	12990.	18548.	2527.	121249.
1887	4269.	46788.	30751.	5437.	3568.	15602.	22196.	2672.	131282.
1888	5953.	50131.	30170.	8888.	6100.	15604.	26793.	2922.	146562.
1889	6239.	50952.	36251.	9723.	8950.	17093.	30672.	3283.	163163.
1890	6503.	51317.	37036.	9638.	6744.	18978.	34574.	3688.	168476.
1891	6999.	58128.	41773.	7599.	8228.	22868.	39115.	6696.	191464.
1892	10461.	67514.	49054.	9407.	10407.	23719.	41794.	7355.	219710.
1893	10390.	78375.	48747.	9201.	11006.	23534.	40624.	7124.	229002.
1894	12616.	80029.	53969.	10144.	11435.	24238.	50405.	7313.	250150.
1895	16752.	80842.	65331.	13953.	16436.	26639.	53303.	8344.	281599.
1896	18738.	81873.	70650.	14049.	16882.	26782.	55641.	9096.	293710.
1897	23424.	96023.	74128.	17661.	19419.	43120.	62119.	10320.	346212.
1898	23363.	114990.	84997.	21651.	19814.	55912.	80176.	20070.	420973.
1899	24543.	133627.	104031.	26876.	21681.	85558.	84184.	30362.	510862.
1900	28025.	156665.	119454.	33900.	28299.	96846.	94299.	33399.	590886.

that the date the first securities appeared in the life
insurance company portfolios. Much of the reluctance
to make these investments may have been attributable to the
riskiness thought to be inherent in them.

Some insurance companies were apparently attracted by
some of the adventures of the day, however. The first holdings
of Union Pacific appeared in the portfolios in 1867, two years
before completion of the transcontinental link at Promontory
Point. The unusual thing about these holdings was that
they were more in evidence in 1868 than in 1870; suggesting
that they were likely more the evidence of succumbing to
a climate of speculation than of reasoned investment for the
long term.

The relationship of life insurance financing to railroad growth has been the subject of some comment. Perhaps
much of this comment has grown up from the wide publicity
given certain findings of the Armstrong commission. These
pictured the insurance companies as being "gorged" with rail
securities, particularly those purchased at the insistence
of J.P. Morgan.

Table 36 indicates that by 1900 rail bonds alone com-
prised nearly one third of total life insurance assets. Rail
stocks brought the total to nearly thirty-six percent. No
doubt, some other classes of assets were partly related to
rail financing as well. The percentage continued to increase
until the time of the Armstrong Commission, where many al-

TABLE 36. RAILROAD BONDS OWNED (PERCENT OF TOTAL ASSETS)

YEAR	REGIONS								TOTAL
	1	2	3	4	5	6	7	8	
1843	0.837	0.279	0.0	0.0	0.0	0.0	0.0	0.0	1.116
1844	1.831	0.845	0.0	0.0	0.0	0.0	0.0	0.0	2.676
1845	1.422	0.669	0.0	0.0	0.0	0.0	0.0	0.0	2.091
1846	1.076	0.461	0.0	0.0	0.0	0.0	0.0	0.0	1.537
1847	0.944	0.567	0.0	0.0	0.0	0.0	0.0	0.0	1.511
1848	0.714	0.517	0.0	0.0	0.0	0.0	0.0	0.0	1.231
1849	0.729	0.729	0.0	0.0	0.0	0.0	0.0	0.0	1.458
1850	0.737	0.380	0.0	0.0	0.0	0.0	0.0	0.0	1.117
1851	0.656	0.665	0.0	0.0	0.0	0.0	0.0	0.0	1.321
1852	0.599	0.955	0.0	0.0	0.0	0.0	0.0	0.0	1.555
1853	0.609	1.092	0.0	0.0	0.0	0.0	0.0	0.0	1.701
1854	0.657	1.223	0.0	0.0	0.0	0.0	0.0	0.0	1.880
1855	0.982	1.042	0.112	0.0	0.0	0.0	0.0	0.0	2.136
1856	0.867	0.941	0.249	0.0	0.0	0.0	0.0	0.0	2.056
1857	0.689	0.722	0.764	0.0	0.0	0.0	0.0	0.0	2.176
1858	0.702	0.763	0.758	0.0	0.014	0.0	0.0	0.0	2.236
1859	0.728	0.763	0.711	0.0	0.022	0.0	0.0	0.0	2.224
1860	0.649	0.671	0.814	0.0	0.019	0.0	0.0	0.0	2.153
1861	0.642	0.653	0.798	0.0	0.018	0.0	0.0	0.0	2.112
1862	0.384	0.425	0.512	0.0	0.011	0.0	0.0	0.0	1.331
1863	0.365	0.345	0.408	0.0	0.008	0.0	0.0	0.0	1.126
1864	0.337	0.322	0.375	0.0	0.009	0.0	0.0	0.0	1.044
1865	0.347	0.355	0.381	0.0	0.012	0.0	0.0	0.0	1.094
1866	0.280	0.307	0.301	0.0	0.012	0.0	0.0	0.0	0.900
1867	0.179	0.254	0.195	0.0	0.015	0.089	0.082	0.052	0.866
1868	0.148	0.202	0.160	0.0	0.017	0.072	0.093	0.070	0.763
1869	0.127	0.207	0.135	0.012	0.018	0.068	0.077	0.057	0.702
1870	0.427	0.330	0.145	0.010	0.019	0.057	0.069	0.050	1.107
1871	0.337	0.265	0.122	0.017	0.014	0.043	0.055	0.060	0.915

TABLE 36 (CONTINUED)

YEAR	REGIONS								TOTAL
	1	2	3	4	5	6	7	8	
1872	0.323	0.251	0.126	0.067	0.013	0.040	0.053	0.056	0.928
1873	0.294	0.234	0.116	0.059	0.011	0.036	0.060	0.054	0.864
1874	0.348	0.659	0.139	0.070	0.013	0.043	0.077	0.064	1.413
1875	0.328	0.640	0.134	0.066	-0.017	0.044	0.079	0.064	1.373
1876	0.341	0.932	0.145	0.068	0.023	0.066	0.089	0.067	1.731
1877	0.327	0.973	0.135	0.064	0.026	0.085	0.068	0.064	1.761
1878	0.367	1.375	0.197	0.069	0.027	0.206	0.103	0.070	2.413
1879	0.370	1.325	0.233	0.067	0.026	0.219	0.098	0.069	2.408
1880	0.566	2.573	0.659	0.072	0.035	0.255	0.111	0.071	4.343
1881	0.763	4.013	1.185	0.103	0.053	0.442	0.245	0.069	6.873
1882	1.110	4.694	2.012	0.377	0.073	0.558	0.872	0.071	9.768
1883	0.757	5.471	3.028	0.395	0.195	0.779	1.332	0.250	12.208
1884	0.806	5.688	4.914	0.454	0.254	0.693	1.683	0.329	14.821
1885	0.715	7.136	4.865	0.500	0.514	1.759	2.633	0.385	18.508
1886	0.686	7.590	4.976	0.800	0.586	2.161	3.114	0.424	20.357
1887	0.675	7.404	4.866	0.860	0.565	2.469	3.512	0.423	20.774
1888	0.826	7.460	4.490	1.323	0.908	2.322	3.987	0.435	21.810
1889	0.846	6.905	4.913	1.318	1.213	2.317	4.157	0.445	22.113
1890	0.817	6.444	4.651	1.210	0.847	2.383	4.342	0.463	21.157
1891	0.808	6.714	4.825	0.878	0.957	2.642	4.518	0.773	22.116
1892	1.101	7.105	5.162	0.990	1.095	2.496	4.398	0.774	23.121
1893	1.020	7.693	4.785	0.903	1.080	2.310	3.988	0.699	22.479
1894	1.135	7.197	4.854	0.912	1.028	2.180	4.533	0.658	22.496
1895	1.401	6.759	5.462	1.167	1.374	2.227	4.457	0.698	23.544
1896	1.464	6.396	5.520	1.098	1.319	2.092	4.347	0.711	22.947
1897	1.690	6.928	5.348	1.274	1.401	3.111	4.482	0.745	24.980
1898	1.548	7.618	5.631	1.434	1.313	3.704	5.311	1.330	27.888
1899	1.495	8.139	6.337	1.637	1.321	5.211	5.128	1.849	31.117
1900	1.549	8.657	6.601	1.873	1.564	5.352	5.211	1.846	32.652

legations were leveled against the companies for their large

holdings. F.W. Cromwell, Treasurer of Mutual Life Insurance

Company of New York, testified as follows.

> "...A. I said to Mr. Fish, 'See here...,
> it is time for us to buy bonds (railroad)
> of you directly...' and he said he could
> not sell the Mutual Life bonds..." Q. So
> the railroads must keep in with the banks
> in order to float their bonds? A. Yes,
> have to, yes, sir. Q. And the insurance
> companies must keep in with the banks
> in order to get the investments they want
> at low prices? A. Yes. Q. So the banks
> control the situation? A. There is no
> question about it...."[3]

The insurance press has done little to change the

impression left by the Armstrong Hearings about the close

ties between the rail and life insurance industries. One of

the most thoroughly researched statements on the subject was

made by A.S. Wing, President of Provident Mutual Life Insurance

Company, before the Group Meeting of the Chamber of Commerce

of The United States. Mr Wing spoke at length on the close

relationship between the two industries and then presented,

as exhibits, certain tables which have been reproduced, in part,

as Table 37 and Table 38.

---

[1] New York State, Armstrong Report..., I, 628.

Table 37. Investments of American Life Insurance Companies in Railroad Securities [4].

	R.R. Mileage	Capital Stock	Bonded Debt	Percent of R.R. Bonds Held by Life Companies	Total Capital	Percent of R.R. Bonds and Stocks Held by Life Companies	Admitted Assets of All Amer. Life Companies
1860	30,626	.....	.....	...	$	......	$ 27,176,339
1870	52,922	.....	.....	.16%	$ 2,664,627,645	.16%	269,520,440
1880	92,147	$2,708,673,375	$2,530,874,943	.78%	5,402,038,257	.39%	417,951,008
1890	163,359	4,590,471,560	5,055,225,025	3.23%	10,020,925,215	1.81%	770,972,061
1900	192,162	5,894,346,250	5,758,592,754	7.26%	11,891,902,339	4.59%	1,742,414,173

Table 38. Railroad Securities Held by Life Companies [5].

	Railroad Stocks	Percent of Assets (b)	Railroad Bonds	Percent of Assets (b)	Railroad Stocks & Bonds	Percent of Assets
1860	$ 135,881.70	.05%	$ 217,410.71	.08%	$ 375,292.41	.13%
1870	1,078,081.76	.04%	3,234,245.00	1.20%	4,312,326.76	1.24%
1880	1,671,804.03	.04%	19,643,697.38	4.70%	21,315,501.41	4.74%
1890	17,732,357.40	2.30%	163,446,076.93	21.20%	181,178,434.33	23.50%
1900	43,??,354.33	2.50%	501,815,281.82	28.80%	545,375,636.15	31.30%

[4] Asa Shove Wing, Life Insurance Investments in Railroads (New York:The Chamber of Commerce of the United States, 1923), p. 12.
[5] Wing, 13. Prepared from Zartman estimates.

These tables may be compared with Table 39 which has been compiled using the insurance data from the present paper.

The more complete accounting of life insurance participation offered by the latter table shows the percentage of rail securities held by life companies larger in each year, of course. But, in this connection, it might be well to return to a point of defense offered in the Armstrong Hearings by Mr. George Walbridge Perkins, Vice-President of New York Life Insurance Company,

> "...J.P. Morgan and Company since I have been in the firm, a matter of four years and a half, have marketed more bonds in the time we are talking about than the New York Life and the Mutual and the Equitable have accomulated in 60 years...."[6]

This is a point worthy of note, particularly in the earlier years which are the subject of this paper. Rail securities were much more of a factor in insurance portfolios than the insurance companies were in financing the railroads. In fact, while virtually all of the important main lines were being laid insurance holdings amounted to but a fractional percentage of railroad capitalization.

The various events of history should now be rather apparent as the general trends in rail bond holdings are viewed

---

[1]New York State, Armstrong Report..., I, 773.

Table 39. Securities of American Railroads Owned by Life Insurance Companies

Year	Bonds[a] (Thousands)	Stocks (Thousands)	Total[b] R.R. Securities Outstanding (Millions)	R.R. Securities as a percent of insurance assets	Percent of R.R. Securities held by insurance companies
1900	590,886	57,589	11,491	35.83	5.643
1899	510,862	50,365	11,034	34.18	5.086
1898	420,973	45,657	11,819	30.91	3.948
1897	346,212	34,191	10,635	27.45	3.577
1896	293,710	31,645	10,567	25.42	3.079
1895	281,599	33,379	10,347	26.33	3.044
1894	250,150	32,174	10,191	25.39	2.770
1893	229,002	28,984	9,895	25.32	2.607
1892	219,710	25,078	9,686	25.76	2.527
1891	191,464	21,762	9,291	24.63	2.295
1890	168,476	18,720	8,984	23.51	2.084
1889	163,163	16,675	9,687	24.37	1.856
1888	146,562	14,605	9,369	23.98	1.720
1887	131,282	14,016	8,673	22.99	1.675
1886	121,249	13,301	8,163	22.59	1.648
1885	104,085	12,617	7,843	20.75	1.488
1884	78,496	10,868	7,676	16.87	1.164
1883	62,119	8,594	7,478	13.90	.946
1882	46,859	2,727	7,107	10.34	.707
1881	32,725	2,162	6,279	7.33	.556
1880	20,077	1,505	6,402	4.67	.400
1879	10,766	1,296	4,872	2.70	.248
1878	10,702	1,114	4,772	2.66	.248
1877	7,746	1,141	4,806	2.02	.185
1876	7,581	875	4,466	1.93	.189
1875	5,968	690	4,658	1.53	.143
1874	6,016	989	4,222	1.64	.166
1873	3,279	698	3,785	1.05	.105
1872	3,386	958	3,159	1.19	.138
1871	3,043	1,014	2,665	1.22	.152
1870	3,146	1,077	2,477	1.47	.170
1869	1,787	1,067	2,041	1.12	.140
1868	1,550	785	1,870	1.15	.125
1867	1,258	255	1,173	1.04	.129
1866	965	127		1.02	
1865	899	97		1.21	
1864	709	66		1.14	
1863	603	308		1.70	
1862	548	89		1.57	
1861	825	129		2.44	

Table 39. (Continued).

Year	Bonds (Thousands)	Stocks (Thousands)	Total R.R. Securities Outstanding (Millions)	R.R. Securities as a percent of insurance assets	Percent of R.R. Securities held by insurance companies
1860	766	120	1,149	2.49	.077
1859	665	119		2.62	
1858	618	148		2.77	
1857	537	104		2.60	
1856	443	152		2.76	
1855	396	208	764	3.26	.079
1854	339	335		3.74	
1853	275	260		3.30	
1852	223	227		3.14	
1851	159	211		3.08	
1850	106	146	318	2.65	.079
1849	113	95		2.69	
1848	53	69		2.85	
1847	51	17		2.01	
1846	49	21		2.17	
1845	54	24		3.03	
1844	59	34		4.21	
1843	22	15		1.89	

[a]The categories "Stocks" and "Bonds" are taken from Table A1.
[b]Total R.R. Securities Outstanding represents the total bonded debt and stock of all classes outstanding in the given year. Years 1850-89: U.S. Department of Commerce, Historical Statistics of the United States, Colonial Times to 1957 (Washington: U.S. Department of Commerce, 1961), Series Q34, p. 428. Years 1890-1900: U.S. Department of Commerce, Historical Statistics..., Series Q97, p. 433.

in Figure 11, and the large percentage changes seen in the
latter years should be in more complete perspective.

Utility Bonds

Table 40 indicates that the entry of utilities into the
portfolios came relatively late in the period. This occurs
in spite of the convention of placing all public utilities
in this category. Actually, the first security of a gas-light
company did not appear until 1871. Prior to that date
virtually every security in this class was for funding a public
water or sewerage system.

The introduction of the gas-light companies, and of the
telegraph, electric, and telephone companies provided the
more attractive investment opportunities that led the life
companies to move rather quickly into purchases effecting a
large part of the country. The purchases of the securities
of the new enterprises produced the large, relative changes
in holdings noted in Figure 12 and Table 41. The percentage
of total assets invested in utilities securities never became
particularly large in this period, however, and the first
large, block purchase ($3,284,000.) did not occur until 1900.

Industrial Bonds

In the classic work, The Investments of Life Insurance
Companies, Mr. Zartman has taken various exceptions to the
effects of regulation upon the life insurance companies. The

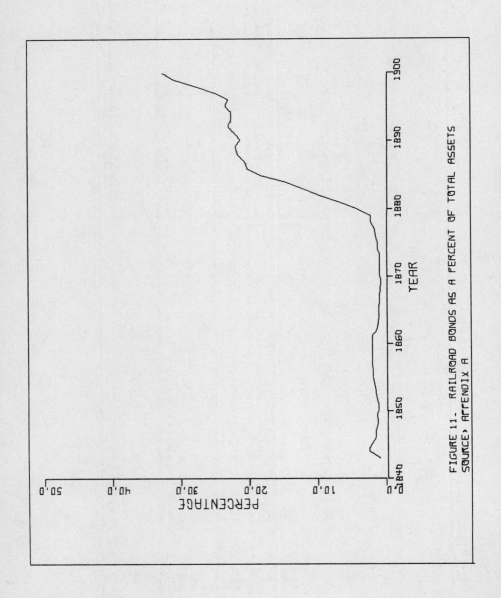

FIGURE 11. RAILROAD BONDS AS A PERCENT OF TOTAL ASSETS
SOURCE: APPENDIX A

TABLE 40. UTILITY BONDS OWNED (THOUSANDS OF DOLLARS)

YEAR	\multicolumn{8}{c}{REGIONS}								TOTAL
	1	2	3	4	5	6	7	8	
1843	0.	0.	0.	0.	0.	0.	0.	0.	0.
1844	0.	0.	0.	0.	0.	0.	0.	0.	0.
1845	0.	0.	0.	0.	0.	0.	0.	0.	0.
1846	0.	0.	0.	0.	0.	0.	0.	0.	0.
1847	0.	0.	0.	0.	0.	0.	0.	0.	0.
1848	0.	0.	0.	0.	0.	0.	0.	0.	0.
1849	0.	0.	0.	0.	0.	0.	0.	0.	0.
1850	0.	0.	0.	0.	0.	0.	0.	0.	0.
1851	0.	0.	0.	0.	0.	0.	0.	0.	0.
1852	0.	0.	0.	0.	0.	0.	0.	0.	0.
1853	0.	0.	0.	0.	0.	0.	0.	0.	0.
1854	0.	0.	0.	0.	0.	0.	0.	0.	0.
1855	0.	0.	0.	0.	0.	0.	0.	0.	0.
1856	0.	0.	0.	0.	0.	0.	0.	0.	0.
1857	0.	0.	0.	0.	0.	0.	0.	0.	0.
1858	0.	0.	0.	0.	0.	0.	0.	0.	0.
1859	0.	0.	0.	0.	0.	0.	0.	0.	0.
1860	0.	0.	0.	0.	0.	0.	0.	0.	0.
1861	0.	0.	0.	0.	0.	0.	0.	0.	0.
1862	0.	4.	0.	0.	0.	0.	0.	0.	4.
1863	0.	4.	0.	0.	0.	0.	0.	0.	4.
1864	0.	6.	0.	0.	0.	0.	0.	0.	6.
1865	0.	8.	0.	0.	0.	0.	0.	0.	8.
1866	19.	8.	64.	0.	0.	0.	0.	0.	91.
1867	27.	6.	54.	0.	0.	0.	0.	0.	88.
1868	41.	7.	59.	0.	0.	0.	0.	0.	107.
1869	50.	375.	154.	0.	0.	0.	0.	0.	579.
1870	124.	487.	174.	0.	0.	0.	0.	0.	786.
1871	112.	395.	162.	0.	0.	0.	0.	0.	669.

TABLE 40 (CONTINUED)

YEAR	1	2	3	4	5	6	7	8	TOTAL
					REGIONS				
1872	140.	1957.	395.	0.	172.	0.	0.	0.	2663.
1873	150.	2112.	720.	0.	157.	134.	47.	0.	3320.
1874	336.	818.	1010.	0.	206.	0.	0.	0.	2370.
1875	388.	730.	1114.	0.	198.	0.	0.	0.	2430.
1876	398.	361.	359.	152.	204.	0.	0.	0.	1473.
1877	1492.	166.	290.	0.	190.	0.	0.	0.	2137.
1878	1257.	305.	308.	0.	201.	0.	0.	0.	2070.
1879	375.	295.	299.	0.	193.	26.	0.	0.	1189.
1880	308.	314.	307.	84.	367.	242.	75.	0.	1702.
1881	261.	372.	292.	0.	373.	469.	175.	0.	1942.
1882	185.	1012.	352.	0.	389.	673.	111.	23.	2745.
1883	477.	735.	660.	0.	294.	855.	442.	100.	3563.
1884	596.	1058.	766.	0.	482.	1575.	968.	120.	5565.
1885	595.	1671.	2403.	0.	531.	1441.	1168.	359.	8169.
1886	605.	1756.	2204.	0.	771.	1470.	1283.	373.	8463.
1887	774.	1775.	2120.	4.	715.	1518.	1472.	356.	8734.
1888	857.	1824.	1702.	26.	141.	1559.	1484.	441.	8034.
1889	541.	1904.	1715.	46.	142.	2093.	2245.	1002.	9686.
1890	491.	1903.	1613.	26.	93.	2091.	2272.	1103.	9592.
1891	369.	3121.	1028.	27.	86.	2261.	2467.	1179.	10539.
1892	527.	4598.	1256.	32.	120.	2534.	3121.	1594.	13783.
1893	630.	4467.	1283.	26.	203.	2571.	3094.	1570.	13843.
1894	777.	4917.	1436.	188.	295.	2680.	3173.	1692.	15156.
1895	1112.	6764.	3242.	260.	377.	2947.	3339.	1824.	19865.
1896	1687.	7996.	3944.	264.	369.	3025.	3396.	1858.	22538.
1897	2194.	9326.	4495.	277.	411.	3748.	3617.	2028.	26096.
1898	3156.	9355.	5328.	315.	409.	3749.	3682.	2039.	28033.
1899	3288.	13704.	5549.	372.	356.	3947.	3848.	2614.	33677.
1900	3681.	18223.	6246.	415.	296.	4388.	4239.	2893.	40381.

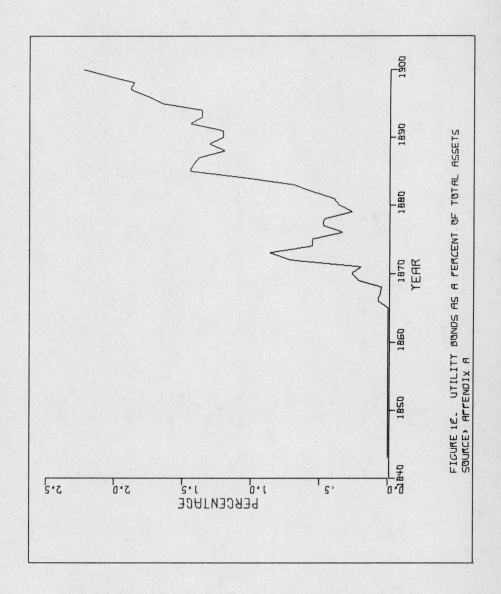

FIGURE 12. UTILITY BONDS AS A PERCENT OF TOTAL ASSETS

SOURCE: APPENDIX A

TABLE 41. UTILITY BONDS OWNED (PERCENT OF TOTAL ASSETS)

YEAR	REGIONS								TOTAL
	1	2	3	4	5	6	7	8	
1843	0.0	0.0	0.0	0.0	0.0	0.0	0.0	0.0	0.0
1844	0.0	0.0	0.0	0.0	0.0	0.0	0.0	0.0	0.0
1845	0.0	0.0	0.0	0.0	0.0	0.0	0.0	0.0	0.0
1846	0.0	0.0	0.0	0.0	0.0	0.0	0.0	0.0	0.0
1847	0.0	0.0	0.0	0.0	0.0	0.0	0.0	0.0	0.0
1848	0.0	0.0	0.0	0.0	0.0	0.0	0.0	0.0	0.0
1849	0.0	0.0	0.0	0.0	0.0	0.0	0.0	0.0	0.0
1850	0.0	0.0	0.0	0.0	0.0	0.0	0.0	0.0	0.0
1851	0.0	0.0	0.0	0.0	0.0	0.0	0.0	0.0	0.0
1852	0.0	0.0	0.0	0.0	0.0	0.0	0.0	0.0	0.0
1853	0.0	0.0	0.0	0.0	0.0	0.0	0.0	0.0	0.0
1854	0.0	0.0	0.0	0.0	0.0	0.0	0.0	0.0	0.0
1855	0.0	0.0	0.0	0.0	0.0	0.0	0.0	0.0	0.0
1856	0.0	0.0	0.0	0.0	0.0	0.0	0.0	0.0	0.0
1857	0.0	0.0	0.0	0.0	0.0	0.0	0.0	0.0	0.0
1858	0.0	0.0	0.0	0.0	0.0	0.0	0.0	0.0	0.0
1859	0.0	0.0	0.0	0.0	0.0	0.0	0.0	0.0	0.0
1860	0.0	0.0	0.0	0.0	0.0	0.0	0.0	0.0	0.0
1861	0.0	0.0	0.0	0.0	0.0	0.0	0.0	0.0	0.0
1862	0.0	0.011	0.0	0.0	0.0	0.0	0.0	0.0	0.011
1863	0.0	0.008	0.0	0.0	0.0	0.0	0.0	0.0	0.008
1864	0.0	0.009	0.0	0.0	0.0	0.0	0.0	0.0	0.009
1865	0.0	0.009	0.0	0.0	0.0	0.0	0.0	0.0	0.009
1866	0.018	0.007	0.060	0.0	0.0	0.0	0.0	0.0	0.085
1867	0.019	0.004	0.037	0.0	0.0	0.0	0.0	0.0	0.060
1868	0.020	0.003	0.029	0.0	0.0	0.0	0.0	0.0	0.052
1869	0.020	0.147	0.061	0.0	0.0	0.0	0.0	0.0	0.227
1870	0.044	0.172	0.061	0.0	0.0	0.0	0.0	0.0	0.277
1871	0.034	0.119	0.049	0.0	0.0	0.0	0.0	0.0	0.201

TABLE 41 (CONTINUED)

YEAR	REGIONS 1	2	3	4	5	6	7	8	TOTAL
1872	0.038	0.536	0.108	0.0	0.047	0.0	0.0	0.0	0.730
1873	0.039	0.556	0.190	0.0	0.041	0.0	0.0	0.0	0.875
1874	0.079	0.192	0.237	0.0	0.048	0.035	0.012	0.0	0.556
1875	0.089	0.168	0.256	0.0	0.046	0.0	0.0	0.0	0.559
1876	0.091	0.082	0.082	0.035	0.047	0.0	0.0	0.0	0.336
1877	0.339	0.038	0.066	0.0	0.043	0.0	0.0	0.0	0.486
1878	0.263	0.069	0.069	0.0	0.045	0.0	0.0	0.0	0.467
1879	0.084	0.066	0.067	0.0	0.043	0.006	0.0	0.0	0.266
1880	0.084	0.068	0.066	0.018	0.043	0.052	0.0	0.0	0.368
1881	0.055	0.078	0.061	0.0	0.079	0.099	0.037	0.0	0.408
1882	0.038	0.211	0.073	0.0	0.081	0.140	0.023	0.005	0.572
1883	0.094	0.145	0.130	0.0	0.058	0.168	0.087	0.020	0.700
1884	0.113	0.145	0.145	0.0	0.091	0.297	0.183	0.023	1.051
1885	0.106	0.297	0.427	0.0	0.094	0.256	0.208	0.064	1.453
1886	0.102	0.295	0.370	0.0	0.129	0.247	0.215	0.063	1.421
1887	0.122	0.261	0.335	0.001	0.113	0.240	0.233	0.056	1.382
1888	0.128	0.271	0.253	0.004	0.021	0.232	0.221	0.066	1.195
1889	0.073	0.258	0.232	0.006	0.019	0.284	0.304	0.136	1.313
1890	0.062	0.239	0.202	0.003	0.012	0.263	0.285	0.139	1.205
1891	0.043	0.361	0.119	0.003	0.010	0.261	0.285	0.136	1.217
1892	0.055	0.484	0.132	0.003	0.013	0.267	0.328	0.168	1.450
1893	0.062	0.438	0.126	0.003	0.020	0.252	0.304	0.154	1.359
1894	0.070	0.442	0.129	0.017	0.026	0.241	0.285	0.152	1.363
1895	0.093	0.566	0.271	0.022	0.032	0.246	0.279	0.152	1.661
1896	0.132	0.625	0.308	0.021	0.029	0.236	0.265	0.145	1.761
1897	0.158	0.673	0.324	0.020	0.035	0.270	0.261	0.146	1.883
1898	0.209	0.620	0.353	0.021	0.027	0.248	0.244	0.135	1.857
1899	0.200	0.835	0.338	0.023	0.022	0.240	0.234	0.159	2.051
1900	0.203	1.007	0.345	0.023	0.016	0.242	0.234	0.160	2.231

present study has made frequent reference to changes probably
effected in response to legal restrictions. The effects of
the laws will be discussed more thoroughly later. (A summary of
legal requirements also appears as Appendix C.) At this point,
however, specific reference should be made to the stringent
legal restrictions that persisted in most states because of
their effects on industrial investments.

Reference to Figure 13 helps to illustrate the trends.
The larger percentages of the earliest years reflected mainly
the holdings of the larger firms, chartered under various
special provisions, before 1840. Of the new mutual firms of
the early period, only New England Mutual Life (chartered
1835) maintained industrial securities worthy of note. The few
issues held by the older companies were not large in value
and were mainly those of a few established textile firms in
Massachusetts. These few holdings were quickly obscured
by the relative expansion of total assets and never reach
even one percent of total assets again in the period 1843-1900.
(See Table 42 and 43.)

In the discussion of other asset categories it has been
quite apparent that many life companies were willing to assume
rather large risks, despite many claims to the contrary.
Further, the long history of solvency of some industrial
firms is a matter of record; particularly as some of the
other securities purchased are reviewed. With these items
in mind, and as the legal sections hereafter are reviewed,

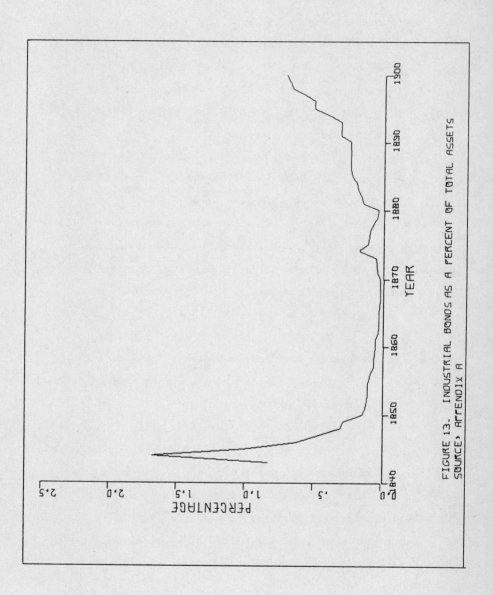

FIGURE 13. INDUSTRIAL BONDS AS A PERCENT OF TOTAL ASSETS
SOURCE, APPENDIX A

TABLE 42. INDUSTRIAL BONDS OWNED (THOUSANDS OF DOLLARS)

YEAR	REGIONS 1	2	3	4	5	6	7	8	TOTAL
1843	16.	0.	0.	0.	0.	0.	0.	0.	16.
1844	37.	0.	0.	0.	0.	0.	0.	0.	37.
1845	26.	0.	0.	0.	0.	0.	0.	0.	26.
1846	20.	0.	0.	0.	0.	0.	0.	0.	20.
1847	15.	0.	0.	0.	0.	0.	0.	0.	15.
1848	13.	0.	0.	0.	0.	0.	0.	0.	13.
1849	21.	0.	0.	0.	0.	0.	0.	0.	21.
1850	13.	0.	0.	0.	0.	0.	0.	0.	13.
1851	14.	0.	0.	0.	0.	0.	0.	0.	14.
1852	15.	0.	0.	0.	0.	0.	0.	0.	15.
1853	16.	0.	0.	0.	0.	0.	0.	0.	16.
1854	20.	0.	0.	0.	0.	0.	0.	0.	20.
1855	17.	0.	0.	0.	0.	0.	0.	0.	17.
1856	17.	0.	0.	0.	0.	0.	0.	0.	17.
1857	14.	0.	0.	0.	0.	0.	0.	0.	14.
1858	15.	0.	0.	0.	0.	0.	0.	0.	15.
1859	16.	0.	0.	0.	0.	0.	0.	0.	16.
1860	16.	0.	0.	0.	0.	0.	0.	0.	16.
1861	17.	0.	0.	0.	0.	0.	0.	0.	17.
1862	10.	0.	0.	0.	0.	0.	0.	0.	10.
1863	11.	0.	0.	0.	0.	0.	0.	0.	11.
1864	12.	0.	0.	0.	0.	0.	0.	0.	12.
1865	15.	0.	0.	0.	0.	0.	0.	0.	15.
1866	15.	0.	0.	0.	0.	0.	0.	0.	15.
1867	13.	0.	0.	0.	0.	0.	0.	0.	13.
1868	14.	27.	0.	0.	0.	0.	0.	0.	41.
1869	14.	28.	0.	0.	0.	23.	0.	0.	65.
1870	13.	31.	0.	0.	0.	22.	0.	0.	65.
1871	11.	82.	47.	0.	0.	20.	0.	0.	161.

TABLE 42 (CCNTINUED)

YEAR	REGIONS								TOTAL
	1	2	3	4	5	6	7	8	
1872	14.	158.	7.	0.	0.	20.	0.	0.	198.
1873	21.	188.	6.	0.	0.	18.	0.	0.	232.
1874	133.	258.	288.	0.	0.	24.	62.	0.	765.
1875	105.	257.	16.	4.	0.	22.	54.	0.	459.
1876	62.	347.	0.	0.	0.	0.	0.	0.	409.
1877	26.	373.	0.	0.	0.	0.	0.	0.	399.
1878	27.	255.	1.	0.	0.	0.	0.	0.	284.
1879	27.	127.	1.	0.	0.	0.	0.	0.	155.
1880	29.	102.	1.	0.	0.	0.	0.	0.	132.
1881	402.	211.	0.	0.	0.	133.	0.	0.	746.
1882	417.	263.	0.	0.	3.	138.	0.	0.	817.
1883	11.	917.	56.	0.	0.	0.	0.	0.	984.
1884	24.	1013.	60.	0.	0.	0.	0.	0.	1097.
1885	38.	1268.	54.	0.	0.	0.	0.	0.	1360.
1886	46.	1299.	53.	0.	0.	102.	0.	0.	1500.
1887	124.	1302.	53.	0.	0.	102.	0.	0.	1581.
1888	150.	1280.	52.	0.	0.	97.	0.	0.	1578.
1889	174.	1431.	124.	0.	0.	98.	0.	0.	1827.
1890	141.	1463.	123.	0.	26.	10.	159.	0.	1923.
1891	157.	2365.	183.	0.	27.	12.	27.	16.	2766.
1892	177.	2436.	206.	0.	28.	12.	0.	26.	2886.
1893	170.	2748.	235.	12.	26.	13.	0.	29.	3232.
1894	187.	3750.	334.	12.	27.	14.	100.	37.	4461.
1895	260.	5336.	418.	12.	27.	14.	19.	55.	6141.
1896	299.	5498.	409.	64.	26.	18.	0.	61.	6374.
1897	1409.	5761.	520.	76.	27.	55.	0.	162.	8010.
1898	1825.	6989.	960.	118.	27.	55.	0.	185.	10158.
1899	1888.	7304.	1728.	171.	28.	55.	0.	200.	11374.
1900	2143.	8173.	2079.	254.	30.	62.	1.	264.	13006.

TABLE 43. INDUSTRIAL BONDS OWNED (PERCENT OF TOTAL ASSETS)

YEAR	REGIONS								TOTAL
	1	2	3	4	5	6	7	8	
1843	0.837	0.0	0.0	0.0	0.0	0.0	0.0	0.0	0.837
1844	1.690	0.0	0.0	0.0	0.0	0.0	0.0	0.0	1.690
1845	1.004	0.0	0.0	0.0	0.0	0.0	0.0	0.0	1.004
1846	0.615	0.0	0.0	0.0	0.0	0.0	0.0	0.0	0.615
1847	0.453	0.0	0.0	0.0	0.0	0.0	0.0	0.0	0.453
1848	0.295	0.0	0.0	0.0	0.0	0.0	0.0	0.0	0.295
1849	0.273	0.0	0.0	0.0	0.0	0.0	0.0	0.0	0.273
1850	0.138	0.0	0.0	0.0	0.0	0.0	0.0	0.0	0.138
1851	0.114	0.0	0.0	0.0	0.0	0.0	0.0	0.0	0.114
1852	0.104	0.0	0.0	0.0	0.0	0.0	0.0	0.0	0.104
1853	0.102	0.0	0.0	0.0	0.0	0.0	0.0	0.0	0.102
1854	0.109	0.0	0.0	0.0	0.0	0.0	0.0	0.0	0.109
1855	0.090	0.0	0.0	0.0	0.0	0.0	0.0	0.0	0.090
1856	0.081	0.0	0.0	0.0	0.0	0.0	0.0	0.0	0.081
1857	0.056	0.0	0.0	0.0	0.0	0.0	0.0	0.0	0.056
1858	0.056	0.0	0.0	0.0	0.0	0.0	0.0	0.0	0.056
1859	0.052	0.0	0.0	0.0	0.0	0.0	0.0	0.0	0.052
1860	0.045	0.0	0.0	0.0	0.0	0.0	0.0	0.0	0.045
1861	0.044	0.0	0.0	0.0	0.0	0.0	0.0	0.0	0.044
1862	0.025	0.0	0.0	0.0	0.0	0.0	0.0	0.0	0.025
1863	0.020	0.0	0.0	0.0	0.0	0.0	0.0	0.0	0.020
1864	0.018	0.0	0.0	0.0	0.0	0.0	0.0	0.0	0.018
1865	0.018	0.0	0.0	0.0	0.0	0.0	0.0	0.0	0.018
1866	0.014	0.0	0.0	0.0	0.0	0.0	0.0	0.0	0.014
1867	0.009	0.0	0.0	0.0	0.0	0.0	0.0	0.0	0.009
1868	0.007	0.013	0.0	0.0	0.0	0.0	0.0	0.0	0.020
1869	0.005	0.011	0.0	0.0	0.0	0.009	0.0	0.0	0.026
1870	0.004	0.011	0.0	0.0	0.0	0.008	0.0	0.0	0.023
1871	0.003	0.025	0.014	0.0	0.0	0.006	0.0	0.0	0.048

TABLE 43 (CONTINUED)

| | | | | REGIONS | | | | | |
YEAR	1	2	3	4	5	6	7	8	TOTAL
1872	0.004	0.043	0.002	0.0	0.0	0.005	0.0	0.0	0.054
1873	0.005	0.049	0.002	0.0	0.0	0.005	0.0	0.0	0.061
1874	0.031	0.061	0.068	0.0	0.0	0.006	0.015	0.0	0.180
1875	0.024	0.059	0.004	0.001	0.0	0.005	0.012	0.0	0.105
1876	0.014	0.079	0.0	0.0	0.0	0.0	0.0	0.0	0.093
1877	0.006	0.085	0.0	0.0	0.0	0.0	0.0	0.0	0.091
1878	0.006	0.058	0.000	0.0	0.0	0.0	0.0	0.0	0.064
1879	0.006	0.028	0.000	0.0	0.0	0.0	0.0	0.0	0.035
1880	0.006	0.022	0.000	0.0	0.0	0.0	0.0	0.0	0.029
1881	0.085	0.044	0.0	0.0	0.0	0.028	0.0	0.0	0.157
1882	0.087	0.055	0.011	0.0	0.0	0.029	0.0	0.0	0.170
1883	0.002	0.180	0.011	0.0	0.0	0.0	0.0	0.0	0.193
1884	0.005	0.191	0.011	0.0	0.0	0.0	0.0	0.0	0.207
1885	0.007	0.225	0.010	0.0	0.0	0.0	0.0	0.0	0.242
1886	0.008	0.218	0.009	0.0	0.0	0.017	0.0	0.0	0.252
1887	0.020	0.206	0.008	0.0	0.0	0.016	0.0	0.0	0.250
1888	0.022	0.190	0.008	0.0	0.0	0.014	0.0	0.0	0.235
1889	0.024	0.194	0.017	0.0	0.0	0.013	0.0	0.0	0.248
1890	0.018	0.184	0.016	0.0	0.003	0.001	0.020	0.0	0.241
1891	0.018	0.273	0.021	0.0	0.003	0.001	0.003	0.002	0.322
1892	0.019	0.256	0.022	0.0	0.003	0.001	0.003	0.003	0.304
1893	0.017	0.270	0.023	0.001	0.003	0.001	0.0	0.003	0.317
1894	0.017	0.337	0.030	0.001	0.002	0.001	0.009	0.003	0.401
1895	0.022	0.446	0.035	0.001	0.002	0.001	0.002	0.005	0.513
1896	0.023	0.430	0.032	0.005	0.002	0.001	0.0	0.005	0.498
1897	0.102	0.416	0.038	0.005	0.002	0.001	0.0	0.005	0.578
1898	0.121	0.463	0.064	0.008	0.002	0.004	0.0	0.012	0.673
1899	0.115	0.445	0.105	0.010	0.002	0.004	0.0	0.012	0.693
1900	0.118	0.452	0.115	0.014	0.002	0.003	0.000	0.015	0.719

it seems quite evident that the legal restrictions imposed
upon the life companies reduced to insignificance any role
that they might have been able to play in mobilizing funds
for industry directly. The other classes of insurance assets
reveal little that might be added to the picture. The
additional industry-related mortgage holdings by Penn Mutual
in the nineties (Table 28) were far from typical, and over
most of the entire period under discussion only a relative
handful of such loans are in evidence in the schedules of all
companies together.

The rebuttal may be made that the states purchased
policyholder security at the price of distorting the capital
market; this remains to be shown.

Canal Bonds

Instances of canal securities in the portfolios are
simply historical curiosities. Total holdings (See Table
44 and 45) never reached three million dollars for the entire
industry. The few investments that were made came late in
canal history. Until 1866 these represent almost solely the
holdings of New York Life in the States of New York and
Pennsylvania. From 1866-1879 New York Life continued to be
the dominant holder of canal securities, but several smaller
firms also purchased smaller amounts. In 1882, Mutual of
New York also began to show some interest in these securities
and the two large firms then held the bulk of such securities
between them.

TABLE 44, CANAL BONDS OWNED (THOUSANDS OF DOLLARS)

| | | | | | REGIONS | | | | | |
YEAR	1	2	3	4	5	6	7	8	TOTAL
1843	0.	0.	0.	0.	0.	0.	0.	0.	0.
1844	0.	0.	0.	0.	0.	0.	0.	0.	0.
1845	0.	0.	0.	0.	0.	0.	0.	0.	0.
1846	0.	0.	0.	0.	0.	0.	0.	0.	0.
1847	0.	0.	0.	0.	0.	0.	0.	0.	0.
1848	0.	0.	0.	0.	0.	0.	0.	0.	0.
1849	0.	0.	0.	0.	0.	0.	0.	0.	0.
1850	0.	0.	0.	0.	0.	0.	0.	0.	0.
1851	0.	0.	0.	0.	0.	0.	0.	0.	0.
1852	0.	0.	0.	0.	0.	0.	0.	0.	0.
1853	0.	0.	0.	0.	0.	0.	0.	0.	0.
1854	0.	0.	0.	0.	0.	0.	0.	0.	0.
1855	0.	0.	0.	0.	0.	0.	0.	0.	0.
1856	0.	0.	0.	0.	0.	0.	0.	0.	0.
1857	0.	15.	0.	0.	0.	0.	0.	0.	15.
1858	0.	17.	0.	0.	0.	0.	0.	0.	17.
1859	0.	17.	0.	0.	0.	0.	0.	0.	17.
1860	0.	18.	0.	0.	0.	0.	0.	0.	18.
1861	0.	18.	0.	0.	0.	0.	0.	0.	18.
1862	0.	11.	0.	0.	0.	0.	0.	0.	11.
1863	0.	12.	0.	0.	0.	0.	0.	0.	12.
1864	0.	14.	0.	0.	0.	0.	0.	0.	14.
1865	0.	16.	0.	0.	0.	0.	0.	0.	16.
1866	0.	17.	0.	0.	0.	0.	0.	0.	17.
1867	0.	14.	0.	0.	0.	0.	0.	0.	14.
1868	8.	15.	0.	0.	0.	0.	0.	0.	15.
1869	8.	630.	0.	0.	0.	0.	0.	0.	638.
1870	7.	622.	0.	0.	0.	0.	0.	0.	630.
1871	7.	467.	3.	3.	0.	0.	0.	0.	479.

TABLE 44 (CONTINUED)

YEAR	REGIONS								TOTAL
	1	2	3	4	5	6	7	8	
1872	45.	379.	1.	2.	0.	0.	0.	0.	427.
1873	0.	426.	1.	2.	0.	0.	0.	0.	428.
1874	0.	496.	1.	2.	0.	0.	0.	0.	500.
1875	0.	534.	0.	0.	0.	0.	0.	0.	534.
1876	0.	391.	0.	0.	0.	0.	0.	0.	391.
1877	0.	336.	0.	0.	0.	0.	0.	0.	336.
1878	0.	330.	0.	0.	0.	0.	0.	0.	330.
1879	0.	323.	0.	0.	0.	0.	0.	0.	323.
1880	0.	1123.	0.	0.	0.	0.	0.	0.	1123.
1881	0.	1543.	0.	0.	0.	0.	0.	0.	1543.
1882	0.	1673.	0.	0.	0.	0.	0.	0.	1673.
1883	0.	2907.	0.	0.	0.	0.	0.	0.	2907.
1884	0.	2368.	0.	0.	0.	0.	0.	0.	2368.
1885	0.	1286.	0.	0.	0.	0.	0.	0.	1286.
1886	0.	1187.	0.	0.	0.	0.	0.	0.	1187.
1887	0.	1343.	0.	0.	0.	0.	0.	0.	1343.
1888	0.	981.	0.	0.	0.	0.	0.	0.	981.
1889	16.	438.	0.	0.	0.	0.	0.	12.	465.
1890	0.	421.	0.	0.	0.	0.	0.	11.	433.
1891	0.	0.	0.	0.	0.	0.	0.	12.	12.
1892	0.	0.	0.	0.	0.	0.	0.	12.	12.
1893	0.	0.	0.	0.	0.	11.	0.	12.	22.
1894	0.	0.	0.	0.	0.	0.	0.	12.	12.
1895	0.	0.	0.	1.	0.	0.	0.	12.	13.
1896	0.	0.	0.	0.	0.	0.	0.	10.	10.
1897	0.	0.	0.	0.	0.	0.	0.	9.	9.
1898	0.	0.	0.	0.	0.	0.	0.	5.	5.
1899	0.	11.	0.	0.	0.	0.	0.	9.	20.
1900	0.	24.	0.	0.	0.	0.	0.	10.	34.

TABLE 45. CANAL BONDS OWNED (PERCENT OF TOTAL ASSETS)

| | | | | REGIONS | | | | | |
YEAR	1	2	3	4	5	6	7	8	TOTAL
1843	0.0	0.0	0.0	0.0	0.0	0.0	0.0	0.0	0.0
1844	0.0	0.0	0.0	0.0	0.0	0.0	0.0	0.0	0.0
1845	0.0	0.0	0.0	0.0	0.0	0.0	0.0	0.0	0.0
1846	0.0	0.0	0.0	0.0	0.0	0.0	0.0	0.0	0.0
1847	0.0	0.0	0.0	0.0	0.0	0.0	0.0	0.0	0.0
1848	0.0	0.0	0.0	0.0	0.0	0.0	0.0	0.0	0.0
1849	0.0	0.0	0.0	0.0	0.0	0.0	0.0	0.0	0.0
1850	0.0	0.0	0.0	0.0	0.0	0.0	0.0	0.0	0.0
1851	0.0	0.0	0.0	0.0	0.0	0.0	0.0	0.0	0.0
1852	0.0	0.0	0.0	0.0	0.0	0.0	0.0	0.0	0.0
1853	0.0	0.0	0.0	0.0	0.0	0.0	0.0	0.0	0.0
1854	0.0	0.0	0.0	0.0	0.0	0.0	0.0	0.0	0.0
1855	0.0	0.0	0.0	0.0	0.0	0.0	0.0	0.0	0.0
1856	0.0	0.061	0.0	0.0	0.0	0.0	0.0	0.0	0.061
1857	0.0	0.060	0.0	0.0	0.0	0.0	0.0	0.0	0.060
1858	0.0	0.060	0.0	0.0	0.0	0.0	0.0	0.0	0.060
1859	0.0	0.057	0.0	0.0	0.0	0.0	0.0	0.0	0.057
1860	0.0	0.049	0.0	0.0	0.0	0.0	0.0	0.0	0.049
1861	0.0	0.047	0.0	0.0	0.0	0.0	0.0	0.0	0.047
1862	0.0	0.028	0.0	0.0	0.0	0.0	0.0	0.0	0.028
1863	0.0	0.022	0.0	0.0	0.0	0.0	0.0	0.0	0.022
1864	0.0	0.020	0.0	0.0	0.0	0.0	0.0	0.0	0.020
1865	0.0	0.020	0.0	0.0	0.0	0.0	0.0	0.0	0.020
1866	0.0	0.016	0.0	0.0	0.0	0.0	0.0	0.0	0.016
1867	0.0	0.010	0.0	0.0	0.0	0.0	0.0	0.0	0.010
1868	0.0	0.007	0.0	0.0	0.0	0.0	0.0	0.0	0.007
1869	0.003	0.248	0.0	0.0	0.0	0.0	0.0	0.0	0.251
1870	0.003	0.219	0.0	0.0	0.0	0.0	0.0	0.0	0.222
1871	0.002	0.140	0.001	0.001	0.0	0.0	0.0	0.0	0.144

TABLE 45 (CCNTINUED)

YEAR	REGIONS								TCTAL
	1	2	3	4	5	6	7	8	
1872	0.012	0.104	0.000	0.001	0.0	0.0	0.0	0.0	0.117
1873	0.0	0.112	0.000	0.000	0.0	0.0	0.0	0.0	0.113
1874	0.0	0.117	0.000	0.001	0.0	0.0	0.0	0.0	0.117
1875	0.0	0.123	0.0	0.0	0.0	0.0	0.0	0.0	0.123
1876	0.0	0.089	0.0	0.0	0.0	0.0	0.0	0.0	0.089
1877	0.0	0.076	0.0	0.0	0.0	0.0	0.0	0.0	0.076
1878	0.0	0.074	0.0	0.0	0.0	0.0	0.0	0.0	0.074
1879	0.0	0.072	0.0	0.0	0.0	0.0	0.0	0.0	0.072
1880	0.0	0.243	0.0	0.0	0.0	0.0	0.0	0.0	0.243
1881	0.0	0.324	0.0	0.0	0.0	0.0	0.0	0.0	0.324
1882	0.0	0.349	0.0	0.0	0.0	0.0	0.0	0.0	0.349
1883	0.0	0.571	0.0	0.0	0.0	0.0	0.0	0.0	0.571
1884	0.0	0.447	0.0	0.0	0.0	0.0	0.0	0.0	0.447
1885	0.0	0.229	0.0	0.0	0.0	0.0	0.0	0.0	0.229
1886	0.0	0.199	0.0	0.0	0.0	0.0	0.0	0.0	0.199
1887	0.0	0.213	0.0	0.0	0.0	0.0	0.0	0.0	0.213
1888	0.0	0.146	0.0	0.0	0.0	0.0	0.0	0.0	0.146
1889	0.002	0.059	0.0	0.0	0.0	0.0	0.0	0.002	0.063
1890	0.0	0.053	0.0	0.0	0.0	0.0	0.0	0.001	0.054
1891	0.0	0.0	0.0	0.0	0.0	0.0	0.0	0.001	0.001
1892	0.0	0.0	0.0	0.0	0.0	0.0	0.0	0.001	0.001
1893	0.0	0.0	0.0	0.0	0.0	0.001	0.0	0.001	0.002
1894	0.0	0.0	0.0	0.000	0.0	0.0	0.0	0.001	0.001
1895	0.0	0.0	0.0	0.000	0.0	0.0	0.0	0.001	0.001
1896	0.0	0.0	0.0	0.0	0.0	0.0	0.0	0.001	0.001
1897	0.0	0.0	0.0	0.0	0.0	0.0	0.0	0.001	0.001
1898	0.0	0.001	0.0	0.0	0.0	0.0	0.0	0.000	0.000
1899	0.0	0.001	0.0	0.0	0.0	0.0	0.0	0.001	0.001
1900	0.0	0.0	0.0	0.0	0.0	0.0	0.0	0.001	0.002

Figure 14 reveals the small percentage involved in this type of holdings. With the small total amount involved, the large relative fluctuations evident in the figure represent almost completely a handful of securities transactions by the two large companies.

Other Domestic Bonds

Inasmuch as most of the principal investment regulations were written from the standpoint of what could be purchased, this category was also relegated to a position of insignificance. Aside from the enumeration of the various securities that occasionally found their way into this classification, given earlier, little remains to be presented that would help in understanding this category.

The increase in the number of financial institutions as subsidiaries and affiliates of life insurance companies in the later years is evidenced in Figure 15. The firms involved in these arrangements were principally in New York City, with a few in Boston and other financial centers. These facts are reflected in the relative importance of the regions containing these centers (Table 46 and 47).

Foreign Bonds

One of the early arguments raised by those seeking to obtain legal provisions for higher amounts of deposits (with regulatory agencies as a reserve against policy commitments)

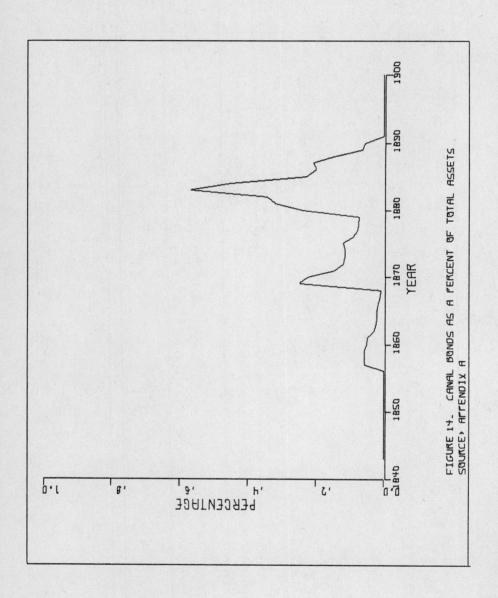

FIGURE 14. CANAL BONDS AS A PERCENT OF TOTAL ASSETS
SOURCE, APPENDIX A

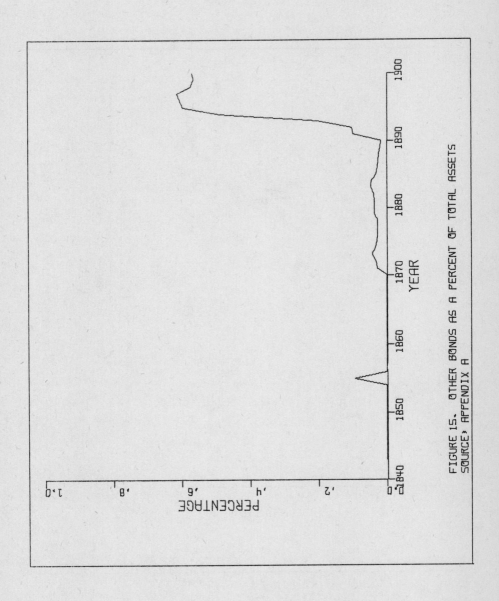

FIGURE 15. OTHER BONDS AS A PERCENT OF TOTAL ASSETS
SOURCE: APPENDIX A

TABLE 46. OTHER BONDS OWNED (THOUSANDS OF DOLLARS)

YEAR	1	2	3	4	5	6	7	8	TOTAL
					REGIONS				
1843	0.	0.	0.	0.	0.	0.	0.	0.	0.
1844	0.	0.	0.	0.	0.	0.	0.	0.	0.
1845	0.	0.	0.	0.	0.	0.	0.	0.	0.
1846	0.	0.	0.	0.	0.	0.	0.	0.	0.
1847	0.	0.	0.	0.	0.	0.	0.	0.	0.
1848	0.	0.	0.	0.	0.	0.	0.	0.	0.
1849	0.	0.	0.	0.	0.	0.	0.	0.	0.
1850	0.	0.	0.	0.	0.	0.	0.	0.	0.
1851	0.	0.	0.	0.	0.	0.	0.	0.	0.
1852	0.	0.	0.	0.	0.	0.	0.	0.	0.
1853	0.	0.	0.	0.	0.	0.	0.	0.	0.
1854	0.	0.	0.	0.	0.	0.	0.	0.	0.
1855	18.	0.	0.	0.	0.	0.	0.	0.	18.
1856	0.	0.	0.	0.	0.	0.	0.	0.	0.
1857	0.	0.	0.	0.	0.	0.	0.	0.	0.
1858	0.	0.	0.	0.	0.	0.	0.	0.	0.
1859	0.	0.	0.	0.	0.	0.	0.	0.	0.
1860	0.	0.	0.	0.	0.	0.	0.	0.	0.
1861	0.	0.	0.	0.	0.	0.	0.	0.	0.
1862	0.	0.	0.	0.	0.	0.	0.	0.	0.
1863	0.	0.	0.	0.	0.	0.	0.	0.	0.
1864	0.	0.	0.	0.	0.	0.	0.	0.	0.
1865	0.	0.	0.	0.	0.	0.	0.	0.	0.
1866	0.	0.	0.	0.	0.	0.	0.	0.	0.
1867	0.	0.	0.	0.	0.	0.	0.	0.	0.
1868	0.	0.	0.	0.	0.	0.	0.	0.	0.
1869	0.	0.	0.	0.	0.	0.	0.	0.	0.
1870	0.	0.	0.	0.	0.	0.	0.	0.	0.
1871	0.	67.	0.	2.	0.	0.	0.	0.	65.

185

TABLE 46 (CONTINUED)

YEAR	REGIONS								TOTAL
	1	2	3	4	5	6	7	8	
1872	1.	115.	0.	2.	0.	3.	0.	0.	121.
1873	1.	166.	0.	2.	0.	0.	0.	0.	169.
1874	0.	127.	0.	9.	0.	0.	0.	0.	136.
1875	0.	120.	0.	0.	0.	0.	0.	0.	120.
1876	0.	118.	0.	0.	0.	0.	0.	0.	118.
1877	0.	112.	0.	0.	0.	0.	0.	0.	112.
1878	0.	118.	0.	0.	0.	0.	0.	0.	118.
1879	0.	166.	0.	0.	0.	0.	0.	0.	166.
1880	0.	177.	0.	0.	0.	0.	0.	0.	177.
1881	0.	179.	0.	0.	0.	0.	0.	0.	179.
1882	0.	136.	0.	0.	0.	0.	0.	0.	136.
1883	0.	241.	0.	0.	0.	0.	0.	0.	241.
1884	0.	233.	0.	0.	0.	0.	0.	0.	233.
1885	0.	164.	0.	0.	0.	0.	0.	0.	164.
1886	0.	155.	0.	0.	0.	0.	0.	0.	155.
1887	0.	150.	0.	0.	0.	0.	0.	0.	150.
1888	0.	143.	0.	0.	0.	0.	0.	0.	143.
1889	0.	143.	0.	0.	0.	0.	0.	0.	143.
1890	0.	139.	0.	0.	0.	0.	0.	0.	139.
1891	0.	873.	0.	0.	0.	0.	0.	0.	873.
1892	0.	985.	0.	0.	0.	0.	0.	0.	985.
1893	183.	1833.	71.	0.	0.	0.	0.	0.	2086.
1894	193.	4962.	140.	0.	54.	11.	87.	0.	5448.
1895	112.	6790.	140.	0.	0.	12.	65.	0.	7118.
1896	98.	7065.	138.	0.	0.	22.	52.	372.	7747.
1897	24.	7991.	145.	0.	0.	0.	0.	355.	8514.
1898	128.	8051.	222.	0.	0.	0.	0.	215.	8616.
1899	267.	8452.	306.	0.	7.	0.	0.	220.	9251.
1900	324.	9407.	339.	0.	7.	2.	0.	239.	10318.

TABLE 47. OTHER BONDS OWNED (PERCENT OF TOTAL ASSETS)

YEAR	1	2	3	REGIONS 4	5	6	7	8	TOTAL
1843	0.0	0.0	0.0	0.0	0.0	0.0	0.0	0.0	0.0
1844	0.0	0.0	0.0	0.0	0.0	0.0	0.0	0.0	0.0
1845	0.0	0.0	0.0	0.0	0.0	0.0	0.0	0.0	0.0
1846	0.0	0.0	0.0	0.0	0.0	0.0	0.0	0.0	0.0
1847	0.0	0.0	0.0	0.0	0.0	0.0	0.0	0.0	0.0
1848	0.0	0.0	0.0	0.0	0.0	0.0	0.0	0.0	0.0
1849	0.0	0.0	0.0	0.0	0.0	0.0	0.0	0.0	0.0
1850	0.0	0.0	0.0	0.0	0.0	0.0	0.0	0.0	0.0
1851	0.0	0.0	0.0	0.0	0.0	0.0	0.0	0.0	0.0
1852	0.0	0.0	0.0	0.0	0.0	0.0	0.0	0.0	0.0
1853	0.0	0.0	0.0	0.0	0.0	0.0	0.0	0.0	0.0
1854	0.0	0.0	0.0	0.0	0.0	0.0	0.0	0.0	0.0
1855	0.C57	0.0	0.0	0.0	0.0	0.0	0.0	0.0	0.C97
1856	0.0	0.0	0.0	0.0	0.0	0.0	0.0	0.0	0.0
1857	0.0	0.0	0.0	0.0	0.0	0.0	0.0	0.0	0.0
1858	0.0	0.0	0.0	0.0	0.0	0.0	0.0	0.0	0.0
1859	0.0	0.0	0.0	0.0	0.0	0.0	0.0	0.0	0.0
1860	0.0	0.0	0.0	0.0	0.0	0.0	0.0	0.0	0.0
1861	0.0	0.0	0.0	0.0	0.0	0.0	0.0	0.0	0.0
1862	0.0	0.0	0.0	0.0	0.0	0.0	0.0	0.0	0.0
1863	0.0	0.0	0.0	0.0	0.0	0.0	0.0	0.0	0.0
1864	0.0	0.0	0.0	0.0	0.0	0.0	0.0	0.0	0.0
1865	0.0	0.0	0.0	0.0	0.0	0.0	0.0	0.0	0.0
1866	0.0	0.0	0.0	0.0	0.0	0.0	0.0	0.0	0.0
1867	0.0	0.0	0.0	0.0	0.0	0.0	0.0	0.0	0.0
1868	0.0	0.0	0.0	0.0	0.0	0.0	0.0	0.0	0.0
1869	0.0	0.0	0.0	0.0	0.0	0.0	0.0	0.0	0.0
1870	0.0	0.0	0.0	0.0	0.0	0.0	0.0	0.0	0.0
1871	0.0	0.020	0.0	100.0	0.0	0.0	0.0	0.0	0.030

TABLE 47 (CONTINUED)

YEAR	REGIONS								TOTAL
	1	2	3	4	5	6	7	8	
1872	0.000	0.032	0.0	0.001	0.0	0.001	0.0	0.0	0.033
1873	0.000	0.044	0.0	0.000	0.0	0.0	0.0	0.0	0.044
1874	0.0	0.030	0.0	0.002	0.0	0.0	0.0	0.0	0.032
1875	0.0	0.028	0.0	0.0	0.0	0.0	0.0	0.0	0.028
1876	0.0	0.027	0.0	0.0	0.0	0.0	0.0	0.0	0.027
1877	0.0	0.025	0.0	0.0	0.0	0.0	0.0	0.0	0.025
1878	0.0	0.027	0.0	0.0	0.0	0.0	0.0	0.0	0.027
1879	0.0	0.037	0.0	0.0	0.0	0.0	0.0	0.0	0.037
1880	0.0	0.038	0.0	0.0	0.0	0.0	0.0	0.0	0.038
1881	0.0	0.038	0.0	0.0	0.0	0.0	0.0	0.0	0.038
1882	0.0	0.039	0.0	0.0	0.0	0.0	0.0	0.0	0.039
1883	0.0	0.047	0.0	0.0	0.0	0.0	0.0	0.0	0.047
1884	0.0	0.044	0.0	0.0	0.0	0.0	0.0	0.0	0.044
1885	0.0	0.029	0.0	0.0	0.0	0.0	0.0	0.0	0.029
1886	0.0	0.026	0.0	0.0	0.0	0.0	0.0	0.0	0.026
1887	0.0	0.024	0.0	0.0	0.0	0.0	0.0	0.0	0.024
1888	0.0	0.021	0.0	0.0	0.0	0.0	0.0	0.0	0.021
1889	0.0	0.019	0.0	0.0	0.0	0.0	0.0	0.0	0.019
1890	0.0	0.017	0.0	0.0	0.0	0.0	0.0	0.0	0.017
1891	0.0	0.101	0.0	0.0	0.0	0.0	0.0	0.0	0.101
1892	0.0	0.104	0.0	0.0	0.0	0.0	0.0	0.0	0.104
1893	0.018	0.180	0.007	0.0	0.0	0.0	0.0	0.0	0.205
1894	0.017	0.446	0.013	0.0	0.005	0.001	0.008	0.0	0.450
1895	0.009	0.568	0.012	0.0	0.0	0.001	0.005	0.0	0.595
1896	0.008	0.552	0.011	0.0	0.0	0.002	0.004	0.029	0.605
1897	0.002	0.577	0.010	0.0	0.0	0.0	0.0	0.026	0.614
1898	0.008	0.533	0.015	0.0	0.0	0.0	0.0	0.014	0.571
1899	0.016	0.515	0.019	0.0	0.000	0.0	0.0	0.013	0.563
1900	0.018	0.520	0.019	0.0	0.000	0.000	0.0	0.013	0.570

was the practice of European governments in requiring such.
Many of the bonds in this category were those purchased
simply to meet the legally required minimum deposit requisite
to doing business in such countries. These are in evidence
in the series beginning with the first entries in 1868.
Part of the percentage influx evidenced by the latter
years, in Figure 16, was the result of expanding foreign
business by the larger companies in those years.

The remainder of the influx may be examined in a comparison with Figure 11. It was accounted for, in large part,
by the allocations made in the rail bond regionalization. Those
allocations made to Canadian and Mexican branches of American
rail lines, and the actual purchases of the securities of
lines wholly within those countries, appeared here.

Stock Categories

The principal characteristics of classes of securities
common to both bonds and stocks have been discussed in connection
with the former. Mostly, those categories unique to stocks,
and the additional characteristics of other categories related
especially to stocks, will be discussed in this section.

Reference to Table 22 and Table 24 reveals that in the
period of the tables, bond holdings reached their maximum,
relative importance in 1900, nearly forty-six percent of
total assets. By contrast, the maximum relative importance
of stock holdings, just over six percent of total assets,

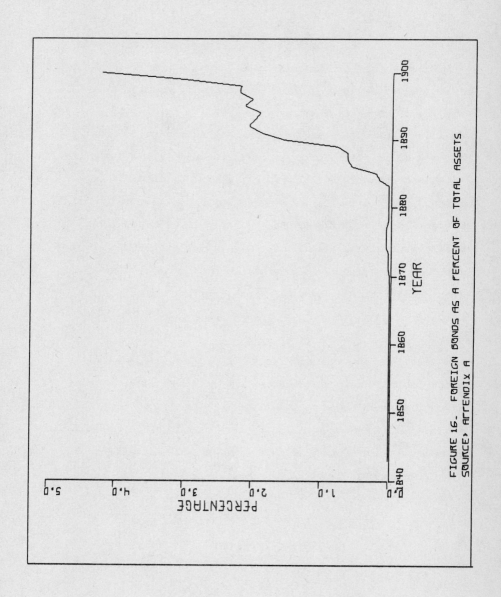

FIGURE 16.- FOREIGN BONDS AS A PERCENT OF TOTAL ASSETS
SOURCE: APPENDIX A

was reached in 1849, before the severe laws limiting such
purchases.

Financial Stocks

The early investment regulations of Massachusetts
specifically permitted purchase of bank stocks. Table 48 and
49 show that most of the early financial stock holdings were
related to institutions in New England. These were virtually
all the stocks of Massachusetts banks, held by life companies
incorporated in that state. Stocks in institutions in the
Middle Atlantic States (Region 2) do not become a consistently
more important part of the portfolios until the period that
included the proliferation of subsidiary institutions. The
stocks secured in the New York City area at that time, to
gain or hold control of various affiliated institutions,
provided the basis of the change.

The two special conditions mentioned seem to have
accounted for most of the purchases of financial stocks. One
exception occurred during the principal period of amalgamation,
the seventies and eighties. During those years stock transfers
seemed to be an important part of many of the mergers and com-
binations that took place. The holdings acquired in this
connection are also evident in Figure 17.

TABLE 48. FINANCIAL STOCK OWNED (THOUSANDS OF DOLLARS)

YEAR	REGIONS								TOTAL
	1	2	3	4	5	6	7	8	
1843	14.	0.	0.	0.	0.	0.	0.	0.	14.
1844	40.	0.	0.	0.	0.	0.	0.	0.	40.
1845	45.	0.	0.	0.	0.	0.	0.	0.	45.
1846	51.	0.	0.	0.	0.	0.	0.	0.	51.
1847	64.	0.	0.	0.	0.	0.	0.	0.	64.
1848	63.	5.	0.	0.	0.	0.	0.	0.	69.
1849	160.	26.	0.	0.	0.	0.	0.	0.	187.
1850	134.	4.	0.	0.	0.	0.	0.	0.	138.
1851	160.	5.	0.	0.	0.	0.	0.	0.	164.
1852	192.	5.	0.	0.	0.	0.	0.	0.	197.
1853	227.	5.	0.	0.	0.	0.	0.	0.	233.
1854	344.	28.	0.	0.	0.	0.	0.	0.	372.
1855	437.	24.	0.	0.	0.	0.	0.	0.	461.
1856	494.	58.	7.	0.	0.	0.	0.	0.	559.
1857	466.	102.	12.	0.	0.	0.	0.	0.	580.
1858	342.	131.	13.	0.	0.	0.	0.	0.	486.
1859	329.	80.	13.	0.	0.	0.	0.	0.	421.
1860	318.	97.	37.	0.	0.	0.	0.	0.	453.
1861	311.	102.	40.	0.	0.	0.	0.	0.	452.
1862	182.	86.	24.	0.	0.	0.	0.	0.	292.
1863	432.	98.	23.	1.	0.	22.	0.	0.	576.
1864	509.	113.	42.	0.	0.	31.	0.	0.	695.
1865	774.	119.	79.	0.	0.	39.	0.	0.	1011.
1866	1523.	178.	90.	0.	0.	41.	0.	0.	1832.
1867	1635.	219.	55.	0.	0.	4.	0.	0.	1914.
1868	1849.	292.	88.	0.	0.	7.	0.	0.	2236.
1869	2233.	249.	72.	0.	0.	8.	0.	0.	2563.
1870	2123.	201.	54.	0.	0.	7.	0.	0.	2386.
1871	1943.	404.	66.	0.	0.	7.	0.	0.	2420.

TABLE 48 (CONTINUED)

				REGIONS					
YEAR	1	2	3	4	5	6	7	8	TOTAL
1872	2060.	695.	64.	0.	0.	2.	0.	0.	2820.
1873	2113.	1054.	47.	0.	0.	8.	0.	34.	3255.
1874	2740.	1388.	1504.	3.	0.	12.	307.	0.	5954.
1875	2602.	1602.	41.	0.	0.	9.	0.	0.	4253.
1876	2857.	2036.	57.	0.	0.	10.	0.	0.	4959.
1877	2637.	1791.	25.	0.	0.	5.	0.	0.	4458.
1878	2766.	1851.	62.	0.	0.	3.	0.	0.	4683.
1879	2634.	1832.	26.	0.	0.	3.	0.	0.	4546.
1880	2519.	2387.	40.	31.	0.	6.	0.	0.	4982.
1881	2083.	3685.	37.	0.	0.	5.	0.	0.	5811.
1882	2126.	4849.	15.	0.	0.	6.	0.	0.	6995.
1883	3565.	2148.	52.	0.	0.	7.	12.	0.	5784.
1884	3927.	2990.	13.	0.	0.	7.	61.	0.	6999.
1885	3579.	2750.	12.	0.	0.	7.	12.	0.	6359.
1886	3517.	3405.	11.	0.	0.	64.	5.	0.	7002.
1887	3433.	3850.	11.	0.	0.	61.	5.	0.	7360.
1888	3381.	3853.	10.	1.	0.	60.	29.	0.	7334.
1889	3484.	5531.	16.	1.	0.	159.	38.	10.	9239.
1890	3490.	6167.	16.	1.	0.	405.	167.	27.	10272.
1891	3676.	8590.	16.	2.	0.	514.	49.	56.	12903.
1892	3726.	12637.	61.	2.	0.	444.	87.	34.	16991.
1893	3588.	14408.	328.	2.	0.	504.	84.	575.	19489.
1894	3668.	14917.	336.	2.	0.	313.	67.	38.	19340.
1895	3658.	17802.	334.	2.	0.	309.	56.	34.	22196.
1896	3650.	19174.	2016.	2.	0.	312.	47.	69.	25270.
1897	4092.	22095.	2078.	2.	0.	350.	51.	76.	28736.
1898	4015.	23449.	2079.	2.	0.	302.	44.	80.	29970.
1899	4520.	26534.	2142.	2.	0.	264.	41.	100.	33603.
1900	4971.	29495.	2333.	2.	0.	288.	15.	120.	37228.

193

TABLE 49. FINANCIAL STOCKS OWNED (PERCENT OF TOTAL ASSETS)

YEAR	REGIONS								TOTAL
	1	2	3	4	5	6	7	8	
1843	0.697	0.0	0.0	0.0	0.0	0.0	0.0	0.0	0.697
1844	1.831	0.0	0.0	0.0	0.0	0.0	0.0	0.0	1.831
1845	1.757	0.0	0.0	0.0	0.0	0.0	0.0	0.0	1.757
1846	1.588	0.0	0.0	0.0	0.0	0.0	0.0	0.0	1.588
1847	1.889	0.0	0.0	0.0	0.0	0.0	0.0	0.0	1.889
1848	1.477	0.123	0.0	0.0	0.0	0.0	0.0	0.0	1.600
1849	2.073	0.342	0.0	0.0	0.0	0.0	0.0	0.0	2.414
1850	1.405	0.046	0.0	0.0	0.0	0.0	0.0	0.0	1.451
1851	1.330	0.038	0.0	0.0	0.0	0.0	0.0	0.0	1.368
1852	1.338	0.035	0.0	0.0	0.0	0.0	0.0	0.0	1.372
1853	1.405	0.034	0.0	0.0	0.0	0.0	0.0	0.0	1.439
1854	1.907	0.155	0.0	0.0	0.0	0.0	0.0	0.0	2.062
1855	2.361	0.127	0.0	0.0	0.0	0.0	0.0	0.0	2.488
1856	2.291	0.269	0.034	0.0	0.0	0.0	0.0	0.0	2.593
1857	1.890	0.413	0.047	0.0	0.0	0.0	0.0	0.0	2.349
1858	1.237	0.474	0.046	0.0	0.0	0.0	0.0	0.0	1.757
1859	1.059	0.266	0.044	0.0	0.0	0.0	0.0	0.0	1.408
1860	0.893	0.274	0.105	0.0	0.0	0.0	0.0	0.0	1.272
1861	0.795	0.261	0.102	0.0	0.0	0.0	0.0	0.0	1.158
1862	0.442	0.208	0.059	0.0	0.0	0.0	0.0	0.0	0.709
1863	0.806	0.182	0.043	0.002	0.0	0.042	0.0	0.0	1.076
1864	0.749	0.167	0.061	0.0	0.0	0.046	0.0	0.0	1.024
1865	0.942	0.145	0.096	0.0	0.0	0.047	0.0	0.0	1.230
1866	1.420	0.166	0.024	0.0	0.0	0.038	0.0	0.0	1.708
1867	1.126	0.151	0.038	0.0	0.0	0.003	0.0	0.0	1.318
1868	0.910	0.144	0.043	0.0	0.0	0.003	0.0	0.0	1.100
1869	0.878	0.098	0.028	0.0	0.0	0.003	0.0	0.0	1.007
1870	0.748	0.071	0.019	0.0	0.0	0.002	0.0	0.0	0.840
1871	0.584	0.121	0.020	0.0	0.0	0.0	0.0	0.0	0.728

TABLE 49 (CONTINUED)

YEAR	REGIONS								TOTAL
	1	2	3	4	5	6	7	8	
1872	0.565	0.190	0.017	0.0	0.0	0.001	0.0	0.0	0.773
1873	0.557	0.278	0.012	0.0	0.0	0.002	0.0	0.009	0.858
1874	0.643	0.326	0.353	0.001	0.0	0.003	0.072	0.0	1.398
1875	0.598	0.368	0.009	0.0	0.0	0.002	0.0	0.0	0.978
1876	0.652	0.465	0.013	0.0	0.0	0.002	0.0	0.0	1.132
1877	0.599	0.407	0.006	0.0	0.0	0.001	0.0	0.0	1.014
1878	0.624	0.417	0.014	0.0	0.0	0.001	0.0	0.0	1.056
1879	0.589	0.421	0.006	0.0	0.0	0.001	0.0	0.0	1.017
1880	0.545	0.516	0.009	0.007	0.0	0.001	0.0	0.0	1.078
1881	0.438	0.774	0.008	0.0	0.0	0.001	0.0	0.0	1.220
1882	0.443	1.011	0.003	0.0	0.0	0.001	0.0	0.0	1.458
1883	0.701	0.422	0.010	0.0	0.0	0.001	0.002	0.0	1.137
1884	0.741	0.565	0.002	0.0	0.0	0.001	0.012	0.0	1.321
1885	0.636	0.489	0.002	0.0	0.0	0.001	0.002	0.0	1.131
1886	0.591	0.572	0.002	0.0	0.0	0.011	0.001	0.0	1.176
1887	0.543	0.609	0.002	0.0	0.0	0.010	0.001	0.0	1.165
1888	0.503	0.573	0.002	0.000	0.0	0.009	0.004	0.0	1.091
1889	0.472	0.750	0.002	0.000	0.0	0.021	0.005	0.001	1.252
1890	0.438	0.774	0.002	0.000	0.0	0.051	0.021	0.003	1.290
1891	0.425	0.992	0.002	0.000	0.0	0.059	0.006	0.006	1.490
1892	0.392	1.330	0.006	0.000	0.0	0.047	0.009	0.004	1.788
1893	0.352	1.414	0.032	0.000	0.0	0.049	0.038	0.056	1.913
1894	0.330	1.342	0.030	0.000	0.0	0.028	0.006	0.003	1.739
1895	0.306	1.488	0.028	0.000	0.0	0.026	0.005	0.003	1.856
1896	0.285	1.498	0.157	0.000	0.0	0.024	0.004	0.005	1.974
1897	0.295	1.594	0.149	0.000	0.0	0.025	0.004	0.005	2.073
1898	0.266	1.553	0.138	0.000	0.0	0.020	0.003	0.005	1.985
1899	0.275	1.616	0.130	0.000	0.0	0.016	0.002	0.006	2.047
1900	0.275	1.630	0.129	0.000	0.0	0.016	0.001	0.007	2.057

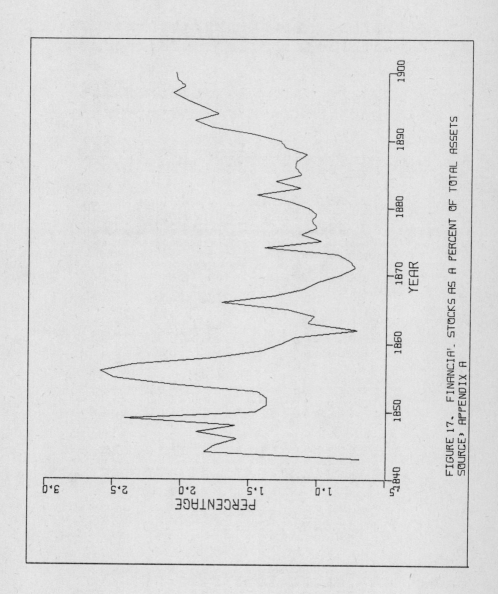

FIGURE 17. FINANCIAL STOCKS AS A PERCENT OF TOTAL ASSETS
SOURCE: APPENDIX A

Railroad Stocks

A comparison of Figure 18 with Figure 11 indicates the
similarity of the trends in bond and stock holdings during
the latter years. The main differences to be noted are in
the early period. The companies of Massachusetts and Connecticut were allowed to hold stocks of various descriptions in
those years, and several instances of small purchases of
rail stocks existed in the records of some of those companies.

The distinct bias in the portfolios of life insurance
companies toward debt issues, as opposed to equities, is
evident in the two categories of rail securities. Some
writers have contended that this simply reflected the conservative, cautious approach of early insurance investment
managers. Others have suggested, more realistically, that
the more or less guaranteed income stream of debt issues was
more suited to the absolute need of life insurance companies
to maintain consistent liquidity. Additionally, it ought
to be suggested that the legal restraints appear to have been
the most important factor. For example, no objection was
evident to the purchase of the legally allowable financial
stocks, even when some rather insecure institutions were involved.

Utility Stocks

The size of the amounts used in generating Figure 19

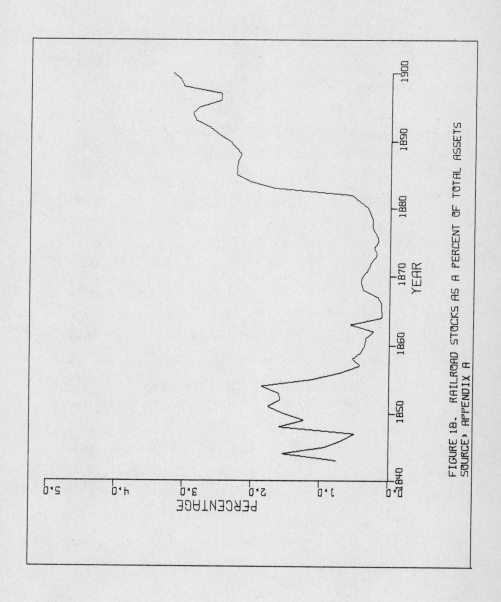

FIGURE 1B. RAILROAD STOCKS AS A PERCENT OF TOTAL ASSETS
SOURCE, APPENDIX A

TABLE 50. RAILROAD STOCK OWNED (THOUSANDS OF DOLLARS)

YEAR	REGIONS								TOTAL
	1	2	3	4	5	6	7	8	
1843	10.	5.	0.	0.	0.	0.	0.	0.	15.
1844	22.	12.	0.	0.	0.	0.	0.	0.	34.
1845	15.	9.	0.	0.	0.	0.	0.	0.	24.
1846	13.	8.	0.	0.	0.	0.	0.	0.	21.
1847	10.	6.	0.	0.	0.	0.	0.	0.	17.
1848	63.	5.	0.	0.	0.	0.	0.	0.	69.
1849	76.	19.	0.	0.	0.	0.	0.	0.	95.
1850	130.	15.	0.	0.	0.	0.	0.	0.	146.
1851	188.	23.	0.	0.	0.	0.	0.	0.	211.
1852	197.	30.	0.	0.	0.	0.	0.	0.	227.
1853	219.	41.	0.	0.	0.	0.	0.	0.	260.
1854	258.	77.	0.	0.	0.	0.	0.	0.	335.
1855	143.	65.	0.	0.	0.	0.	0.	0.	208.
1856	64.	71.	17.	0.	0.	0.	0.	0.	152.
1857	38.	65.	1.	0.	0.	0.	0.	0.	104.
1858	75.	73.	0.	0.	0.	0.	0.	0.	148.
1859	35.	83.	0.	0.	0.	0.	0.	0.	119.
1860	33.	87.	0.	0.	0.	0.	0.	0.	120.
1861	35.	94.	0.	0.	0.	0.	0.	0.	129.
1862	26.	63.	0.	0.	0.	0.	0.	0.	69.
1863	47.	262.	0.	0.	0.	0.	0.	0.	308.
1864	66.	0.	0.	0.	0.	0.	0.	0.	66.
1865	79.	0.	18.	0.	0.	0.	0.	0.	97.
1866	109.	0.	18.	0.	0.	0.	0.	0.	127.
1867	147.	92.	16.	0.	0.	0.	0.	0.	255.
1868	404.	250.	131.	0.	0.	0.	0.	0.	785.
1869	488.	278.	188.	13.	7.	46.	46.	0.	1067.
1870	593.	302.	182.	0.	0.	0.	0.	0.	1077.
1871	585.	265.	119.	44.	0.	0.	0.	0.	1014.

TABLE 50 (CONTINUED)

YEAR	1	2	3	4	REGIONS 5	6	7	8	TOTAL
1872	601.	226.	131.	0.	0.	0.	0.	0.	958.
1873	456.	158.	84.	0.	0.	0.	0.	0.	698.
1874	668.	208.	98.	16.	0.	0.	0.	0.	989.
1875	452.	157.	81.	0.	0.	0.	0.	0.	690.
1876	554.	232.	89.	0.	0.	0.	0.	0.	875.
1877	607.	275.	153.	0.	0.	93.	12.	0.	1141.
1878	672.	313.	129.	0.	0.	0.	0.	0.	1114.
1879	804.	324.	159.	0.	0.	8.	0.	0.	1296.
1880	843.	376.	284.	0.	0.	1.	1.	0.	1505.
1881	1076.	680.	298.	0.	0.	1.	81.	26.	2162.
1882	1109.	935.	516.	0.	0.	1.	105.	60.	2727.
1883	907.	4196.	2460.	4.	3.	147.	846.	31.	8594.
1884	1064.	4770.	3099.	5.	4.	183.	1711.	32.	10868.
1885	2064.	5096.	3175.	4.	5.	189.	2055.	28.	12617.
1886	2126.	5036.	3570.	5.	7.	469.	2064.	24.	13301.
1887	2429.	5139.	3615.	35.	7.	433.	2293.	22.	14016.
1888	2416.	5102.	3815.	413.	9.	564.	2261.	24.	14605.
1889	3019.	5919.	4634.	174.	20.	573.	2311.	25.	16675.
1890	3007.	5926.	4679.	168.	342.	666.	3898.	33.	18720.
1891	3170.	7502.	4951.	109.	367.	1478.	4141.	44.	21762.
1892	3591.	7696.	6619.	248.	391.	2096.	4393.	45.	25078.
1893	3188.	9238.	6998.	396.	392.	1532.	7189.	51.	28984.
1894	4232.	10822.	8553.	440.	747.	1137.	5768.	475.	32174.
1895	5437.	11104.	8561.	672.	746.	1215.	5137.	506.	33379.
1896	5322.	11012.	8418.	706.	772.	1308.	3542.	566.	31645.
1897	5897.	11656.	8720.	732.	813.	1659.	3901.	813.	34191.
1898	8555.	19004.	8714.	846.	811.	1713.	5206.	809.	45657.
1899	10193.	20320.	9827.	912.	896.	1794.	5588.	836.	50365.
1900	11379.	24175.	10823.	1000.	1073.	2029.	6194.	915.	57589.

TABLE 51. RAILROAD STOCK OWNED (PERCENT CF TCTAL ASSETS)

YEAR	REGIONS								TOTAL
	1	2	3	4	5	6	7	8	
1843	0.488	0.279	0.0	0.0	0.0	0.0	0.0	0.0	0.767
1844	0.986	0.563	0.0	0.0	0.0	0.0	0.0	0.0	1.549
1845	0.586	0.335	0.0	0.0	0.0	0.0	0.0	0.0	0.920
1846	0.410	0.256	0.0	0.0	0.0	0.0	0.0	0.0	0.666
1847	0.302	0.189	0.0	0.0	0.0	0.0	0.0	0.0	0.491
1848	1.477	0.123	0.0	0.0	0.0	0.0	0.0	0.0	1.600
1849	0.979	0.251	0.0	0.0	0.0	0.0	0.0	0.0	1.230
1850	1.370	0.161	0.0	0.0	0.0	0.0	0.0	0.0	1.532
1851	1.568	0.190	0.0	0.0	0.0	0.0	0.0	0.0	1.758
1852	1.372	0.208	0.0	0.0	0.0	0.0	0.0	0.0	1.581
1853	1.354	0.254	0.0	0.0	0.0	0.0	0.0	0.0	1.608
1854	1.433	0.429	0.0	0.0	0.0	0.0	0.0	0.0	1.861
1855	0.772	0.352	0.0	0.0	0.0	0.0	0.0	0.0	1.124
1856	0.296	0.329	0.081	0.0	0.0	0.0	0.0	0.0	0.705
1857	0.155	0.263	0.005	0.0	0.0	0.0	0.0	0.0	0.422
1858	0.270	0.265	0.0	0.0	0.0	0.0	0.0	0.0	0.535
1859	0.118	0.279	0.0	0.0	0.0	0.0	0.0	0.0	0.397
1860	0.094	0.244	0.0	0.0	0.0	0.0	0.0	0.0	0.338
1861	0.091	0.240	0.0	0.0	0.0	0.0	0.0	0.0	0.330
1862	0.064	0.153	0.0	0.0	0.0	0.0	0.0	0.0	0.217
1863	0.087	0.488	0.0	0.0	0.0	0.0	0.0	0.0	0.575
1864	0.097	0.0	0.0	0.0	0.0	0.0	0.0	0.0	0.097
1865	0.096	0.0	0.021	0.0	0.0	0.0	0.0	0.0	0.118
1866	0.101	0.0	0.017	0.0	0.0	0.0	0.0	0.0	0.118
1867	0.101	0.063	0.011	0.0	0.0	0.0	0.0	0.0	0.176
1868	0.199	0.123	0.065	0.0	0.0	0.0	0.0	0.0	0.386
1869	0.192	0.109	0.074	0.005	0.003	0.018	0.018	0.0	0.419
1870	0.209	0.106	0.064	0.0	0.0	0.0	0.0	0.0	0.379
1871	0.176	0.080	0.036	0.013	0.0	0.0	0.0	0.0	0.305

TABLE 51 (CONTINUED)

| | | | | REGIONS | | | | | |
YEAR	1	2	3	4	5	6	7	8	TOTAL
1872	0.165	0.062	0.036	0.0	0.0	0.0	0.0	0.0	0.263
1873	0.120	0.042	0.022	0.0	0.0	0.0	0.0	0.0	0.184
1874	0.157	0.049	0.023	0.004	0.0	0.0	0.0	0.0	0.232
1875	0.104	0.036	0.019	0.0	0.0	0.0	0.0	0.0	0.159
1876	0.126	0.053	0.020	0.0	0.0	0.0	0.0	0.0	0.200
1877	0.138	0.062	0.035	0.0	0.0	0.021	0.003	0.0	0.259
1878	0.151	0.071	0.029	0.0	0.0	0.0	0.0	0.0	0.251
1879	0.180	0.072	0.036	0.0	0.0	0.002	0.0	0.0	0.290
1880	0.182	0.081	0.061	0.0	0.0	0.000	0.000	0.0	0.326
1881	0.226	0.143	0.063	0.0	0.0	0.000	0.017	0.006	0.454
1882	0.231	0.195	0.108	0.0	0.0	0.000	0.022	0.013	0.568
1883	0.178	0.825	0.483	0.001	0.001	0.029	0.166	0.006	1.689
1884	0.201	0.901	0.585	0.001	0.001	0.035	0.323	0.006	2.052
1885	0.367	0.906	0.565	0.001	0.001	0.034	0.365	0.005	2.244
1886	0.357	0.845	0.599	0.001	0.001	0.075	0.347	0.004	2.233
1887	0.384	0.813	0.579	0.006	0.001	0.068	0.363	0.004	2.218
1888	0.360	0.759	0.568	0.062	0.001	0.084	0.337	0.004	2.173
1889	0.409	0.802	0.628	0.024	0.003	0.078	0.313	0.003	2.260
1890	0.378	0.744	0.588	0.021	0.043	0.084	0.490	0.004	2.351
1891	0.366	0.867	0.572	0.013	0.042	0.171	0.478	0.005	2.514
1892	0.378	0.810	0.696	0.026	0.041	0.221	0.462	0.005	2.639
1893	0.313	0.907	0.687	0.039	0.038	0.150	0.706	0.005	2.845
1894	0.381	0.973	0.769	0.040	0.067	0.102	0.519	0.043	2.893
1895	0.455	0.928	0.716	0.056	0.062	0.102	0.429	0.042	2.791
1896	0.416	0.860	0.658	0.055	0.060	0.102	0.277	0.044	2.472
1897	0.426	0.841	0.629	0.053	0.059	0.120	0.281	0.059	2.467
1898	0.567	1.259	0.577	0.056	0.054	0.113	0.345	0.054	3.025
1899	0.621	1.238	0.599	0.056	0.055	0.109	0.340	0.051	3.068
1900	0.629	1.336	0.598	0.055	0.059	0.112	0.342	0.051	3.182

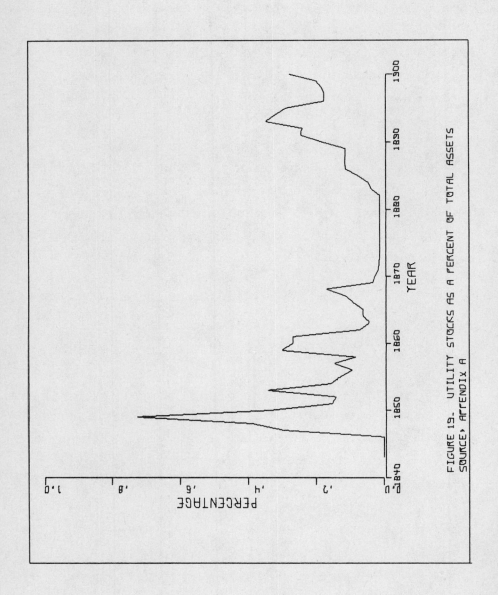

FIGURE 19. UTILITY STOCKS AS A PERCENT OF TOTAL ASSETS

SOURCE, APPENDIX A

was so small that the seemingly drastic fluctuations ought to
be ignored. They represent only the portfolio changes of
the few companies who held significant amounts of these securities. The items held in the early period were principally
the stocks of water companies and were mostly in the New
England area.

Much later, with the innovation of other utilities,
stock holdings generally increased their importance. The
securities accounting for this change were principally those
of the telegraph companies. Table 52 indicates that prior
to the purchases involving the latter companies the amounts
involved in this class of investments were scarcely worth
mentioning.

Industrial Stocks

Table 54 indicates that the dollar amount of industrial
stocks held in 1849 was not surpassed until 1894. The holdings
of the early years were akin to those mentioned for the bonds.
They mainly represented holdings in a few of the Massachusetts
textile mills by a few of the earliest chartered companies.
The relative importance of these meager holdings was reduced
to insignificance by the growth of the value of total assets
held, as indicated in Figure 20.

As the holdings of the pre-mutual companies passed from
the scene the only consistent basis of the whole series is a
small purchase of textile stock by New England Mutual Life.

TABLE 52. UTILITY STOCK CWNED (THCUSANDS CF CCLLARS)

YEAR	REGIONS								
	1	2	3	4	5	6	7	8	TCTAL
1843	0.	0.	0.	0.	0.	0.	0.	0.	0.
1844	0.	0.	0.	0.	0.	0.	0.	0.	0.
1845	0.	0.	0.	0.	0.	0.	0.	0.	0.
1846	0.	0.	0.	0.	0.	0.	0.	0.	0.
1847	10.	0.	0.	0.	0.	0.	0.	0.	10.
1848	17.	0.	0.	0.	0.	0.	0.	0.	17.
1849	28.	28.	0.	0.	0.	0.	0.	0.	56.
1850	18.	14.	0.	0.	0.	0.	0.	0.	32.
1851	18.	0.	0.	0.	0.	0.	0.	0.	18.
1852	20.	0.	0.	0.	0.	0.	0.	0.	20.
1853	56.	0.	0.	0.	0.	0.	0.	0.	56.
1854	28.	0.	0.	0.	0.	0.	0.	0.	28.
1855	24.	0.	0.	0.	0.	0.	0.	0.	24.
1856	20.	0.	0.	0.	0.	0.	0.	0.	20.
1857	16.	0.	0.	0.	21.	0.	0.	0.	37.
1858	23.	0.	0.	0.	0.	0.	0.	0.	23.
1859	26.	65.	0.	0.	0.	0.	0.	0.	91.
1860	29.	67.	0.	0.	0.	0.	0.	0.	96.
1861	34.	71.	0.	0.	0.	0.	0.	0.	105.
1862	23.	6.	0.	0.	0.	0.	0.	0.	29.
1863	23.	0.	0.	0.	0.	0.	0.	0.	23.
1864	46.	0.	0.	0.	0.	0.	0.	0.	46.
1865	55.	0.	0.	0.	0.	0.	0.	0.	55.
1866	104.	0.	0.	0.	0.	0.	0.	0.	104.
1867	116.	0.	54.	0.	0.	0.	0.	0.	170.
1868	202.	18.	132.	0.	0.	0.	0.	0.	352.
1869	78.	0.	0.	0.	0.	0.	0.	0.	78.
1870	70.	0.	0.	0.	0.	0.	0.	0.	70.
1871	58.	0.	0.	0.	0.	0.	0.	0.	58.

TABLE 52 (CONTINUED)

					REGIONS				
YEAR	1	2	3	4	5	6	7	8	TOTAL
1872	52.	0.	0.	0.	0.	0.	0.	0.	52.
1873	49.	0.	0.	0.	0.	0.	0.	0.	49.
1874	62.	0.	0.	0.	0.	0.	0.	0.	62.
1875	66.	0.	0.	0.	0.	0.	0.	0.	66.
1876	74.	0.	0.	0.	0.	0.	0.	0.	74.
1877	72.	0.	0.	0.	0.	0.	0.	0.	72.
1878	72.	0.	0.	0.	0.	0.	0.	0.	72.
1879	72.	0.	0.	0.	0.	0.	0.	0.	72.
1880	77.	0.	0.	0.	0.	0.	0.	0.	72.
1881	75.	0.	0.	0.	0.	0.	0.	0.	75.
1882	79.	0.	0.	0.	0.	0.	0.	0.	79.
1883	62.	0.	0.	0.	0.	46.	56.	47.	211.
1884	67.	0.	0.	0.	0.	61.	67.	78.	273.
1885	64.	0.	0.	0.	0.	130.	130.	137.	461.
1886	63.	53.	62.	0.	53.	182.	125.	168.	707.
1887	67.	71.	71.	0.	0.	197.	177.	177.	760.
1888	69.	72.	63.	0.	0.	195.	196.	179.	775.
1889	73.	126.	0.	0.	0.	254.	206.	192.	852.
1890	105.	306.	0.	0.	0.	362.	373.	327.	1472.
1891	126.	932.	0.	0.	0.	383.	351.	351.	2144.
1892	129.	992.	0.	0.	0.	393.	391.	377.	2262.
1893	194.	1022.	3.	0.	0.	778.	783.	785.	3563.
1894	247.	1167.	3.	0.	0.	721.	713.	713.	3564.
1895	334.	1176.	6.	0.	0.	716.	612.	612.	3457.
1896	361.	1202.	6.	0.	0.	246.	194.	245.	2256.
1897	483.	1389.	13.	0.	0.	225.	151.	195.	2457.
1898	486.	1477.	516.	0.	0.	190.	85.	84.	2637.
1899	872.	1614.	456.	0.	11.	150.	94.	145.	3341.
1900	1544.	1885.	506.	0.	12.	395.	345.	423.	5111.

TABLE 53. UTILITY STOCK OWNED (PERCENT OF TOTAL ASSETS)

YEAR	REGIONS								TOTAL
	1	2	3	4	5	6	7	8	
1843	0.0	0.0	0.0	0.0	0.0	0.0	0.0	0.0	0.0
1844	0.0	0.0	0.0	0.0	0.0	0.0	0.0	0.0	0.0
1845	0.0	0.0	0.0	0.0	0.0	0.0	0.0	0.0	0.0
1846	0.0	0.0	0.0	0.0	0.0	0.0	0.0	0.0	0.0
1847	0.302	0.0	0.0	0.0	0.0	0.0	0.0	0.0	0.302
1848	0.394	0.0	0.0	0.0	0.0	0.0	0.0	0.0	0.394
1849	0.364	0.364	0.0	0.0	0.0	0.0	0.0	0.0	0.729
1850	0.184	0.150	0.0	0.0	0.0	0.0	0.0	0.0	0.334
1851	0.152	0.0	0.0	0.0	0.0	0.0	0.0	0.0	0.152
1852	0.139	0.0	0.0	0.0	0.0	0.0	0.0	0.0	0.139
1853	0.347	0.0	0.0	0.0	0.0	0.0	0.0	0.0	0.347
1854	0.155	0.0	0.0	0.0	0.0	0.0	0.0	0.0	0.155
1855	0.127	0.0	0.0	0.0	0.0	0.0	0.0	0.0	0.127
1856	0.094	0.0	0.0	0.0	0.0	0.0	0.0	0.0	0.094
1857	0.066	0.0	0.0	0.0	0.084	0.0	0.0	0.0	0.150
1858	0.084	0.0	0.0	0.0	0.0	0.0	0.0	0.0	0.084
1859	0.087	0.218	0.0	0.0	0.0	0.0	0.0	0.0	0.305
1860	0.083	0.188	0.0	0.0	0.0	0.0	0.0	0.0	0.270
1861	0.087	0.181	0.0	0.0	0.0	0.0	0.0	0.0	0.269
1862	0.055	0.015	0.0	0.0	0.0	0.0	0.0	0.0	0.070
1863	0.043	0.0	0.0	0.0	0.0	0.0	0.0	0.0	0.043
1864	0.067	0.0	0.0	0.0	0.0	0.0	0.0	0.0	0.067
1865	0.067	0.0	0.0	0.0	0.0	0.0	0.0	0.0	0.067
1866	0.097	0.0	0.0	0.0	0.0	0.0	0.0	0.0	0.097
1867	0.080	0.0	0.037	0.0	0.0	0.0	0.0	0.0	0.117
1868	0.099	0.009	0.065	0.0	0.0	0.0	0.0	0.0	0.173
1869	0.031	0.0	0.0	0.0	0.0	0.0	0.0	0.0	0.031
1870	0.025	0.0	0.0	0.0	0.0	0.0	0.0	0.0	0.025
1871	0.017	0.0	0.0	0.0	0.0	0.0	0.0	0.0	0.017

TABLE 53 (CONTINUED)

YEAR	REGIONS								TOTAL
	1	2	3	4	5	6	7	8	
1872	0.014	0.0	0.0	0.0	0.0	0.0	0.0	0.0	0.014
1873	0.013	0.0	0.0	0.0	0.0	0.0	0.0	0.0	0.013
1874	0.015	0.0	0.0	0.0	0.0	0.0	0.0	0.0	0.015
1875	0.015	0.0	0.0	0.0	0.0	0.0	0.0	0.0	0.015
1876	0.017	0.0	0.0	0.0	0.0	0.0	0.0	0.0	0.017
1877	0.016	0.0	0.0	0.0	0.0	0.0	0.0	0.0	0.016
1878	0.016	0.0	0.0	0.0	0.0	0.0	0.0	0.0	0.016
1879	0.016	0.0	0.0	0.0	0.0	0.0	0.0	0.0	0.016
1880	0.017	0.0	0.0	0.0	0.0	0.0	0.0	0.0	0.017
1881	0.016	0.0	0.0	0.0	0.0	0.0	0.0	0.0	0.016
1882	0.017	0.0	0.0	0.0	0.0	0.0	0.0	0.0	0.017
1883	0.012	0.0	0.0	0.0	0.0	0.009	0.011	0.009	0.041
1884	0.013	0.0	0.0	0.0	0.0	0.012	0.013	0.015	0.052
1885	0.011	0.0	0.0	0.0	0.0	0.023	0.023	0.024	0.082
1886	0.011	0.009	0.010	0.0	0.009	0.031	0.021	0.028	0.119
1887	0.011	0.011	0.011	0.0	0.0	0.031	0.028	0.028	0.120
1888	0.010	0.011	0.009	0.0	0.0	0.029	0.029	0.027	0.115
1889	0.010	0.017	0.0	0.0	0.0	0.034	0.026	0.026	0.115
1890	0.013	0.038	0.0	0.0	0.0	0.045	0.047	0.041	0.185
1891	0.015	0.108	0.0	0.0	0.0	0.044	0.041	0.041	0.248
1892	0.014	0.104	0.0	0.0	0.0	0.041	0.041	0.040	0.240
1893	0.019	0.100	0.0	0.0	0.0	0.076	0.077	0.077	0.350
1894	0.022	0.105	0.000	0.0	0.0	0.065	0.064	0.064	0.321
1895	0.028	0.098	0.001	0.0	0.0	0.060	0.061	0.051	0.289
1896	0.028	0.094	0.000	0.0	0.0	0.019	0.015	0.019	0.176
1897	0.035	0.100	0.001	0.0	0.0	0.016	0.011	0.014	0.177
1898	0.032	0.098	0.034	0.0	0.0	0.013	0.006	0.006	0.188
1899	0.053	0.098	0.028	0.0	0.001	0.009	0.006	0.009	0.204
1900	0.085	0.104	0.028	0.0	0.001	0.022	0.019	0.023	0.282

TABLE 54. INDUSTRIAL STOCK OWNED (THOUSANDS OF DOLLARS)

	REGIONS								
YEAR	1	2	3	4	5	6	7	8	TOTAL
1843	7.	0.	0.	0.	0.	0.	0.	0.	7.
1844	19.	0.	0.	0.	0.	0.	0.	0.	19.
1845	24.	0.	0.	0.	0.	0.	0.	0.	24.
1846	23.	0.	0.	0.	0.	0.	0.	0.	23.
1847	45.	0.	0.	0.	0.	0.	0.	0.	45.
1848	71.	0.	0.	0.	0.	0.	0.	0.	71.
1849	100.	32.	0.	0.	0.	0.	0.	0.	132.
1850	50.	12.	0.	0.	0.	0.	0.	0.	62.
1851	54.	0.	0.	0.	0.	0.	0.	0.	54.
1852	51.	0.	0.	0.	0.	0.	0.	0.	51.
1853	33.	0.	0.	0.	0.	0.	0.	0.	33.
1854	39.	0.	0.	0.	0.	0.	0.	0.	39.
1855	29.	0.	0.	0.	0.	0.	0.	0.	29.
1856	30.	0.	0.	0.	0.	0.	0.	0.	30.
1857	12.	0.	0.	0.	0.	0.	0.	0.	12.
1858	13.	0.	0.	0.	0.	0.	0.	0.	13.
1859	9.	5.	0.	0.	0.	0.	0.	0.	14.
1860	9.	0.	0.	0.	0.	0.	0.	0.	9.
1861	10.	0.	0.	0.	0.	0.	0.	0.	10.
1862	8.	0.	0.	0.	0.	0.	0.	0.	8.
1863	7.	0.	0.	0.	0.	0.	0.	0.	7.
1864	7.	0.	0.	0.	0.	0.	0.	0.	7.
1865	10.	0.	0.	0.	0.	0.	0.	0.	10.
1866	10.	0.	0.	0.	0.	0.	0.	0.	10.
1867	6.	0.	0.	0.	0.	0.	0.	0.	6.
1868	9.	9.	0.	0.	0.	0.	0.	0.	19.
1869	6.	13.	0.	0.	0.	0.	0.	0.	19.
1870	7.	10.	22.	0.	0.	0.	0.	0.	39.
1871	8.	12.	6.	0.	0.	0.	0.	0.	26.

209

TABLE 54 (CONTINUED)

YEAR	REGIONS								TOTAL
	1	2	3	4	5	6	7	8	
1872	8.	9.	0.	0.	0.	0.	0.	0.	18.
1873	7.	9.	4.	0.	0.	0.	0.	0.	21.
1874	8.	0.	17.	0.	0.	0.	0.	0.	25.
1875	8.	0.	0.	0.	0.	0.	0.	0.	8.
1876	23.	0.	0.	0.	0.	0.	0.	0.	23.
1877	7.	0.	1.	0.	0.	0.	0.	0.	8.
1878	8.	0.	0.	0.	0.	0.	0.	0.	8.
1879	9.	0.	1.	0.	0.	0.	0.	0.	11.
1880	11.	0.	0.	0.	0.	0.	0.	0.	11.
1881	12.	0.	0.	0.	0.	0.	0.	0.	12.
1882	12.	0.	0.	0.	0.	0.	0.	0.	12.
1883	19.	0.	0.	0.	0.	0.	0.	0.	19.
1884	22.	0.	0.	0.	0.	0.	0.	0.	22.
1885	20.	0.	0.	0.	0.	0.	0.	0.	20.
1886	21.	0.	0.	0.	0.	0.	0.	0.	21.
1887	38.	0.	0.	0.	0.	0.	0.	0.	38.
1888	41.	0.	0.	0.	0.	0.	0.	0.	41.
1889	44.	0.	0.	0.	0.	0.	0.	0.	44.
1890	46.	0.	0.	0.	0.	0.	0.	0.	46.
1891	27.	0.	0.	0.	0.	0.	0.	15.	51.
1892	11.	0.	0.	0.	0.	0.	0.	0.	11.
1893	10.	0.	0.	26.	0.	0.	0.	0.	36.
1894	10.	16.	268.	0.	0.	0.	0.	0.	293.
1895	29.	17.	288.	0.	0.	0.	0.	0.	334.
1896	51.	88.	277.	0.	0.	9.	0.	9.	425.
1897	53.	91.	291.	0.	0.	0.	0.	12.	447.
1898	58.	91.	333.	0.	0.	0.	0.	19.	502.
1899	117.	95.	354.	0.	0.	1.	0.	20.	588.
1900	514.	220.	399.	0.	0.	0.	0.	24.	1157.

TABLE 55. INDUSTRIAL STOCK OWNED (PERCENT OF TOTAL ASSETS)

YEAR	1	2	3	4	5	6	7	8	TOTAL
					REGIONS				
1843	0.349	0.0	0.0	0.0	0.0	0.0	0.0	0.0	0.349
1844	0.845	0.0	0.0	0.0	0.0	0.0	0.0	0.0	0.845
1845	0.920	0.0	0.0	0.0	0.0	0.0	0.0	0.0	0.920
1846	0.717	0.0	0.0	0.0	0.0	0.0	0.0	0.0	0.717
1847	1.322	0.0	0.0	0.0	0.0	0.0	0.0	0.0	1.322
1848	1.650	0.0	0.0	0.0	0.0	0.0	0.0	0.0	1.650
1849	1.298	0.410	0.0	0.0	0.0	0.0	0.0	0.0	1.708
1850	0.530	0.127	0.0	0.0	0.0	0.0	0.0	0.0	0.656
1851	0.447	0.0	0.0	0.0	0.0	0.0	0.0	0.0	0.447
1852	0.356	0.0	0.0	0.0	0.0	0.0	0.0	0.0	0.356
1853	0.203	0.0	0.0	0.0	0.0	0.0	0.0	0.0	0.203
1854	0.219	0.0	0.0	0.0	0.0	0.0	0.0	0.0	0.219
1855	0.157	0.0	0.0	0.0	0.0	0.0	0.0	0.0	0.157
1856	0.141	0.0	0.0	0.0	0.0	0.0	0.0	0.0	0.141
1857	0.047	0.0	0.0	0.0	0.0	0.0	0.0	0.0	0.047
1858	0.046	0.0	0.0	0.0	0.0	0.0	0.0	0.0	0.046
1859	0.031	0.017	0.0	0.0	0.0	0.0	0.0	0.0	0.048
1860	0.026	0.0	0.0	0.0	0.0	0.0	0.0	0.0	0.026
1861	0.025	0.0	0.0	0.0	0.0	0.0	0.0	0.0	0.025
1862	0.019	0.0	0.0	0.0	0.0	0.0	0.0	0.0	0.019
1863	0.013	0.0	0.0	0.0	0.0	0.0	0.0	0.0	0.013
1864	0.011	0.0	0.0	0.0	0.0	0.0	0.0	0.0	0.011
1865	0.012	0.0	0.0	0.0	0.0	0.0	0.0	0.0	0.012
1866	0.010	0.0	0.0	0.0	0.0	0.0	0.0	0.0	0.010
1867	0.004	0.0	0.0	0.0	0.0	0.0	0.0	0.0	0.004
1868	0.005	0.005	0.0	0.0	0.0	0.0	0.0	0.0	0.009
1869	0.002	0.005	0.0	0.0	0.0	0.0	0.0	0.0	0.007
1870	0.003	0.003	0.008	0.0	0.0	0.0	0.0	0.0	0.014
1871	0.002	0.004	0.002	0.0	0.0	0.0	0.0	0.0	0.008

TABLE 55 (CONTINUED)

YEAR	REGIONS								TOTAL
	1	2	3	4	5	6	7	8	
1872	0.002	0.003	0.0	0.0	0.0	0.0	0.0	0.0	0.005
1873	0.002	0.002	0.001	0.0	0.0	0.0	0.0	0.0	0.005
1874	0.002	0.0	0.004	0.0	0.0	0.0	0.0	0.0	0.006
1875	0.002	0.0	0.0	0.0	0.0	0.0	0.0	0.0	0.002
1876	0.005	0.0	0.0	0.0	0.0	0.0	0.0	0.0	0.005
1877	0.002	0.0	0.000	0.0	0.0	0.0	0.0	0.0	0.002
1878	0.002	0.0	0.0	0.0	0.0	0.0	0.0	0.0	0.002
1879	0.002	0.0	0.000	0.0	0.0	0.0	0.0	0.0	0.002
1880	0.002	0.0	0.0	0.0	0.0	0.0	0.0	0.0	0.002
1881	0.003	0.0	0.0	0.0	0.0	0.0	0.0	0.0	0.003
1882	0.003	0.0	0.0	0.0	0.0	0.0	0.0	0.0	0.003
1883	0.004	0.0	0.0	0.0	0.0	0.0	0.0	0.0	0.004
1884	0.004	0.0	0.0	0.0	0.0	0.0	0.0	0.0	0.004
1885	0.003	0.0	0.0	0.0	0.0	0.0	0.0	0.0	0.003
1886	0.004	0.0	0.0	0.0	0.0	0.0	0.0	0.0	0.004
1887	0.006	0.0	0.0	0.0	0.0	0.0	0.0	0.0	0.006
1888	0.006	0.0	0.0	0.0	0.0	0.0	0.0	0.0	0.006
1889	0.006	0.0	0.0	0.0	0.0	0.0	0.0	0.0	0.006
1890	0.006	0.0	0.0	0.0	0.0	0.0	0.0	0.0	0.006
1891	0.003	0.0	0.0	0.0	0.0	0.001	0.0	0.002	0.006
1892	0.001	0.0	0.0	0.0	0.0	0.0	0.0	0.0	0.001
1893	0.001	0.0	0.0	0.003	0.0	0.0	0.0	0.0	0.004
1894	0.001	0.001	0.024	0.0	0.0	0.0	0.0	0.0	0.026
1895	0.002	0.001	0.024	0.0	0.0	0.0	0.0	0.0	0.028
1896	0.004	0.007	0.022	0.0	0.0	0.0	0.0	0.001	0.033
1897	0.004	0.007	0.021	0.0	0.0	0.0	0.0	0.001	0.032
1898	0.004	0.006	0.022	0.0	0.0	0.000	0.0	0.001	0.033
1899	0.007	0.006	0.022	0.0	0.0	0.0	0.0	0.001	0.036
1900	0.028	0.012	0.022	0.0	0.0	0.0	0.0	0.001	0.064

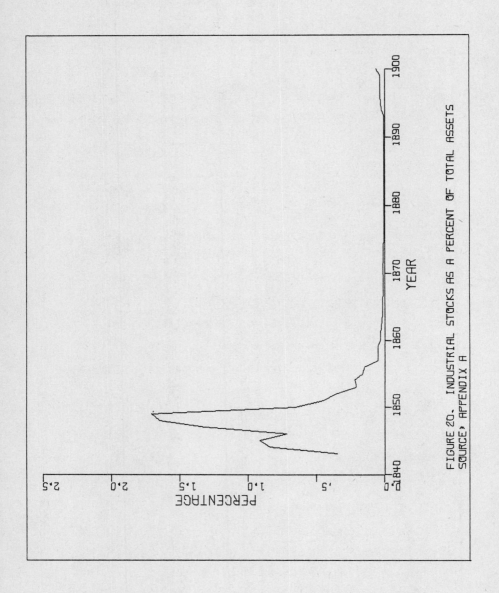

FIGURE 20. INDUSTRIAL STOCKS AS A PERCENT OF TOTAL ASSETS

SOURCE: APPENDIX A

This stock appears year after year at various market valuations and is variously joined by the small holdings of other companies.

Whatever the reasons were for the reluctance to hold industrial securities, and the reluctance to hold stocks, the combined effect of these tendencies permitted few issues of this category to reach life insurance portfolios.

Other Stock Categories

Perhaps the most significant point to be made about the remaining stock classifications is their lack of significance. As in the case of bonds, the early purchases of canal stocks represented mostly the passing interest of a single large company, New York Life. That company's holdings predominate until a sizable purchase was made by Equitable in 1883. These securities do not appear after 1884.

The few purchases made were in the canals of New York and Pennsylvania.

The principal purchase of the entire series of "Other Stocks" was made by the Life Association of America in 1874. About ten thousand dollars worth of stock in the St. Louis Chamber of Commerce were involved.

Income

As in the case of assets, the Institute of Life Insurance has prepared summary information on the total income of life

215

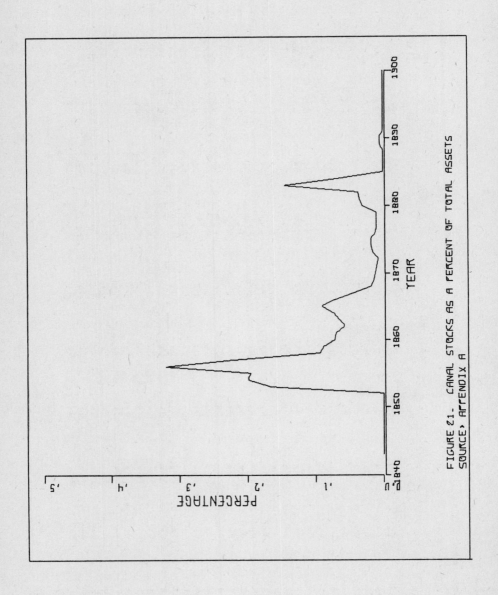

FIGURE 21. CANAL STOCKS AS A PERCENT OF TOTAL ASSETS

SOURCE: APPENDIX A

TABLE 56. CANAL STOCK OWNED (THOUSANDS OF DOLLARS)

	REGIONS								
YEAR	1	2	3	4	5	6	7	8	TOTAL
1843	0.	0.	0.	0.	0.	0.	0.	0.	0.
1844	0.	0.	0.	0.	0.	0.	0.	0.	0.
1845	0.	0.	0.	0.	0.	0.	0.	0.	0.
1846	0.	0.	0.	0.	0.	0.	0.	0.	0.
1847	0.	0.	0.	0.	0.	0.	0.	0.	0.
1848	0.	0.	0.	0.	0.	0.	0.	0.	0.
1849	0.	0.	0.	0.	0.	0.	0.	0.	0.
1850	0.	0.	0.	0.	0.	0.	0.	0.	0.
1851	0.	0.	0.	0.	0.	0.	0.	0.	0.
1852	0.	0.	0.	0.	0.	0.	0.	0.	0.
1853	0.	27.	0.	0.	0.	0.	0.	0.	27.
1854	0.	36.	0.	0.	0.	0.	0.	0.	36.
1855	0.	36.	0.	0.	0.	0.	0.	0.	36.
1856	0.	69.	0.	0.	0.	0.	0.	0.	69.
1857	0.	54.	0.	0.	0.	0.	0.	0.	54.
1858	0.	26.	0.	0.	0.	0.	0.	0.	26.
1859	0.	26.	0.	0.	0.	0.	0.	0.	26.
1860	0.	25.	0.	0.	0.	0.	0.	0.	25.
1861	0.	27.	0.	0.	0.	0.	0.	0.	27.
1862	0.	24.	0.	0.	0.	0.	0.	0.	24.
1863	0.	36.	0.	0.	0.	0.	0.	0.	36.
1864	0.	51.	0.	0.	0.	0.	0.	0.	51.
1865	0.	75.	0.	0.	0.	0.	0.	0.	75.
1866	0.	77.	0.	0.	0.	0.	0.	0.	77.
1867	0.	66.	0.	0.	0.	0.	0.	0.	66.
1868	0.	36.	0.	0.	0.	0.	0.	0.	36.
1869	0.	34.	0.	0.	0.	0.	0.	0.	34.
1870	0.	31.	0.	0.	0.	0.	0.	0.	31.
1871	0.	28.	0.	0.	0.	0.	0.	0.	28.

TABLE 56 (CONTINUED)

				REGIONS					
YEAR	1	2	3	4	5	6	7	8	TOTAL
1872	0.	27.	0.	0.	0.	0.	0.	0.	27.
1873	0.	63.	0.	0.	0.	0.	0.	0.	63.
1874	0.	83.	0.	0.	0.	0.	0.	0.	83.
1875	0.	84.	0.	0.	0.	0.	0.	0.	84.
1876	0.	50.	0.	0.	0.	0.	0.	0.	50.
1877	0.	46.	0.	0.	0.	0.	0.	0.	46.
1878	0.	49.	0.	0.	0.	0.	0.	0.	49.
1879	0.	51.	0.	0.	0.	0.	0.	0.	51.
1880	0.	152.	0.	0.	0.	0.	0.	0.	152.
1881	0.	178.	0.	0.	0.	0.	0.	0.	178.
1882	0.	187.	0.	0.	0.	0.	0.	0.	187.
1883	0.	748.	0.	0.	0.	0.	0.	0.	748.
1884	0.	361.	0.	0.	0.	0.	0.	0.	361.
1885	0.	0.	0.	0.	0.	0.	0.	0.	0.
1886	0.	0.	0.	0.	0.	0.	0.	0.	0.
1887	0.	0.	0.	0.	0.	8.	0.	0.	8.
1888	0.	0.	0.	0.	0.	40.	0.	14.	54.
1890	0.	0.	0.	0.	0.	39.	13.	0.	53.
1891	0.	0.	0.	0.	0.	0.	0.	0.	0.
1892	0.	0.	0.	0.	0.	0.	0.	0.	0.
1893	0.	0.	0.	0.	0.	8.	0.	15.	23.
1894	0.	0.	0.	0.	0.	0.	0.	0.	0.
1895	0.	0.	0.	0.	0.	0.	0.	0.	0.
1896	0.	0.	0.	0.	0.	0.	0.	0.	0.
1897	0.	0.	0.	0.	0.	0.	0.	0.	0.
1898	0.	0.	0.	0.	0.	0.	0.	0.	0.
1899	0.	0.	0.	0.	0.	0.	0.	0.	0.
1900	0.	0.	0.	0.	0.	0.	0.	0.	0.

TABLE 57. CANAL STOCK OWNED (PERCENT OF TOTAL ASSETS)

| | REGIONS | | | | | | | | |
YEAR	1	2	3	4	5	6	7	8	TOTAL
1843	0.0	0.0	0.0	0.0	0.0	0.0	0.0	0.0	0.0
1844	0.0	0.0	0.0	0.0	0.0	0.0	0.0	0.0	0.0
1845	0.0	0.0	0.0	0.0	0.0	0.0	0.0	0.0	0.0
1846	0.0	0.0	0.0	0.0	0.0	0.0	0.0	0.0	0.0
1847	0.0	0.0	0.0	0.0	0.0	0.0	0.0	0.0	0.0
1848	0.0	0.0	0.0	0.0	0.0	0.0	0.0	0.0	0.0
1849	0.0	0.0	0.0	0.0	0.0	0.0	0.0	0.0	0.0
1850	0.0	0.0	0.0	0.0	0.0	0.0	0.0	0.0	0.0
1851	0.0	0.0	0.0	0.0	0.0	0.0	0.0	0.0	0.0
1852	0.0	0.0	0.0	0.0	0.0	0.0	0.0	0.0	0.0
1853	0.0	0.169	0.0	0.0	0.0	0.0	0.0	0.0	0.169
1854	0.0	0.201	0.0	0.0	0.0	0.0	0.0	0.0	0.201
1855	0.0	0.195	0.0	0.0	0.0	0.0	0.0	0.0	0.195
1856	0.0	0.322	0.0	0.0	0.0	0.0	0.0	0.0	0.322
1857	0.0	0.220	0.0	0.0	0.0	0.0	0.0	0.0	0.220
1858	0.0	0.093	0.0	0.0	0.0	0.0	0.0	0.0	0.093
1859	0.0	0.087	0.0	0.0	0.0	0.0	0.0	0.0	0.087
1860	0.0	0.071	0.0	0.0	0.0	0.0	0.0	0.0	0.071
1861	0.0	0.069	0.0	0.0	0.0	0.0	0.0	0.0	0.069
1862	0.0	0.057	0.0	0.0	0.0	0.0	0.0	0.0	0.057
1863	0.0	0.067	0.0	0.0	0.0	0.0	0.0	0.0	0.067
1864	0.0	0.075	0.0	0.0	0.0	0.0	0.0	0.0	0.075
1865	0.0	0.092	0.0	0.0	0.0	0.0	0.0	0.0	0.092
1866	0.0	0.072	0.0	0.0	0.0	0.0	0.0	0.0	0.072
1867	0.0	0.045	0.0	0.0	0.0	0.0	0.0	0.0	0.045
1868	0.0	0.018	0.0	0.0	0.0	0.0	0.0	0.0	0.018
1869	0.0	0.013	0.0	0.0	0.0	0.0	0.0	0.0	0.013
1870	0.0	0.011	0.0	0.0	0.0	0.0	0.0	0.0	0.011
1871	0.0	0.009	0.0	0.0	0.0	0.0	0.0	0.0	0.009

TABLE 57 (CONTINUED)

YEAR	REGIONS								TOTAL
---	1	2	3	4	5	6	7	8	
1872	0.0	0.007	0.0	0.0	0.0	0.0	0.0	0.0	0.007
1873	0.0	0.017	0.0	0.0	0.0	0.0	0.0	0.0	0.017
1874	0.0	0.020	0.0	0.0	0.0	0.0	0.0	0.0	0.020
1875	0.0	0.019	0.0	0.0	0.0	0.0	0.0	0.0	0.019
1876	0.0	0.011	0.0	0.0	0.0	0.0	0.0	0.0	0.011
1877	0.0	0.010	0.0	0.0	0.0	0.0	0.0	0.0	0.010
1878	0.0	0.011	0.0	0.0	0.0	0.0	0.0	0.0	0.011
1879	0.0	0.011	0.0	0.0	0.0	0.0	0.0	0.0	0.011
1880	0.0	0.033	0.0	0.0	0.0	0.0	0.0	0.0	0.033
1881	0.0	0.037	0.0	0.0	0.0	0.0	0.0	0.0	0.037
1882	0.0	0.039	0.0	0.0	0.0	0.0	0.0	0.0	0.039
1883	0.0	0.147	0.0	0.0	0.0	0.0	0.0	0.0	0.147
1884	0.0	0.068	0.0	0.0	0.0	0.0	0.0	0.0	0.068
1885	0.0	0.0	0.0	0.0	0.0	0.0	0.0	0.0	0.0
1886	0.0	0.0	0.0	0.0	0.0	0.0	0.0	0.0	0.0
1887	0.0	0.0	0.0	0.0	0.0	0.0	0.0	0.0	0.0
1888	0.0	0.0	0.0	0.0	0.0	0.0	0.001	0.0	0.001
1889	0.0	0.0	0.0	0.0	0.0	0.005	0.0	0.002	0.007
1890	0.0	0.0	0.0	0.0	0.0	0.005	0.002	0.0	0.007
1891	0.0	0.0	0.0	0.0	0.0	0.0	0.0	0.0	0.0
1892	0.0	0.0	0.0	0.0	0.0	0.0	0.0	0.0	0.0
1893	0.0	0.0	0.0	0.0	0.0	0.001	0.0	0.001	0.002
1894	0.0	0.0	0.0	0.0	0.0	0.0	0.0	0.0	0.0
1895	0.0	0.0	0.0	0.0	0.0	0.0	0.0	0.0	0.0
1896	0.0	0.0	0.0	0.0	0.0	0.0	0.0	0.0	0.0
1897	0.0	0.0	0.0	0.0	0.0	0.0	0.0	0.0	0.0
1898	0.0	0.0	0.0	0.0	0.0	0.0	0.0	0.0	0.0
1899	0.0	0.0	0.0	0.0	0.0	0.0	0.0	0.0	0.0
1900	0.0	0.0	0.0	0.0	0.0	0.0	0.0	0.0	0.0

TABLE 58. OTHER STOCK OWNED (THOUSANDS OF DOLLARS)

REGIONS

YEAR	1	2	3	4	5	6	7	8	TOTAL
1843	0.	0.	0.	0.	0.	0.	0.	0.	0.
1844	0.	0.	0.	0.	0.	0.	0.	0.	0.
1845	0.	0.	0.	0.	0.	0.	0.	0.	0.
1846	0.	0.	0.	0.	0.	0.	0.	0.	0.
1847	0.	0.	0.	0.	0.	0.	0.	0.	0.
1848	0.	0.	0.	0.	0.	0.	0.	0.	0.
1849	0.	0.	0.	0.	0.	0.	0.	0.	0.
1850	0.	0.	0.	0.	0.	0.	0.	0.	0.
1851	0.	0.	0.	0.	0.	0.	0.	0.	0.
1852	0.	0.	0.	0.	0.	0.	0.	0.	0.
1853	0.	0.	0.	0.	0.	0.	0.	0.	0.
1854	0.	0.	0.	0.	0.	0.	0.	0.	0.
1855	0.	0.	0.	0.	0.	0.	0.	0.	0.
1856	0.	0.	0.	0.	0.	0.	0.	0.	0.
1857	0.	0.	0.	0.	0.	0.	0.	0.	0.
1858	0.	0.	0.	0.	0.	0.	0.	0.	0.
1859	0.	0.	0.	0.	0.	0.	0.	0.	0.
1860	0.	0.	0.	0.	0.	0.	0.	0.	0.
1861	0.	0.	0.	0.	0.	0.	0.	0.	0.
1862	0.	0.	0.	0.	0.	0.	0.	0.	0.
1863	0.	0.	0.	0.	0.	0.	0.	0.	0.
1864	0.	0.	0.	0.	0.	0.	0.	0.	0.
1865	0.	0.	0.	0.	0.	0.	0.	0.	0.
1866	0.	0.	0.	0.	0.	0.	0.	0.	0.
1867	0.	0.	0.	0.	0.	0.	0.	0.	0.
1868	0.	0.	0.	0.	0.	0.	0.	0.	0.
1869	0.	0.	0.	0.	0.	0.	0.	0.	0.
1870	0.	0.	0.	0.	0.	0.	0.	0.	0.
1871	0.	0.	0.	0.	0.	0.	0.	0.	0.

TABLE 58 (CONTINUED)

YEAR	REGIONS								TOTAL
	1	2	3	4	5	6	7	8	
1872	0.	0.	0.	0.	0.	0.	0.	0.	0.
1873	0.	0.	0.	0.	0.	3.	0.	0.	3.
1874	0.	0.	0.	0.	0.	11.	0.	0.	11.
1875	0.	0.	0.	0.	0.	11.	0.	0.	11.
1876	0.	0.	0.	0.	0.	0.	0.	0.	0.
1877	0.	0.	0.	0.	0.	0.	0.	0.	0.
1878	0.	0.	0.	0.	0.	0.	0.	0.	0.
1879	0.	0.	0.	0.	0.	0.	0.	0.	0.
1880	0.	0.	0.	0.	0.	0.	0.	0.	0.
1881	0.	0.	0.	0.	0.	0.	0.	0.	0.
1882	0.	0.	0.	0.	0.	0.	0.	0.	0.
1883	0.	0.	0.	0.	0.	0.	0.	0.	0.
1884	0.	0.	0.	0.	0.	0.	0.	0.	0.
1885	0.	0.	0.	0.	0.	0.	0.	0.	0.
1886	0.	0.	0.	0.	0.	0.	0.	0.	0.
1887	0.	0.	0.	0.	0.	0.	0.	0.	0.
1888	0.	0.	0.	0.	0.	0.	0.	0.	0.
1889	0.	0.	0.	0.	0.	0.	0.	0.	0.
1890	0.	0.	0.	0.	0.	0.	0.	0.	0.
1891	0.	0.	0.	0.	0.	0.	0.	0.	0.
1892	0.	0.	0.	0.	0.	0.	0.	0.	0.
1893	0.	0.	0.	0.	0.	0.	0.	0.	0.
1894	0.	0.	0.	0.	0.	0.	0.	0.	0.
1895	0.	0.	0.	0.	0.	0.	0.	0.	0.
1896	0.	0.	0.	0.	0.	0.	0.	0.	0.
1897	0.	0.	0.	0.	0.	0.	0.	0.	0.
1898	0.	0.	0.	0.	0.	0.	0.	0.	0.
1899	0.	0.	0.	0.	0.	0.	0.	0.	0.
1900	0.	0.	0.	0.	0.	0.	0.	0.	0.

TABLE 59. OTHER STOCK OWNED (PERCENT OF TOTAL ASSETS)

| YEAR | | | | | REGIONS | | | | | |
	1	2	3	4	5	6	7	8	8	TOTAL
1843	0.0	0.0	0.0	0.0	0.0	0.0	0.0	0.0	0.0	0.0
1844	0.0	0.0	0.0	0.0	0.0	0.0	0.0	0.0	0.0	0.0
1845	0.0	0.0	0.0	0.0	0.0	0.0	0.0	0.0	0.0	0.0
1846	0.0	0.0	0.0	0.0	0.0	0.0	0.0	0.0	0.0	0.0
1847	0.0	0.0	0.0	0.0	0.0	0.0	0.0	0.0	0.0	0.0
1848	0.0	0.0	0.0	0.0	0.0	0.0	0.0	0.0	0.0	0.0
1849	0.0	0.0	0.0	0.0	0.0	0.0	0.0	0.0	0.0	0.0
1850	0.0	0.0	0.0	0.0	0.0	0.0	0.0	0.0	0.0	0.0
1851	0.0	0.0	0.0	0.0	0.0	0.0	0.0	0.0	0.0	0.0
1852	0.0	0.0	0.0	0.0	0.0	0.0	0.0	0.0	0.0	0.0
1853	0.0	0.0	0.0	0.0	0.0	0.0	0.0	0.0	0.0	0.0
1854	0.0	0.0	0.0	0.0	0.0	0.0	0.0	0.0	0.0	0.0
1855	0.0	0.0	0.0	0.0	0.0	0.0	0.0	0.0	0.0	0.0
1856	0.0	0.0	0.0	0.0	0.0	0.0	0.0	0.0	0.0	0.0
1857	0.0	0.0	0.0	0.0	0.0	0.0	0.0	0.0	0.0	0.0
1858	0.0	0.0	0.0	0.0	0.0	0.0	0.0	0.0	0.0	0.0
1859	0.0	0.0	0.0	0.0	0.0	0.0	0.0	0.0	0.0	0.0
1860	0.0	0.0	0.0	0.0	0.0	0.0	0.0	0.0	0.0	0.0
1861	0.0	0.0	0.0	0.0	0.0	0.0	0.0	0.0	0.0	0.0
1862	0.0	0.0	0.0	0.0	0.0	0.0	0.0	0.0	0.0	0.0
1863	0.0	0.0	0.0	0.0	0.0	0.0	0.0	0.0	0.0	0.0
1864	0.0	0.0	0.0	0.0	0.0	0.0	0.0	0.0	0.0	0.0
1865	0.0	0.0	0.0	0.0	0.0	0.0	0.0	0.0	0.0	0.0
1866	0.0	0.0	0.0	0.0	0.0	0.0	0.0	0.0	0.0	0.0
1867	0.0	0.0	0.0	0.0	0.0	0.0	0.0	0.0	0.0	0.0
1868	0.0	0.0	0.0	0.0	0.0	0.0	0.0	0.0	0.0	0.0
1869	0.0	0.0	0.0	0.0	0.0	0.0	0.0	0.0	0.0	0.0
1870	0.0	0.0	0.0	0.0	0.0	0.0	0.0	0.0	0.0	0.0
1871	0.0	0.0	0.0	0.0	0.0	0.0	0.0	0.0	0.0	0.0

TABLE 59 (CONTINUED)

YEAR	REGIONS								TOTAL
	1	2	3	4	5	6	7	8	
1872	0.0	0.0	0.0	0.0	0.0	0.0	0.0	0.0	0.0
1873	0.0	0.0	0.0	0.0	0.0	0.001	0.0	0.0	0.001
1874	0.0	0.0	0.0	0.0	0.0	0.003	0.0	0.0	0.003
1875	0.0	0.0	0.0	0.0	0.0	0.002	0.0	0.0	0.002
1876	0.0	0.0	0.0	0.0	0.0	0.0	0.0	0.0	0.0
1877	0.0	0.0	0.0	0.0	0.0	0.0	0.0	0.0	0.0
1878	0.0	0.0	0.0	0.0	0.0	0.0	0.0	0.0	0.0
1879	0.0	0.0	0.0	0.0	0.0	0.0	0.0	0.0	0.0
1880	0.0	0.0	0.0	0.0	0.0	0.0	0.0	0.0	0.0
1881	0.0	0.0	0.0	0.0	0.0	0.0	0.0	0.0	0.0
1882	0.0	0.0	0.0	0.0	0.0	0.0	0.0	0.0	0.0
1883	0.0	0.0	0.0	0.0	0.0	0.0	0.0	0.0	0.0
1884	0.0	0.0	0.0	0.0	0.0	0.0	0.0	0.0	0.0
1885	0.0	0.0	0.0	0.0	0.0	0.0	0.0	0.0	0.0
1886	0.0	0.0	0.0	0.0	0.0	0.0	0.0	0.0	0.0
1887	0.0	0.0	0.0	0.0	0.0	0.0	0.0	0.0	0.0
1888	0.0	0.0	0.0	0.0	0.0	0.0	0.0	0.0	0.0
1889	0.0	0.0	0.0	0.0	0.0	0.0	0.0	0.0	0.0
1890	0.0	0.0	0.0	0.0	0.0	0.0	0.0	0.0	0.0
1891	0.0	0.0	0.0	0.0	0.0	0.0	0.0	0.0	0.0
1892	0.0	0.0	0.0	0.0	0.0	0.0	0.0	0.0	0.0
1893	0.0	0.0	0.0	0.0	0.0	0.0	0.0	0.0	0.0
1894	0.0	0.0	0.0	0.0	0.0	0.0	0.0	0.0	0.0
1895	0.0	0.0	0.0	0.0	0.0	0.0	0.0	0.0	0.0
1896	0.0	0.0	0.0	0.0	0.0	0.0	0.0	0.0	0.0
1897	0.0	0.0	0.0	0.0	0.0	0.0	0.0	0.0	0.0
1898	0.0	0.0	0.0	0.0	0.0	0.0	0.0	0.0	0.0
1899	0.0	0.0	0.0	0.0	0.0	0.0	0.0	0.0	0.0
1900	0.0	0.0	0.0	0.0	0.0	0.0	0.0	0.0	0.0

insurance companies. The conventions employed in compiling
the information are similar to those discussed in connection
with Table 16. Further information on these conventions
may be obtained from the section on methodology associated
with the Institute's presentation. Extracts from the
Institute's income information have been reproduced here
for reference as Table 60.

Table 61 presents data from the present study corresponding to that of the Institute. The values of Table 61
are mostly larger in each year reflecting the general
increase in insurance in force. Some of the same trends
are generally evident. Notice, for example, the contraction
of the amount of income during the seventies, the period
ending the heyday of the "Tontine Revolution." The story
of the losses of that period, which was begun in the discussion of the asset tables, may be extended in connection
with income. One might expect that the income series would
be more responsive to changes in business conditions than
would the asset series because of its larger percentage
relationship to current income. Recall the high percentages
of terminations that took place. The income from new
premiums was a large part of total income.

Table 61 suggests that it took from 1874 to 1886 to
regain the total income stream enjoyed before the depression.
Premium income peaks in 1871 and does not reach that level
again until 1888.

Table 60 . Income of U.S. Life Insurance Companies[a] (Millions of dollars).

Year	Total	Life Premiums	Annuity Premiums	Other Income
1900	400.6	318.4	6.3	75.9
1899	365.4	285.6	6.2	73.6
1898	325.5	252.6	5.1	67.8
1897	304.9	237.3	6.0	61.6
1896	283.7	222.9	5.0	55.8
1895	271.9	216.1	3.6	52.2
1894	262.0	207.1	2.6	52.3
1893	241.7	195.0	2.0	44.7
1892	227.6	181.9	2.6	43.1
1891	213.4	170.0	2.9	40.5
1890	195.6	153.6	3.2	38.8
1889	176.2	137.2	2.9	36.1
1888	153.9	117.9	2.4	33.6
1887	133.7	101.6	1.9	30.2
1886	119.1	89.1	1.7	28.3
1885	107.0	78.8	1.2	27.0
1884	98.1	71.8	1.3	25.0
1883	93.4	66.0	2.2	25.2
1882	85.7	59.4	1.7	24.6
1881	80.2	54.9	1.9	23.4
1880	77.7	53.0	1.2	23.5
1879	77.8	53.1	.7	24.0
1878	80.5	56.8	.5	23.2
1877	86.2	62.7	.3	23.2
1876	96.4	71.8	.3	24.3
1875	108.6	83.4	.4	24.8
1874	115.7	89.2	.2	26.3
1873	118.4	95.8	.2	22.4
1872	117.3	96.5	.1	20.7
1871	113.5	96.6	.1	16.8
1870	105.0	90.2	.1	14.7
1869	98.5	86.0	.1	12.4
1868	77.4	67.8	.1	9.5
1867	56.5	50.4	.1[b]	6.1
1866	40.4	35.8	.1[b]	4.6
1865	24.9	21.6	.1[c]	3.3
1864	16.1	13.1	.1[c]	3.0
1863	10.6	8.5	.1[c]	2.1
1862	7.4	5.7	.1[c]	1.7
1861	6.3	4.9	.1[c]	1.4
1860	6.0	4.8	.1[c]	1.2
1859	5.2	4.0	.1[c]	1.2
1858	4.5	3.6	.1[c]	.9
1857	4.0	3.2	.1[c]	.8
1856	3.8	3.0	.1[c]	.8
1855	3.5	3.0	.1[c]	.5
1854	3.2	2.6	.1[c]	.6

[a]Institute of Life Insurance, The Historical Statistics of the United States, 1759 to 1958 (New York:Institute of Life Insurance, 1960), p. 11.
[b]Less than $50,000.
[c]Included with "Life Premiums."

TABLE 61. PREMIUM INCOME RECEIVED (THOUSANDS OF DOLLARS)

YEAR	REGIONS									TOTAL	TOTAL INCOME
	1	2	3	4	5	6	7	8	9		
1843	0.	0.	0.	0.	0.	0.	0.	0.	0.	266.	393.
1844	0.	0.	0.	0.	0.	0.	0.	0.	0.	418.	541.
1845	0.	0.	0.	0.	0.	0.	0.	0.	0.	731.	854.
1846	0.	0.	0.	0.	0.	0.	0.	0.	0.	1212.	1389.
1847	0.	0.	0.	0.	0.	0.	0.	0.	0.	1627.	1772.
1848	0.	0.	0.	0.	0.	0.	0.	0.	0.	1924.	2129.
1849	0.	0.	0.	0.	0.	0.	0.	0.	0.	3197.	3541.
1850	0.	0.	0.	0.	0.	0.	0.	0.	0.	3739.	4293.
1851	0.	0.	0.	0.	0.	0.	0.	0.	0.	4115.	4655.
1852	0.	0.	0.	0.	0.	0.	0.	0.	0.	4163.	4948.
1853	0.	0.	0.	0.	0.	0.	0.	0.	0.	4535.	5751.
1854	0.	0.	0.	0.	0.	0.	0.	0.	0.	4604.	5537.
1855	0.	0.	0.	0.	0.	0.	0.	0.	0.	4949.	6080.
1856	0.	0.	0.	0.	0.	0.	0.	0.	0.	5169.	6439.
1857	0.	0.	0.	0.	0.	0.	0.	0.	0.	5448.	6922.
1858	0.	0.	0.	0.	0.	0.	0.	0.	0.	7291.	8925.
1859	0.	0.	0.	0.	0.	0.	0.	0.	0.	6050.	7070.
1860	0.	0.	0.	0.	0.	0.	0.	0.	0.	7173.	6896.
1861	0.	0.	0.	0.	0.	0.	0.	0.	0.	7323.	9295.
1862	0.	0.	0.	0.	0.	0.	0.	0.	0.	6794.	8423.
1863	0.	0.	0.	0.	0.	0.	0.	0.	0.	15379.	18023.
1864	0.	0.	0.	0.	0.	0.	0.	0.	0.	17412.	20392.
1865	0.	0.	0.	0.	0.	0.	0.	0.	0.	27366.	30964.
1866	0.	0.	0.	0.	0.	0.	0.	0.	0.	46703.	49249.
1867	0.	0.	0.	0.	0.	0.	0.	0.	0.	65914.	70241.
1868	0.	0.	0.	0.	0.	0.	0.	0.	0.	77057.	88964.
1869	0.	0.	0.	0.	0.	0.	0.	0.	0.	91944.	105496.
1870	0.	0.	0.	0.	0.	0.	0.	0.	0.	102190.	117101.
1871	0.	0.	0.	0.	0.	0.	0.	0.	0.	107261.	125567.

TABLE 61 (CONTINUED)

YEAR	REGIONS									TOTAL	TOTAL INCOME
	1	2	3	4	5	6	7	8	9		
1872	0.	0.	0.	0.	0.	0.	0.	0.	0.	106675.	128811.
1873	0.	0.	0.	0.	0.	0.	0.	0.	0.	103803.	127806.
1874	21613.	48191.	21758.	656.	1824.	980.	1950.	1381.	2566.	100919.	131570.
1875	19094.	41876.	19415.	699.	1786.	1009.	1924.	1454.	2239.	89497.	115232.
1876	15471.	36099.	16515.	729.	1728.	1037.	1711.	1490.	1943.	76724.	102210.
1877	11815.	32371.	15040.	815.	1855.	1113.	1632.	1625.	1714.	67980.	93400.
1878	10920.	28184.	12601.	847.	1712.	1121.	1489.	1636.	1588.	60300.	85007.
1879	9622.	26491.	12017.	920.	1667.	1237.	1536.	1905.	1504.	56901.	82197.
1880	9368.	25426.	11478.	1022.	1757.	1458.	1628.	2162.	1517.	55015.	81556.
1881	9576.	27773.	13142.	1167.	1932.	1875.	1746.	2209.	1919.	61340.	86527.
1882	9604.	28142.	13481.	1239.	1991.	2448.	1862.	2119.	2679.	63583.	89965.
1883	10819.	30756.	14837.	1441.	2462.	3303.	2172.	2357.	4276.	72424.	111886.
1884	10457.	32327.	14968.	1511.	2817.	3778.	2267.	2188.	6509.	76822.	103329.
1885	11242.	33361.	15876.	1804.	3365.	4504.	2606.	2377.	8800.	83935.	112365.
1886	13190.	37464.	18045.	2093.	4108.	5947.	3160.	2648.	10469.	97124.	124171.
1887	14318.	40272.	19943.	2295.	4495.	7024.	3650.	2978.	10520.	105496.	134691.
1888	16481.	45600.	21722.	2941.	5308.	8299.	4636.	4061.	14840.	123887.	161709.
1889	19382.	53837.	22867.	3160.	6227.	10339.	5836.	5005.	18099.	144753.	181562.
1890	20708.	59542.	27880.	3565.	7291.	12338.	6923.	5314.	21118.	164680.	204728.
1891	22495.	62537.	31186.	4678.	8089.	12919.	7858.	5972.	23254.	175989.	219385.
1892	23575.	65892.	33089.	5388.	8375.	14408.	8655.	6280.	24650.	190311.	234420.
1893	25484.	71338.	36429.	6253.	9553.	15690.	9368.	6762.	26107.	206975.	253069.
1894	26265.	75500.	37526.	6883.	10251.	16056.	9354.	6503.	27825.	216164.	269621.
1895	27861.	79423.	39714.	7812.	10910.	16375.	9487.	6664.	28811.	227056.	278952.
1896	28237.	83727.	40653.	8816.	11446.	16089.	9391.	6868.	28317.	233545.	294816.
1897	30381.	96784.	42743.	9499.	12087.	16684.	9671.	7110.	30073.	258032.	320027.
1898	31248.	99404.	45495.	11099.	12894.	16997.	10505.	7481.	30486.	265611.	336990.
1899	33766.	109324.	51680.	12482.	14647.	19266.	12378.	9084.	32533.	295161.	371380.
1900	37955.	124511.	58775.	14528.	16947.	21099.	13776.	10448.	37940.	335979.	415431.

The period of the contraction is approximately the
same in the series of Table 60.

Table 62 presents premium income as a percent of total
income and does this by region after 1873. There are
numerous minor fluctuations in the figures of the total; but
the percentage seems to be generally higher during the forties
and early fifties, and during the mid-sixties and early
seventies, than in adjacent periods. These years were
described in the general history as being periods of rapid
expansion and intense competition. One would expect the
influx of new premiums during these periods to induce such
an effect. One would also expect the series to generally
decrease over the growth of the industry as the number of
terminations decreased and as the amount of income from
the accumulated assets became a more important part of
total income. Any relaxation of legal restrictions which
permitted higher yield investments would increase the
latter's importance.

TABLE 62. PREMIUM INCOME RECEIVED (PERCENT OF TOTAL INCOME)

					REGIONS					
YEAR	1	2	3	4	5	6	7	8	9	TOTAL
1843	0.0	0.0	0.0	0.0	0.0	0.0	0.0	0.0	0.0	67.778
1844	0.0	0.0	0.0	0.0	0.0	0.0	0.0	0.0	0.0	77.395
1845	0.0	0.0	0.0	0.0	0.0	0.0	0.0	0.0	0.0	85.682
1846	0.0	0.0	0.0	0.0	0.0	0.0	0.0	0.0	0.0	87.228
1847	0.0	0.0	0.0	0.0	0.0	0.0	0.0	0.0	0.0	91.808
1848	0.0	0.0	0.0	0.0	0.0	0.0	0.0	0.0	0.0	90.385
1849	0.0	0.0	0.0	0.0	0.0	0.0	0.0	0.0	0.0	90.296
1850	0.0	0.0	0.0	0.0	0.0	0.0	0.0	0.0	0.0	87.090
1851	0.0	0.0	0.0	0.0	0.0	0.0	0.0	0.0	0.0	88.401
1852	0.0	0.0	0.0	0.0	0.0	0.0	0.0	0.0	0.0	84.141
1853	0.0	0.0	0.0	0.0	0.0	0.0	0.0	0.0	0.0	78.863
1854	0.0	0.0	0.0	0.0	0.0	0.0	0.0	0.0	0.0	83.150
1855	0.0	0.0	0.0	0.0	0.0	0.0	0.0	0.0	0.0	81.395
1856	0.0	0.0	0.0	0.0	0.0	0.0	0.0	0.0	0.0	80.267
1857	0.0	0.0	0.0	0.0	0.0	0.0	0.0	0.0	0.0	78.714
1858	0.0	0.0	0.0	0.0	0.0	0.0	0.0	0.0	0.0	81.689
1859	0.0	0.0	0.0	0.0	0.0	0.0	0.0	0.0	0.0	85.566
1860	0.0	0.0	0.0	0.0	0.0	0.0	0.0	0.0	0.0	80.631
1861	0.0	0.0	0.0	0.0	0.0	0.0	0.0	0.0	0.0	78.780
1862	0.0	0.0	0.0	0.0	0.0	0.0	0.0	0.0	0.0	80.663
1863	0.0	0.0	0.0	0.0	0.0	0.0	0.0	0.0	0.0	85.329
1864	0.0	0.0	0.0	0.0	0.0	0.0	0.0	0.0	0.0	85.369
1865	0.0	0.0	0.0	0.0	0.0	0.0	0.0	0.0	0.0	88.380
1866	0.0	0.0	0.0	0.0	0.0	0.0	0.0	0.0	0.0	94.630
1867	0.0	0.0	0.0	0.0	0.0	0.0	0.0	0.0	0.0	93.840
1868	0.0	0.0	0.0	0.0	0.0	0.0	0.0	0.0	0.0	86.616
1869	0.0	0.0	0.0	0.0	0.0	0.0	0.0	0.0	0.0	87.154
1870	0.0	0.0	0.0	0.0	0.0	0.0	0.0	0.0	0.0	87.266
1871	0.0	0.0	0.0	0.0	0.0	0.0	0.0	0.0	0.0	85.421

TABLE 62 (CONTINUED)

YEAR	REGIONS									TOTAL
	1	2	3	4	5	6	7	8	9	
1872	0.0	0.0	0.0	0.0	0.0	0.0	0.0	0.0	0.0	83.203
1873	0.0	0.0	0.0	0.0	0.0	0.0	0.0	0.0	0.0	81.220
1874	16.427	36.628	16.537	0.498	1.386	0.745	1.482	1.050	1.950	76.704
1875	16.570	36.341	16.848	0.607	1.550	0.876	1.670	1.262	1.943	77.667
1876	15.137	35.319	16.158	0.714	1.691	1.015	1.674	1.458	1.901	75.066
1877	12.650	34.659	16.103	0.873	1.986	1.192	1.747	1.740	1.635	72.784
1878	12.846	33.155	15.059	0.996	2.014	1.319	1.752	1.925	1.868	70.935
1879	11.706	32.229	14.620	1.120	2.028	1.505	1.869	2.318	1.830	69.225
1880	11.487	31.176	14.074	1.253	2.154	1.788	1.997	2.651	1.860	68.438
1881	11.068	32.098	15.189	1.348	2.233	2.167	2.018	2.653	2.218	70.891
1882	10.675	31.283	14.984	1.377	2.213	2.721	2.092	2.356	2.978	70.675
1883	9.670	27.489	13.260	1.288	2.201	2.952	1.941	2.107	3.822	64.731
1884	10.120	31.286	14.486	1.462	2.726	3.656	2.194	2.117	6.299	74.346
1885	10.005	29.690	14.129	1.605	2.994	4.008	2.319	2.116	7.832	74.698
1886	10.622	30.171	14.533	1.685	3.308	4.789	2.545	2.133	8.431	78.218
1887	10.638	29.922	14.817	1.705	3.340	5.219	2.712	2.213	7.816	78.383
1888	10.192	28.199	13.433	1.819	3.282	5.132	2.867	2.512	9.177	76.611
1889	10.675	29.652	12.594	1.740	3.429	5.655	3.214	2.756	5.969	79.726
1890	10.115	29.083	13.618	1.741	3.561	6.027	3.382	2.596	10.315	80.438
1891	10.254	28.506	14.215	2.132	3.687	5.869	3.582	2.722	10.600	81.587
1892	10.057	28.108	14.115	2.298	3.573	6.146	3.692	2.679	10.515	81.184
1893	10.070	28.189	14.395	2.471	3.775	6.200	3.698	2.672	10.316	81.786
1894	9.741	28.002	13.918	2.553	3.802	5.955	3.469	2.412	10.320	80.174
1895	9.988	28.472	14.237	2.800	3.911	5.870	3.401	2.389	10.328	81.396
1896	9.578	28.400	13.789	2.990	3.883	5.457	3.185	2.330	9.605	79.217
1897	9.493	30.242	13.356	2.968	3.777	5.213	3.022	2.222	9.397	79.691
1898	9.273	29.497	13.500	3.294	3.826	5.044	3.117	2.220	9.047	78.819
1899	9.092	29.437	13.916	3.361	3.944	5.168	3.333	2.446	8.760	79.477
1900	9.136	29.971	14.148	3.497	4.079	6.079	3.316	2.515	9.133	80.875

CONCLUSION

Regional Considerations

Up to this point a large number of tables have been presented which have listed various items of data by region. Much has been left unsaid about these portions of the tables, with the thought of handling some of the considerations in the more general context of regional capital flows.

Historical Brief

In the early 1900's a great deal of debate took place in connection with legislation proposed in the various states to further direct the investment decisions of insurance companies with regard to the location of their investments. While these particular discussions took place later than the period herein under discussion, the arguments presented were not unlike the many which had preceded them. Additionally, the documentation involved is more complete and aids in setting forth the elements of the controversy. One may recall having seen references made to Southern or Western resentment to alleged capital exportation by Northern or Eastern financial institutions. The discussions mentioned here took place in the spirit of this sort of controversy.

As a vehicle for providing historical context to the

regional analysis made in this study, the reader may examine
the following lengthy quotes from a gentleman who was then
Insurance Commissioner of the State of South Carolina, Fitz
Hugh McMaster. His comments are presented as summarizing
much of the sentiment current at his time, and previously,
upon this subject. By way of rebuttal, some of the principal
proponents of the contrary position will be presented. Both
positions will then be contrasted with the findings made
herein.

"From my earliest childhood I had heard my father
lament the constant outflow of money from South
Carolina to insurance companies in a few centers
in distant states. His sentiments were those of
great numbers of the thoughtful men of the State.
I recall having heard one of the most conservative,
patriotic and intelligent men in South Carolina
say that in his opinion it would have been better
for the State if it had never admitted a life
insurance company of another State within its
bounds; that regardless of the fact that a few
widows and orphans had been benefited, the great
drain upon the people of the State as a whole had
been such that their exclusion would have been of
material benefit to the State. This man for a
number of years occupied one of the highest positions
in our State and now occupies a high position with
the Federal Government and his talents and his
good judgment are recognized by all who know him."[1]

"I believe it may be stated...as an axiom, that
there is no other single agency in the United
States comparable to life insurance making for
the concentration of wealth in certain centers
and putting the control of money in so very few
hands."[2]

[1]Fitz High McMaster, Life Insurance Companies Should
Be Compelled to Invest in the Securities of those States in
Which the Funds Originate (Columbia, S.C.:The State Company,
1914), p.1.
[2]Fitz High McMaster, In Consideration of Requiring Local
Investments by Life Insurance Companies (Columbia, S.C.:The
State Company, 1911), p. 1.

"Let us consider this matter of concentration of
wealth and control of money as affected by the life
insurance companies of the United States. Mark
these figures: the total income of all of the life
insurance companies of the United States for the
year 1913 amounted in round figures to $962,000,000.
Of this huge sum, approximating the total income
of the national government, $665,000,000 went to
the four cities of New York, Hartford, Newark and
Philadelphia. Here is a great country of more than
three million square miles of area pouring in
more than two-thirds of its life insurance funds
into one little corner of less than 100 miles
radius from Wall Street, New York City.

In the matter of assets the figures are still
more impressive. The total assets of all of the
life insurance companies of the United States on
December 31, 1913, amounted to $4,667,000,000.
The assets of the companies with home offices in
the four States named amounted to $3,556,000,000
or 75 percent of the total. Here are assets be-
longing to some millions of people living throughout the United States, which are controlled by,
I suppose it is no exaggeration to say, about a
score of men. Indeed, when we read the testimony
of Mr. Mellen as to the disbursement of some eleven
millions of dollars of the New York, New Haven and
Hartford Railroad Company by Mr. J. Pierpont Morgan,
without question one is encouraged to believe that
possibly these great insurance funds are ultimately
controlled by less than a score of men. Of course,
it is to laugh to say that those to whom these
funds belong have any voice in the control over
them or even in the election of the managements
of the so-called mutual companies. The situation
becomes the more ridiculous when regarded from a
policyholder's controlling standpoint when it is
further realized that of the insurance in force
in such companies as the New York Life and the
Mutual Life only about 14 percent is in force in
New York State; that of the insurance in force in
the Mutual Benefit about 6 percent is New Jersey
business; that of the Connecticut companies about
4 percent is Connecticut business and of the
Philadelphia companies relatively about 20 percent
is Pennsylvania business. In other words, from
about 80 to 95 percent of the business of these
companies comes from beyond the borders of the State
in which they have their home offices..."[3]

---

[3]McMaster, Life Insurance Companies..., p. 5.

"A life insurance company never brings any money
into any State except its home State save in the few
instances of those companies which have invested
largely in real estate mortgages and which have
taken large columns of money from other States and
have invested them in mortgages in a few selected
States. With these exceptions life insurance companies have drawn money from all sections of the United
States and have used it very largely for investment in the securities nearby to their home offices
or for the purpose of enabling groups of financiers
to get control of the great quasi public corporations of the country. Of necessity life insurance
companies must take money out of a State, even
though they invest the full reserves of the people
of the State in securities of the State, for the
tribute laid upon the people of the State by way of
managerial expenses, including within this term
the home office expenses, amounts to a very much
larger percentage of the income than the average
man is apt to realize. Excluding municipal, State
and federal taxes and license fees, the total
expenses, agency, administrative and clerical, of
the average life insurance company runs from about
10 to 20 percent of the gross income, interest income as well as premium. Of necessity a large
portion of this is spent at the home office.
So the statement may be repeated with assurance that
life insurance companies always take money out
of a State...."[4]

"It is equally as absurd to make an argument to
prove that in every State from which insurance
funds are drawn, there are absolutely safe securities in which to invest the reserves. To say
otherwise is to utter a silly paradox. It is to
chatter in twaddle. It is to assert that the whole
is not greater than a part, or that land is not
good surety for a portion of its yield.
The records show that those companies which
have invested their funds in other securities
than those generally listed on Wall street, and
away from the money centers, have, as a rule, re-

---

[4]McMaster, p. 7.

ceived higher rates of interest than those whose
investments are largely confined to the active market securities...."[5]

"It is submitted that each State should pass laws exactly
detailing the class of securities in which not only
its domestic companies, but all others doing
business therein should invest.

Of course, I appreciate that while it is not
indicated in the text of the program that as
stated there compulsory investment means whether
each State shall require the companies operating
in it to invest in securities of that State or not.

I am content to let that question answer
itself. Such States as Massachusetts, New York,
Connecticut, Pennsylvania and New Jersey, which
have laid the whole country under tribute to them
through their insurance organizations, of necessity
must permit their companies to invest in the
securities of other States, though they do compel
them to invest in only certain classes of securities.
If the other States of the Union are content
forever to pay tribute to a handful of States and
not require the capital which is collected in
those States to be invested in the securities of
the State in which it originates, then all that
I have to say is that these States are altruistic
to the point of folly..."[6]

"The natural channel for the investment of the
savings of the people of South Carolina is in
South Carolina securities. The same is true of
every other State in the Union. How will these
investments find their natural channels if they
are controlled by men in Boston, Mass., New York
City or Newark, New Jersey or other points 1,000
miles away from South Carolina and by men who
know little of and care less for the particular
interest of such distant States.

Nearby securities of even less interest rates
will be exhausted first before securities of more
distant localities are sought, regardless of the
locus of the policyholders. The securities on the
spot will be taken as a general rule, unless legislation compels otherwise...."[7]

---

[5]McMaster, In Consideration..., p. 4.
[6]McMaster, Life Insurance Companies..., pp. 11,12.
[7]McMaster, In Consideration..., p. 8.

As one might expect, it was not within the character of a large and powerful industry of this period to take this sort of agitation without reply, particularly if it had the potential of finding expression in the form of regulatory legislation. For example, when the Robertson Law went into effect in Texas, requiring regional investment of funds arising therein, "...twenty-six of the largest life insurance companies operating in that state..."[8], immediately withdrew rather than attempt to comply. For the most part, such drastic action was not taken. The reason and influence of the companies were usually sufficient to prevent the passage of laws found overly undesirable by them.

Consider the following as representative of the industry's point of view.

> "For several years it has been a common belief that life insurance companies were causing a depletion of the wealth of certain States by withdrawing therefrom and retaining the money required to make up and maintain the reserve funds necessarily incident to providing life insurance on the level premium plant. This belief has been particularly common in the Southern and Western portions of the United States. The fact that the payment of premiums was a voluntary act on the part of the citizens of the State, was an expenditure of their own money for their own purposes, and was necessary if they were to be insured in the companies of their choice, was not sufficient to overcome objection to the supposed result of the transaction upon the locality in which they lived.
> Within the last two or three years no less than

---

[8] Thomas Monroe Henry, Compulsory Local Investments, (Asheville, N.C.: Convention of Insurance Commissioners, 1914), p. 2.

fifteen States have given more or less consideration to the question of whether or not an effort
should be made to compel, if possible, the
investment of life insurance reserves within the
State from which they had been drawn. In one
State only has a compulsory investment law been
enacted. In most of the States it has not been
difficult to show them that to the extent that a
company had already made the required investment
the legislation would be unnecessary and without
immediate effect, either to the State or the company, and that as to other companies such a law
should not be made effective. Argument has never
been made for the law as a means of getting more
than a fair share of investments, but always on
the assumption that the locality in question was
being discriminated against and, therefore, was
being gradually but surely deprived of its working
capital. This presumption of fact has afforded
the justification offered for the proposed inter-
ference with the natural laws of supply and demand
which have controlled heretofore.

An examination of the investments of individual
life insurance companies seemed to show that with
few exceptions their investments had not been as
widely distributed throughout the United States
as their contracts of insurance had been, and that
their money had been permitted to follow the
natural demand for it without much regard to the
matter of locality from which its premium receipts
had been drawn....

Since the geographical distribution of investments has become a matter of concern to the several
States in connection with the accumulation of
reserve funds, we have, by careful estimate, calculated these reserves by States for comparison
with investments by States. Such a separation of
reserves is not required in ordinary reports, and
has not been shown so far as we know, in any prior
contribution upon this subject...

It will surely be conceded that a comparison
of reserves with investments under this grouping
will determine whether or not any considerable
section of the United States has been seriously
discriminated against or has been impoverished
even temporarily by the operation of life insurance
companies. Though discrimination has been charged
by States individually, the statements made to
sustain proposed compulsory investment legislation
have been general statements applicable to sections
of the country, as, for example, the "West", or
the "South", or the "South and West", as compared

with the "North" or "East", etc. Petty jealousies
between States are hardly worthy of notice in a
discussion of the broad question before us, and
the grouping adopted herein has enabled us to
largely eliminate them from our discussion.
Summarizing the investments and reserves of the
fourteen companies under examination we adduce a
table, as follows:

Table 63.   Regional Reserves and Investments Compared

Group	Reserves	Investment	Ratio of Investment to Reserves
Northwestern	$70,978,674	$144,847,826	204%
Middle Atlantic	550,438,080	898,775,257	163%
Southwestern	141,010,733	175,778,501	124%
Pacific	65,933,495	81,314,499	123%
Central Northern	267,828,893	304,850,890	114%
South Atlantic	91,534,649	101,769,061	111%
Gulf & Miss. Valley	103,711,638	101,417,762	98%
New England	129,490,576	80,335,014	62%
Total	$1,420,926,738	$1,889,088,810	

it would seem to be proven that the companies have
not drawn money from the South and West to invest in
"Wall Street" as is so frequently charged against
them, even assuming that railroad bonds are merely
Wall Street investments."[9]

[9]Robert Lynn Cox, The Geographical Distribution of the
Investments of Life Insurance Companies, An address delivered
at the bi-monthly meeting of the Association of Life Insurance
Presidents by Its General Counsel and President (New York:The Ass'c.
of Life Insurance Presidents, 1909), pp. 1-12.

Particular notice should be taken of the extent to which
the conclusions which have been drawn by the two gentlemen
quoted above have been altered by the measures of geographical
concentration which each chose. Mr Hughs included the monies
subsequently used in payment of expenses in his presentation
and concluded that all states without a substantial insurance
industry must unavoidably be drained of funds by the sale
of policies.

Expenses were certainly no small part of the insurance
operation, particularly in the earlier years, as the
following extract illustrates:

Table 64. Percentage of Expenditures on Cash Premium Receipts[10]

Company	Percentage[11]
Equitable	37.02
Mutual Life	43.10
Mutual Benefit	55.60
Aetna (four years only)	59.30
Connecticut Mutual	66.22
Manhattan	82.05
New York Life	52.15
Knickerbocker	79.70
North America	61.75
New England Mutual	70.72
Home Life	70.97
Guardian	75.70
Germania	54.41
Washington	59.90
United States	53.67

Table 64. (Continued).

Company	Percentage
Security	73.93
Berkshire	53.01
Charter Oak	58.59
Massachusetts Mutual	62.81
National (Vt.)	54.10
Phoenix	64.26
Union Mutual	66.11

The presentation of Mr. McMaster is, of course, in marked contrast to that given by Mr. Cox. He chose to relate that portion of premium collections which constituted reserves to the total investments with the region. This permitted him to show virtually all regions as gainers, with the noticeable exception of New England, which contains the insurance centers Boston and Hartford.

The regions defined in the report by Mr. Cox are the same as those used in this study.

Perhaps a minor disservice has been done the reader by drawing an account of the extremes of the argument and allowing him to enterpolate the middle ground on his own. The section just presented was not intended to call attention to the ex-

---

[10] The Equitable Life Assurance Society of the United States, Annual Report, 1869 (New York:The Equitable Life Assurance Society of the U.S., 1869), p. 5.

[11] The definition used in this table is also unortho-dox: "The...statement exhibits the percentage of the total cash premium receipts which has been expended in all ways, excepting only the profit dividends to policyholders, for the five years next preceding the last report of the Super-intendent of Insurance for the State of New York."

tremes, but rather to sketch a wide spectrum of opinion as quickly, yet as completely, as possible. As a brief example of one more moderate proposal, consider the following:

> "In view of the fact that there is more or less advocacy of the view that a State should require a life insurance company doing business in its borders to invest a fixed percentage of its reserve held against policies issued to citizens of that State in securities which are local to that State, I think it important to emphasize the proposition that railroad securities ought to be treated as local securities for the purposes of complying with any such State requirement."[12]

Perhaps, even here we may find the livelihood of the speaker revealed in his sentiments.

Regional Income

Recall from the section on methodology that "Premium Income" and "Regional Investments" are to be used as proxies in determining the relative flows of funds between regions as a result of the influence of the life insurance industry as an intermediary. This method is not as favorable to the industry as the method Mr. Cox employed. Neither is it as unfavorable as the reasoning used by Mr. McMaster.

Table 65 is presented to give some indication of the number of persons that were included in the potential market provided by the various regions defined in this study. It has been redefined from census data, by state.

[12]Walker D. Hines, Railroads should be Treated as Local Investments for Life Insurance Companies, An address delivered at the Sixth Annual Meeting of the Association of Life Insurance Presidents in New York City, Dec. 5, 1912, by the Chairman of the Executive Committee, Atchison, Topeka and Santa Fe Railway, (New York:The Ass'n of Life Insurance Presidents, 1913), p.1.

At some point the company records of every life company must have contained information which would, given sufficient effort, have allowed the geographical source of every dollar of premium income to have been disclosed. This situation is not a general condition among the company records still available. As an example of such a complete record, however, Table 66 has been prepared year by year from the original accountant's ledgers at Connecticut Mutual Life Insurance Company. The example provided is particularly good; since, Connecticut Mutual was active early in the period and was one of the major companies during most of the years prior to the publication of more complete regional data in the Spectator and elsewhere.

Table 66 indicates that Connecticut Mutual was able to obtain a wide range of operation rather early. Within its first twenty years the company was operating within all eight of domestic regions under discussion.

Unfortunately, the presentation of premium income for the entire industry is not as lengthy. Beginning with 1874, Table 67 gives that percentage of premium income coming from each of the regions. Premiums were being received from every region throughout the period covered. The Middle Atlantic states dominated throughout the period and were followed in this dominance by the Central Northern and then the New England States. However, the relative prominence of these groups decreased over the period in each case.

Table 65 . Population by Region[a] 1840-1900[b].

Region	1840	1850	1860	1870	1880	1890	1900
New England (Region 1)	2,234,822	2,728,116	3,135,283	3,487,924	4,010,529	4,700,749	5,592,017
Middle Atlantic (Region 2)	5,108,109	6,624,988	8,333,330	9,848,415	11,756,053	14,147,495	17,106,175
Central Northern (Region 3)	2,924,728	4,523,260	6,926,884	9,124,517	11,206,668	13,478,305	15,985,581
South Atlantic (Region 4)	3,343,450	3,952,837	4,490,358	4,816,001	6,338,022	7,406,647	8,791,983
Gulf and Miss. Valley (Region 5)	2,927,856	3,881,033	4,728,997	5,161,360	6,525,097	7,547,742	8,929,382
South-Western (Region 6)	833,687	1,166,080	2,456,676	3,520,482	5,952,642	8,303,219	9,672,444
North-Western (Region 7)	43,112	198,291	880,614	1,813,018	3,013,770	5,030,298	6,160,123
Pacific (Region 8)	-	117,271	491,183	832,059	1,363,833	2,323,259	3,020,479

Table 65 . Population by Region[a] 1840-1900[b].

[a] The regions presented here have been constructed to match those used elsewhere in the study.

[b] U.S. Department of Commerce, Historical Statistics of the United States, Colonial Times to 1957 (Washington:U.S. Department of Commerce, 1961), pp. 12-13.

Table 66. Business by Region, Connecticut Mutual Life.[a]

Year	Region 1	Region 2	Region 3	Region 4	Region 5	Region 6	Region 7	Region 8
				Number of Policies				
1846	42	12						
1847	385	87	18		2			
				Premium Income (thousands)				
1848	$ 174	$ 82	$ 3		$ 1	$ 3		
1849	89	94	5			6		
1850	212	92	14	4	1	3		
1851	263	151	55	5	2	18		
1852	191	101	17	4	1			
1853	134	89	18	1				
1854	35	213	9					
1855	65	388	6					
1856	72	317	9					
1857	251	187	18	4	5	14		
1858	303	167	55	4	5		1	
1859	344	187	77	4	5		1	
1860	338	260	97	5	5	1		
1861	408	172	149	5	41	1		
1862	397	975	271				5	
1863	329	1899	833			25	1	6
1864	379	2757	1126				1	33
1865	2376	1450	1468	16	16	31	1	51
1866	901	1989	2331			184	1	107
1867	1025	2637	2628	24		134		209
1868	1278	5252	2291	24		355		87
1869	1282	6828	2433	59		488	7	262
1870	1224	6765	3196	47	338	2	25	157
1871	3151	4331		215	703	507	190	225

Table 66 . Business by Region, Connecticut Mutual Life[a].

| Year | Region 1 | Region 2 | Premium Income (thousands) | | | | | |
			Region 3	Region 4	Region 5	Region 6	Region 7	Region 8
1872	2602	2535	2103	164	288	392	238	217
1873	2546	1878	2128	68	128	412	172	210
1874	2426	1906	1531	217	276	349	173	212
1875	2326	2079	2050	211	451	371	157	190
1876	2105	1667	1972	626	306	383	149	144
1877	2566	1235	1952	73	446	352	138	160
1878	1777	3170	108	188	465	136	147	
1879	1622	1350	2237	228	171	360	122	125
1880	1567	1291	1990	181	114	343	121	128
1881	1387	1326	1907	167	103	477	122	121
1882	1495	1153	2429	206	150	756	121	104
1883	1459	1137	2109	154	95	847	103	
1884	1418	1098	1797	152	93	923	116	98
1885	1385	1095	1627	125	90	959	121	93
1886	1323	1137	1389	99	84	1296	44	
1887	991	1369	1449	309	83	1373	84	22
1888	1045	1397	1860	137	81	2075	113	115
1889	1027	1748	1567	136	81	1515	120	165
1890	1025	1260	1399	138	82	1705	117	99
1891	1346	1582	1286	139	80	1663	117	106
1892	825	1209	1370	167	80	1664	125	116
1893	1018	1516	1554	154	75	1598	196	140
1894	1114	1541	1640	154	72	1548	152	146
1895	1406	1692	1453	130	63	1605	178	174
1896	1400	1645	1454	66	63	2005	196	172
1897	1441	1657	1308	132	61	1730	209	151
1898	1104	1556	1498	127	60	1431	450	165
1899	1052	1786	960	115	57	1299	376	186
1900	957	1850	849	113	54	970		188

Table 66 . Business by Region, Connecticut Mutual Life[a].

[a] Connecticut Mutual Life Insurance Company, "Ledger", Vols. A-F. The values appearing here were computed from the original ledger entries. These were ordinarily the reports of general agents.

TABLE67. PREMIUM INCOME RECEIVED (PERCENT OF PREMIUM INCOME)

| YEAR | | | | | REGIONS | | | | | |
	1	2	3	4	5	6	7	8	9	TOTAL
1874	21.416	47.752	21.560	0.650	1.808	0.971	1.933	1.368	2.543	76.704
1875	21.335	46.791	21.693	0.781	1.996	1.128	2.150	1.624	2.502	77.667
1876	20.165	47.050	21.525	0.951	2.253	1.352	2.230	1.943	2.532	75.066
1877	17.380	47.619	22.124	1.199	2.729	1.637	2.400	2.391	2.521	72.784
1878	18.110	46.740	21.230	1.404	2.840	1.859	2.470	2.713	2.634	70.935
1879	16.910	46.557	21.120	1.618	2.930	2.174	2.699	3.348	2.644	69.225
1880	16.784	45.554	20.564	1.831	3.147	2.612	2.918	3.873	2.717	68.438
1881	15.612	45.277	21.425	1.902	3.150	3.057	2.847	3.601	3.128	70.891
1882	15.104	44.259	21.201	1.948	3.131	3.850	2.960	3.333	4.213	70.675
1883	14.939	42.467	20.486	1.990	3.400	4.561	2.999	3.255	5.904	64.731
1884	13.612	42.081	19.485	1.967	3.667	4.918	2.951	2.848	8.473	74.346
1885	13.394	39.746	18.914	2.149	4.009	5.366	3.105	2.832	10.485	74.698
1886	13.560	38.573	18.580	2.155	4.229	6.123	3.254	2.727	10.779	78.218
1887	13.572	38.174	18.904	2.175	4.261	6.658	3.460	2.823	9.972	78.383
1888	13.303	36.807	17.533	2.374	4.284	6.699	3.742	3.278	11.978	76.611
1889	13.390	37.193	15.797	2.183	4.302	7.143	4.032	3.457	12.504	79.726
1890	12.575	36.156	16.930	2.165	4.427	7.492	4.204	3.227	12.824	80.438
1891	12.568	34.939	17.423	2.614	4.519	7.218	4.390	3.337	12.992	81.587
1892	12.388	34.623	17.387	2.387	4.401	7.571	4.548	3.300	12.952	81.184
1893	12.313	34.467	17.601	3.021	4.615	7.580	4.521	3.267	12.614	81.786
1894	12.150	34.927	17.360	3.184	4.742	7.428	4.327	3.009	12.872	80.174
1895	12.271	34.979	17.491	3.441	4.805	7.212	4.178	2.935	12.689	81.396
1896	12.090	35.850	17.407	3.775	4.901	6.889	4.021	2.941	12.125	79.217
1897	11.913	37.950	16.760	3.725	4.739	6.542	3.792	2.788	11.792	79.691
1898	11.765	37.424	17.128	4.179	4.855	6.399	3.955	2.817	11.478	78.819
1899	11.440	37.039	17.509	4.229	4.962	6.527	4.194	3.078	11.022	79.477
1900	11.297	37.059	17.494	4.324	5.044	6.280	4.100	3.110	11.292	80.875

Regional Investment

As in the case of premium income, the regionalization presented for investment is not complete prior to 1874. Table 68 presents regional data for 1843-1900. Only stock and bond holdings are included for the earlier years. After 1873 mortgages and real estate holdings are also included. Column eleven of the table may be compared with column twelve to obtain an idea of the portion of total assets included in the regionalization. Recall that only stocks and bonds are in the series prior to 1874. Regionally identifiable assets as a percentage of total assets are presented in Table 69.

Table 68 compares rather closely with the presentation of Connecticut Mutual income with regard to the dates of entry into the various regions and their relative importance, suggesting that its use as an example in that connection was probably justified.

Virtually no securities were evidenced in all the Southern and Western regions in the ante-bellum years, and only recent inroads had been made in the Central Northern States. Such as is known about early mortgage and real estate holdings would soften this characterized somewhat, but not significantly.

The early laws of the state which included the principal insurance centers all specified state and local bonds, and mortgages of the home state, as acceptable securities for investment purposes. Beyond that, states such as New York

TABLE 68. REGIONAL INVESTMENTS OF LIFE INSURANCE COMPANIES (THOUSANDS OF DOLLARS)

YEAR	1	2	3	4	5	6	7	8	9	TOTAL	TOTAL ASSETS
1843	77.	22.	0.	0.	0.	0.	0.	0.	0.	98.	1961.
1844	190.	65.	0.	0.	0.	0.	0.	0.	0.	255.	2208.
1845	170.	110.	0.	0.	0.	0.	0.	0.	0.	280.	2578.
1846	166.	153.	0.	0.	0.	0.	0.	0.	0.	318.	3202.
1847	200.	152.	0.	0.	0.	0.	0.	0.	0.	352.	3387.
1848	279.	146.	2.	0.	0.	0.	0.	0.	0.	427.	4283.
1849	481.	375.	4.	35.	0.	0.	0.	0.	0.	894.	7727.
1850	452.	271.	2.	22.	0.	0.	0.	0.	0.	746.	9519.
1851	578.	324.	2.	23.	0.	0.	0.	0.	0.	927.	12007.
1852	643.	412.	2.	0.	0.	0.	0.	0.	0.	1057.	14339.
1853	754.	525.	3.	0.	0.	0.	0.	0.	0.	1281.	16189.
1854	945.	694.	5.	0.	0.	0.	0.	0.	0.	1644.	18020.
1855	982.	600.	25.	0.	0.	0.	0.	0.	0.	1607.	18529.
1856	983.	705.	83.	1.	0.	0.	0.	0.	0.	1772.	21550.
1857	863.	678.	268.	0.	21.	0.	6.	0.	0.	1836.	24674.
1858	829.	823.	298.	0.	4.	0.	0.	0.	0.	1954.	27628.
1859	807.	1000.	306.	0.	7.	0.	0.	0.	0.	2120.	29908.
1860	876.	1051.	414.	0.	7.	0.	0.	0.	0.	2348.	35597.
1861	915.	1125.	451.	0.	7.	0.	0.	0.	0.	2497.	39073.
1862	642.	1378.	307.	0.	7.	0.	0.	0.	0.	2334.	41194.
1863	1311.	1846.	316.	5.	24.	22.	0.	0.	0.	3526.	53586.
1864	1962.	1956.	429.	5.	30.	54.	0.	22.	0.	4458.	67933.
1865	2903.	4402.	628.	6.	41.	107.	0.	28.	0.	8115.	82192.
1866	5301.	5725.	776.	101.	70.	124.	0.	147.	0.	12245.	107257.
1867	5415.	6704.	1012.	89.	99.	209.	119.	218.	0.	13865.	145261.
1868	6437.	8426.	1349.	203.	230.	236.	189.	304.	0.	17372.	203288.
1869	7029.	11995.	1440.	296.	264.	343.	283.	306.	83.	22042.	254380.
1870	8172.	12354.	2466.	548.	376.	282.	244.	297.	100.	24839.	284063.
1871	8235.	15371.	2394.	839.	853.	343.	255.	340.	164.	28794.	332642.

TABLE 68 (CONTINUED)

YEAR	REGIONS									TOTAL	TOTAL ASSETS
	1	2	3	4	5	6	7	8	9		
1872	8865.	17725.	4272.	738.	904.	435.	328.	393.	178.	33838.	364876.
1873	8630.	18629.	4378.	714.	766.	591.	425.	497.	162.	34792.	379534.
1874	46710.	169690.	44697.	1164.	1230.	5461.	25079.	960.	611.	295801.	425918.
1875	47451.	181424.	50021.	1076.	1242.	6367.	25525.	1001.	570.	314677.	434787.
1876	50398.	186558.	53956.	1143.	1327.	7444.	23050.	1078.	581.	325533.	438000.
1877	48353.	177193.	66089.	956.	1953.	8377.	22527.	1003.	465.	326916.	439878.
1878	47742.	171807.	71152.	1464.	1533.	10961.	24488.	1053.	395.	330594.	443544.
1879	41116.	167879.	81464.	1261.	1366.	11842.	22698.	1016.	589.	329229.	447144.
1880	39503.	165302.	83056.	1234.	1506.	13555.	21609.	1042.	915.	327723.	462291.
1881	37801.	178056.	85450.	1348.	1679.	14904.	21577.	1062.	1165.	343043.	476135.
1882	34730.	177187.	93262.	2614.	1932.	15562.	24651.	1096.	1312.	352345.	479715.
1883	34908.	187148.	112969.	2850.	2659.	16634.	32995.	2051.	1614.	393827.	508822.
1884	36239.	192818.	128809.	3586.	3450.	17114.	39573.	2614.	3499.	427703.	529634.
1885	36585.	203958.	136339.	3685.	5411.	24619.	48511.	3263.	5148.	467518.	562365.
1886	35816.	205480.	152266.	5450.	6844.	31536.	54359.	3537.	8673.	503963.	595608.
1887	36171.	218614.	151068.	6350.	7053.	37274.	60190.	3662.	10263.	530645.	631949.
1888	36414.	234120.	137625.	11488.	9358.	51704.	66508.	3993.	11883.	563093.	671592.
1889	39027.	249350.	153721.	13235.	14939.	58348.	74917.	5203.	14600.	623340.	737860.
1890	40444.	264978.	165823.	12846.	14190.	66597.	91806.	7418.	24963.	689065.	796326.
1891	42362.	285429.	174984.	10812.	16611.	73861.	104787.	11865.	27293.	748003.	865720.
1892	46844.	318718.	183725.	13103.	20223.	75845.	117033.	17574.	32190.	825255.	950266.
1893	49184.	344850.	191712.	15122.	21277.	90359.	124959.	19214.	34842.	891519.	1018732.
1894	57696.	365898.	205373.	16840.	23332.	96459.	136798.	22175.	38097.	962668.	1111959.
1895	66799.	388843.	226036.	21712.	30456.	99640.	142729.	24134.	42374.	1042723.	1196060.
1896	70408.	411505.	238886.	21754.	32241.	104774.	152541.	25734.	44092.	1101935.	1279969.
1897	79176.	433968.	246281.	26444.	36983.	124409.	160562.	28431.	48921.	1185174.	1385968.
1898	84879.	468971.	256509.	31430.	37133.	140364.	183308.	37915.	51992.	1292499.	1509495.
1899	95821.	493762.	279188.	36915.	37911.	169457.	188440.	48639.	69359.	1419492.	1641755.
1900	106941.	527544.	311768.	44501.	45989.	189339.	211115.	52419.	96368.	1585980.	1809659.

TABLE 69. REGIONAL INVESTMENTS OF LIFE INSURANCE COMPANIES (PERCENT OF TOTAL ASSETS)

| | | | | | REGIONS | | | | | |
YEAR	1	2	3	4	5	6	7	8	9	TOTAL
1843	3.906	1.116	0.0	0.0	0.0	0.0	0.0	0.0	0.0	5.022
1844	8.590	2.957	0.0	0.0	0.0	0.0	0.0	0.0	0.0	11.547
1845	6.609	4.266	0.0	0.0	0.0	0.0	0.0	0.0	0.0	10.875
1846	5.174	4.764	0.0	0.0	0.0	0.0	0.0	0.0	0.0	9.938
1847	5.893	4.496	0.0	0.0	0.0	0.0	0.0	0.0	0.0	10.389
1848	6.525	3.398	0.049	0.0	0.0	0.0	0.0	0.0	0.0	9.972
1849	6.218	4.852	0.046	0.456	0.0	0.0	0.0	0.0	0.0	11.571
1850	4.744	2.844	0.023	0.230	0.0	0.0	0.0	0.0	0.0	7.842
1851	4.817	2.698	0.019	0.190	0.0	0.0	0.0	0.0	0.0	7.724
1852	4.482	2.875	0.017	0.0	0.0	0.0	0.0	0.0	0.0	7.374
1853	4.654	3.241	0.017	0.0	0.0	0.0	0.0	0.0	0.0	7.913
1854	5.247	3.851	0.027	0.0	0.0	0.0	0.0	0.0	0.0	9.125
1855	5.299	3.238	0.135	0.0	0.0	0.0	0.0	0.0	0.0	8.671
1856	4.562	3.272	0.383	0.007	0.0	0.0	0.0	0.0	0.0	8.224
1857	3.498	2.748	1.088	0.0	0.084	0.0	0.023	0.0	0.0	7.441
1858	2.999	2.980	1.079	0.0	0.014	0.0	0.0	0.0	0.0	7.072
1859	2.699	3.344	1.025	0.0	0.022	0.0	0.0	0.0	0.0	7.089
1860	2.461	2.952	1.163	0.0	0.019	0.0	0.0	0.0	0.0	6.595
1861	2.341	2.878	1.154	0.0	0.018	0.0	0.0	0.0	0.0	6.392
1862	1.558	3.346	0.745	0.0	0.017	0.0	0.0	0.0	0.0	5.666
1863	2.447	3.446	0.590	0.010	0.045	0.042	0.0	0.0	0.0	6.581
1864	2.888	2.879	0.631	0.008	0.044	0.060	0.0	0.032	0.0	6.563
1865	3.532	5.356	0.764	0.008	0.050	0.130	0.0	0.034	0.0	9.874
1866	4.942	5.338	0.723	0.094	0.066	0.116	0.0	0.137	0.0	11.416
1867	3.728	4.615	0.696	0.061	0.068	0.144	0.082	0.150	0.0	9.545
1868	3.167	4.145	0.664	0.100	0.113	0.116	0.093	0.149	0.0	8.546
1869	2.763	4.715	0.566	0.116	0.104	0.135	0.111	0.121	0.033	8.665
1870	2.877	4.349	0.868	0.193	0.132	0.059	0.086	0.104	0.035	8.744

TABLE 69 (CONTINUED)

| | | | | | REGIONS | | | | | |
YEAR	1	2	3	4	5	6	7	8	9	TCTAL
1872	2.430	4.858	1.171	0.202	0.248	0.119	0.090	0.108	0.049	9.274
1873	2.274	4.908	1.154	0.188	0.202	0.156	0.112	0.131	0.043	9.167
1874	10.967	39.888	10.494	0.273	0.289	1.282	5.888	0.225	0.143	69.450
1875	10.914	41.727	11.505	0.248	0.286	1.464	5.871	0.230	0.131	72.375
1876	11.506	42.593	12.319	0.261	0.303	1.700	5.262	0.246	0.133	74.323
1877	10.992	40.282	15.024	0.217	0.444	1.905	5.121	0.228	0.106	74.320
1878	10.764	38.735	16.042	0.330	0.346	2.471	5.521	0.237	0.089	74.535
1879	9.195	37.545	18.219	0.282	0.305	2.648	5.076	0.227	0.132	73.629
1880	8.545	35.757	17.966	0.267	0.326	2.932	4.674	0.225	0.198	70.891
1881	7.939	37.396	17.947	0.283	0.353	3.130	4.532	0.245	0.245	72.048
1882	7.240	36.936	19.441	0.545	0.403	3.244	5.139	0.228	0.274	73.449
1883	6.861	36.781	22.202	0.560	0.523	3.269	6.484	0.403	0.317	77.400
1884	6.842	36.406	24.320	0.677	0.651	3.231	7.472	0.494	0.661	80.754
1885	6.506	36.268	24.244	0.655	0.962	4.378	8.626	0.580	0.915	83.134
1886	6.014	34.499	25.565	0.915	1.149	5.295	9.127	0.594	1.456	84.613
1887	5.724	34.594	23.905	1.005	1.116	5.898	9.524	0.579	1.624	83.970
1888	5.419	34.840	20.480	1.710	1.393	7.654	9.897	0.594	1.768	83.755
1889	5.289	33.794	20.833	1.794	2.025	7.908	10.153	0.705	1.979	84.479
1890	5.079	33.275	20.824	1.613	1.782	8.363	11.529	0.932	3.135	86.531
1891	4.893	32.970	20.213	1.249	1.919	8.532	12.104	1.371	3.153	86.402
1892	4.930	33.540	19.334	1.379	2.128	7.981	12.316	1.849	3.388	86.845
1893	4.828	33.851	18.819	1.484	2.089	8.873	12.266	1.686	3.420	87.513
1894	5.189	32.906	18.469	1.514	2.098	8.675	12.302	1.994	3.426	86.574
1895	5.585	32.510	18.898	1.815	2.546	8.331	11.933	2.018	3.543	87.180
1896	5.501	32.150	18.663	1.700	2.519	8.186	11.918	2.051	3.445	86.091
1897	5.713	31.312	17.770	1.908	2.668	8.976	11.585	2.051	3.530	85.512
1898	5.623	31.068	16.993	2.082	2.460	9.299	12.144	2.512	3.444	85.625
1899	5.837	30.075	17.005	2.249	2.309	10.322	11.478	2.963	4.225	86.462
1900	5.909	29.152	17.228	2.459	2.541	10.463	11.666	2.897	5.325	87.640

required that fifty percent of the investments be in federal
securities, the bonds of New York or its cities, and mortgages
within the state. The combined effects of such provincial laws,
together with the expected regional bias, and poor communications,
may be seen hereafter.

Comparison of the amount of premium income (Table 61)
taken from a region in a year with total regional investment
(Table 68) for that year does not seem to be a particularly
useful enterprise. The stock of investment is larger than the
flow of income in every case and all regions are winners by
such a measure, as in the example from Mr. Cox. Comparison
of the percent of total premium income (Table 67) derived within
a region with the percentage of total assets allocated to
it (Table 69) seems a little more appropriate. But, notice
that if this were done, the investment percentages would sum
to less than 100%. They, in fact, would sum to the percentage
of total assets regionalized, i.e., to the last column of
Table 69.

Such biased comparison could give some unusual results.
The Middle Atlantic States would be seen to provide a larger
percentage of premium income, by several points in each year,
than the percentage of total insurance investments that they
contained.

The percentage differential would be even greater in
the case of the New England States, as, indeed, it was shown
to be in the table presented by Mr. Cox. The Central Northern

States would exhibit a similar differential early, but the
tremendous influx of mortgage and real estate holdings to
these areas would have more than offset this later in the
period.

Even in what the author would consider to be a biased
approach, the South Atlantic, Gulf and Mississippi Valley,
Pacific and Foreign Regions would still be able to salvage
much of their lament. Each of these regions would be seen to
have produced a larger percentage of premium income in each
year than their percentage of life insurance investment
calculated by this method. The consistent, net recipient
would be Region 7, the Northwestern States. The percentage
of total assets held in rail bonds alone would be enough
to offset the small percentage of premiums from that region.
The same would be true, to a much lesser degree, for the
Southwestern States.

Table 70 and the subsequent tables in this section
have been calculated using total regionalized assets as a
base, as described in the section on methodology. That is,
the entries of the tables are the percentage of assets
allocated to a region relative to the total of all assets
which were able to be allocated for that year.

The regional comparisons thought to be most valid in
this study, then, are to be made between Table 67 and Table 70;
that is, the comparisons to be made between the percent of
premium income arising in a region and the percent of regionalized
assets allocated to that region.

TABLE 70. REGIONAL INVESTMENTS OF LIFE INSURANCE COMPANIES (PERCENT OF TOTAL)

YEAR					REGIONS				
	1	2	3	4	5	6	7	8	9
1874	15.791	57.434	15.110	0.393	0.416	1.846	8.478	0.325	0.206
1875	15.079	57.654	15.896	0.342	0.395	2.023	8.111	0.318	0.181
1876	15.482	57.308	16.575	0.351	0.408	2.287	7.081	0.331	0.178
1877	14.791	54.201	20.216	0.293	0.597	2.563	6.891	0.307	0.142
1878	14.441	51.969	21.522	0.443	0.464	3.316	7.407	0.319	0.119
1879	12.488	50.991	24.744	0.383	0.415	3.597	6.894	0.308	0.179
1880	12.054	50.440	25.343	0.377	0.459	4.136	6.594	0.318	0.279
1881	11.019	51.905	24.910	0.393	0.490	4.345	6.290	0.310	0.340
1882	9.857	50.288	26.469	0.742	0.548	4.417	6.996	0.311	0.372
1883	8.864	47.520	28.685	0.724	0.675	4.224	8.378	0.521	0.410
1884	8.473	45.082	30.116	0.839	0.807	4.001	9.253	0.611	0.818
1885	7.825	43.626	29.162	0.788	1.157	5.266	10.376	0.698	1.101
1886	7.107	40.773	30.214	1.081	1.358	6.258	10.786	0.702	1.721
1887	6.816	41.198	28.469	1.197	1.329	7.024	11.343	0.690	1.934
1888	6.467	41.577	24.441	2.040	1.662	9.182	11.811	0.705	2.110
1889	6.261	40.002	24.661	2.123	2.397	9.361	12.019	0.835	2.342
1890	5.869	38.455	24.065	1.864	2.059	9.665	13.323	1.077	3.023
1891	5.663	38.159	23.393	1.445	2.221	9.874	14.009	1.586	3.649
1892	5.676	38.621	22.263	1.588	2.451	9.190	14.181	2.130	3.901
1893	5.517	38.681	21.504	1.696	2.387	10.135	14.016	2.155	3.908
1894	5.993	38.009	21.334	1.749	2.424	10.020	14.210	2.304	3.957
1895	6.406	37.291	21.677	2.082	2.921	9.556	13.688	2.314	4.064
1896	6.390	37.344	21.679	1.974	2.926	9.508	13.843	2.335	4.001
1897	6.681	36.616	20.780	2.231	3.120	10.457	13.548	2.399	4.128
1898	6.567	36.284	19.846	2.432	2.873	10.860	14.162	2.933	4.023
1899	6.750	34.784	19.668	2.601	2.671	11.938	13.275	3.426	4.886
1900	6.743	33.263	19.658	2.806	2.900	11.936	13.311	3.305	6.076

Using this approach, New England consistently yielded a
larger percentage of premiums than it held in assets, even
as it would have been seen to do using the previous approach.
The Middle Atlantic States, however, consistently provided a
smaller percentage of income than they held in assets
through nearly the entire period. The differential was
rather large in the earliest years, over 10% in 1874. (Recall,
at this point, that Mr. McMaster would also like to have
had us consider the large percentage of income going to home
office expenses in these figures).

The two Southern regions consistently provided a larger
part of income than the portion of assets they held, as did
foreign areas. The same was generally true for the Pacific
region.   The Southwestern and Northwestern States consistently
paid a smaller proportion of premiums than they were allocated
in assets, with the difference increasing throughout the
period. Some of the particulars of these trends may be
examined through the use of Tables 71-74, which relate the
various classes of assets held in each region to the total
of assets regionalized.

As the insurance industry extended its sphere of in-
fluences from the insurance centers to the rest of the country,
the proportion of premium income generated in New England
decreased by about one-half from 21% to 11%. In the same
period, the proportion of assets allocated to the region
fell similarly, from 16% to 7%. Over the period the relative

TABLE 71. REAL ESTATE OWNED IN EACH REGION (PERCENT OF TOTAL REGIONAL INVESTMENT)

REGIONS

YEAR	1	2	3	4	5	6	7	8	9
1874	2.320	4.116	0.285	0.026	0.001	0.448	0.010	0.0	0.089
1875	2.179	4.531	0.684	0.027	0.002	0.560	0.015	0.0	0.081
1876	2.417	5.564	1.095	0.045	0.003	0.738	0.026	0.0	0.083
1877	2.083	6.024	1.752	0.067	0.018	0.816	0.077	0.0	0.079
1878	2.413	7.975	3.190	0.212	0.049	1.420	0.147	0.0	0.086
1879	2.422	8.475	4.009	0.197	0.048	1.468	0.152	0.0	0.156
1880	2.202	8.123	4.367	0.165	0.043	1.373	0.142	0.0	0.253
1881	2.042	7.917	4.682	0.140	0.039	1.303	0.135	0.0	0.314
1882	1.908	7.574	4.205	0.086	0.033	1.183	0.108	0.0	0.348
1883	1.826	7.437	3.865	0.038	0.028	1.098	0.086	0.0	0.384
1884	1.650	7.219	3.347	0.055	0.020	0.967	0.077	0.0	0.590
1885	1.599	7.470	3.077	0.073	0.014	0.913	0.073	0.0	0.806
1886	1.473	7.345	2.732	0.016	0.006	0.882	0.088	0.0	1.022
1887	1.324	7.137	2.162	0.010	0.002	0.892	0.105	0.0	1.154
1888	1.253	7.068	1.663	0.006	0.001	0.986	0.364	0.0	1.339
1889	1.175	6.957	1.557	0.013	0.002	0.980	0.550	0.002	1.388
1890	1.084	6.607	1.197	0.016	0.000	0.894	0.648	0.102	1.772
1891	1.083	6.742	1.039	0.023	0.000	0.912	0.581	0.096	1.405
1892	0.998	7.381	0.850	0.039	0.000	0.860	0.572	0.086	1.449
1893	0.996	7.505	0.848	0.043	0.000	0.943	0.611	0.097	1.546
1894	0.941	7.639	0.739	0.043	0.009	0.986	0.618	0.079	1.673
1895	0.846	7.247	0.631	0.037	0.029	1.011	0.875	0.088	1.517
1896	0.865	7.505	0.631	0.035	0.029	1.064	0.873	0.132	1.543
1897	0.758	6.784	0.563	0.040	0.038	1.280	0.975	0.153	1.396
1898	0.700	6.468	0.629	0.057	0.033	1.215	1.079	0.166	1.334
1899	0.656	6.003	0.598	0.051	0.028	1.081	1.173	0.164	1.239
1900	0.581	5.584	0.525	0.033	0.016	0.973	1.068	0.154	1.126

TABLE 72. MORTGAGES HELD IN EACH REGION (PERCENT OF TOTAL REGIONAL INVESTMENT)

YEAR	1	2	3	4	5	6	7	8	9
1874	9.506	44.676	11.747	0.020	0.029	1.113	8.128	0.025	75.243
1875	9.307	43.513	12.634	0.018	0.035	1.082	7.888	0.023	74.499
1876	8.930	41.730	13.096	0.016	0.038	1.030	6.876	0.022	71.738
1877	8.269	36.388	15.794	0.011	0.046	0.938	6.642	0.020	68.108
1878	7.239	30.984	15.448	0.006	0.047	0.878	7.085	0.018	61.706
1879	5.441	27.570	17.842	0.005	0.045	1.034	6.533	0.016	58.487
1880	4.637	25.494	16.981	0.004	0.046	1.104	6.212	0.014	54.492
1881	3.939	25.365	15.647	0.002	0.045	1.222	5.584	0.011	51.815
1882	3.640	24.836	15.861	0.005	0.060	1.294	5.539	0.010	51.245
1883	3.244	23.497	17.361	0.008	0.086	1.226	6.015	0.008	51.446
1884	2.870	21.803	17.809	0.010	0.106	1.101	6.204	0.007	49.908
1885	2.611	20.101	17.483	0.014	0.123	1.211	5.976	0.006	47.526
1886	2.276	18.617	18.838	0.044	0.135	1.735	5.778	0.005	47.430
1887	2.143	19.778	17.823	0.048	0.161	2.100	5.616	0.004	47.675
1888	1.766	21.069	14.708	0.063	0.187	3.890	5.122	0.003	46.811
1889	1.814	20.401	14.678	0.067	0.228	4.106	4.930	0.038	46.270
1890	1.783	20.335	14.769	0.077	0.272	4.510	5.713	0.126	47.604
1891	1.666	18.834	13.952	0.084	0.292	4.241	6.312	0.271	45.696
1892	1.488	17.802	12.534	0.087	0.366	3.795	6.517	0.373	43.022
1893	1.632	16.837	12.415	0.124	0.373	4.908	6.571	0.394	43.348
1894	1.568	15.995	12.097	0.147	0.341	4.998	6.325	0.396	41.952
1895	1.673	15.192	11.773	0.170	0.354	4.523	5.781	0.434	39.994
1896	1.640	15.473	11.735	0.202	0.387	4.418	6.359	0.433	40.801
1897	1.503	14.598	11.133	0.255	0.432	4.071	5.883	0.474	38.483
1898	1.451	13.845	9.597	0.285	0.509	4.020	5.484	0.431	36.164
1899	1.503	12.634	9.190	0.260	0.512	3.729	4.983	0.355	33.293
1900	1.439	10.825	9.195	0.272	0.613	3.731	5.144	0.332	31.669

REGIONS

TABLE 73. BONDS OWNED IN EACH REGION (PERCENT OF TOTAL REGIONAL INVESTMENT)

					REGIONS				
YEAR	1	2	3	4	5	6	7	8	9
1874	2.789	8.074	2.532	0.340	0.385	0.278	0.236	0.300	0.117
1875	2.599	9.024	2.539	0.297	0.358	0.375	0.209	0.295	0.101
1876	3.057	9.302	2.338	0.291	0.367	0.516	0.179	0.309	0.095
1877	3.422	11.144	2.615	0.214	0.533	0.778	0.168	0.286	0.063
1878	3.725	12.340	2.826	0.225	0.368	1.016	0.175	0.301	0.033
1879	3.555	14.261	2.836	0.181	0.321	1.091	0.210	0.292	0.023
1880	4.162	15.932	3.897	0.198	0.370	1.657	0.240	0.304	0.027
1881	4.092	17.299	4.483	0.250	0.406	1.818	0.548	0.291	0.026
1882	3.365	16.183	6.252	0.651	0.456	1.937	1.319	0.284	0.025
1883	2.637	14.786	6.821	0.677	0.560	1.848	2.045	0.493	0.025
1884	2.765	14.162	8.233	0.773	0.680	1.874	2.542	0.579	0.228
1885	2.390	14.376	7.921	0.700	1.019	3.072	3.857	0.657	0.294
1886	2.221	13.125	7.921	1.021	1.205	3.499	4.485	0.659	0.698
1887	2.225	12.575	7.779	1.132	1.165	3.902	5.155	0.649	0.778
1888	2.398	11.838	7.379	1.898	1.473	4.160	5.892	0.670	0.770
1889	2.210	10.787	7.680	2.015	2.164	4.109	6.129	0.757	0.944
1890	2.038	9.713	7.417	1.747	1.738	4.047	6.317	0.792	1.832
1891	1.979	10.307	7.738	1.324	1.880	4.403	6.508	1.156	2.200
1892	2.287	10.854	8.069	1.431	2.037	4.180	6.503	1.616	2.391
1893	2.107	11.572	7.419	1.482	1.970	3.968	5.930	1.504	2.269
1894	2.637	11.578	7.546	1.514	1.997	3.810	6.587	1.701	2.200
1895	2.980	11.966	8.392	1.810	2.466	3.807	6.475	1.682	2.453
1896	3.033	11.509	8.340	1.674	2.440	3.857	6.228	1.689	2.344
1897	3.531	12.262	8.148	1.874	2.582	4.958	6.343	1.679	2.598
1898	3.401	12.566	8.319	2.024	2.268	5.454	7.207	2.260	2.546
1899	3.485	12.726	8.980	2.225	2.067	6.972	6.716	2.830	3.520
1900	3.563	13.338	9.052	2.437	2.203	7.063	6.686	2.725	4.831

TABLE 74. STOCK OWNED IN EACH REGION (PERCENT OF TOTAL REGIONAL INVESTMENT)

YEAR	REGIONS							
	1	2	3	4	5	6	7	8
1874	1.176	0.567	0.547	0.006	0.0	0.008	0.104	0.0
1875	0.994	0.586	0.039	0.0	0.0	0.006	0.0	0.0
1876	1.077	0.712	0.045	0.0	0.0	0.003	0.0	0.0
1877	1.017	0.646	0.055	0.0	0.0	0.030	0.004	0.0
1878	1.064	0.669	0.058	0.0	0.0	0.001	0.0	0.0
1879	1.069	0.685	0.057	0.0	0.0	0.004	0.0	0.0
1880	1.053	0.890	0.099	0.009	0.0	0.002	0.000	0.0
1881	0.946	1.324	0.098	0.0	0.0	0.002	0.024	0.008
1882	0.944	1.695	0.151	0.0	0.0	0.002	0.030	0.017
1883	1.156	1.801	0.638	0.001	0.001	0.051	0.232	0.020
1884	1.187	1.899	0.726	0.001	0.001	0.059	0.430	0.026
1885	1.225	1.678	0.682	0.001	0.001	0.070	0.470	0.035
1886	1.136	1.685	0.723	0.001	0.012	0.142	0.435	0.038
1887	1.125	1.707	0.705	0.007	0.001	0.130	0.467	0.038
1888	1.049	1.603	0.690	0.074	0.002	0.146	0.443	0.036
1889	1.062	1.857	0.746	0.028	0.003	0.165	0.410	0.039
1890	0.965	1.799	0.681	0.025	0.050	0.214	0.646	0.056
1891	0.936	2.276	0.664	0.015	0.049	0.319	0.607	0.062
1892	0.904	2.584	0.809	0.030	0.047	0.355	0.590	0.055
1893	0.783	2.767	0.822	0.048	0.044	0.317	0.904	0.160
1894	0.847	2.797	0.951	0.046	0.078	0.225	0.680	0.127

decline in the importance of New England mortgage and real estate
holdings was not offset. The gradual shift of the industry
generally into more bond holdings did not involve many
securities from New England. Large numbers of the new
securities were rail bonds and many were related to the rail
expansions of the great central plains. The three central
regions involved also reflected this shift. In fact, the
largest part of the increased investments in the Central Northern,
Northwestern and Southwestern Regions seems to have been
the result of the rail assets allocated there.

By contrast, the decrease in the relative importance
of premium income from the Central Atlantic States was much
less than for New England, from 48% to 37%. At the same
time, its relative importance in asset holdings decreased
by nearly one-half, from 57% to 33%. The amount of Premium
income from New England nearly doubled over the twenty-six
year period; whereas, the amount of premium income from
the Central Atlantic Region came nearer to tripling. The
relative loss of importance in real estate related assets
that affected New England were not quite as severe in the
Central Atlantic States; real estate holdings were a fairly
stable proportion of the assets, and the relative decline
in mortgage importance was less.

During the period it appears that we must generally
agree with those who invisioned their funds being extracted
from their states and taken to New York. At least, if the

complainer lived in the South Atlantic, the Gulf and Mississippi
Valley, the Pacific or the Foreign Region. Since the combined
efforts of Boston and Hartford were not able to make New
England equally guilty it might be suggested that the provincial aspects of New York investment law had a good deal
to do with this phenomenon. However, if the complainer
lived in the central regions, one would at least have to
check the exceptional nature of his specific locality before
listening to his lamentations.

Legal Considerations

This paper has made points from time to time that
should have caused the reader to become rather suspect of
the principles of insurance regulation that persisted in
the last century or, of century-old thought in today's
regulations for that matter. It has been indicated that legal
restrictions were active participants in causing the distortions, both geographically and by class, that took place
in the course of the intermediation performed by the Life
Insurance Industry. Of course, these distortions have only
been spoken of as relative to some undefined norm of homogeneity
among regions or among alternative types of assets. Comparisons have not been made with the records of distortion
in other intermediaries (Goldsmith suggests these were severe)
nor have possible positive aspects of such distortions been
considered; nor shall they be.

More specific attention should be given the various
legal considerations that have been referred to. The work
of Zartman, cited previously, contains an excellent review of
the history of regulation. The reader is also directed to
Appendix C which contains a series of brief reviews of laws
and charters written in each state.

Beginnings

"The regulation of life insurance companies has historically been a state matter. The United States Supreme
Court in 1868 adopted the position that insurance was
not 'commerce' and therefore not subject to federal
government regulation under the interstate commerce
clause of the U.S. Constitution. (Paul v. Virginia,
75 U.S., 168, 183 (1868)). However, in June, 1944,
the Court reversed its earlier stand and thus opened
the way for Congress to establish machinery for
federal supervision of the insurance business."[1]

The states of Massachusetts and New York have been
particularly prominent in the history of insurance regulation.
The history of the regulation initiated by these states was
very noticeable in the trends of some of the asset categories
discussed. Massachusetts was regulating insurance investments
as early as 1836. The law of that year permitted the companies to invest as they desired in the stock of any corporation established in Massachusetts, whose corporate property consisted entirely of real estate, or in the funded

---

[1]Andrew F. Brimmer, Life Insurance Companies in the
Capital Market (East Lansing, Mich.:Bureau of Business and
Economic Research, Graduate School of Business Administration,
Michigan State University, 1962), p. 52.

debt of any city or town in the state. In 1838 the provisions were expanded to permit one-third of the capital to be invested in the stocks of railroad companies incorporated within Massachusetts, as long as not more than one-fifth of the capital went into any one railroad corporation. In 1845 the "one-fifth" restriction was removed. An 1864 law extended the investment provisions to include U.S. chartered banks. Each of these laws has had effects noted previously.

The first New York law regulating investment was passed in 1848 and restricted investment to bonds of the U.S. Government, the State and cities of New York, or mortgages on cultivated farms in New York worth double the amount of the loan. This type of restriction persisted through various revisions and was restated in the charters of various New York companies. The empirical path of these regulations has also been noted as various series have been discussed. Exposition along such lines could proceed ad. nausium but deference is given rather to Appendix C.

Endings

This paper has pointed out some of the restrictions and distortions in intermediation activities of life insurance companies. It has been contended that these were largely the price paid for various regulations placed upon the industry. The blanket laws restricting investments by location and by class had particularly pronounced effects. The wisdom of using laws framed in this way might well be thought over by any generation of legislators.

Some have suggested that such regulations were a small price to pay for policy holder security. Whether the trade-off was indeed, a sound one is subject to question.

"In general, this regulation must be termed strict; comparison need only be made with insurance invest-ment regulation in England, a country with a generally similar cultural and economic background, to point up this strictness. In England there is relatively little regulation of investment; wide latitude is allowed to investment officers. Yet historically the record of English life insurance for safety has been equally as good as that in the United States. And in the United States there has been no correlation between investment safety and the stringency of investment laws. In the nineteenth century, failures occurred in states with very strict investment laws as well as in those with liberal laws...."[1]

The fact that the degree of restriction inherent in a law and the degree of safety it provides are not equivalent notions appears to have historically escaped many legislators. Even today a clear distinction is not always made.

Many of the lessons of history have passed unnoticed. The New York restrictions limiting certain investments to mortgages and real estate of specified character within the State of New York, must be considered quite strict. An Annual Report of Equitable reads as follows,

---

[1]George T. Conklin, in The Investment of Life Insurance Funds, David McCahan, ed. (Philadelphia:University of Pennsylvania Press, 1953), p. 253.

"One of the great dangers which would beset the business of Life Insurance, if the safeguards were less certain than they now are, would be that those having the management of the affairs of a company might not be sufficiently cautious in confining the investments of the accumulated funds to those descriptions of securities which would make the company proof against loss. The laws of the State of New York are so stringent as to make it almost impossible for the assets of a Life Insurance Company to be squandered in this way...
The provisions of the Insurance Law of the State of New York confine Life Insurance Companies in their investments principally to Bonds of the United States, Bonds and Mortgages on Real Estate, and Bonds and Stocks of the State of New York and cities and counties within that State. These limits would seem to be comparatively safe...."[2]

The New York Insurance Department also seemed to be confident of its regulations. In 1869 the Superintendent wrote,

"Are the companies, to whose care and management is confided the investment and payment of such vast amounts of capital and which to this extent are trustees for so many millions of our people, honest, reliable and solvent, and is there an abiding assurance of their faithfully executing these important trusts?
This is a most serious question, and one, the responsibility of answering which, the Superintendent feels to be very grave. The Insurance Department was organized to act as a constant guard and check upon companies and to furnish the public as perfect protection as possible against loss through ignorance, error or fraud. In short, to see to it that the laws were rigidly complied with and the public interests duly protected. From this department an answer to the above great question may reasonably be expected, which will be entitled to confidence and respect. It will be the earnest effort of the

---

[2]Equitable, 18-19.

Superintendent to give such information as will
enable all to arrive at a correct conclusion.
Thus far the business of the different companies
seems to have proved eminently successful. Without an exception, all the companies doing
business in this State appear, from their statements rendered under the oaths of officers, to be
in a sound and prosperous condition."[3]

The gentlemen of the day involved in these actions appear
to have so convinced one another of the correctness of their
course that even when half of the companies failed in the decade of the seventies, coincident with the decimation of the
New York real estate and mortgage markets, the only possible
explanation for them was fraud and mismanagement. This interpretation persists even though the tremendous changes of the
period, discussed in this paper must have been at least as
apparent to those involved.

In 1871, at the first hints of disaster, the Superintendent suggested in his report that the previous departmental
administration had permitted the problem to form.[4] In 1873
the situation was still a debatable point for some, and the
following appeared:

"There has been a disposition of late by a portion
of the press to create the impression that Life Insurance was deteriorating in this country, and that it
is not as well organized as formerly. Ex parte
figures have been compiled from the reports in proof
of this."
"The statistics in the following pages not only

---

[3] New York State, <u>Annual Report of the Superintendent of
the Insurance Department</u>, 1869, vi.

[4] New York State, 1871, xi.

completely and emphatically disprove this, but show
a marked improvement in all points of life insurance
management...."[5]

By 1881 the situation was an established fact but
those in the regulatory offices were ready with an
interpretation:

"The business of life insurance has become one
of the established and settled institutions of
the country. It was perhaps inevitable in passing
through the fires of experiment and speculation
incident to the extraordinary condition of affairs
during the past twenty or twenty-five years that,
some failures should have occurred. More companies
were started than the business demanded, and,
as a matter of course, the weaker went to the wall.
Some companies were managed imprudently, some
dishonestly, and some on false principles. More
than fifty companies, from one cause and another,
have thus ceased doing business in the last twenty
years."[6]

In most states the interpretation of the wholesale
failures was essentially the same. This statement by
Massachusetts Commissioner was quite representative:

"The failures in life insurance have been the
results of gross mismanagement, occasioned by in-
competency or something worse. Few, if any,
branches of business ever suffered as this has
done during the past decade. Reckless managers
have wasted its substance by extravagent salaries
and office expenses; by foolish, fruitless efforts
to secure new business; by dividends when there
was no surplus; by expending money not to do good,
but to avert an evil, usually more imaginary than
real; in short, by ways almost innumerable."

---

[5]William W. Byington, A Synopsis of Life Insurance Statistics,
(New York:Francis Hart and Company, 1873), p.3.
[6]New York State, 1881, i.

Just prior to these remarks, in the same report, the
Commissioner had praised the managers of the surviving
companies as follows:

> "There is a manifest improvement in the tone
> of the business. By the disappearance of badly
> managed Companies, which have by their recklessness
> demoralized the public, and caused a general dis-
> trust in regard to the stability of life insurance
> the greatest obstacle which well-managed Companies
> have had to contend with, is removed. Officers
> of Companies are wide awake and fully realize their
> responsibilities. Probably never, within the history
> of life insurance, have there been such determined
> efforts on the part of managers to perfect and
> strengthen their Companies, as are manifest at the
> present time. Such efforts, if continued must inevi-
> tably restore that public confidence which is essential
> to the successful prosecution of the business."[7]

Unfortunately, many of the managers thus praised also
had occasion to be denounced for their fraudulent activities
in just the next few years as their companies took their
turn upon the block. In other words, it appears that
failure was sufficient evidence of dishonesty. Liquidity
was sufficient evidence of uprightness. The first of these
was a necessary conclusion, given the tacit assumption of
a perfect legal structure.

Without having attempted to say what might have been
the outcome had different regulations, or none at all, persisted over the last century, it is hardly possible to assess

---

[7]Clarke, 90-91.

the value of various state's regulations, other than relatively.
Examination of Table B1 indicates, that of the number of
companies included there, many had ceased to function as
active, independent units by the end of the period.
Seventy-seven percent of those with New York charters were
in that class. Eighty-two percent of Pennsylvania companies
and fifty-six percent of Connecticut companies had ceased
to function. The Massachusetts record was better by comparison, only thirteen percent mortality occurred among
the commonwealth's companies. These figures may be compared
with seventy-nine percent for all other states and
seventy-six percent for all states combined.

Admittedly, the number of unsuccessful companies may
not be the best measure of effective regulation. Nevertheless, one would be hard-pressed to explain what increase
in security policyholders of companies chartered in New
York, for example, may have received relative to policyholders
with companies of other states. Recall that this ethereal
increase of security was to have been the benefit received
in return for the regulatory impediments to capital mobilization.
On the other hand, it would be relatively more easy to explain
what benefits the monied interests lobbying in the New
York (again, as an example) Legislature may have received
from the laws concentrating life insurance investment there.

Even at time some of the regulatory practices were not
universally received or practiced. The following is taken

from the statement of the Connecticut Commissioner in his

1875 report:

"In the light of actual experience an important
question arises in regard to the investments of
life insurance companies. Should there be absolutely no restriction upon them, or if restricted
where should the line be drawn? An obvious answer
to this question would be - place them under the
same restraints that are applied to our savings
banks. But this would be clearly unjust and im-
practicable. Our savings banks are purely local
institutions. They agree to pay to their depositors
only their earnings. If they cannot successfully
use their deposits they can return them. Life
insurance companies have the whole country for a
field. They make specific contracts to pay
specific sums of money. They must keep all their
income actively employed in order to be able to
fulfill their contracts. Their agencies are
wide spread, and they are thus brought into active
business relations with nearly every conspicuous
town in the Union. Why then should they not be allowed
a wide range in selecting locations for loaning
their money, especially upon real estate? It is
easier to designate a few things that they should be
prohibited from investing in than it is to specify
the securities in which they may invest. They
should not be allowed to invest in the bonds of a
non-dividend paying railroad on any terms, or in
any security that has not a recognized intrinsic
or market value. In loaning upon real estate they
cannot be restricted, as our savings banks are, to
loans in this State, for the very good reason that
the demand for such loans is too limited to absorb
the deposits of our savings banks, much less the
enormous amounts accumulated by other corporations.
Our life insurance companies have sought loans of
this character, and are still seeking them, but
with poor success. To compel them to loan any
considerable portion of their funds upon this class
of securities would be equivalent to directing
them not to loan them at all.
    One thing should be embodied in our laws and
strictly enforced. No life insurance company
should be permitted to loan or invest any money,
even to the value of a dollar, except at a regular
meeting of the board of directors, and then each
director's vote should be taken on any such loan
or investment, yea or nay and recorded. This

would create a personal responsibility in each
case, which is now wholly wanting and be most
salutary in its effects."[8]

Rather than moving toward the advice of the Connecticut

Commissioner; however, virtually all states moved in the

direction of passing provincial legislation of their own.

The sentiment which Mr. McMaster was quoted as representing

in the case of South Carolina became the prevailing one

in framing many state investment statutes. States not

overtly active in the fray and others, in second round

legislation, usually passed laws which were generally worded

along these lines, "whatever regulations or payments

are expected of our companies shall be expected of yours."

Happily, some states wearied of this game of retaliatory

legislation and moved to what might be worthy of the euphemism

"reciprocal" legislation. The general wording of such laws

might be paraphrased, "We shall respond in kind to your

legislation. If it shall be that you extricate our com-

panies from the morass of your legislation, your companies

shall be similarly benefitted."

Again, one might be inclined to wonder about the official

attitude of the insurance centers toward all this. Quotations

of the time from the New York and Massachusetts Insurance

---

[8] State of Connecticut, Annual Report of the Commissioner
of Insurance of Connecticut (Hartford:Press of Case Lockwood
and Brainard, 1875), p. 147-48.

Departments follow:

"It will be seen that this amendment does not in
any way increase the fees heretofore required to be
paid by companies of other States. It imposes no
new burden anywhere. On the other hand, by virtue
of its provisions, any state can relieve its companies
from paying here, by just so much as it will relieve
New York companies from paying there. It is thus
left to the companies of each State to say, through
its Legislature, how much they will reduce their
own payments to this Department. It is believed
that the fees collectible under the reciprocal law
as it is termed, will be sufficient to meet necessary
expenses here; but if not, the fund in the Treasury
will make up any little deficiency for many years
unless (which is hoped and which indeed is the chief
thing sought) the Legislatures of other states
shall see fit to reduce their charges against New
York companies. The proper place to tax insurance
corporations is at home. If they do not directly
benefit any State they may enter, shut them out. Do
not admit them, upon the apparent theory that they
are an injury rather than a benefit, by taxation.
The attempt by one State to forage upon insurance
corporations of other States, is not founded upon
any correct principle, nor indeed is it justifiable
or expedient upon any ground."[9]

"Their laws are of two sorts and have two purposes
in view. First, those which are designed to
protect their own citizens from imposition by
fraudulent or ill-managed corporations; second
those which are designed to aid their own corporations when acting in other States. A State creates
corporations, and then feels itself bound to
fight their battles wherever they may go.
   "As to legislation of the first class, a State
has clearly a right to protect its citizens
against fraud and imposition, whether by external
or internal corporations. Any reasonable security
for fair dealing it must have a right to require.
It has a right to know the truth, on the best
evidence, as to the means and resources of every

---

[9]New York State, 1874, xvii.

corporation seeking business within its limits....
"But state legislation of the second class,
retaliatory or otherwise, is, for the most part
absurd, if not unconstitutional. Laws which only
embarrass sound institutions of other States
without any tendency to exclude unsound ones,
such as exorbitant license fees, do not protect
the citizen, but injure him. They serve no
imaginable purpose but to avert competition from the
home corporations, and thus obstruct the freedom
of trade. Massachusetts has done nothing of this
sort aggressively, but she has done it in retaliation
for such attacks on her corporations in other
States."[10]

In retrospect, one has trouble finding defense for

some of even the most universally accepted provisions. For

example, virtually every state, in its general law and in

its charters, required a minimum capital accumulation of

companies before allowing them to commense business. The

figure named was usually $100,000, though some states re-

quired more. Yet, the average capital required of the

defunct companies identified in Table B1 was $150,000.

By contrast, some of the largest companies, which have

survived the entire period, predated such requirements and

started with much less. Even some of later origin started

with some other line of insurance, such as assessment, which

required little capital and changed their charters after

---

[10]Clarke, p. 58.

accumulating the necessary minimum. All of which proves
little except that a minimum capital requirement was neither
a necessary or sufficient requirement for success. This generalization might be applied to some other regulations as aptly.

Summary

This study was undertaken with the hope of casting
some light upon the process of capital mobilization during
a critical period in the development of this nation. To do
this required rather complete knowledge of the sources and
the uses of the funds of the companies involved. Knowledge
of this sort is not available in the studies that have been
compiled heretofore. As well done as they are, their
emphasis has not been upon the subject at hand. Neither
has their length, detail, and documentation been sufficiently
complete along these lines.

Having been over the ground of the previous studies in
this paper both the reader and the author should be sufficiently
aware of the causes of problems inherent in any study of a
similar nature. So much must be done before anything at all
may be said that to deal with all possible points in an
exacting way would be to fail as badly as to become subject
to serious omissions. An effort has been made to preserve
sufficient references and detail of methodology that the
series presented herein may be thought valid for use by
others. At the same time, treatment of the subject of inter-

mediation has required presentation of a rather broad financial history of the Life Insurance Industry. Each aspect of the paper has suffered at the expense of the other though, perhaps not mortally.

The financial history that has been presented has tended to reinforce some traditional interpretations of events in the period and has reduced the credence of others. The events connected with the introduction of Tontine insurance have been played down and those connected with the early period of mutualization elevated for honors as the most significant and permanent revolution in life insurance history. The idea that life insurance has done much to encourage saving among the lower income groups and to lend regularity to the saving pattern of all policyholders has been generally upheld. On the other hand, little support has been given to the idea that direct life insurance investments were critical or even of great importance to the earliest development of basic American industries. Regulation, provincialism, liquidity requirements, some risk aversion, and, possibly, certain banking interest structured the general investment patterns of the companies too rigidly for that. Investments came late to most industries, after their positions in the world had been established and riskiness decimated. They also came in small amounts relative to the need, partly because of diversification, partly because the industries had already become large, and mostly because the laws had relegated the money to other purposes.

Zartman suggested some years ago that the price the nation paid for the historical pattern of investment regulation was great. The attitude of this paper toward the regulations has supported the basic attitudes of Zartman, but has attempted to do so with a little more empirical justification. Little has been found in the way of benefits to the policy-holders or to the companies that would offset the price paid through the reduction of capital mobility.

Support has been given to the traditional idea that geo-graphically, insurance companies were much more broadly based in their income patterns than in their investments. This was done even though high expenses in the home office states were ignored, and the holdings of railroad securities and other interstate assets carefully allocated geographically. However, the geographical distortion was found to be a decreasing phenomenon and less severe than some have indicated. Further, New England was seen to have been benefited much less, and the states between the Ohio River and the Rocky Mountains much more, by insurance investments than some have suggested.

In short, it seems that there can be little doubt that the product and methods of the American Life Insurance Industry have done much to encourage grass-roots savings and to make such savings, together with those of the more well-to-do generally available for investment. However, as one seeks to justify the regulation to which the actual investments

were subjected or to show that the direct investments were
critical to the development of a particular industry in
the period, the burden of proof becomes very large indeed.

BIBLIOGRAPHY

1. Aetna Life Insurance Company. Annual Statement. Hartford, Conn.:
   Aetna Life Insurance Company, 1854-1900.

2. Alabama, State of. Annual Report of the Insurance Commissioner of
   the State of Alabama. Montgomery, Ala.: State Printer, 1898-1901.

3. Association of American Railroads, Railroads of America.
   Washington, D. C.: Association of American Railroads, 1966.

4. Barnes, William. New York Insurance Reports. 7 Vols. Albany,
   N. Y.: Weed Parsons and Co., 1873.

5. Berkshire Life Insurance Company. Annual Statement. Pittsfield,
   Mass.: Berkshire Life Insurance Company, 1852-1900.

6. Bliss, George. The Law of Life Insurance. New York: Voorhis and
   Co., 1874.

7. Brimmer, Andrew F., Life Insurance Companies In The Capital Market.
   East Lansing, Mich.: Bureau of Business and Economic Research,
   Michigan State University, 1962.

8. Buley, R. Carlyle. The American Life Convention. 2 Vols.
   New York: Appleton Century-Crofts, Inc., 1968.

9. Byington, William W. A Synopsis of Life Insurance Statistics.
   New York: Francis Hart and Co., 1873.

10. California, State of. Annual Report of the Insurance Commissioner,
    Sacramento, Calif.: State Printer, 1868-1901.

11. Chandler, Alfred D., Jr. "Patterns of Finance, 1830-1850." The
    Business History Review, XXVIII (September, 1954.)

12. Clarke, Julius L. History of the Massachusetts Insurance Department:
    Including a Sketch of the Origin and Progress of Insurance and of
    the Legislation of the State from 1780 to 1876. Boston, Mass:
    Wright and Potter, State Printers, 1876.

13. Colorado, State of. Annual Report of the Superintendent of
    Insurance of the State of Colorado. Denver, Colo: State Printing
    Office, 1882-1900.

14. Connecticut Mutual Life Insurance Company. Annual Report, Hartford, Conn: Connecticut Mutual Life Insurance Company, 1848-1900.

15. Connecticut Mutual Life Insurance Company. Ledger. 6 Vols. Hartford, Conn.: Connecticut Mutual Life Insurance Company, 1846-1900.

16. Connecticut, State of. Annual Report of the Commissioner of Insurance of Connecticut. Hartford, Conn.: State Printer, 1866-1901.

17. Cooke, Fredrick Hale. The Law of Life Insurance. New York: Baker, Voorhis and Co., 1891.

18. Cox, Robert Lynn. The Geographical Distribution of the Investments of Life Insurance Companies. New York: The Association of Life Presidents, 1909.

19. Davidson, John M. In Chancery Before the Chancellor, In the Matter of the New York Life Insurance and Trust Company, Answer and Report. New York: New York Life Insurance and Trust Company, 1841.

20. Davis, Lance E., Hughes, J. R. T., and McDougall, Duncan M., American Economic History. Homewood, Ill.: Richard D. Irwin, Inc., 1965.

21. Davis, Lance E. "Stock Ownership in the Early New England Textile Industry," The Business History Review, XXXII (1958).

22. Davis, Lance E. "The New England Textile Mills and the Capital Markets," The Journal of Economic History, March, 1960.

23. Davis, Lance E. "United States Financial Intermediaries in the Early Nineteenth Century," Unpublished Dissertation, Johns Hopkins University, 1956.

24. Delaware, State of. Biennial Report of the Insurance Commissioner. Dover, Del.: State Printer, 1881-1901.

25. Easterlin, Richard A., "Interregional Differences In Per Capita Income, Population, and Total Income, 1840-1950," Trends in the American Economy in the Nineteenth Century, Princeton: Princeton University Press, 1960.

26. Easterlin, Richard A., "Regional Income Trends, 1840-1950," American Economic History. Edited by Seymore E. Harris. New York: McGraw Hill Book Co., Inc., 1961, 525-547.

27. Engineering News. Atlas of Railway Progress. New York: Engineering News, 1889.

28. Equitable Life Assurance Society of the United States. Annual Statement. New York,: Equitable Life Assurance Society of the United States, 1862-1900.

29. Federal Reserve Bank of Boston. A History of Investment Banking in New England. Boston, Mass.: Federal Reserve Bank of Boston, 1965.

30. Fowler, J. A. The History of Insurance in Philadelphia for Two Centuries. Philadelphia, Pa.: Review and Printing Co., 1888.

31. Georgia, State of. Report of the Insurance Department of the Comptroller General's Office. Augusta, Ga.: State Printer, 1890-1900.

32. Goldsmith, Raymond W. A Study of Saving In the United States. Princeton: Princeton University Press, 1956.

33. Goldsmith, Raymond W. Financial Intermediaries in the American Economy Since 1900. Princeton, N. J.: Princeton University Press, 1958.

34. Goldsmith, Raymond W. Financial Intermediaries in the American Economy Since 1900, Supplementary Appendicies. New York: National Bureau of Economic Research, 1958.

35. Goldsmith, Raymond W. "The Share of Financial Intermediaries in National Wealth and National Assets, 1900-1940," Studies In Capital Formation and Financing, Occasional Paper No. 42. Princeton, N. J.: Princeton University Press, 1954.

36. Hamilton, Andrew. Statutory Revision of the Laws of New York Affecting Insurance Companies. Albany, N. Y.: Banks and Co., 1903.

37. Henry, Thomas Monroe. Compulsory Local Investments. Asheville, N. C.: National Convention of Insurance Commissioners, 1914.

38. Hines, Walker D. Railroad Securities Should Be Treated as Local Investments for Life Insurance Companies. New York: Association of Life Presidents, 1912.

39. Hoffman, Frederick L. "Fifty Years of America Life Insurance Progress," Publications of the American Statistical Association, XII (1910-1911), 677-760.

40. Home Life Insurance Company, Annual Statement. New York: Home Mutual Life Insurance Company, 1861-1900.

41. Huse, Charles Phillips. The Financial History of Boston. Cambridge, Mass.: Harvard University Press, 1916.

42. Illinois, State of. Annual Report of the Auditor of Public Accounts of the State of Illinois. Springfield, Ill.: State Printer, 1869-1901.

43. Indiana, State of. <u>Annual Report of the Insurance Department</u>. Indianapolis, Ind. State Printer, 1888-1900.

44. Institute of Life Insurance. <u>The Historical Statistics of the United States, 1759 to 1958</u>. New York: Institute of Life Insurance, 1960.

45. Iowa, State of. <u>Annual Report of the Insurance Department of the State of Iowa</u>. Des Moines, Ia.: State Printer, 1871-1901.

46. Jones, Lawrence D. <u>Investment Policies of Life Insurance Companies</u>. Cambridge, Mass.: Harvard University Press, 1968.

47. Kansas, State of. <u>Annual Report of the Superintendent of Insurance of the State of Kansas</u>. Topeka, Kan.: Public Printer, 1872-1901.

48. Keller, Morton. <u>The Life Insurance Enterprise</u>. Cambridge, Mass.: Harvard University Press, 1963.

49. Kentucky, State of. <u>Annual Report of the Commissioner of the Insurance Bureau of Kentucky to the Auditor of Public Accounts</u>. Frankfort, Ky.: State Printer, 1871-1901.

50. Knight, Charles K. <u>The History of Life Insurance in the United States to 1870</u>. Philadelphia, Pa.: University of Pennsylvania, 1920.

51. Kuznets, Simon, and Goldsmith, Raymond W. <u>Income and Wealth in the United States</u>. Baltimore, Md.: The Johns Hopkins Press, 1952.

52. Kuznets, Simon. <u>Capital in the American Economy, Its Formation and Financing</u>. Princeton, N. J.: Princeton University Press, 1961.

53. Kuznets, Simon. "Long-term Changes in the National Income of the United States of America." <u>Income and Wealth Series II</u>, 1955, 24-246.

54. Kuznets, Simon. <u>National Product Since 1869</u>. New York: National Bureau of Economic Research, 1946.

55. Louisiana, State of. <u>Secretary of State's Annual Report of the Condition and Affairs of the Insurance Companies</u>. Baton Rouge, La.: State Printer, 1887-1900.

56. Mackie, Alexander. Facile Princeps. <u>The Story of the Beginnings of Life Insurance in America</u>. Lancaster, Pa.: Lancaster Press, 1956.

57. Maine, State of. <u>Annual Report of the Bank and Insurance Examiner of the State of Maine</u>. Augusta, Me.: Printers to the State, 1869-1901.

58. Manhattan Life Insurance Company, Annual Statement. New York: Manhattan Life Insurance Company, 1851-1900.

59. Martin, Joseph G. A Century of Finance: Martin's History of the Boston Stock and Money Markets. Boston, Mass.: 1898.

60. Martin, Robert F. National Income For the United States, 1799-1938. New York: National Industrial Conference Board, 1939.

61. Maryland, State of. Annual Report of the Insurance Commissioner. Baltimore, Md.: State Printer, 1880-1900.

62. Massachusetts, Commonwealth of. Annual Report of the Insurance Commissioner of the Commonwealth of Massachusetts. Boston, Mass.: State Printers, 1857-1901.

63. Massachusetts, Commonwealth of. Supplement to the General Statutes of the Commonwealth of Massachusetts. Boston, Mass.: Wright and Potter, State Printers, 1860-1872.

64. Massachusetts Mutual Life Insurance Company, Annual Statement. Springfield, Mass.: Massachusetts Mutual Life Insurance Company, 1851-1900.

65. Metcalf, Theron, and Mann, Horace, The Revised Statutes of the Commonwealth of Massachusetts. Boston, Mass.: Dutton and Wentworth, State Printers, 1836.

66. McCahan, David (ed.) Investment of Life Insurance Funds. Philadelphia, Pa.: University of Pennsylvania Press, 1953.

67. McMaster, Fitz Hugh. Life Insurance Companies Should Be Compelled to Invest in the Securities of Those States in Which the Funds Originate. Columbia, S. C.: The State Company, 1914.

68. Michigan, State of. Annual Report of the Secretary of State of Michigan Relating to Insurance. Lansing, Mich.: State Printer, 1870-1900.

69. Minnesota, State of. Annual Report of the Insurance Commissioner of the State of Minnesota. Saint Paul, Minn.: State Printer, 1870-1901.

70. Missouri, State of. Annual Report of the Superintendent of the Insurance Department of the State of Missouri. Jefferson City, Mo.: State Printers and Binders, 1870-1901.

71. Montgomery, Thomas H. A History of the Insurance Company of North America. Philadelphia, Pa.: Press of Review Publishing and Printing Co., 1885.

72. Mutual Benefit Life Insurance Company. Annual Statement. Newark, N. J.: Mutual Benefit Life Insurance Company, 1846-1900.

73. Mutual Life Insurance Company of New York. Annual Statement. New York: Mutual Life Insurance Company of New York, 1846-1900.

74. National Life Insurance Company. Annual Statement. Montpelier, Vt.: National Life Insurance Company, 1851-1900.

75. Navin, Thomas R. and Sears, Marian V. "The Rise of a Market for Industrial Securities 1887-1902," The Business History Review, XXIX (June, 1955.)

76. Nebraska, State of. Biennial Report of the Auditor of Public Accounts. Lincoln, Neb.: State Printer, 1890-1901.

77. New England Mutual Life Insurance Company, Annual Statement. Boston, Mass: New England Mutual Life Insurance Company, 1847-1900.

78. New Hampshire, State Of. Annual Report of the Insurance Commissioners to the Legislature of New Hampshire. Concord, N. H.: 1860-1901.

79. New Jersey, State of. Report By The Secretary of State as Commissioner of Insurance. Trenton, N. J.: State Printer, 1877-1901.

80. New York Life Insurance Company. Annual Statement. New York: New York Life Insurance Company, 1945-1900.

81. New York Life Insurance and Trust Company, "Report of the Trustees," New York: The New York Life Insurance and Trust Company, 1831. (Handwritten.)

82. New York, State of. Annual Report of The Superintendent of the Insurance Department of New York. Albany, N. Y.: State Printer, 1860-1910.

83. New York, State of. "Insurance Laws of Other States," Albany: New York Insurance Department, 1867. (Scrapbook.)

84. New York, State of. "Letter Books," Albany, N. Y.: Comptroller's Office, 1859. (Scrapbooks.)

85. New York, State of. "Taxes Against Mutual Life Insurance Companies in the City of New York, Returned to the Comptroller's Office, from 1843 to 1849 Inclusive," Albany, N. Y.: Office of the Attorney General. (Handwritten.)

86. New York, State of. Testimony Taken Before the Joint Committee of the Senate and Assembly of the State of New York to Investigate and Examine into the Business and Affairs of Life Insurance Companies Doing Business in the State of New York. 7 Vols. Albany, N. Y.: Brandow Printing Co., 1906.

87. New York Stock Exchange, The. Understanding the New York Stock Exchange. New York: The New York Stock Exchange, 1967.

88. North Carolina, State of. Annual Report of the Insurance Commissioner of the State of North Carolina. Raleigh, N. C.: State Printer & Binder, 1900.

89. North, Douglass C. "Capital Accumulation in Life Insurance Between the Civil War and the Investigation of 1905," Men In Business. Edited By William Miller. Cambridge, Mass.: Harvard University Press, 1952.

90. North, Douglas C. Growth and welfare in the American Past, Englewood Cliffs, N. J.: Prentice-Hall, 1966.

91. North, Douglas C. The Economic Growth of the United States, 1790-1860. Englewood Cliffs, N. J.: Prentice-Hall, 1961.

92. North, Douglass C. "The Large Life Insurance Companies Before 1906," Unpublished Dissertation, University of California, 1952.

93. Ohio, State of. Annual Report of the Superintendent of the Insurance Department. Columbus, Ohio: State Printer, 1868-1901.

94. Palmer, Charles G. "Schedule of Real Estate," New York: New York Life Insurance and Trust Company, 1843-1846. (Handwritten.)

95. Penn Mutual Life Insurance Company. Annual Statement. Philadelphia, Pa.: Penn Mutual Life Insurance Company, 1947-1900.

96. Penn Mutual Life Insurance Company, Ledger. 2 Vols. Philadelphia, Pa.: Penn Mutual Life Insurance Company, 1945-1900.

97. Pennsylvania, State of. Annual Report of the Insurance Commissioner of the State of Pennsylvania. Harrisburg, Pa.: State Printers, 1874-1901.

98. Pierce, R. H. "Aetna Mortgage Report," Hartford, Conn.: Aetna Life Insurance Company, 1948. (typewritten.)

99. Poor, Henry V. and Poor, H. W. Manual of the Railroads of the United States. New York: Journeymen Printers' Co-operative Association, 1868-1901.

100. Rhode Island, State of. Annual Report of the Insurance Commissioner of the State of Rhode Island. Providence, R. I.: Printers to the State, 1867-1901.

101. South Dakota, State of. Annual Report of the Commissioner of Insurance to the Governor of South Dakota. Huron, S. D.: State Printer, 1898-1901.

102. Spectator Company. Charters of American Life Insurance Companies. New York: Spectator Company, 1906.

103. Spectator Company. Life Insurance History, 1843-1910, Yearly Business of ALL Active United States Life Insurance Companies from Organization. New York: Spectator Company, 1911.

104. Spectator Company. The Insurance Yearbook. New York: Spectator Company, 1874-1911.

105. Stalson, J. Owen. Marketing Life Insurance, Its History in America. Cambridge, Mass.: Harvard University Press, 1942.

106. State Mutual Life Insurance Company, Annual Statement. Worchester, Mass., State Mutual Life Insurance Company, 1845-1900.

107. Tennessee, State of. Annual Report of the Insurance Commissioner of the State of Tennessee. State Printer, 1874-1901.

108. Texas, State of. Annual Report of Commissioner of Agriculture, Insurance, Statistics and History. Austin, State printer, 1876-1901.

109. Vermont, State of. Annual Report of the Insurance Commissioners of the State of Vermont. Montpelier, Vt.: State Printer, 1869-1901.

110. Washington, State of. Annual Report of the Commissioner of Insurance of the State of Washington. Olympia, Wash.: State printer, 1891-1901.

111. Wisconsin, State of. Annual Report of the Insurance Department of the State of Wisconsin. Madison, Wis.: 1870-1901.

112. Wright, Elizar. Massachusetts Reports on Life Insurance, 1859-1865. Boston, Mass.: Wright and Potter, 1865.

113. Union Mutual Life Insurance Company. Annual Statement. Boston, Mass.: Union Mutual Life Insurance Company, 1850-1900.

114. U. S. Bureau of the Census. Preliminary Report on the Eighth Census. 1862.

115. U. S. Department of Commerce. Historical Statistics of the United States, Colonial Times to 1957. Washington, D. C.: US Department of Commerce, 1961.

116. U. S. Department of Commerce. Historical Statistics of the United States, 1789-1945. Washington, D. C., U. S. Department of Commerce, 1949.

117. Virginia, State of. Reports of Life Insurance Companies. Richmond, Va.: State printer, 1895-1901.

118. Walford, C. Insurance Guide and Handbook. New York: Wynkoop and Hallenbeck, 1868.

119. Warren, George W. Review of Life Insurance Investment. Boston, Mass.: Cupples, Upham and Co., 1884.

120. White, Gerald T. A History of the Massachusetts Life Insurance Company. Cambridge, Mass: Harvard University Press, 1955.

121. Williamson, Harold F. and Smalley, Orange A. Northwestern Mutual Life, A Century of Trusteeship. Evanston, Ill.: Northwestern University Press, 1957.

122. Wing, Asa Shove. Life Insurance Investments In Railroads. New York: The Chamber of Commerce of the United States, 1923.

123. Woodward, P. Henry. Insurance In Connecticut. Boston, Mass.: D. H. Hard and Co., 1897.

124. Zartman, Lester W. The Investments of Life Insurance Companies. New York: Henry Holt and Co., 1906.

APPENDICES

APPENDIX A

INCOME AND ASSETS

APPENDIX A

INCOME AND ASSETS

This section presents the major portion of the data used in preparing the tables and figures original to this study. Each page of Table Al, presented herein, gives the various items calculated for each corresponding year in the period 1843-1900. Additional details appear beginning with the year 1874.

Table Al does not present the original data items of the study, the volume of which precludes their inclusion at all. These may be discovered by making reference to the section on methodology which discusses the preparation of this appendix.

TABLE A1. INCOME AND ASSETS, 1843 THROUGH 1900 (THOUSANDS)

ASSET CATEGORY DATA OF 1843	REGIONS									TOTAL
	1	2	3	4	5	6	7	8	9	
PREMIUM INCOME										266.
TOTAL INCOME										393.
REAL ESTATE										349.
BONDS										
UNITED STATES										14.
STATE, LOCAL	14.	11.	0.	0.	0.	0.	0.	0.		25.
RAILROAD	16.	5.	0.	0.	0.	0.	0.	0.		22.
UTILITY	0.	0.	0.	0.	0.	0.	0.	0.		0.
INDUSTRIAL	16.	0.	0.	0.	0.	0.	0.	0.		16.
CANAL	0.		0.	0.	0.	0.	0.	0.		0.
FOREIGN	0.	0.	0.	0.	0.	0.	0.	0.	0.	0.
ALL OTHER	0.	0.	0.	0.	0.	0.	0.	0.	0.	0.
TOTAL BONDS	47.	16.	0.	0.	0.	0.	0.	0.		77.
STOCKS										
FINANCIAL	14.	0.	0.	0.	0.	0.	0.	0.		14.
RAILROAD	10.	5.	0.	0.	0.	0.	0.	0.		15.
UTILITY	0.	0.	0.	0.	0.	0.	0.	0.		0.
INDUSTRIAL	7.	0.	0.	0.	0.	0.	0.	0.		7.
CANAL	0.	0.	0.	0.	0.	0.	0.	0.		0.
ALL OTHER	0.	0.	0.	0.	0.	0.	0.	0.		0.
TOTAL STOCKS	30.	5.	0.	0.	0.	0.	0.	0.		36.
MORTGAGES										636.
LOANS										650.
PREMIUM NOTES										17.
PREMIUMS DUE										53.
CASH										73.
OTHER ASSETS										70.
TOTAL ASSETS										1961.

TABLE A1 (CONTINUED)

ASSET CATEGORY	REGIONS 1	2	3	4	5	6	7	8	9	TOTAL
DATA OF 1844										
PREMIUM INCOME										418.
TOTAL INCOME										541.
REAL ESTATE										361.
BONDS										
UNITED STATES										12.
STATE, LOCAL	31.	34.	0.	0.	0.	0.	0.	0.		65.
RAILROAD	40.	19.	0.	0.	0.	0.	0.	0.		59.
UTILITY	0.	0.	0.	0.	0.	0.	0.	0.		0.
INDUSTRIAL	37.	0.	0.	0.	0.	0.	0.	0.		37.
CANAL	0.	0.	0.	0.	0.	0.	0.	0.		0.
FOREIGN	0.	0.	0.	0.	0.	0.	0.	0.	0.	0.
ALL OTHER	0.	0.	0.	0.	0.	0.	0.	0.	0.	0.
TOTAL BONDS	109.	53.	0.	0.	0.	0.	0.	0.	0.	174.
STOCKS										
FINANCIAL	40.	0.	0.	0.	0.	0.	0.	0.		40.
RAILROAD	22.	12.	0.	0.	0.	0.	0.	0.		34.
UTILITY	19.	0.	0.	0.	0.	0.	0.	0.		0.
INDUSTRIAL	0.	0.	0.	0.	0.	0.	0.	0.		19.
CANAL	0.	0.	0.	0.	0.	0.	0.	0.		0.
ALL OTHER	0.	0.	0.	0.	0.	0.	0.	0.		0.
TOTAL STOCKS	81.	12.								93.
MORTGAGES										750.
LOANS										602.
PREMIUM NOTES										37.
PREMIUMS DUE										57.
CASH										64.
OTHER ASSETS										69.
TOTAL ASSETS										2208.

TABLE A1 (CONTINUED)

ASSET CATEGORY	1	2	3	REGIONS 4	5	6	7	8	9	TOTAL
DATA OF 1845										
PREMIUM INCOME										731.
TOTAL INCOME										854.
REAL ESTATE										387.
BONDS										
UNITED STATES										11.
STATE, LOCAL	24.	84.	0.	0.	0.	0.	0.	0.		108.
RAILROAD	37.	17.	0.	0.	0.	0.	0.	0.		54.
UTILITY	0.	0.	0.	0.	0.	0.	0.	0.		0.
INDUSTRIAL	26.	0.	0.	0.	0.	0.	0.	0.		26.
CANAL	0.	0.	0.	0.	0.	0.	0.	0.		0.
FOREIGN	0.	0.	0.	0.	0.	0.	0.	0.	0.	0.
ALL OTHER	0.	0.	0.	0.	0.	0.	0.	0.	0.	0.
TOTAL BONDS	86.	101.	0.	0.	0.	0.	0.	0.		199.
STOCKS										
FINANCIAL	45.	0.	0.	0.	0.	0.	0.	0.		45.
RAILROAD	15.	9.	0.	0.	0.	0.	0.	0.		24.
UTILITY	0.	0.	0.	0.	0.	0.	0.	0.		0.
INDUSTRIAL	24.	0.	0.	0.	0.	0.	0.	0.		24.
CANAL	0.	0.	0.	0.	0.	0.	0.	0.		0.
ALL OTHER	0.	0.	0.	0.	0.	0.	0.	0.		0.
TOTAL STOCKS	84.	9.	0.	0.	0.	0.	0.	0.		93.
MORTGAGES										1026.
LOANS										558.
PREMIUM NOTES										82.
PREMIUMS DUE										62.
CASH										96.
OTHER ASSETS										75.
TOTAL ASSETS										2578.

TABLE A1 (CONTINUED)

| ASSET CATEGORY | | | | REGIONS | | | | | | |
DATA OF 1846	1	2	3	4	5	6	7	8	9	TOTAL
PREMIUM INCOME										1212.
TOTAL INCOME										1389.
REAL ESTATE										342.
BONDS										
UNITED STATES										
STATE, LOCAL	25.	130.	0.	0.	0.	0.	0.	0.		24.
RAILROAD	34.	15.	0.	0.	0.	0.	0.	0.		154.
UTILITY	0.	0.	0.	0.	0.	0.	0.	0.		49.
INDUSTRIAL	20.	0.	0.	0.	0.	0.	0.	0.		20.
CANAL	0.	0.	0.	0.	0.	0.	0.	0.		0.
FOREIGN									0.	0.
ALL OTHER	0.	0.	0.	0.	0.	0.	0.	0.	0.	0.
TOTAL BONDS	79.	144.	0.	0.	0.	0.	0.	0.	0.	247.
STOCKS										
FINANCIAL	51.	0.	0.	0.	0.	0.	0.	0.		51.
RAILROAD	13.	8.	0.	0.	0.	0.	0.	0.		21.
UTILITY	0.	0.	0.	0.	0.	0.	0.	0.		0.
INDUSTRIAL	23.	0.	0.	0.	3.	0.	0.	0.		23.
CANAL	0.	0.	0.	0.	0.	0.	0.	0.		0.
ALL OTHER	0.	0.	0.	0.	0.	0.	0.	0.		0.
TOTAL STOCKS	87.	8.	0.	0.	0.	0.	0.	0.		95.
MORTGAGES										1241.
LOANS										634.
PREMIUM NOTES										410.
PREMIUMS DUE										60.
CASH										91.
OTHER ASSETS										82.
TOTAL ASSETS										3202.

TABLE A1 (CONTINUED)

ASSET CATEGORY DATA OF 1847	1	2	3	4	5	6	7	8	9	TOTAL
					REGIONS					
PREMIUM INCOME										1627.
TOTAL INCOME										1772.
REAL ESTATE										266.
BONDS										
UNITED STATES										129.
STATE, LOCAL	23.	127.	0.	0.	0.	0.	0.	0.		150.
RAILROAD	32.	19.	0.	0.	0.	0.	0.	0.		51.
UTILITY	0.	0.	0.	0.	0.	0.	0.	0.		0.
INDUSTRIAL	15.	0.	0.	0.	0.	0.	0.	0.		15.
CANAL										0.
FOREIGN									0.	0.
ALL OTHER	0.	0.	0.	0.	0.	0.	0.	0.	0.	0.
TOTAL BONDS	70.	146.	0.	0.	0.	0.	0.	0.	0.	345.
STOCKS										
FINANCIAL	64.	0.	0.	0.	0.	0.	0.	0.		64.
RAILROAD	10.	6.	0.	0.	0.	0.	0.	0.		17.
UTILITY	10.	0.	0.	0.	0.	0.	0.	0.		10.
INDUSTRIAL	45.	0.	0.	0.	0.	0.	0.	0.		45.
CANAL	0.	0.	0.	0.	0.	0.	0.	0.		0.
ALL OTHER	0.	0.	0.	0.	0.	0.	0.	0.		0.
TOTAL STOCKS	129.	6.								136.
MORTGAGES										1193.
LOANS										707.
PREMIUM NOTES										511.
PREMIUMS DUE										42.
CASH										107.
OTHER ASSETS										80.
TOTAL ASSETS										3387.

TABLE A1 (CONTINUED)

ASSET CATEGORY DATA OF 1848	1	2	3	4	5	6	7	8	9	TOTAL
PREMIUM INCOME										1924.
TOTAL INCOME										2129.
REAL ESTATE										258.
BONDS										
UNITED STATES	22.	113.	2.	0.	0.	0.	0.	0.		241.
STATE, LOCAL										137.
RAILROAD	31.	22.	0.	0.	0.	0.	0.	0.		53.
UTILITY	0.	0.	0.	0.	3.	0.	0.	0.		0.
INDUSTRIAL	13.	0.	0.	0.	0.	0.	0.	0.		13.
CANAL	0.	0.	0.	0.	0.	0.	0.	0.		0.
FOREIGN									0.	0.
ALL OTHER	0.	0.	0.	0.	0.	0.	0.	0.	0.	0.
TOTAL BONDS	65.	135.	2.	0.	0.	0.	0.	0.	0.	444.
STOCKS										
FINANCIAL	63.	5.	0.	0.	0.	0.	0.	0.		69.
RAILROAD	63.	5.	0.	0.	0.	0.	0.	0.		69.
UTILITY	17.	0.	0.	0.	0.	0.	0.	0.		17.
INDUSTRIAL	71.	0.	0.	0.	0.	0.	0.	0.		71.
CANAL	0.	0.	0.	0.	0.	0.	0.	0.		0.
ALL OTHER	0.	0.	0.	0.	0.	0.	0.	0.		0.
TOTAL STOCKS	214.	11.	0.	0.	0.					225.
MORTGAGES										1455.
LOANS										769.
PREMIUM NOTES										829.
PREMIUMS DUE										46.
CASH										127.
OTHER ASSETS										131.
TOTAL ASSETS										4283.

REGIONS

TABLE A1 (CONTINUED)

ASSET CATEGORY	REGIONS									
	1	2	3	4	5	6	7	8	9	TOTAL
DATA OF 1849										
PREMIUM INCOME										3197.
TOTAL INCOME										3541.
REAL ESTATE	39.									362.
BONDS										
UNITED STATES		213.								395.
STATE, LOCAL	56.	56.	4.	35.	0.	0.	0.	0.		290.
RAILROAD	0.	0.	0.	0.	0.	0.	0.	0.		113.
UTILITY	21.	0.	0.	0.	0.	0.	0.	0.		0.
INDUSTRIAL	0.	0.	0.	0.	0.	0.	0.	0.		21.
CANAL										0.
FOREIGN									0.	0.
ALL OTHER	0.	0.	0.	0.	0.	0.	0.	0.	0.	0.
TOTAL BONDS	116.	269.	4.	35.	0.	0.	0.	0.	0.	819.
STOCKS										
FINANCIAL	160.	26.	0.	0.	0.	0.	0.	0.		187.
RAILROAD	76.	19.	0.	0.	0.	0.	0.	0.		95.
UTILITY	28.	28.	0.	0.	0.	0.	0.	0.		56.
INDUSTRIAL	100.	32.	0.	0.	0.	0.	0.	0.		132.
CANAL	0.	0.	0.	0.	0.	0.	0.	0.		0.
ALL OTHER	0.	0.	0.	0.	0.	0.	0.	0.		0.
TOTAL STOCKS	364.	106.	0.	0.	0.	0.	0.	0.		470.
MORTGAGES										2688.
LOANS										1096.
PREMIUM NOTES										1727.
PREMIUMS DUE										80.
CASH										273.
OTHER ASSETS										212.
TOTAL ASSETS										7727.

TABLE A1 (CONTINUED)

ASSET CATEGORY	REGIONS									TOTAL
	1	2	3	4	5	6	7	8	9	
DATA OF 1850										
PREMIUM INCOME										3739.
TOTAL INCOME										4293.
REAL ESTATE										327.
BONDS										
UNITED STATES	36.	189.	2.	22.	0.	0.	0.	0.		367.
STATE, LOCAL	70.	36.	0.	0.	0.	0.	0.	0.		249.
RAILROAD	0.	0.	0.	0.	0.	0.	0.	0.		106.
UTILITY	13.	0.	0.	0.	0.	0.	0.	0.		0.
INDUSTRIAL	0.	0.	0.	0.	0.	0.	0.	0.		13.
CANAL										0.
FOREIGN	0.	0.	0.	0.	0.	0.	0.	0.	0.	0.
ALL OTHER	0.	0.	0.	0.	0.	0.	0.	0.	0.	0.
TOTAL BONDS	119.	225.	2.	22.	0.	0.	0.	0.		735.
STOCKS										
FINANCIAL	134.	4.	0.	0.	0.	0.	0.	0.		138.
RAILROAD	130.	15.	0.	0.	0.	0.	0.	0.		146.
UTILITY	18.	14.	0.	0.	0.	0.	0.	0.		32.
INDUSTRIAL	50.	12.	0.	0.	0.	0.	0.	0.		62.
CANAL	0.	0.	0.	0.	0.	0.	0.	0.		0.
ALL OTHER	0.	0.	0.	0.	0.	0.	0.	0.		0.
TOTAL STOCKS	332.	46.	0.	0.	0.	0.	0.	0.		378.
MORTGAGES										3911.
LOANS										1261.
PREMIUM NOTES										1995.
PREMIUMS DUE										71.
CASH										610.
OTHER ASSETS										232.
TOTAL ASSETS										9519.

TABLE A1 (CONTINUED)

| | | | | | REGIONS | | | | | |
ASSET CATEGORY	1	2	3	4	5	6	7	8	9	TOTAL
DATA OF 1851										
PREMIUM INCOME										4115.
TOTAL INCOME										4655.
REAL ESTATE										369.
BONDS										
UNITED STATES										
STATE, LOCAL	66.	217.	2.	23.	0.	0.	0.	0.		437.
RAILROAD	79.	80.	0.	0.	0.	0.	0.	0.		308.
UTILITY	0.	0.	0.	0.	0.	0.	0.	0.		159.
INDUSTRIAL	14.	0.	0.	0.	0.	0.	0.	0.		0.
CANAL	0.	0.	0.	0.	0.	0.	0.	0.		0.
FOREIGN	0.	0.	0.	0.	0.	0.	0.	0.	0.	0.
ALL OTHER	0.	0.	0.	0.	0.	0.	0.	0.	0.	0.
TOTAL BONDS	159.	297.	2.	23.	0.	0.	0.	0.	0.	918.
STOCKS										
FINANCIAL	160.	5.	0.	0.	0.	0.	0.	0.		164.
RAILROAD	188.	23.	0.	0.	0.	0.	0.	0.		211.
UTILITY	18.	0.	0.	0.	0.	0.	0.	0.		18.
INDUSTRIAL	54.	0.	0.	0.	0.	0.	0.	0.		54.
CANAL	0.	0.	0.	0.	0.	0.	0.	0.		0.
ALL OTHER	0.	0.	0.	0.	0.	0.	0.	0.	0.	0.
TOTAL STOCKS	420.	27.	0.	0.	0.	0.	0.	0.	0.	447.
MORTGAGES										4901.
LOANS										1635.
PREMIUM NOTES										2806.
PREMIUMS DUE										95.
CASH										555.
OTHER ASSETS										280.
TOTAL ASSETS										12007.

TABLE A1 (CONTINUED)

ASSET CATEGORY	\<REGIONS\> 1	2	3	4	5	6	7	8	9	TOTAL
DATA OF 1852										
PREMIUM INCOME										4163.
TOTAL INCOME										4948.
REAL ESTATE										352.
BONDS										
UNITED STATES	82.	240.	2.	0.	0.	0.	0.	0.		428.
STATE, LOCAL	86.	137.	0.	0.	0.	0.	0.	0.		325.
RAILROAD	0.	0.	0.	0.	0.	0.	0.	0.		223.
UTILITY	0.	0.	0.	0.	0.	0.	0.	0.		0.
INDUSTRIAL	15.	0.	0.	0.	0.	0.	0.	0.		15.
CANAL	0.	0.	0.	0.	0.	0.	0.	0.		0.
FOREIGN	0.	0.	0.	0.	0.	0.	0.	0.	0.	0.
ALL OTHER	0.	0.	0.	0.	0.	0.	0.	0.	0.	0.
TOTAL BONDS	183.	377.	2.	0.	0.	0.	0.	0.		990.
STOCKS										
FINANCIAL	192.	5.	0.	0.	0.	0.	0.	0.		197.
RAILROAD	197.	30.	0.	0.	0.	0.	0.	0.		227.
UTILITY	20.	0.	0.	0.	0.	0.	0.	0.		20.
INDUSTRIAL	51.	0.	0.	0.	0.	0.	0.	0.		51.
CANAL	0.	0.	0.	0.	0.	0.	0.	0.		0.
ALL OTHER	0.	0.	0.	0.	0.	0.	0.	0.		0.
TOTAL STOCKS	460.	35.	0.	0.	0.	0.	0.	0.		494.
MORTGAGES										6434.
LOANS										1726.
PREMIUM NOTES										3329.
PREMIUMS DUE										188.
CASH										543.
OTHER ASSETS										282.
TOTAL ASSETS										14339.

TABLE A1 (CONTINUED)

ASSET CATEGORY	1	2	3	4	5	6	7	8	9	TOTAL
					REGIONS					
DATA OF 1853										
PREMIUM INCOME										4535.
TOTAL INCOME										5751.
REAL ESTATE										364.
BONDS										
UNITED STATES	103.	274.	3.	0.	0.	0.	0.	0.		434.
STATE, LOCAL	99.	177.	0.	0.	0.	0.	0.	0.		379.
RAILROAD	0.	0.	0.	0.	0.	0.	0.	0.		275.
UTILITY	0.	0.	0.	0.	0.	0.	0.	0.		0.
INDUSTRIAL	16.	0.	0.	0.	0.	0.	0.	0.		16.
CANAL	0.	0.	0.	0.	0.	0.	0.	0.		0.
FOREIGN	0.	0.	0.	0.	0.	0.	0.	0.	0.	0.
ALL OTHER	0.	0.	0.	0.	0.	0.	0.	0.	0.	0.
TOTAL BONDS	218.	451.	3.	0.	0.	0.	0.	0.		1105.
STOCKS										
FINANCIAL	227.	5.	0.	0.	0.	0.	0.	0.		233.
RAILROAD	219.	41.	0.	0.	0.	0.	0.	0.		260.
UTILITY	56.	0.	0.	0.	0.	0.	0.	0.		56.
INDUSTRIAL	33.	0.	0.	0.	0.	0.	0.	0.		33.
CANAL	0.	27.	0.	0.	0.	0.	0.	0.		27.
ALL OTHER	0.	0.	0.	0.	0.	0.	0.	0.		0.
TOTAL STOCKS	536.	74.	0.	0.	0.	0.	0.	0.		610.
MORTGAGES										7774.
LOANS										1544.
PREMIUM NOTES										3802.
PREMIUMS DUE										212.
CASH										468.
OTHER ASSETS										311.
TOTAL ASSETS										16189.

TABLE A1 (CONTINUED)

ASSET CATEGORY	REGIONS									TOTAL
	1	2	3	4	5	6	7	8	9	
DATA OF 1854										
PREMIUM INCOME										4604.
TOTAL INCOME										5537.
REAL ESTATE										391.
BONDS										
UNITED STATES										471.
STATE, LOCAL	138.	332.	5.	0.	0.	0.	0.	0.		475.
RAILROAD	118.	220.	0.	0.	0.	0.	0.	0.		339.
UTILITY	0.	0.	0.	0.	0.	0.	0.	0.		0.
INDUSTRIAL	20.	0.	0.	0.	0.	0.	0.	0.		20.
CANAL	0.	0.	0.	0.	0.	0.	0.	0.		0.
FOREIGN	0.	0.	0.	0.	0.	0.	0.	0.	0.	0.
ALL OTHER	0.	0.	0.	0.	0.	0.	0.	0.	0.	0.
TOTAL BONDS	276.	552.	5.	0.	0.	0.	0.	0.	0.	1305.
STOCKS										
FINANCIAL	344.	28.	0.	0.	0.	0.	0.	0.		372.
RAILROAD	258.	77.	0.	0.	0.	0.	0.	0.		335.
UTILITY	28.	0.	0.	0.	0.	0.	0.	0.		28.
INDUSTRIAL	39.	0.	0.	0.	0.	0.	0.	0.		39.
CANAL	0.	36.	0.	0.	0.	0.	0.	0.		36.
ALL OTHER	0.	0.	0.	0.	0.	0.	0.	0.		0.
TOTAL STOCKS	669.	141.	0.	0.	0.	0.	0.	0.		811.
MORTGAGES										9183.
LOANS										1102.
PREMIUM NOTES										4111.
PREMIUMS DUE										222.
CASH										556.
OTHER ASSETS										340.
TOTAL ASSETS										18020.

TABLE A1 (CONTINUED)

ASSET CATEGORY	REGIONS									TOTAL
	1	2	3	4	5	6	7	8	9	
DATA OF 1855										
PREMIUM INCOME										4949.
TOTAL INCOME										6080.
REAL ESTATE										372.
BONDS										
UNITED STATES										473.
STATE, LOCAL	132.	282.	4.	0.	0.	0.	0.	0.		418.
RAILROAD	182.	193.	21.	0.	0.	0.	0.	0.		396.
UTILITY	17.	0.	0.	0.	0.	0.	0.	0.		0.
INDUSTRIAL	0.	0.	0.	0.	0.	0.	0.	0.		17.
CANAL	0.	0.	0.	0.	0.	0.	0.	0.		0.
FOREIGN	18.	0.	0.	0.	0.	0.	0.	0.	0.	0.
ALL OTHER		0.	25.	0.	0.	0.	0.	0.		18.
TOTAL BONDS	349.	475.	25.	0.	0.	0.	0.	0.	0.	1322.
STOCKS										
FINANCIAL	437.	24.	0.	0.	0.	0.	0.	0.		461.
RAILROAD	143.	65.	0.	0.	0.	0.	0.	0.		208.
UTILITY	24.	0.	0.	0.	0.	0.	0.	0.		24.
INDUSTRIAL	29.	0.	0.	0.	0.	0.	0.	0.		29.
CANAL	0.	36.	0.	0.	0.	0.	0.	0.		36.
ALL OTHER	0.	0.	0.	0.	0.	0.	0.	0.		0.
TOTAL STOCKS	633.	125.	0.							758.
MORTGAGES										9758.
LOANS										1087.
PREMIUM NOTES										4167.
PREMIUMS DUE										256.
CASH										476.
OTHER ASSETS										332.
TOTAL ASSETS										18529.

TABLE A1 (CONTINUED)

ASSET CATEGORY	1	2	3	4	REGIONS 5	6	7	8	9	TOTAL
DATA OF 1856										
PREMIUM INCOME										5169.
TOTAL INCOME										6439.
REAL ESTATE										401.
BONDS										
UNITED STATES										
STATE, LOCAL	171.	304.	4.	1.	0.	0.	0.	0.		529.
RAILROAD	187.	203.	54.	0.	0.	0.	0.	0.		481.
UTILITY	0.	0.	0.	0.	0.	0.	0.	0.		0.
INDUSTRIAL	17.	0.	0.	0.	0.	0.	0.	0.		17.
CANAL	0.	0.	0.	0.	0.	0.	0.	0.		0.
FOREIGN	0.	0.	0.	0.	0.	0.	0.	0.		0.
ALL OTHER	0.	0.	0.	0.	0.	0.	0.	0.	0.	0.
TOTAL BONDS	375.	507.	58.	1.	0.	0.	0.	0.	0.	1471.
STOCKS										
FINANCIAL	494.	58.	7.	0.	0.	0.	0.	0.		559.
RAILROAD	64.	71.	17.	0.	0.	0.	0.	0.		152.
UTILITY	20.	0.	0.	0.	0.	0.	0.	0.		20.
INDUSTRIAL	30.	0.	0.	0.	0.	0.	0.	0.		30.
CANAL	0.	69.	0.	0.	0.	0.	0.	0.		69.
ALL OTHER	0.	0.	0.	0.	0.	0.	0.	0.		0.
TOTAL STOCKS	608.	198.	25.	0.	0.	0.	0.	0.		831.
MORTGAGES										11660.
LOANS										1163.
PREMIUM NOTES										4675.
PREMIUMS DUE										303.
CASH										624.
OTHER ASSETS										422.
TOTAL ASSETS										21550.

TABLE A1 (CONTINUED)

ASSET CATEGORY	REGIONS									TOTAL
DATA OF 1857	1	2	3	4	5	6	7	8	9	
PREMIUM INCOME										5448.
TOTAL INCOME										6922.
REAL ESTATE										428.
BONDS										
UNITED STATES										591.
STATE, LOCAL	147.	264.	67.	0.	0.	0.	6.	0.		484.
RAILROAD	170.	178.	189.	0.	0.	0.	0.	0.		537.
UTILITY	0.	0.	0.	0.	0.	0.	0.	0.		0.
INDUSTRIAL	14.	0.	0.	0.	0.	0.	0.	0.		14.
CANAL	0.	15.	0.	0.	0.	0.	0.	0.		15.
FOREIGN									0.	0.
ALL OTHER	0.	0.	0.	0.	0.	0.	0.	0.	0.	0.
TOTAL BONDS	331.	457.	256.	0.	0.	0.	6.	0.	0.	1640.
STOCKS										
FINANCIAL	466.	102.	12.	0.	0.	0.	0.	0.		580.
RAILROAD	38.	65.	1.	0.	0.	0.	0.	0.		104.
UTILITY	16.	0.	0.	0.	21.	0.	0.	0.		37.
INDUSTRIAL	12.	0.	0.	0.	0.	0.	0.	0.		12.
CANAL	0.	54.	0.	0.	0.	0.	0.	0.		54.
ALL OTHER	0.	0.	0.	0.	0.	0.	0.	0.		0.
TOTAL STOCKS	532.	221.	13.	0.	21.	0.	0.	0.		787.
MORTGAGES										13413.
LOANS										1387.
PREMIUM NOTES										5487.
PREMIUMS DUE										377.
CASH										585.
OTHER ASSETS										570.
TOTAL ASSETS										24674.

TABLE A1 (CONTINUED)

ASSET CATEGORY	REGIONS 1	2	3	4	5	6	7	8	9	TOTAL
DATA OF 1858										
PREMIUM INCOME										7291.
TOTAL INCOME										8925.
REAL ESTATE										675.
BONDS										
UNITED STATES										630.
STATE, LOCAL	167.	366.	76.	0.	0.	0.	0.	0.		609.
RAILROAD	194.	211.	209.	0.	4.	0.	0.	0.		618.
UTILITY	0.	0.	0.	0.	0.	0.	0.	0.		0.
INDUSTRIAL	15.	0.	0.	0.	0.	0.	0.	0.		15.
CANAL	0.	17.	0.	0.	0.	0.	0.	0.		17.
FOREIGN									0.	0.
ALL OTHER	0.	0.	0.	0.	0.	0.	0.	0.	0.	0.
TOTAL BONDS	376.	593.	285.	0.	4.	0.	0.	0.	0.	1889.
STOCKS										
FINANCIAL	342.	131.	13.	0.	0.	0.	0.	0.		486.
RAILROAD	75.	73.	0.	0.	0.	0.	0.	0.		148.
UTILITY	23.	0.	0.	0.	0.	0.	0.	0.		23.
INDUSTRIAL	13.	0.	0.	0.	0.	0.	0.	0.		13.
CANAL	0.	26.	0.	0.	0.	0.	0.	0.		26.
ALL OTHER	0.	0.	0.	0.	0.	0.	0.	0.		0.
TOTAL STOCKS	452.	230.	13.	0.	0.	0.	0.	0.		695.
MORTGAGES										15741.
LOANS										1445.
PREMIUM NOTES										5371.
PREMIUMS DUE										252.
CASH										983.
OTHER ASSETS										577.
TOTAL ASSETS										27628.

TABLE A1 (CONTINUED)

ASSET CATEGORY DATA OF 1859	1	2	3	4	REGIONS 5	6	7	8	9	TOTAL
PREMIUM INCOME										6050.
TOTAL INCOME										7070.
REAL ESTATE										705.
BONDS										
UNITED STATES										681.
STATE, LOCAL	175.	496.	81.	0.	0.	0.	0.	0.		751.
RAILROAD	218.	228.	213.	0.	7.	0.	0.	0.		665.
UTILITY	0.	0.	0.	0.	0.	0.	0.	0.		0.
INDUSTRIAL	16.	0.	0.	0.	0.	0.	0.	0.		16.
CANAL	0.	17.	0.	0.	0.	0.	0.	0.		17.
FOREIGN									0.	0.
ALL OTHER	0.	0.	0.	0.	0.	0.	0.	0.	0.	0.
TOTAL BONDS	408.	741.	293.	0.	7.	0.	0.	0.	0.	2129.
STOCKS										
FINANCIAL	329.	80.	13.	0.	0.	0.	0.	0.		421.
RAILROAD	35.	83.	0.	0.	0.	0.	0.	0.		119.
UTILITY	26.	65.	0.	0.	0.	0.	0.	0.		91.
INDUSTRIAL	9.	5.	0.	0.	0.	0.	0.	0.		14.
CANAL	0.	26.	0.	0.	0.	0.	0.	0.		26.
ALL OTHER	0.	0.	0.	0.	0.	0.	0.	0.		0.
TOTAL STOCKS	399.	259.	13.	0.	0.	0.	0.	0.		672.
MORTGAGES										17318.
LOANS										1463.
PREMIUM NOTES										5879.
PREMIUMS DUE										253.
CASH										840.
OTHER ASSETS										649.
TOTAL ASSETS										29908.

TABLE A1 (CONTINUED)

ASSET CATEGORY	REGIONS									TOTAL
DATA OF 1860	1	2	3	4	5	6	7	8	9	
PREMIUM INCOME										7173.
TOTAL INCOME										8896.
REAL ESTATE										1087.
BONDS										
UNITED STATES										1134.
STATE, LOCAL	239.	518.	87.	0.	0.	0.	0.	0.		844.
RAILROAD	231.	239.	290.	0.	7.	0.	0.	0.		766.
UTILITY	0.	0.	0.	0.	0.	0.	0.	0.		0.
INDUSTRIAL	16.	0.	0.	0.	0.	0.	0.	0.		16.
CANAL	0.	17.	0.	0.	0.	0.	0.	0.		17.
FOREIGN	0.	0.	0.	0.	0.	0.	0.	0.	0.	0.
ALL OTHER	0.	0.	0.	0.	0.	0.	0.	0.	0.	0.
TOTAL BONDS	486.	774.	377.	0.	7.	0.	0.	0.	0.	2777.
STOCKS										
FINANCIAL	318.	97.	37.	0.	0.	0.	0.	0.		453.
RAILROAD	33.	87.	0.	0.	0.	0.	0.	0.		120.
UTILITY	29.	67.	0.	0.	0.	0.	0.	0.		96.
INDUSTRIAL	9.	0.	0.	0.	0.	0.	0.	0.		9.
CANAL	0.	25.	0.	0.	0.	0.	0.	0.		25.
ALL OTHER	0.	0.	0.	0.	0.	0.	0.	0.		0.
TOTAL STOCKS	390.	276.	37.	0.	0.	0.	0.	0.		704.
MORTGAGES										19887.
LOANS										1612.
PREMIUM NOTES										6893.
PREMIUMS DUE										657.
CASH										1258.
OTHER ASSETS										722.
TOTAL ASSETS										35597.

TABLE A1 (CONTINUED)

ASSET CATEGORY	REGIONS									TOTAL
DATA OF 1861	1	2	3	4	5	6	7	8	9	
PREMIUM INCOME										7323.
TOTAL INCOME										9295.
REAL ESTATE										1119.
BONDS										
UNITED STATES										3049.
STATE, LOCAL	257.	557.	99.	0.	0.	0.	0.	0.		913.
RAILROAD	251.	255.	312.	0.	7.	0.	0.	0.		825.
UTILITY	0.	0.	0.	0.	0.	0.	0.	0.		0.
INDUSTRIAL	17.	0.	0.	0.	0.	0.	0.	0.		17.
CANAL	0.	18.	0.	0.	0.	0.	0.	0.		18.
FOREIGN									0.	0.
ALL OTHER	0.	0.	0.	0.	0.	0.	0.	0.	0.	0.
TOTAL BONDS	525.	831.	411.	0.	7.	0.	0.	0.	0.	4823.
STOCKS										
FINANCIAL	311.	102.	40.	0.	0.	0.	0.	0.		452.
RAILROAD	35.	94.	0.	0.	0.	0.	0.	0.		129.
UTILITY	34.	71.	0.	0.	0.	0.	0.	0.		105.
INDUSTRIAL	10.	0.	0.	0.	0.	0.	0.	0.		10.
CANAL	0.	27.	0.	0.	0.	0.	0.	0.		27.
ALL OTHER	0.	0.	0.	0.	0.	0.	0.	0.		0.
TOTAL STOCKS	390.	294.	40.	0.	0.	0.	0.	0.		723.
MORTGAGES										20528.
LOANS										1713.
PREMIUM NOTES										7016.
PREMIUMS DUE										763.
CASH										1449.
OTHER ASSETS										919.
TOTAL ASSETS										39073.

TABLE A1 (CONTINUED)

ASSET CATEGORY	REGIONS									TOTAL
	1	2	3	4	5	6	7	8	9	
DATA OF 1862										
PREMIUM INCOME										6794.
TOTAL INCOME										8423.
REAL ESTATE										1124.
BONDS										
UNITED STATES										6826.
STATE, LOCAL	234.	1009.	72.	0.	3.	0.	0.	0.		1318.
RAILROAD	158.	175.	211.	0.	4.	0.	0.	0.		548.
UTILITY	0.	4.	0.	0.	0.	0.	0.	0.		4.
INDUSTRIAL	10.	0.	0.	0.	0.	0.	0.	0.		10.
CANAL	0.	11.	0.	0.	0.	0.	0.	0.		11.
FOREIGN	0.	0.	0.	0.	0.	0.	0.	0.	0.	0.
ALL OTHER	0.	0.	0.	0.	0.	0.	0.	0.	0.	0.
TOTAL BONDS	403.	1200.	282.	0.	7.	0.	0.	0.	0.	8719.
STOCKS										
FINANCIAL	182.	86.	24.	0.	0.	0.	0.	0.		292.
RAILROAD	26.	63.	0.	0.	0.	0.	0.	0.		89.
UTILITY	23.	6.	0.	0.	0.	0.	0.	0.		29.
INDUSTRIAL	8.	0.	0.	0.	0.	0.	0.	0.		8.
CANAL	0.	24.	0.	0.	0.	0.	0.	0.		24.
ALL OTHER	0.	0.	0.	0.	0.	0.	0.	0.		0.
TOTAL STOCKS	239.	178.	24.							442.
MORTGAGES										18637.
LOANS										1599.
PREMIUM NOTES										6751.
PREMIUMS DUE										755.
CASH										2338.
OTHER ASSETS										831.
TOTAL ASSETS										41194.

TABLE A1 (CONTINUED)

ASSET CATEGORY	REGIONS									TOTAL
	1	2	3	4	5	6	7	8	9	
DATA OF 1863										
PREMIUM INCOME										15379.
TOTAL INCOME										18023.
REAL ESTATE										1272.
BONDS										
UNITED STATES										14664.
STATE, LOCAL	596.	1250.	74.	4.	20.	0.	0.	0.		1945.
RAILROAD	195.	185.	219.	0.	4.	0.	0.	0.		603.
UTILITY	0.	4.	0.	0.	0.	0.	0.	0.		4.
INDUSTRIAL	11.	0.	0.	0.	0.	0.	0.	0.		11.
CANAL	0.	12.	0.	0.	0.	0.	0.	0.		12.
FOREIGN									0.	0.
ALL OTHER	0.	0.	0.	4.	0.	0.	0.	0.	0.	0.
TOTAL BONDS	802.	1451.	293.	4.	24.	0.	0.	0.	0.	17239.
STOCKS										
FINANCIAL	432.	98.	23.	1.	0.	22.	0.	0.		576.
RAILROAD	47.	262.	0.	0.	0.	0.	0.	0.		308.
UTILITY	23.	0.	0.	0.	0.	0.	0.	0.		23.
INDUSTRIAL	7.	0.	0.	0.	0.	0.	0.	0.		7.
CANAL	0.	36.	0.	0.	0.	0.	0.	0.		36.
ALL OTHER	0.	0.	0.	0.	0.	0.	0.	0.		0.
TOTAL STOCKS	509.	395.	23.	1.	0.	22.	0.	0.		951.
MORTGAGES										19987.
LOANS										1707.
PREMIUM NOTES										7780.
PREMIUMS DUE										1146.
CASH										2515.
OTHER ASSETS										988.
TOTAL ASSETS										53586.

TABLE A1 (CONTINUED)

ASSET CATEGORY	REGIONS 1	2	3	4	5	6	7	8	9	TOTAL
DATA OF 1864										
PREMIUM INCOME										17412.
TOTAL INCOME										20392.
REAL ESTATE										2301.
BONDS										
UNITED STATES										20705.
STATE, LOCAL	1093.	1553.	132.	5.	24.	23.	0.	22.		2852.
RAILROAD	229.	219.	255.	0.	6.	0.	0.	0.		709.
UTILITY	0.	6.	0.	0.	0.	0.	0.	0.		6.
INDUSTRIAL	12.	0.	0.	0.	0.	0.	0.	0.		12.
CANAL	0.	14.	0.	0.	0.	0.	0.	0.		14.
FOREIGN	0.	0.	0.	0.	0.	0.	0.	0.	0.	0.
ALL OTHER	0.	0.	0.	0.	0.	0.	0.	0.		0.
TOTAL BONDS	1335.	1791.	387.	5.	30.	23.	0.	22.	C.	24298.
STOCKS										
FINANCIAL	509.	113.	42.	0.	0.	31.	0.	0.		695.
RAILROAD	66.	0.	0.	0.	0.	0.	0.	0.		66.
UTILITY	46.	0.	0.	0.	0.	0.	0.	0.		46.
INDUSTRIAL	7.	0.	0.	0.	0.	0.	0.	0.		7.
CANAL	0.	51.	0.	0.	0.	0.	0.	0.		51.
ALL OTHER	0.	0.	0.	0.	0.	0.	0.	0.		0.
TOTAL STOCKS	628.	164.	42.	0.	0.	31.	0.	0.		865.
MORTGAGES										20618.
LOANS										1924.
PREMIUM NOTES										11619.
PREMIUMS DUE										2606.
CASH										2562.
OTHER ASSETS										1140.
TOTAL ASSETS										67933.

TABLE A1 (CONTINUED)

ASSET CATEGORY				REGIONS						
DATA OF 1865	1	2	3	4	5	6	7	8	9	TOTAL
PREMIUM INCOME										27366.
TOTAL INCOME										30964.
REAL ESTATE										2330.
BONDS										
UNITED STATES	1685.	3892.	219.	6.	31.	68.	0.	28.		20832.
STATE, LOCAL	285.	291.	313.	0.	10.	0.	0.	0.		5928.
RAILROAD	6.	8.	0.	0.	0.	0.	0.	0.		859.
UTILITY	15.	0.	0.	0.	0.	0.	0.	0.		8.
INDUSTRIAL	0.	16.	0.	0.	0.	0.	0.	0.		15.
CANAL	0.	0.	0.	0.	0.	0.	0.	0.		16.
FOREIGN									0.	0.
ALL OTHER	0.	0.	0.	0.	0.	0.	0.	0.		0.
TOTAL BONDS	1985.	4207.	531.	6.	41.	68.	0.	28.	0.	27659.
STOCKS										
FINANCIAL	774.	119.	79.	0.	0.	39.	0.	0.		1011.
RAILROAD	79.	0.	18.	0.	0.	0.	0.	0.		97.
UTILITY	55.	0.	0.	0.	0.	0.	0.	0.		55.
INDUSTRIAL	10.	0.	0.	0.	0.	0.	0.	0.		10.
CANAL	0.	75.	0.	0.	0.	0.	0.	0.		75.
ALL OTHER	0.	0.	0.	0.	0.	0.	0.	0.		0.
TOTAL STOCKS	918.	195.	97.	0.	0.	39.	0.	0.		1249.
MORTGAGES										20700.
LOANS										1980.
PREMIUM NOTES										17717.
PREMIUMS DUE										5780.
CASH										3428.
OTHER ASSETS										1310.
TOTAL ASSETS										82192.

TABLE A1 (CONTINUED)

ASSET CATEGORY	REGIONS									TOTAL
	1	2	3	4	5	6	7	8	9	
DATA OF 1866										
PREMIUM INCOME										46703.
TOTAL INCOME										49249.
REAL ESTATE										2934.
BONDS										
UNITED STATES										22479.
STATE, LOCAL	3220.	5117.	282.	101.	58.	83.	0.	147.		9007.
RAILROAD	301.	329.	323.	0.	13.	0.	0.	0.		965.
UTILITY	19.	8.	64.	0.	0.	0.	0.	0.		91.
INDUSTRIAL	15.	0.	0.	0.	0.	0.	0.	0.		15.
CANAL	0.	17.	0.	0.	0.	0.	0.	0.		17.
FOREIGN	0.	0.	0.	0.	0.	0.	0.	0.	0.	0.
ALL OTHER	0.	0.	0.	0.	0.	0.	0.	0.		0.
TOTAL BONDS	3555.	5470.	668.	101.	70.	83.	3.	147.	0.	32574.
STOCKS										
FINANCIAL	1523.	178.	90.	0.	0.	41.	0.	0.		1832.
RAILROAD	109.	0.	18.	0.	0.	0.	0.	0.		127.
UTILITY	104.	0.	0.	0.	0.	0.	0.	0.		104.
INDUSTRIAL	10.	0.	0.	0.	0.	0.	0.	0.		10.
CANAL	0.	77.	0.	0.	0.	0.	0.	0.		77.
ALL OTHER	0.	0.	0.	0.	0.	0.	0.	0.		0.
TOTAL STOCKS	1746.	255.	108.	0.	0.	41.	0.	0.		2149.
MORTGAGES										29512.
LOANS										2036.
PREMIUM NOTES										21367.
PREMIUMS DUE										9139.
CASH										5540.
OTHER ASSETS										2005.
TOTAL ASSETS										107257.

TABLE A1 (CONTINUED)

ASSET CATEGORY				REGIONS						
DATA OF 1867	1	2	3	4	5	6	7	8	9	TOTAL
PREMIUM INCOME										65914.
TOTAL INCOME										70241.
REAL ESTATE										4212.
BONDS										
UNITED STATES										24619.
STATE, LOCAL	3210.	5938.	549.	89.	78.	75.	0.	143.		10081.
RAILROAD	260.	369.	283.	0.	22.	130.	119.	76.		1258.
UTILITY	27.	6.	54.	0.	0.	0.	0.	0.		88.
INDUSTRIAL	13.	0.	0.	0.	0.	0.	0.	0.		13.
CANAL	0.	14.	0.	0.	0.	0.	0.	0.		14.
FOREIGN					0.				0.	0.
ALL OTHER	0.	0.	0.	0.	0.	0.	0.	0.	0.	0.
TOTAL BONDS	3510.	6327.	886.	89.	99.	204.	119.	218.	0.	36073.
STOCKS										
FINANCIAL	1635.	219.	55.	0.	0.	4.	0.	0.		1914.
RAILROAD	147.	92.	16.	0.	0.	0.	0.	0.		255.
UTILITY	116.	0.	54.	0.	0.	0.	0.	0.		170.
INDUSTRIAL	6.	0.	0.	0.	0.	0.	0.	0.		6.
CANAL	0.	66.	0.	0.	0.	0.	0.	0.		66.
ALL OTHER	0.	0.	0.	0.	0.	0.	0.	0.		0.
TOTAL STOCKS	1904.	377.	125.	0.	0.	4.	0.	0.		2411.
MORTGAGES										40502.
LOANS										2515.
PREMIUM NOTES										37212.
PREMIUMS DUE										12575.
CASH										5101.
OTHER ASSETS										4660.
TOTAL ASSETS										145261.

TABLE A1 (CONTINUED)

ASSET CATEGORY	1	2	3	4	REGIONS 5	6	7	8	9	TOTAL
DATA OF 1868										
PREMIUM INCOME										77057.
TOTAL INCOME										88964.
REAL ESTATE										5609.
BONDS										
UNITED STATES										26139.
STATE, LOCAL	3616.	7361.	614.	203.	195.	82.	0.	161.		12231.
RAILROAD	301.	411.	325.	0.	35.	146.	189.	143.		1550.
UTILITY	41.	7.	59.	0.	0.	0.	0.	0.		107.
INDUSTRIAL	14.	27.	0.	0.	0.	0.	0.	0.		41.
CANAL	0.	15.	0.	0.	0.	0.	0.	0.		15.
FOREIGN										0.
ALL OTHER	0.	0.	0.	0.	0.	0.	0.	0.	0.	0.
TOTAL BONDS	3973.	7821.	997.	203.	230.	229.	189.	304.	0.	40083.
STOCKS										
FINANCIAL	1849.	292.	88.	0.	0.	7.	0.	0.		2236.
RAILROAD	404.	250.	131.	0.	0.	0.	0.	0.		785.
UTILITY	202.	18.	132.	0.	0.	0.	0.	0.		352.
INDUSTRIAL	9.	9.	0.	0.	0.	0.	0.	0.		19.
CANAL	0.	36.	0.	0.	0.	0.	0.	0.		36.
ALL OTHER	0.	0.	0.	0.	0.	7.	0.	0.		0.
TOTAL STOCKS	2464.	605.	352.	0.	0.					3428.
MORTGAGES										67410.
LOANS										4402.
PREMIUM NOTES										51755.
PREMIUMS DUE										21291.
CASH										5374.
OTHER ASSETS										3937.
TOTAL ASSETS										203288.

TABLE A1 (CONTINUED)

ASSET CATEGORY	REGIONS									TOTAL
DATA OF 1869	1	2	3	4	5	6	7	8	9	
PREMIUM INCOME										91944.
TOTAL INCOME										105496.
REAL ESTATE										8823.
BONDS										
UNITED STATES										29116.
STATE, LOCAL	3830.	9862.	682.	252.	211.	92.	41.	162.		15131.
RAILROAD	322.	526.	344.	31.	46.	174.	196.	146.		1787.
UTILITY	50.	375.	154.	0.	0.	0.	0.	0.		579.
INDUSTRIAL	14.	28.	0.	0.	0.	23.	0.	0.		65.
CANAL	8.	630.	0.	0.	0.	0.	0.	0.		638.
FOREIGN									83.	83.
ALL OTHER	0.	0.	0.	0.	0.	0.	0.	0.		0.
TOTAL BONDS	4224.	11421.	1180.	283.	257.	289.	237.	308.	83.	47359.
STOCKS										
FINANCIAL	2233.	249.	72.	0.	0.	8.	0.	0.		2563.
RAILROAD	488.	278.	188.	13.	7.	46.	46.	0.		1067.
UTILITY	78.	0.	0.	0.	0.	0.	0.	0.		78.
INDUSTRIAL	6.	13.	0.	0.	0.	0.	0.	0.		19.
CANAL	0.	34.	0.	0.	0.	0.	0.	0.		34.
ALL OTHER	0.	0.	0.	0.	0.	0.	0.	0.		0.
TOTAL STOCKS	2805.	574.	260.	13.	7.	54.	46.	0.		3759.
MORTGAGES										97402.
LOANS										4591.
PREMIUM NOTES										54532.
PREMIUMS DUE										24431.
CASH										7428.
OTHER ASSETS										5699.
TOTAL ASSETS										254380.

TABLE A1 (CONTINUED)

ASSET CATEGORY	1	2	3	4	5	6	7	8	9	TOTAL
DATA OF 1870										
PREMIUM INCOME										102190.
TOTAL INCOME										117101.
REAL ESTATE										10302.
BONDS										
UNITED STATES										24086.
STATE, LOCAL	4020.	9732.	1621.	519.	322.	90.	48.	154.		16508.
RAILROAD	1214.	938.	412.	29.	53.	162.	196.	143.		3146.
UTILITY	12.	487.	174.	0.	0.	0.	0.	0.		786.
INDUSTRIAL	13.	31.	0.	0.	0.	22.	0.	0.		66.
CANAL	7.	622.	0.	0.	0.	0.	0.	0.		630.
FOREIGN									100.	100.
ALL OTHER	0.	0.	0.	0.	0.	0.	0.	0.	100.	0.
TOTAL BONDS	5379.	11811.	2207.	548.	376.	274.	244.	297.	100.	45321.
STOCKS										
FINANCIAL	2123.	201.	54.	0.	0.	7.	0.	0.		2386.
RAILROAD	593.	302.	182.	0.	0.	0.	0.	0.		1077.
UTILITY	70.	0.	0.	0.	0.	0.	0.	0.		70.
INDUSTRIAL	7.	10.	22.	0.	0.	0.	0.	0.		39.
CANAL	0.	31.	0.	0.	0.	0.	0.	0.		31.
ALL OTHER	0.	0.	0.	0.	0.	0.	0.	0.		0.
TOTAL STOCKS	2794.	544.	259.	0.	0.	7.	0.	0.		3603.
MORTGAGES										113205.
LOANS										5534.
PREMIUM NOTES										64044.
PREMIUMS DUE										24628.
CASH										11354.
OTHER ASSETS										5971.
TOTAL ASSETS										284063.

TABLE A1 (CONTINUED)

| | | | | REGIONS | | | | | | |
ASSET CATEGORY	1	2	3	4	5	6	7	8	9	TOTAL
DATA OF 1871										
PREMIUM INCOME										107261.
TOTAL INCOME										125567.
REAL ESTATE										12129.
BONDS										
UNITED STATES										24855.
STATE, LOCAL	12737.		1584.	733.	806.	172.	71.	142.		20634.
RAILROAD	1123.	882.	407.	57.	47.	145.	184.	199.		3043.
UTILITY	112.	395.	162.	0.	0.	20.	0.	0.		669.
INDUSTRIAL	11.	82.	47.	0.	0.	0.	0.	0.		161.
CANAL	7.	467.	3.	3.	0.	0.	0.	0.		479.
FOREIGN									164.	164.
ALL OTHER	0.	97.	0.	2.	0.	0.	0.	0.	164.	99.
TOTAL BONDS	5641.	14662.	2203.	794.	853.	337.	255.	340.	164.	50104.
STOCKS										
FINANCIAL	1943.	404.	66.	0.	0.	7.	0.	0.		2420.
RAILROAD	585.	265.	119.	44.	0.	0.	0.	0.		1014.
UTILITY	58.	0.	0.	0.	0.	0.	0.	0.		58.
INDUSTRIAL	8.	12.	6.	0.	0.	0.	0.	0.		26.
CANAL	0.	28.	0.	0.	0.	0.	0.	0.		28.
ALL OTHER	0.	0.	0.	0.	0.	0.	0.	0.		0.
TOTAL STOCKS	2594.	709.	191.	44.	0.	7.	0.	0.		3545.
MORTGAGES										149298.
LOANS										7778.
PREMIUM NOTES										69031.
PREMIUMS DUE										20228.
CASH										14353.
OTHER ASSETS										6339.
TOTAL ASSETS										332642.

TABLE A1 (CONTINUED)

| ASSET CATEGORY | REGIONS | | | | | | | | | TOTAL |
DATA OF 1872	1	2	3	4	5	6	7	8	9	
PREMIUM INCOME										106675.
TOTAL INCOME										128211.
REAL ESTATE										14659.
BONDS										
UNITED STATES										24196.
STATE. LOCAL	4766.	13245.	3215.	490.	685.	266.	136.	188.		22591.
RAILROAD	1179.	915.	459.	244.	47.	144.	192.	205.		3386.
UTILITY	140.	1957.	395.	0.	172.	0.	0.	0.		2663.
INDUSTRIAL	14.	158.	7.	0.	0.	20.	0.	0.		198.
CANAL	45.	379.	1.	2.	0.	0.	0.	0.		427.
FOREIGN									178.	178.
ALL OTHER	1.	115.	0.	2.	0.	3.	0.	0.		121.
TOTAL BONDS	6144.	16768.	4077.	738.	904.	433.	328.	393.	178.	54159.
STOCKS										
FINANCIAL	2060.	695.	64.	0.	0.	2.	0.	0.		2820.
RAILROAD	601.	226.	131.	0.	0.	0.	0.	0.		958.
UTILITY	52.	9.	0.	0.	0.	0.	0.	0.		52.
INDUSTRIAL	8.	0.	0.	0.	0.	0.	0.	0.		18.
CANAL	0.	27.	0.	0.	0.	0.	0.	0.		27.
ALL OTHER	0.	0.	0.	0.	0.	0.	0.	0.		0.
TOTAL STOCKS	2721.	957.	195.	0.	0.	2.	0.	0.		3875.
MORTGAGES										177430.
LOANS										7763.
PREMIUM NOTES										67971.
PREMIUMS DUE										17782.
CASH										14373.
OTHER ASSETS										7042.
TOTAL ASSETS										364876.

TABLE A1 (CONTINUED)

					REGIONS					
ASSET CATEGORY	1	2	3	4	5	6	7	8	9	TOTAL
DATA OF 1873										
PREMIUM INCOME										103803.
TOTAL INCOME										127805.
REAL ESTATE										15882.
BONDS										
UNITED STATES										22317.
STATE, LOCAL	4720.	13563.	3077.	487.	566.	290.	151.	257.		23113.
RAILROAD	1115.	889.	439.	224.	43.	138.	227.	206.		3279.
UTILITY	150.	2112.	720.	0.	157.	134.	47.	0.		3320.
INDUSTRIAL	21.	188.	6.	0.	0.	18.	0.	0.		232.
CANAL	0.	426.	1.	2.	0.	0.	0.	0.		428.
FOREIGN									162.	162.
ALL OTHER	1.	166.	0.	2.	0.	0.	0.	0.		169.
TOTAL BONDS	6006.	17344.	4243.	714.	766.	580.	425.	463.	162.	63019.
STOCKS										
FINANCIAL	2113.	1054.	47.	0.	0.	8.	0.	34.		3255.
RAILROAD	456.	158.	84.	0.	0.	0.	0.	0.		698.
UTILITY	49.	0.	0.	0.	0.	0.	0.	0.		49.
INDUSTRIAL	7.	9.	4.	0.	0.	0.	0.	0.		21.
CANAL	0.	63.	0.	0.	0.	0.	0.	0.		63.
ALL OTHER	0.	0.	0.	0.	0.	3.	0.	0.		3.
TOTAL STOCKS	2624.	1285.	135.	0.	0.	11.	0.	34.		4090.
MORTGAGES										197982.
LOANS										7468.
PREMIUM NOTES										61345.
PREMIUMS DUE										13930.
CASH										19847.
OTHER ASSETS										6433.
TOTAL ASSETS										379534.

TABLE A1 (CONTINUED)

ASSET CATEGORY
DATA OF 1874

ASSET CATEGORY	1	2	3	4	5	6	7	8	9	TOTAL
PREMIUM INCOME	21613.	48191.	21758.	656.	1824.	980.	1950.	1381.	2566.	100919.
TOTAL INCOME										131570.
REAL ESTATE	6863.	12176.	843.	78.	4.	1326.	31.	0.	263.	21583.
BONDS										
UNITED STATES										23535.
STATE, LOCAL	6298.	19377.	5600.	696.	877.	614.	311.	616.		34389.
RAILROAD	1483.	2807.	590.	299.	56.	184.	326.	271.		6016.
UTILITY	336.	818.	1010.	0.	206.	0.	0.	0.		2370.
INDUSTRIAL	133.	258.	288.	0.	0.	24.	62.	0.		765.
CANAL	0.	496.	1.	2.	0.	0.	0.	0.		500.
FOREIGN									347.	347.
ALL OTHER	0.	127.	0.	9.	0.	0.	0.	0.		136.
TOTAL BONDS	8251.	23884.	7488.	1006.	1139.	821.	699.	887.	347.	68059.
STOCKS										
FINANCIAL	2740.	1388.	1504.	3.	0.	12.	307.	0.		5954.
RAILROAD	668.	208.	98.	16.	0.	0.	0.	0.		989.
UTILITY	62.	0.	0.	0.	0.	0.	0.	0.		62.
INDUSTRIAL	8.	0.	17.	0.	0.	0.	0.	0.		25.
CANAL	0.	83.	0.	0.	0.	0.	0.	0.		83.
ALL OTHER	0.	0.	0.	0.	0.	11.	0.	0.		11.
TOTAL STOCKS	3478.	1679.	1619.	19.	0.	24.	307.	0.		7125.
MORTGAGES	28118.	132152.	34747.	61.	86.	3291.	24042.	73.	0.	222570.
LOANS										6631.
PREMIUM NOTES										59267.
PREMIUMS DUE										13255.
CASH										18978.
OTHER ASSETS										8797.
TOTAL ASSETS										425918.

TABLE A1 (CONTINUED)

ASSET CATEGORY				REGIONS						
DATA OF 1875	1	2	3	4	5	6	7	8	9	TOTAL
PREMIUM INCOME	19094.	41876.	19415.	699.	1786.	1009.	1924.	1454.	2239.	89497.
TOTAL INCOME										115232.
REAL ESTATE	6856.	14258.	2153.	86.	5.	1763.	47.	0.	254.	25423.
BONDS										
UNITED STATES										24800.
STATE, LOCAL	6260.	23975.	6279.	641.	853.	967.	258.	649.		39882.
RAILROAD	1425.	2781.	581.	289.	760.	192.	345.	279.		5968.
UTILITY	388.	730.	1114.	0.	198.	0.	0.	0.		2430.
INDUSTRIAL	105.	257.	16.	4.	0.	22.	54.	0.		459.
CANAL	0.	534.	0.	0.	0.	0.	0.	0.		534.
FOREIGN									317.	317.
ALL OTHER	0.	120.	0.	0.	0.	0.	0.	0.		120.
TOTAL BONDS	8179.	28398.	7989.	934.	1127.	1181.	657.	928.	317.	74510.
STOCKS										
FINANCIAL	2602.	1602.	41.	0.	0.	9.	0.	0.		4253.
RAILROAD	452.	157.	81.	0.	0.	0.	0.	0.		690.
UTILITY	66.	0.	0.	0.	0.	0.	0.	0.		66.
INDUSTRIAL	8.	0.	0.	0.	0.	0.	0.	0.		8.
CANAL	0.	84.	0.	0.	0.	0.	0.	0.		84.
ALL OTHER	0.	0.	0.	0.	0.	11.	0.	0.		11.
TOTAL STOCKS	3127.	1843.	122.	0.	0.	19.	0.	0.		5112.
MORTGAGES	29288.	136925.	39756.	56.	110.	3404.	24820.	73.	0.	234433.
LOANS										6252.
PREMIUM NOTES										54618.
PREMIUMS DUE										9559.
CASH										15594.
OTHER ASSETS										9202.
TOTAL ASSETS										434787.

TABLE A1 (CONTINUED)

ASSET CATEGORY

	1	2	3	4	5	6	7	8	9	TOTAL
DATA OF 1876				REGIONS						
PREMIUM INCOME	15471.	36099.	16515.	729.	1728.	1037.	1711.	1490.	1943.	76724.
TOTAL INCOME										102210.
REAL ESTATE	7869.	18112.	3566.	145.	10.	2402.	84.	0.	271.	32460.
BONDS										
UNITED STATES										32465.
STATE, LOCAL	7996.	24982.	6618.	497.	890.	1393.	193.	711.		43280.
RAILROAD	1494.	4082.	634.	299.	100.	287.	390.	294.	0.	7581.
UTILITY	398.	361.	359.	152.	204.	0.	0.	0.	0.	1473.
INDUSTRIAL	62.	347.	0.	0.	0.	0.	0.	0.	0.	409.
CANAL	0.	391.	0.	0.	0.	0.	0.	0.	0.	391.
FOREIGN	0.	0.	0.	0.	0.	0.	0.	0.	310.	310.
ALL OTHER	0.	118.	0.	0.	0.	0.	0.	0.	0.	118.
TOTAL BONDS	9951.	30281.	7611.	947.	1194.	1680.	583.	1005.	310.	86027.
STOCKS										
FINANCIAL	2857.	2036.	57.	0.	0.	10.	0.	0.	0.	4959.
RAILROAD	554.	232.	89.	0.	0.	0.	0.	0.	0.	875.
UTILITY	74.	0.	0.	0.	0.	0.	0.	0.	0.	74.
INDUSTRIAL	23.	0.	0.	0.	0.	0.	0.	0.	0.	23.
CANAL	0.	50.	0.	0.	0.	0.	0.	0.	0.	50.
ALL OTHER	0.	0.	0.	0.	0.	0.	0.	0.	0.	0.
TOTAL STOCKS	3507.	2317.	146.	0.	0.	10.	0.	0.	0.	5981.
MORTGAGES	29070.	135847.	42633.	50.	123.	3352.	22383.	73.	0.	233531.
LOANS										6666.
PREMIUM NOTES										42984.
PREMIUMS DUE										7473.
CASH										13635.
OTHER ASSETS										9553.
TOTAL ASSETS										438000.

TABLE A1 (CONTINUED)

ASSET CATEGORY	REGIONS									
DATA OF 1877	1	2	3	4	5	6	7	8	9	TOTAL
PREMIUM INCOME	11815.	32371.	15040.	815.	1855.	1113.	1632.	1625.	1714.	67980.
TOTAL INCOME										93400.
REAL ESTATE	6810.	19692.	5728.	220.	58.	2668.	252.	0.	258.	35687.
BONDS										
UNITED STATES										41814.
STATE, LOCAL	8234.	31162.	7665.	421.	1440.	2172.	163.	654.		51910.
RAILROAD	1437.	4282.	593.	280.	114.	373.	386.	282.	0.	7746.
UTILITY	1492.	166.	290.	0.	190.	0.	0.	0.	0.	2137.
INDUSTRIAL	26.	373.	0.	0.	0.	0.	0.	0.	0.	399.
CANAL	0.	336.	0.	0.	0.	0.	0.	0.	0.	336.
FOREIGN									207.	207.
ALL OTHER	0.	112.	0.	0.	0.	0.	0.	0.		112.
TOTAL BONDS	11188.	36430.	8548.	701.	1743.	2545.	548.	936.	207.	104661.
STOCKS										
FINANCIAL	2637.	1791.	25.	0.	0.	5.	0.	0.	0.	4458.
RAILROAD	607.	275.	153.	0.	0.	93.	12.	0.	0.	1141.
UTILITY	72.	0.	0.	0.	0.	0.	0.	0.	0.	72.
INDUSTRIAL	7.	0.	1.	0.	0.	0.	0.	0.	0.	8.
CANAL	0.	46.	0.	0.	0.	0.	0.	0.	0.	46.
ALL OTHER	0.	0.	0.	0.	0.	0.	0.	0.	0.	0.
TOTAL STOCKS	3323.	2111.	179.	0.	C.	98.	12.	0.	0.	5725.
MORTGAGES	27032.	118959.	51634.	35.	151.	3066.	21714.	67.	0.	222657.
LOANS										7286.
PREMIUM NOTES										37829.
PREMIUMS DUE										5194.
CASH										11246.
OTHER ASSETS										10100.
TOTAL ASSETS										439878.

TABLE A1 (CONTINUED)

ASSET CATEGORY DATA OF 1878	REGIONS 1	2	3	4	5	6	7	8	9	TOTAL
PREMIUM INCOME	10920.	28184.	12801.	847.	1712.	1121.	1489.	1636.	1588.	60300.
TOTAL INCOME										85007.
REAL ESTATE	7977.	26364.	10547.	701.	162.	4696.	486.	0.	285.	51218.
BONDS										
UNITED STATES										44471.
STATE, LOCAL	9405.	33688.	8162.	436.	895.	2448.	123.	685.		55842.
RAILROAD	1626.	6100.	872.	307.	121.	912.	456.	309.	0.	10702.
UTILITY	1257.	305.	308.	0.	201.	0.	0.	0.	0.	2070.
INDUSTRIAL	27.	255.	1.	0.	0.	0.	0.	0.	0.	284.
CANAL	0.	330.	0.	0.	0.	0.	0.	0.	0.	330.
FOREIGN	0.	0.	0.	0.	0.	0.	0.	0.	110.	110.
ALL OTHER	0.	118.	0.	0.	0.	0.	0.	0.	0.	118.
TOTAL BONDS	12315.	40797.	9344.	743.	1216.	3359.	578.	994.	110.	113926.
STOCKS										
FINANCIAL	2766.	1851.	62.	0.	0.	3.	0.	0.	0.	4683.
RAILROAD	672.	313.	129.	0.	0.	0.	0.	0.	0.	1114.
UTILITY	72.	0.	0.	0.	0.	0.	0.	0.	0.	72.
INDUSTRIAL	8.	0.	0.	0.	0.	0.	0.	0.	0.	8.
CANAL	0.	49.	0.	0.	0.	0.	0.	0.	0.	49.
ALL OTHER	0.	0.	0.	0.	0.	0.	0.	0.	0.	0.
TOTAL STOCKS	3518.	2213.	192.	0.	0.	3.	0.	0.	0.	5926.
MORTGAGES	23932.	102432.	51070.	20.	154.	2903.	23424.	60.	0.	203995.
LOANS										7317.
PREMIUM NOTES										34036.
PREMIUMS DUE										4556.
CASH										13494.
OTHER ASSETS										9184.
TOTAL ASSETS										443544.

TABLE A1 (CONTINUED)

ASSET CATEGORY	1	2	3	4	REGIONS 5	6	7	8	9	TOTAL
DATA OF 1879										
PREMIUM INCOME	9622.	26491.	12017.	920.	1667.	1237.	1536.	1905.	1504.	56901.
TOTAL INCOME										82197.
REAL ESTATE	7975.	27902.	13199.	649.	159.	4835.	499.	0.	512.	65731.
BONDS										
UNITED STATES										46752.
STATE, LOCAL	9649.	40114.	7994.	295.	747.	2588.	251.	654.		62292.
RAILROAD	1654.	5927.	1043.	300.	117.	977.	440.	309.		10766.
UTILITY	375.	295.	299.	0.	193.	26.	0.	0.		1189.
INDUSTRIAL	27.	127.	1.	0.	0.	0.	0.	0.		155.
CANAL	0.	323.	0.	0.	0.	0.	0.	0.		323.
FOREIGN									77.	77.
ALL OTHER	0.	166.	0.	0.	0.	0.	0.	0.		166.
TOTAL BONDS	11706.	46951.	9337.	596.	1057.	3592.	690.	962.	77.	121720.
STOCKS										
FINANCIAL	2634.	1882.	26.	0.	0.	3.	0.	0.		4546.
RAILROAD	804.	324.	159.	0.	0.	8.	0.	0.		1296.
UTILITY	72.	0.	0.	0.	0.	0.	0.	0.		72.
INDUSTRIAL	9.	0.	1.	0.	0.	0.	0.	0.		11.
CANAL	0.	51.	0.	0.	0.	0.	0.	0.		61.
ALL OTHER	0.	0.	0.	0.	0.	0.	0.	0.		0.
TOTAL STOCKS	3520.	2256.	187.	0.	0.	12.	0.	0.		5974.
MORTGAGES	17915.	90770.	58741.	17.	149.	3404.	21508.	53.	0.	192557.
LOANS										13869.
PREMIUM NOTES										29400.
PREMIUMS DUE										4400.
CASH										15203.
OTHER ASSETS										8366.
TOTAL ASSETS										447144.

TABLE A1 (CONTINUED)

ASSET CATEGORY DATA OF 1880	REGIONS									TOTAL
	1	2	3	4	5	6	7	8	9	
PREMIUM INCOME	9368.	25426.	11478.	1022.	1757.	1458.	1628.	2162.	1517.	55815.
TOTAL INCOME										81856.
REAL ESTATE	7216.	26622.	14311.	541.	141.	4499.	464.	0.	828.	54623.
BONDS										
UNITED STATES										40025.
STATE, LOCAL	10607.	38603.	9416.	234.	682.	4010.	272.	669.		64493.
RAILROAD	2617.	11895.	3047.	332.	164.	1179.	515.	328.		20077.
UTILITY	388.	314.	307.	84.	367.	242.	0.	0.		1702.
INDUSTRIAL	29.	102.	1.	0.	0.	0.	0.	0.		132.
CANAL	0.	1123.	0.	0.	0.	0.	0.	0.		1123.
FOREIGN	0.	0.	0.	0.	0.	0.	0.		87.	87.
ALL OTHER	0.	177.	0.	0.	0.	0.	0.	0.	87.	177.
TOTAL BONDS	13641.	52214.	12772.	650.	1213.	5431.	787.	997.	87.	127816.
STOCKS										
FINANCIAL	2519.	2387.	40.	31.	0.	6.	0.	0.		4982.
RAILROAD	843.	376.	284.	0.	0.	1.	1.	0.		1505.
UTILITY	77.	0.	0.	0.	0.	0.	0.	0.		77.
INDUSTRIAL	11.	0.	0.	0.	0.	0.	0.	0.		11.
CANAL	0.	152.	0.	0.	0.	0.	0.	0.		152.
ALL OTHER	0.	0.	0.	0.	0.	0.	0.	0.		0.
TOTAL STOCKS	3450.	2915.	323.	31.	0.	7.	1.	0.		6727.
MORTGAGES	15197.	83551.	55650.	12.	152.	3618.	20357.	45.	0.	178583.
LOANS										32336.
PREMIUM NOTES										28759.
PREMIUMS DUE										4551.
CASH										21902.
OTHER ASSETS										7082.
TOTAL ASSETS										462291.

TABLE A1 (CONTINUED)

ASSET CATEGORY	REGIONS									TOTAL
DATA OF 1881	1	2	3	4	5	6	7	8	9	
PREMIUM INCOME	9576.	27773.	13142.	1167.	1932.	1875.	1746.	2209.	1919.	61340.
TOTAL INCOME										86527.
REAL ESTATE	7004.	27157.	16060.	481.	134.	4469.	462.	0.	1076.	56843.
BONDS										
UNITED STATES										32050.
STATE, LOCAL	9743.	37933.	9446.	369.	766.	3529.	539.	667.		62992.
RAILROAD	3632.	19107.	5641.	489.	253.	2106.	1165.	330.		32725.
UTILITY	261.	372.	292.	0.	373.	469.	175.	0.		1942.
INDUSTRIAL	402.	211.	0.	0.	0.	133.	0.	0.		746.
CANAL	0.	1543.								1543.
FOREIGN									89.	89.
ALL OTHER	0.	179.	0.	0.	0.	0.	0.	0.		179.
TOTAL BONDS	14038.	59343.	15378.	858.	1392.	6237.	1880.	997.	89.	132265.
STOCKS										
FINANCIAL	2083.	3685.	37.	0.	0.	5.	0.	0.		5811.
RAILROAD	1076.	680.	298.	0.	0.	1.	81.	26.		2162.
UTILITY	75.	0.	0.	0.	0.	0.	0.	0.		75.
INDUSTRIAL	12.	0.	0.	0.	0.	0.	0.	0.		12.
CANAL	0.	178.	0.	0.	0.	0.	0.	0.		178.
ALL OTHER	0.	0.	0.	0.	0.	0.	0.	0.		0.
TOTAL STOCKS	3245.	4542.	336.	0.	0.	7.	81.	26.		8237.
MORTGAGES	13513.	87013.	53676.	8.	153.	4191.	19154.	39.	0.	177749.
LOANS										44351.
PREMIUM NOTES										26688.
PREMIUMS DUE										4876.
CASH										18585.
OTHER ASSETS										6629.
TOTAL ASSETS										476135.

TABLE A1 (CONTINUED)

ASSET CATEGORY
DATA OF 1882

	REGIONS									
	1	2	3	4	5	6	7	8	9	TOTAL
PREMIUM INCOME	9604.	28142.	13481.	1239.	1991.	2448.	1882.	2119.	2679.	63583.
TOTAL INCOME										89965.
REAL ESTATE	6722.	26688.	14817.	303.	116.	4169.	381.	0.	1225.	54419.
BONDS										
UNITED STATES										16109.
STATE, LOCAL	5930.	31371.	12024.	482.	866.	3338.	353.	636.		55001.
RAILROAD	5326.	22517.	9652.	1810.	351.	2677.	4185.	342.		46859.
UTILITY	185.	1012.	352.	0.	389.	673.	111.	23.		2745.
INDUSTRIAL	417.	263.	0.	0.	0.	138.	0.	0.		817.
CANAL	0.	1673.	0.	0.	0.	0.	0.	0.		1673.
FOREIGN	0.	0.	0.	0.	0.	0.	0.	0.	87.	87.
ALL OTHER	0.	186.	0.	0.	0.	0.	0.	0.		186.
TOTAL BONDS	11857.	57021.	22028.	2292.	1606.	6827.	4649.	1001.	87.	123476.
STOCKS										
FINANCIAL	2126.	4849.	15.	0.	0.	6.	0.	0.	0.	6995.
RAILROAD	1109.	935.	516.	0.	0.	1.	105.	60.	0.	2727.
UTILITY	79.	0.	0.	0.	0.	0.	0.	0.	0.	79.
INDUSTRIAL	12.	0.	0.	0.	0.	0.	0.	0.	0.	12.
CANAL	0.	187.	0.	0.	0.	0.	0.	0.	0.	187.
ALL OTHER	0.	0.	0.	0.	0.	0.	0.	0.	0.	0.
TOTAL STOCKS	3327.	5971.	531.	0.	0.	7.	105.	60.	0.	10000.
MORTGAGES	12825.	87507.	55886.	19.	210.	4560.	19517.	35.	0.	180659.
LOANS										62067.
PREMIUM NOTES										22911.
PREMIUMS DUE										5185.
CASH										15584.
OTHER ASSETS										5600.
TOTAL ASSETS										479715.

TABLE A1 (CONTINUED)

ASSET CATEGORY
DATA OF 1883

					REGIONS					
	1	2	3	4	5	6	7	8	9	TOTAL
PREMIUM INCOME	10819.	30756.	14837.	1441.	2462.	3303.	2172.	2357.	4276.	72424.
TOTAL INCOME										111886.
REAL ESTATE	7193.	29288.	15221.	149.	110.	4325.	340.	0.	1514.	58139.
BONDS										
UNITED STATES										14206.
STATE. LOCAL	6044.	25595.	10741.	655.	919.	2459.	832.	567.		47812.
RAILROAD	3853.	27837.	15408.	2012.	993.	3966.	6778.	1273.		62119.
UTILITY	477.	735.	660.	0.	294.	855.	442.	100.		3563.
INDUSTRIAL	11.	917.	56.	0.	0.	0.	0.	0.		984.
CANAL	0.	2907.	0.	0.	0.	0.	0.	0.		2907.
FOREIGN	0.	0.	0.	0.	0.	0.	0.	0.	100.	100.
ALL OTHER	0.	241.	0.	0.	0.	0.	0.	0.		241.
TOTAL BONDS	10384.	58231.	26864.	2667.	2226.	7279.	8053.	1941.	100.	131932.
STOCKS										
FINANCIAL	3565.	2148.	52.	0.	0.	7.	12.	0.		5784.
RAILROAD	907.	4196.	2460.	4.	3.	147.	846.	31.		8594.
UTILITY	62.	0.	0.	0.	0.	46.	56.	47.		211.
INDUSTRIAL	19.	0.	0.	0.	0.	0.	0.	0.		19.
CANAL	0.	748.	0.	0.	0.	0.	0.	0.		748.
ALL OTHER	0.	0.	0.	0.	0.	0.	0.	0.		0.
TOTAL STOCKS	4553.	7091.	2512.	4.	3.	199.	914.	78.		15355.
MORTGAGES	12778.	92538.	68371.	30.	340.	4830.	23688.	33.	0.	202607.
LOANS										48079.
PREMIUM NOTES										22478.
PREMIUMS DUE										6210.
CASH										17907.
OTHER ASSETS										6213.
TOTAL ASSETS										508822.

TABLE A1 (CONTINUED)

ASSET CATEGORY	REGIONS									TOTAL
	1	2	3	4	5	6	7	8	9	
DATA OF 1884										
PREMIUM INCOME	10457.	32327.	14968.	1511.	2817.	3778.	2267.	2188.	6509.	76622.
TOTAL INCOME					...					103329.
REAL ESTATE	7059.	30877.	14315.	235.	85.	4138.	328.	0.	2524.	59561.
BONDS										
UNITED STATES										12886.
STATE, LOCAL	6941.	25772.	8359.	902.	1084.	2770.	990.	610.		47429.
RAILROAD	4267.	30126.	26027.	2404.	1343.	3671.	8913.	1745.		78496.
UTILITY	596.	1058.	766.	0.	482.	1575.	968.	120.	0.	5565.
INDUSTRIAL	24.	1013.	60.	0.	0.	0.	0.	0.		1097.
CANAL	0.	2368.								2368.
FOREIGN									975.	975.
ALL OTHER	0.	233.	0.	0.	0.	0.	0.	0.		233.
TOTAL BONDS	11828.	60570.	35212.	3306.	2909.	8016.	10871.	2475.	975.	149048.
STOCKS										
FINANCIAL	3927.	2990.	13.	0.	0.	7.	61.	0.	0.	6999.
RAILROAD	1064.	4770.	3099.	5.	4.	183.	1711.	32.	0.	10868.
UTILITY	67.	0.	0.	0.	0.	61.	67.	78.	0.	273.
INDUSTRIAL	22.	0.	0.	0.	0.	0.	0.	0.	0.	22.
CANAL	0.	361.								361.
ALL OTHER	0.	0.	0.	0.	0.	0.	0.	0.	0.	0.
TOTAL STOCKS	5079.	8121.	3113.	5.	4.	252.	1839.	110.	0.	18522.
MORTGAGES	12273.	93251.	76169.	41.	452.	4708.	26534.	29.	0.	213458.
LOANS										35419.
PREMIUM NOTES										20349.
PREMIUMS DUE										6612.
CASH										21314.
OTHER ASSETS										6325.
TOTAL ASSETS										529634.

TABLE A1 (CONTINUED)

ASSET CATEGORY	REGIONS 1	2	3	4	5	6	7	8	9	TOTAL
DATA OF 1885										
PREMIUM INCOME	11242.	33361.	15876.	1804.	3365.	4504.	2606.	2377.	8800.	83935.
TOTAL INCOME										112365.
REAL ESTATE	7477.	34924.	14383.	341.	65.	4268.	342.	0.	3770.	65571.
BONDS										
UNITED STATES										16159.
STATE, LOCAL	6517.	22689.	7215.	459.	1343.	3032.	2056.	550.		43860.
RAILROAD	4023.	40133.	27361.	2813.	2891.	9891.	14810.	2164.		104085.
UTILITY	595.	1671.	2403.	0.	531.	1441.	1168.	359.		8169.
INDUSTRIAL	38.	1268.	54.	0.	0.	0.	0.	0.		1360.
CANAL	0.	1286.	0.	0.	0.	0.	0.	0.		1286.
FOREIGN	0.	0.	0.	0.	0.	0.	0.	0.	1374.	1374.
ALL OTHER	0.	164.	0.	0.	0.	0.	0.	0.		164.
TOTAL BONDS	11173.	67210.	37033.	3272.	4765.	14364.	18034.	3072.	1374.	176458.
STOCKS										
FINANCIAL	3579.	2750.	12.	0.	0.	7.	12.	0.		6359.
RAILROAD	2064.	5096.	3175.	4.	5.	189.	2055.	28.		12617.
UTILITY	64.	0.	0.	0.	0.	130.	130.	137.		461.
INDUSTRIAL	20.	0.	0.	0.	0.	0.	0.	0.		20.
CANAL	0.	0.	0.	0.	0.	0.	0.	0.		0.
ALL OTHER	0.	0.	0.	0.	0.	0.	0.	0.		0.
TOTAL STOCKS	5726.	7846.	3187.	4.	5.	325.	2197.	165.		19457.
MORTGAGES	12209.	93977.	81736.	67.	576.	5662.	27937.	26.	4.	222193.
LOANS										18581.
PREMIUM NOTES										21092.
PREMIUMS DUE										7372.
CASH										26790.
OTHER ASSETS										6225.
TOTAL ASSETS										562365.

TABLE A1 (CONTINUED)

ASSET CATEGORY

	1	2	3	4	REGIONS 5	6	7	8	9	TOTAL
DATA OF 1886										
PREMIUM INCOME	13190.	37464.	18045.	2093.	4108.	5947.	3160.	2648.	10469.	97124.
TOTAL INCOME										124171.
REAL ESTATE	7425.	37015.	13768.	78.	28.	4444.	441.	0.	5150.	68349.
BONDS										
UNITED STATES										14341.
STATE, LOCAL	6460.	16541.	8024.	382.	1813.	3071.	2771.	422.		39484.
RAILROAD	4084.	45209.	29635.	4765.	3491.	12990.	18548.	2527.		121249.
UTILITY	505.	1756.	2204.	771.	1470.	1283.	373.			8463.
INDUSTRIAL	46.	1299.	53.	0.	102.	0.	0.			1500.
CANAL	0.	1187.	0.	0.	0.	0.	0.			1187.
FOREIGN									3517.	3517.
ALL OTHER	0.	155.	0.	0.	0.	0.	0.			155.
TOTAL BONDS	11195.	66147.	39917.	5147.	6075.	17633.	22602.	3323.	3517.	189897.
STOCKS										
FINANCIAL	3517.	3405.	11.	0.	0.	64.	5.	0.		7002.
RAILROAD	2126.	5036.	3570.	5.	7.	2064.	469.	24.		13301.
UTILITY	63.	53.	62.	0.	53.	125.	182.	168.		707.
INDUSTRIAL	21.	0.	0.	0.	0.	0.	0.			21.
CANAL	0.	0.	0.	0.	0.	0.	0.			0.
ALL OTHER	0.	0.	0.	0.	0.	0.	0.			0.
TOTAL STOCKS	5727.	8494.	3642.	5.	61.	715.	2194.	191.		21031.
MORTGAGES	11471.	93824.	94939.	220.	680.	8743.	29121.	23.	6.	239027.
LOANS										23558.
PREMIUM NOTES										19805.
PREMIUMS DUE										8054.
CASH										22912.
OTHER ASSETS										6490.
TOTAL ASSETS										595608.

TABLE A1 (CONTINUED)

ASSET CATEGORY	1	2	3	4	5	6	7	8	9	TOTAL
DATA OF 1887				REGIONS						
PREMIUM INCOME	14318.	40272.	19943.	2295.	4495.	7024.	3650.	2978.	10520.	105496.
TOTAL INCOME										134591.
REAL ESTATE	7025.	37873.	11472.	52.	8.	4735.	558.	0.	6126.	67849.
BONDS										
UNITED STATES										12559.
STATE, LOCAL	6640.	15372.	8356.	565.	1901.	3486.	3689.	414.		40423.
RAILROAD	4269.	46788.	30751.	5437.	3568.	15602.	22196.	2672.		131282.
UTILITY	774.	1775.	2120.	4.	715.	1518.	1472.	356.	0.	8734.
INDUSTRIAL	124.	1302.	53.	0.	0.	102.	0.	0.	0.	1581.
CANAL	0.	1343.	0.							1343.
FOREIGN									4126.	4126.
ALL OTHER	0.	150.	0.	0.	0.	0.	0.	0.		150.
TOTAL BONDS	11806.	66730.	41280.	6007.	6183.	20708.	27357.	3442.	4126.	200198.
STOCKS										
FINANCIAL	3433.	3850.	11.	0.	0.	61.	5.	0.		7360.
RAILROAD	2429.	5139.	3657.	35.	7.	433.	2293.	22.		14016.
UTILITY	67.	71.	71.	0.	0.	197.	177.	177.		760.
INDUSTRIAL	38.	0.	0.	0.	0.	0.	0.	0.		38.
CANAL	0.	0.	0.	0.	0.	0.	0.	0.		0.
ALL OTHER	0.	0.	0.	0.	0.	0.	0.	0.		0.
TOTAL STOCKS	5967.	9060.	3739.	35.	7.	690.	2476.	200.		22174.
MORTGAGES	11373.	104952.	94578.	256.	854.	11141.	29799.	20.	10.	252984.
LOANS										33028.
PREMIUM NOTES										18814.
PREMIUMS DUE										9073.
CASH										25286.
OTHER ASSETS										6669.
TOTAL ASSETS										631949.

TABLE A1 (CONTINUED)

ASSET CATEGORY

					REGIONS					
	1	2	3	4	5	6	7	8	9	TOTAL
DATA OF 1888										
PREMIUM INCOME	16481.	45600.	21722.	2941.	5308.	8299.	4636.	4061.	14840.	123887.
TOTAL INCOME										161709.
REAL ESTATE	7057.	39799.	9362.	31.	3.	5554.	1993.	0.	7538.	71338.
BONDS										
UNITED STATES										
STATE, LOCAL	6544.	12299.	9628.	1776.	2054.	6163.	4900.	410.		11462.
RAILROAD	5953.	50131.	30170.	8888.	6100.	15604.	26793.	2922.		146562.
UTILITY	857.	1824.	1702.	26.	141.	1559.	1484.	441.		8034.
INDUSTRIAL	150.	1280.	52.	0.	0.	97.	0.	0.		1578.
CANAL	0.	981.	0.	0.	0.	0.	0.	0.		981.
FOREIGN	0.	0.	0.	0.	0.	0.	0.	0.	4334.	4334.
ALL OTHER	0.	143.	0.	0.	0.	0.	0.	0.		143.
TOTAL BONDS	13504.	66658.	41552.	10690.	8294.	23423.	33177.	3773.	4334.	216867.
STOCKS										
FINANCIAL	3381.	3853.	10.	1.	0.	60.	29.	0.		7334.
RAILROAD	2416.	5102.	3815.	413.	9.	564.	2261.	24.		14605.
UTILITY	69.	72.	63.	0.	0.	195.	196.	179.		775.
INDUSTRIAL	41.	0.	0.	0.	0.	0.	0.	0.		41.
CANAL	0.	0.	0.	0.	0.	0.	0.	0.		8.
ALL OTHER	0.	0.	0.	0.	0.	0.	0.	0.		0.
TOTAL STOCKS	5908.	9027.	3888.	414.	9.	820.	2495.	203.		22763.
MORTGAGES	9945.	118637.	82623.	353.	1052.	21907.	28843.	17.	12.	263588.
LOANS										32496.
PREMIUM NOTES										18587.
PREMIUMS DUE										12131.
CASH										30859.
OTHER ASSETS										7696.
TOTAL ASSETS										671592.

TABLE A1 (CONTINUED)

ASSET CATEGORY	REGIONS									TOTAL
	1	2	3	4	5	6	7	8	9	
DATA OF 1889										
PREMIUM INCOME	19382.	53837.	22867.	3160.	6227.	10339.	5836.	5005.	18099.	144753.
TOTAL INCOME										181562.
REAL ESTATE	7323.	43366.	9707.	83.	13.	6111.	3427.	10.	8651.	78691.
BONDS										
UNITED STATES										9180.
STATE, LOCAL	6808.	12373.	9784.	2791.	4396.	6332.	5290.	420.		48195.
RAILROAD	6239.	50952.	36251.	9723.	8950.	17093.	30672.	3283.		163163.
UTILITY	541.	1904.	1715.	46.	142.	2093.	2245.	1002.		9686.
INDUSTRIAL	174.	1431.	124.	0.	0.	98.	0.	0.		1827.
CANAL	16.	438.	0.	0.	0.	0.	0.	12.		465.
FOREIGN	0.	0.	0.	0.	0.	0.	0.	0.	5887.	5887.
ALL OTHER	0.	143.	0.	0.	0.	0.	0.	0.		143.
TOTAL BONDS	13778.	67240.	47873.	12560.	13488.	25616.	38207.	4717.	5887.	238546.
STOCKS										
FINANCIAL	3484.	5531.	16.	1.	0.	159.	38.	10.		9239.
RAILROAD	3019.	5919.	4634.	174.	20.	573.	2311.	25.		16675.
UTILITY	73.	126.	0.	0.	0.	254.	206.	192.		852.
INDUSTRIAL	44.	0.	0.	0.	0.	0.	0.	0.		44.
CANAL	0.	0.	0.	0.	0.	40.	0.	14.		54.
ALL OTHER	0.	0.	0.	0.	0.	0.	0.	0.		0.
TOTAL STOCKS	6620.	11576.	4649.	175.	20.	1026.	2555.	241.		26863.
MORTGAGES	11306.	127168.	91491.	417.	1418.	25596.	30728.	234.	61.	288420.
LOANS										36968.
PREMIUM NOTES										19577.
PREMIUMS DUE										12389.
CASH										34792.
OTHER ASSETS										7501.
TOTAL ASSETS										737860.

TABLE A1 (CONTINUED)

ASSET CATEGORY

DATA OF 1890

	REGIONS									TOTAL
	1	2	3	4	5	6	7	8	9	
PREMIUM INCOME	20708.	59542.	27880.	3565.	7291.	12338.	6923.	5314.	21118.	164680.
TOTAL INCOME										204728.
REAL ESTATE	7467.	45528.	8250.	107.	2.	6162.	4466.	706.	12211.	84899.
BONDS										
UNITED STATES										6501.
STATE, LOCAL	6911.	11684.	12337.	2376.	5111.	6805.	6520.	655.		52398.
RAILROAD	6503.	51317.	37036.	9638.	6744.	18978.	34574.	3688.		168476.
UTILITY	491.	1903.	1613.	26.	93.	2091.	2272.	1103.		9592.
INDUSTRIAL	141.	1463.	123.	0.	26.	10.	159.	0.		1923.
CANAL	0.	421.	0.	0.	0.	0.	0.	11.		433.
FOREIGN	0.	0.	0.	0.	0.	0.	0.	0.	12621.	12621.
ALL OTHER	0.	139.	0.	0.	0.	0.	0.	0.		139.
TOTAL BONDS	14046.	66927.	51108.	12040.	11974.	27884.	43525.	5457.	12621.	252082.
STOCKS										
FINANCIAL	3490.	6167.	16.	1.	0.	405.	167.	27.		10272.
RAILROAD	3007.	5926.	4679.	168.	342.	666.	3898.	33.		18720.
UTILITY	105.	306.	0.	0.	0.	362.	373.	327.		1472.
INDUSTRIAL	46.	0.	0.	0.	0.	0.	0.	0.		46.
CANAL	0.	0.	0.	0.	0.	39.	13.	0.		53.
ALL OTHER	0.	0.	0.	0.	0.	0.	0.	0.		0.
TOTAL STOCKS	6647.	12399.	4694.	169.	342.	1472.	4452.	387.		30563.
MORTGAGES	12284.	140124.	101771.	530.	1871.	31079.	39364.	869.	131.	328022.
LOANS										39257.
PREMIUM NOTES										20345.
PREMIUMS DUE										13345.
CASH										32999.
OTHER ASSETS										7435.
TOTAL ASSETS										796326.

TABLE A1 (CONTINUED)

ASSET CATEGORY	REGIONS									TOTAL
	1	2	3	4	5	6	7	8	9	
DATA OF 1891										
PREMIUM INCOME	22495.	62537.	31186.	4678.	8089.	12919.	7858.	5972.	23254.	178989.
TOTAL INCOME										219385.
REAL ESTATE	8104.	50431.	7774.	169.	1.	6820.	4349.	719.	10511.	88879.
BONDS										
UNITED STATES										6721.
STATE, LOCAL	7276.	12608.	14897.	2274.	5658.	7793.	7074.	745.		58325.
RAILROAD	6999.	58128.	41773.	7599.	8288.	22868.	39115.	6696.		191464.
UTILITY	369.	3121.	1028.	27.	86.	2261.	2467.	1179.		10539.
INDUSTRIAL	157.	2365.	183.	0.	27.	12.	27.	16.		2786.
CANAL	0.	0.	0.	0.	0.	0.	0.	12.		12.
FOREIGN	0.	0.	0.	0.	0.	0.	0.	0.	16457.	16457.
ALL OTHER	0.	873.	0.	0.	0.	0.	0.	0.		873.
TOTAL BONDS	14801.	77095.	57880.	9900.	14059.	32934.	48682.	8648.	16457.	287178.
STOCKS										
FINANCIAL	3676.	8590.	16.	2.	0.	514.	49.	56.		12903.
RAILROAD	3170.	7502.	4951.	109.	367.	1478.	4141.	44.		21762.
UTILITY	126.	932.	0.	0.	0.	383.	351.	351.		2144.
INDUSTRIAL	27.	0.	0.	0.	0.	9.	0.	15.		51.
CANAL	0.	0.	0.	0.	0.	0.	0.	0.		0.
ALL OTHER	0.	0.	0.	0.	0.	0.	0.	0.		0.
TOTAL STOCKS	6999.	17024.	4967.	111.	367.	2385.	4540.	467.		36860.
MORTGAGES	12458.	140879.	104363.	631.	2184.	31722.	47215.	2030.	325.	341807.
LOANS										49171.
PREMIUM NOTES										20444.
PREMIUMS DUE										15225.
CASH										35273.
OTHER ASSETS										7340.
TOTAL ASSETS										865720.

TABLE A1 (CONTINUED)

| ASSET CATEGORY | REGIONS | | | | | | | | | |
DATA OF 1892	1	2	3	4	5	6	7	8	9	TOTAL
PREMIUM INCOME	23575.	65892.	33089.	5388.	8375.	14408.	8655.	6280.	24650.	190311.
TOTAL INCOME										234420.
REAL ESTATE	8235.	60911.	7016.	324.	1.	7094.	4719.	706.	11961.	100967.
BONDS										
UNITED STATES										6840.
STATE, LOCAL	7710.	14039.	16074.	2371.	6256.	8231.	8748.	4348.		67778.
RAILROAD	10461.	67514.	49054.	9407.	10407.	23719.	41794.	7355.		219710.
UTILITY	527.	4598.	1256.	32.	120.	2534.	3121.	1594.		13783.
INDUSTRIAL	177.	2436.	206.		28.		12.	26.		2886.
CANAL	0.	0.	0.	0.	0.	0.	0.	12.		12.
FOREIGN									19731.	19731.
ALL OTHER	0.	985.								985.
TOTAL BONDS	18875.	89573.	66590.	11810.	16810.	34495.	53664.	13335.	19731.	331724.
STOCKS										
FINANCIAL	3726.	12637.	61.	2.	0.	444.	87.	34.		16991.
RAILROAD	3591.	7696.	6619.	248.	391.	2096.	4393.	45.		25078.
UTILITY	129.	992.	0.	0.	0.	393.	391.	377.		2282.
INDUSTRIAL	11.	0.	0.	0.	0.	0.	0.	0.		11.
CANAL	0.	0.	0.	0.	0.	0.	0.	0.		0.
ALL OTHER	0.	0.	0.	0.	0.	0.	0.	0.		0.
TOTAL STOCKS	7457.	21324.	6679.	250.	391.	2933.	4871.	456.		44362.
MORTGAGES	12277.	146910.	103439.	718.	3021.	31322.	53780.	3077.	499.	355042.
LOANS										45256.
PREMIUM NOTES										23628.
PREMIUMS DUE										18228.
CASH										42807.
OTHER ASSETS										7981.
TOTAL ASSETS										950266.

TABLE A1 (CONTINUED)

ASSET CATEGORY

DATA OF 1893	1	2	3	4	REGIONS 5	6	7	8	9	TOTAL
PREMIUM INCOME	25484.	71338.	36429.	6253.	9553.	15690.	9358.	6762.	26107.	206575.
TOTAL INCOME										253069.
REAL ESTATE	8878.	66910.	7563.	385.	1.	8408.	5447.	862.	13780.	112234.
BONDS										
UNITED STATES										7957.
STATE, LOCAL	7407.	15743.	15803.	3970.	6324.	9250.	9152.	4677.		72327.
RAILROAD	10390.	78375.	48747.	9201.	11006.	23534.	40624.	7124.		229002.
UTILITY	630.	4467.	1283.	26.	203.	2571.	3094.	1570.		13843.
INDUSTRIAL	170.	2748.	235.	12.	26.	13.	0.	29.		3232.
CANAL	0.	0.	0.	0.	0.	11.	0.	12.		22.
FOREIGN									20225.	20225.
ALL OTHER	183.	1833.	71.	0.	0.	0.	0.	0.		2086.
TOTAL BONDS	18781.	103165.	66139.	13209.	17560.	35377.	52871.	13411.	20225.	348696.
STOCKS										
FINANCIAL	3588.	14408.	328.	2.	0.	504.	84.	575.		19489.
RAILROAD	3188.	9238.	6998.	396.	392.	1532.	7189.	51.		28984.
UTILITY	194.	1022.	0.	0.	0.	778.	783.	785.		3563.
INDUSTRIAL	10.	0.	0.	26.	0.	0.	0.	0.		36.
CANAL	0.	0.	0.	0.	0.	8.	0.	15.		23.
ALL OTHER	0.	0.	0.	0.	0.	0.	0.	0.		0.
TOTAL STOCKS	6980.	24668.	7326.	425.	392.	2822.	8055.	1426.		52095.
MORTGAGES	14545.	150107.	110684.	1103.	3325.	43752.	58585.	3515.	837.	386452.
LOANS										34636.
PREMIUM NOTES										27198.
PREMIUMS DUE										21940.
CASH										45617.
OTHER ASSETS										10089.
TOTAL ASSETS										1018732.

TABLE A1 (CONTINUED)

ASSET CATEGORY DATA OF 1894	1	2	3	4	REGIONS 5	6	7	8	9	TOTAL
PREMIUM INCOME	26265.	75500.	37526.	6883.	10251.	16056.	9354.	6503.	27825.	216164.
TOTAL INCOME										269621.
REAL ESTATE	9055.	73542.	7112.	410.	82.	9491.	5951.	760.	16103.	122606.
BONDS										
UNITED STATES										15849.
STATE, LOCAL	11616.	17798.	16768.	4227.	7410.	9737.	9645.	7326.		84526.
RAILROAD	12616.	80029.	53969.	10144.	11435.	24238.	50405.	7313.		250150.
UTILITY	777.	4917.	1436.	188.	295.	2680.	3173.	1692.		15156.
INDUSTRIAL	187.	3750.	334.	12.	27.	14.	100.	37.		4461.
CANAL	0.	0.	0.	0.	0.	0.	0.	12.		12.
FOREIGN								21178.		21178.
ALL OTHER	193.	4962.	140.	0.	54.	11.	87.	0.		5448.
TOTAL BONDS	25388.	111456.	72647.	14570.	19221.	36680.	63411.	16379.	21178.	396779.
STOCKS										
FINANCIAL	3668.	14917.	336.	2.	0.	313.	67.	38.		19340.
RAILROAD	4232.	10822.	8553.	440.	747.	1137.	5768.	475.		32174.
UTILITY	247.	1167.	3.	0.	0.	721.	713.	713.		3564.
INDUSTRIAL	10.	16.	268.	0.	0.	14.	0.	0.		293.
CANAL	0.	0.	0.	0.	0.	0.	0.	0.		0.
ALL OTHER	0.	0.	0.	0.	0.	0.	0.	0.		0.
TOTAL STOCKS	8157.	26923.	9159.	442.	747.	2171.	6548.	1225.		55372.
MORTGAGES	15096.	153976.	116455.	1418.	3283.	48118.	60888.	3811.	817.	403862.
LOANS										40399.
PREMIUM NOTES										29972.
PREMIUMS DUE										21680.
CASH										52155.
OTHER ASSETS										10412.
TOTAL ASSETS										1111959.

TABLE A1 (CONTINUED)

ASSET CATEGORY	REGIONS									TOTAL
	1	2	3	4	5	6	7	8	9	
DATA OF 1895										
PREMIUM INCOME	27861.	79423.	39714.	7812.	10910.	16375.	9487.	6664.	28811.	227056.
TOTAL INCOME										278952.
REAL ESTATE	8825.	75566.	6580.	391.	302.	10538.	9125.	917.	15814.	128058.
BONDS										
UNITED STATES										17036.
STATE, LOCAL	12838.	25038.	18370.	4651.	8875.	10087.	10789.	7306.		97954.
RAILROAD	16752.	80842.	65331.	13953.	16436.	26639.	53303.	8344.		281599.
UTILITY	1112.	6764.	3242.	260.	377.	2947.	3339.	1824.		19865.
INDUSTRIAL	260.	5336.	418.	12.	27.	14.	19.	55.		6141.
CANAL	0.	0.	0.	1.	0.	0.	0.	12.		13.
FOREIGN									25579.	25579.
ALL OTHER	112.	6790.	140.	0.	0.	12.	65.	0.		7118.
TOTAL BONDS	31074.	124769.	87501.	18877.	25715.	39698.	67515.	17540.	25579.	455305.
STOCKS										
FINANCIAL	3658.	17802.	334.	2.	0.	309.	56.	34.		22196.
RAILROAD	5437.	11104.	8561.	672.	746.	1215.	5137.	506.		33379.
UTILITY	334.	1176.	6.	0.	0.	716.	612.	612.		3457.
INDUSTRIAL	29.	17.	288.	0.	0.	0.	0.	0.		334.
CANAL	0.	0.	0.	0.	0.	0.	0.	0.		0.
ALL OTHER	0.	0.	0.	0.	0.	0.	0.	0.		0.
TOTAL STOCKS	9459.	30100.	9190.	674.	746.	2240.	5805.	1153.		59367.
MORTGAGES	17441.	158408.	122764.	1770.	3693.	47164.	60284.	4524.	982.	417030.
LOANS										41726.
PREMIUM NOTES										34564.
PREMIUMS DUE										21806.
CASH										51265.
OTHER ASSETS										12517.
TOTAL ASSETS										1196060.

TABLE A1 (CONTINUED)

ASSET CATEGORY	1	2	3	4	5	6	7	8	9	TOTAL
DATA OF 1896										
PREMIUM INCOME	28237.	83727.	40653.	8816.	11446.	16089.	9391.	6868.	28317.	233545.
TOTAL INCOME										294816.
REAL ESTATE	9537.	82702.	6950.	383.	320.	11721.	9615.	1452.	17004.	139684.
BONDS										
UNITED STATES										21644.
STATE, LOCAL	12595.	24395.	16764.	4065.	9605.	12660.	9544.	7220.		96848.
RAILROAD	18738.	81873.	70650.	14049.	16882.	26782.	55641.	9096.		293710.
UTILITY	1687.	7996.	3944.	264.	369.	3025.	3396.	1858.		22538.
INDUSTRIAL	299.	5498.	409.	64.	26.	18.	0.	61.		6374.
CANAL	0.	0.	0.	0.	0.	0.	0.	10.		10.
FOREIGN									25827.	25827.
ALL OTHER	98.	7065.	138.	0.	0.	22.	52.	372.		7747.
TOTAL BONDS	33417.	126826.	91905.	18442.	26682.	42506.	68634.	18616.	25827.	474699.
STOCKS										
FINANCIAL	3650.	19174.	2016.	2.	0.	312.	47.	69.		25270.
RAILROAD	5322.	11012.	8418.	706.	772.	1308.	3542.	566.		31645.
UTILITY	361.	1202.	6.	0.	0.	246.	194.	245.		2256.
INDUSTRIAL	51.	88.	277.	0.	0.	0.	0.	9.		425.
CANAL	0.	0.	0.	0.	0.	0.	0.	0.		0.
ALL OTHER	0.	0.	0.	0.	0.	0.	0.	0.		0.
TOTAL STOCKS	9385.	31476.	10717.	708.	772.	1866.	3783.	890.		59597.
MORTGAGES	18070.	170500.	129315.	2221.	4268.	46680.	70510.	4776.	1261.	449601.
LOANS										50099.
PREMIUM NOTES										43651.
PREMIUMS DUE										23929.
CASH										50595.
OTHER ASSETS										13940.
TOTAL ASSETS										1279969.

REGIONS

TABLE A1 (CONTINUED)

ASSET CATEGORY	1	2	3	4	5	6	7	8	9	TOTAL
DATA OF 1897										
PREMIUM INCOME	30381.	96784.	42743.	9499.	12087.	16684.	9671.	7110.	30073.	255032.
TOTAL INCOME										320027.
REAL ESTATE	8986.	80396.	6674.	480.	445.	15171.	11554.	1813.	16549.	142069.
BONDS										
UNITED STATES										14797.
STATE, LOCAL	14797.	26227.	17276.	4193.	10744.	11837.	9444.	7027.		101545.
RAILROAD	23424.	96023.	74128.	17661.	19419.	43120.	62119.	10320.		346212.
UTILITY	2194.	9326.	4495.	277.	411.	3748.	3617.	2028.		26096.
INDUSTRIAL	1409.	5761.	520.	76.	27.	55.	56.	162.		8010.
CANAL	0.	0.	0.	0.	0.	0.	0.	9.		9.
FOREIGN									30796.	30796.
ALL OTHER	24.	7991.	145.	0.	0.	350.	0.	355.		8514.
TOTAL BONDS	41848.	145327.	96563.	22206.	30600.	58759.	75180.	19901.	30796.	535978.
STOCKS										
FINANCIAL	4092.	22095.	2071.	2.	0.	350.	51.	76.		28736.
RAILROAD	5897.	11656.	8720.	732.	813.	1659.	3901.	813.		34191.
UTILITY	483.	1389.	13.	0.	0.	225.	151.	195.		2457.
INDUSTRIAL	53.	91.	291.	0.	0.	0.	0.	12.		447.
CANAL	0.	0.	0.	0.	0.	0.	0.	0.		0.
ALL OTHER	0.	0.	0.	0.	0.	0.	0.	0.		0.
TOTAL STOCKS	10525.	35232.	11094.	734.	813.	2234.	4103.	1095.		65831.
MORTGAGES	17817.	173013.	131949.	3024.	5125.	48245.	69725.	5621.	1576.	456095.
LOANS										93720.
PREMIUM NOTES										14196.
PREMIUMS DUE										24016.
CASH										71174.
OTHER ASSETS										13683.
TOTAL ASSETS										1385968.

TABLE A1 (CONTINUED)

ASSET CATEGORY	REGIONS									TOTAL
DATA OF 1898	1	2	3	4	5	6	7	8	9	
PREMIUM INCOME	31248.	59404.	45495.	11099.	12894.	16997.	10505.	7481.	30488.	265611.
TOTAL INCOME										336990.
REAL ESTATE	9049.	83599.	8134.	735.	430.	15707.	13942.	2141.	17246.	160984.
BONDS										
UNITED STATES										13322.
STATE, LOCAL	15487.	23026.	16017.	4078.	9058.	10778.	9297.	6703.		94445.
RAILROAD	23363.	114990.	84997.	21651.	19814.	55912.	80176.	20070.		420973.
UTILITY	3156.	9355.	5328.	315.	409.	3749.	3682.	0.	185.	28023.
INDUSTRIAL	1825.	6989.	960.	118.	27.	55.	0.	0.	5.	10158.
CANAL	0.	0.	0.	0.	0.	0.	0.	0.	5.	5.
FOREIGN									32906.	32906.
ALL OTHER	128.	8051.	222.	0.	0.	0.	0.	215.	32906.	8616.
TOTAL BONDS	43959.	162410.	107525.	26162.	29308.	70493.	93165.	29217.	32906.	608458.
STOCKS										
FINANCIAL	4015.	23449.	2078.	2.	0.	302.	44.	80.		29970.
RAILROAD	8555.	19004.	8714.	846.	811.	1713.	5206.	809.		45657.
UTILITY	486.	1477.	516.	0.	0.	190.	85.	84.		2837.
INDUSTRIAL	58.	91.	333.	0.	0.	0.	0.	19.		502.
CANAL	0.	0.	0.	0.	0.	0.	0.	0.		0.
ALL OTHER	0.	0.	0.	0.	0.	0.	0.	0.		0.
TOTAL STOCKS	13113.	44020.	11641.	848.	811.	2205.	5335.	992.		78966.
MORTGAGES	18758.	178941.	129209.	3685.	6584.	61958.	70875.	5566.	1840.	467416.
LOANS										103792.
PREMIUM NOTES										14522.
PREMIUMS DUE										26415.
CASH										77672.
OTHER ASSETS										14175.
TOTAL ASSETS										1509495.

TABLE A1 (CONTINUED)

ASSET CATEGORY
DATA OF 1899

	__				REGIONS					
	1	2	3	4	5	6	7	8	9	TOTAL
PREMIUM INCOME	33766.	109324.	51680.	12482.	14647.	19266.	12378.	9084.	32533.	295161.
TOTAL INCOME										371380.

	1	2	3	4	5	6	7	8	9	TOTAL
REAL ESTATE	9307.	85214.	8495.	728.	394.	15345.	16646.	2330.	17593.	156052.
BONDS										
UNITED STATES										8558.
STATE, LOCAL	19487.	17550.	15851.	4165.	7273.	9407.	7306.	6769.		87810.
RAILROAD	24543.	133627.	104031.	26876.	21681.	65558.	84184.	30362.		510862.
UTILITY	3288.	13704.	5549.	372.	356.	3947.	3848.	2614.		33677.
INDUSTRIAL	1888.	7304.	1728.	171.	28.	55.	0.	200.		11374.
CANAL	0.	11.	0.	0.	0.	0.	0.	9.		20.
FOREIGN									49965.	49965.
ALL OTHER	267.	8452.	306.	0.	7.	0.	0.	220.	49965.	9281.
TOTAL BONDS	49474.	180648.	127465.	31584.	29344.	98968.	95338.	40175.	49965.	711517.
STOCKS										
FINANCIAL	4520.	26534.	2142.	2.	0.	264.	41.	100.		33603.
RAILROAD	10193.	20320.	9827.	912.	896.	1794.	5588.	836.		50365.
UTILITY	872.	1614.	456.	0.	11.	150.	94.	145.		3341.
INDUSTRIAL	117.	95.	354.	0.	0.	1.	0.	20.		588.
CANAL	0.	0.	0.	0.	0.	0.	0.	0.		0.
ALL OTHER	0.	0.	0.	0.	0.	0.	0.	0.		0.
TOTAL STOCKS	15702.	48563.	12780.	914.	907.	2208.	5723.	1101.		87898.
MORTGAGES	21339.	179337.	130449.	3690.	7265.	52936.	70734.	5033.	1802.	472585.
LOANS										129334.
PREMIUM NOTES										15231.
PREMIUMS DUE										28868.
CASH										74156.
OTHER ASSETS										16076.
TOTAL ASSETS										1641755.

TABLE A1 (CONTINUED)

ASSET CATEGORY	REGIONS									TOTAL
DATA OF 1900	1	2	3	4	5	6	7	8	9	
PREMIUM INCOME	37955.	124511.	58775.	14528.	16947.	21099.	13776.	10448.	37940.	335979.
TOTAL INCOME										416431.
REAL ESTATE	9209.	88558.	8321.	531.	247.	15425.	16934.	2448.	17863.	159537.
BONDS										
UNITED STATES										7460.
STATE, LOCAL	22336.	19039.	15441.	4088.	6309.	10727.	7496.	6413.		91850.
RAILROAD	28025.	156665.	119454.	33900.	28299.	96846.	94299.	33399.		590886.
UTILITY	3681.	18223.	6246.	415.	296.	4388.	4239.	2893.		40381.
INDUSTRIAL	2143.	8173.	2079.	254.	30.	62.	1.	264.		13006.
CANAL	0.	24.	0.	0.	0.	0.	0.	10.		34.
FOREIGN									76615.	76615.
ALL OTHER	324.	9407.	339.	0.	7.	2.	0.	239.		10318.
TOTAL BONDS	56509.	211530.	143559.	38656.	34942.	112024.	106034.	43218.	76615.	830550.
STOCKS										
FINANCIAL	4971.	29495.	2333.	2.	0.	288.	19.	120.		37228.
RAILROAD	11379.	24175.	10823.	1000.	1073.	2029.	6194.	915.		57589.
UTILITY	1544.	1885.	506.	0.	12.	395.	345.	423.		5111.
INDUSTRIAL	514.	220.	399.	0.	0.	0.	0.	24.		1157.
CANAL	0.	0.	0.	0.	0.	0.	0.	0.		0.
ALL OTHER	0.	0.	0.	0.	0.	0.	0.	0.		0.
TOTAL STOCKS	18408.	55776.	14060.	1003.	1085.	2713.	6558.	1483.		101086.
MORTGAGES	22815.	171679.	145828.	4311.	9714.	59177.	81588.	5270.	1890.	502272.
LOANS										147637.
PREMIUM NOTES										16566.
PREMIUMS DUE										33261.
CASH										77528.
OTHER ASSETS										17837.
TOTAL ASSETS										1809659.

APPENDIX B

ENUMERATION OF COMPANIES

APPENDIX B

ENUMERATION OF COMPANIES

This appendix contains a complete list of all companies
for which data is included in this study. These are the
"legal-reserve" and "industrial" companies of the industry
or companies that have been authorized to handle either of
these lines of insurance at any time prior to 1901. Also
included in the list, but not in the data, are some companies
for which some information is known, but not sufficient to
warrant inclusion, and some companies which have appeared in
various reports as having transacted business of the designated
type but which have not, in fact, done so.

Appearing with the names of the companies are: the date
and state of incorporation, the years of asset and income
data included in the study, the years of mortgage and real
estate data for which regional breakdowns were achieved, and
comments upon other key items in the companies history. The
comments include such information as: previous names, date
and method of termination of business (if it occurred before
1901), amalgamations, capital at incorporation and other
items.

Appendix Table B1. Enumeration of Companies Included in the Study.

Company	Incor- porated	Assets, Income	Mort- gages	Real Estate	Comments
Acacia Mutual Life Insurance Company	1869 D.C.				
Aetna Life Insurance Company	1853 Conn.	1851- 1900	1874- 1900	1874- 1900	Incoporations: Aetna Fire, 1820; Annuity, 1850; Life, 1853.
Alabama Gold Insurance Company	1868 Ala.	1869- 1888			Failed, 1888
Alabama Mutual Life Insurance Company	Ala.				Failed, 1868
Alliance Mutual Life Assurance Company of the United States	1873 Kan.	1873- 1876			Retired, 1877 (Captial, $100,000)
American Central Life Insurance Company	1899 Ind.	1899- 1900			
American Life and Accident Insurance Company	La.				Reinsured in Life In- surance Co. of Virginia, 1896

Appendix Table B1. (Continued).

Company	Incor-porated	Assets, Income	Mort-gages	Real Estate	Comments
American Life Insurance and Trust Company	1834 Md.				Retired, 1840
American Life Insurance Company	1850 Pa.	1850-1889			Failed, 1889. Also called American Life and Health early (Capital, $500,000)
American Mutual Life Insurance Company	1847 Conn.	851-1872			Reinsured in American Life and Trust Co., 1873
American National Life and Trust Company	1866 Conn.	1867-1874			Failed, 1875 (Capital, $100,000)
American Popular Life Insurance Company	1866 N.Y.	1866-1875			Failed, 1877 (Capital, $284,500)
American Temperance Life Insurance Company	1851 Conn.	1851-1900	1874-1900	1874-1900	Renamed Phoenix Mutual Life Insurance Company
American Tontine Life and Savings Insurance Company	1868 N.Y.	1868 1870			Reinsured in Empire Mutual Life Insurance Co. (N.Y.). 1871
American Union Life Insurance Company	1894 N.Y.	1894-1900			
Amicable Mutual Life Insurance Company	1869 N.Y.	1869-1871			Reinsured in Guardian Life Insurance Co., 1872 (Capital, $130,000)

Appendix Table B1. (Continued)

Company	Incor-porated	Assets, Income	Mort-gages	Real Estate	Comments
Anchor Life Insurance Company	1866 N.J.	1867-1871			Failed, 1872 (Capital, $130,000)
Asbury Life Insurance Company	1868 N.J.	1868-1873			Failed, 1873 (Capital, $180,000)
Atlantic Mutual Life Insurance Company	1895 Mass.	1896-1900			
Atlantic Mutual Life Insurance Company	1866 N.Y.	1866-1876			Failed, 1877 (Capital, $110,000)
Atlas Insurance Company	Nd.				Reinsured in Fidelity Mutual Life Insurance Company, 1893 (Capital, $100,000)
Atlas Mutual Life Insurance Company	Md.				Reinsured in St. Louis Mutual Life Insurance Company, 1872
Baltimore Fire Insurance Company	1787 Md.				Withdrew, 1791
Baltimore Life Insurance Company	1830 Md.				Reinsured in Equitable Life Assurance Society, 1877

Appendix Table Bl. (Continued)

Company	Incor-porated	Assets, Income	Mort-gages	Real Estate	Comments
Baltimore Life Insurance Company	1900 Md.	1900			1900 is a re-incorpora-tion as a legal reserve company; (1883, Md).
Baltimore Mutual Aid Society	1882 Md.	1882-1899			
Bankers Life Insurance Company	1887 Neb.	1887-1900			
Bankers Life Insurance Company of the City of N.Y.	1869 N.Y.	1897-1900			Reopened in 1897, after being inactive
Ben Franklin Life Insurance Company	1870 N.Y.	1870			Reinsured after first yr. in United States Life (N.Y.), 1870
Berkshire Life Insurance Company	1851 Mass.	1852-1900		1874-1900	
Boston Mutual Life Insurance Company	1892 Mass.	1899-1900			Believed to have operated as an assessment company before 1899
Brooklyn Life Insurance Company	1864 N.Y.	1864-1900	1874-1900		
California Mutual Life Insurance Company	1867 Cal.	1868-1871			Reinsured in Republic Life Insurance Company, 1872

Appendix Table B1. (Continued)

Company	Incorporated	Assets, Income	Mortgages	Real Estate	Comments
Carolina Life Insurance Company					Reinsured in Southern Life Insurance Co. (Tenn.), 1873
Centennial Mutual Life Association	1876 Ia.				Not included; Iowa report lists as an assessment company only
Central Life and Accident Insurance Company	1865 N.Y.	1866-1868			Reinsured in New York Life Insurance Co, 1869
Central Life Assurance Society of the United States	1896 Ia.	1896-1900			
Central Life Insurance Company	1895 Mo.	1896-1899			
Charter Oak Life Insurance Company	1850 Conn.	1850-1885	1874-1885	1874-1885	Failed, 1886 (Capital, $200,000)
Chicago Life Insurance Company	1895 Ia.	1900			
Chicago Life Insurance Company	1867 Ill.	1868-1876		.	Failed, 1877

Appendix Table B1. (Continued).

Company	Incor-porated	Assets, Income	Mort-gages	Real Estate	Comments
Chicago Mutual Life Insurance Company	1861 Ill.				Reinsured in Union Mutual Life Insurance Company, 1884
Chicago Mutual Life Insurance Company	1892 Ill.				
Cincinnati Mutual Life Insurance Company					Reinsured in Union Central Life Insurance Co, 1871
Citizens Life Insurance Company	1900 Cal.	1900			
Citizens Mutual Life Insurance Company	1900 Conn.	1900			
Citizens Mutual Life Insurance Company of N.J.	1870 N.J.	1892-1899			Retired, 1900
Colonial Life Insurance Company of America	1897 N.J.	1898-1900			
Columbia Life Insurance Company	1892 R.I.	1892			Reinsured in Commercial Alliance Life Insurance Company, 1893

Appendix Table B1. (Continued).

Company	Incorporated	Assets, Income	Mortgages	Real Estate	Comments
Columbia Mutual Life Assurance Company	Mo.				Failed, 1876 (Capital, $100,000)
Commercial Alliance Life Insurance Company	1888 N.Y.	1889-1893			Failed, 1894 (Called Commercial Union Life during first year). (Capital, $200,000)
Commercial Life Insurance and Casualty Company	1900 Ga.				
Commonwealth Life Insurance Company	1868 N.Y.	1869-1873			Reinsured in New Jersey Mutual Life Insurance Company, 1873
Connecticut General Life Insurance Company	1865 Conn.	1865-1900	1874-1900	1874-1900	
Connecticut Mutual Life Insurance Company	1846 Conn.	1847-1900	1874-1900	1874-1900	
Conservative Life Insurance Company	1900 Cal.	1900			
Continental Life Insurance Company	1862 Conn.	1864-1886	1874-1886	1874-1886	Failed, 1887 (Capital, $300,000)

Appendix Table B1. (Continued).

Company	Incor-porated	Assets, Income	Mort-gages	Real Estate	Comments
Continental Life Insurance Company	1866 N.Y.	1866-1875		1874-1875	Failed, 1876 (Capital, $100,000)
Cotton States Life Insurance Company	1868 Ga.	1869-1884			Retired, 1888 (Became inactive in 1885)
Covenant Mutaul Life Insurance Company	1853 Mo.	1868-1898			Reinsured in Metropolitan Life Insurance Company, 1900 (Capital, $100,000)
Craftsman Life Assurance Company	1868 N.Y.	1868-1871			Reinsured in Hope Mutual Life Insurance Company, 1872 (Capital, $200,000)
Crescent Mutual Life Insurance Company	1849 La.				Failed, 1850
Delaware Mutual Life Insurance Company	1867 Del.	1867-1872			Reinsured in National Life Insurance Company of U.S.A., 1873
Des Moines Life Insurance Company	1885 Ia.				
DeSoto Life Insurance Company	Mo.				Reinsured in Republic Life Insurance Co., 1871
Diamond State Insurance Company	Del.				

Appendix Table B1. (Continued).

Company	Incor-porated	Assets, Income	Mort-gages	Real Estate	Comments
Dutchess County Fire, Marine and Life Insurance Company	1814 N.Y.				Withdrew, 1818
Eagle Life and Health Insurance Company	1847 N.J.	1848-1852			Reinsured in Knickerbocker Life Insurance Company, 1853
Eagle Life Insurance Company	Ill.				Reinsured in Great Western Life Insurance Company (Ill.), 1869
Eastern Mutual Life Insurance Company	1896 N.J.	1896			Retired, 1897
Eclectic Life Insurance Company	1868 N.Y.	1868-1872			Failed, 1873 (also called First National Eclectic Life) (Capital, $150,000)
Economical Mutual Life Insurance Company	1866 R.I.	1866-1872			Reinsured in Republis Life Insurance Company, 1873 (Capital, $100,000)
Economic Insurance Company of America	1898 Del.	1899			
Empire Mutual Life Insurance Company	1869 N.Y.	1869-1871			Reinsured in Continental Life Insurance Company, 1872 (Capital, $100,000)

Appendix Table B1. (Continued).

Company	Incorporated	Assets, Income	Mortgages	Real Estate	Comments
Empire Mutual Life Insurance Company	Ill.				Reinsured in International Life Insurance Company, 1869
Empire State Life Insurance Company	1869 N.Y.	1869–1872			Reinsured in Life Association of America 1872 (Capital, $100,000)
Episcopal Corporation	1769 Mass.				Insurance of Episcopal Ministers, no public business
Equality Life Insurance Company	Va.				Retired, 1889
Equitable Life and Trust Company	1841 Pa.				Reinsured in Aetna, 1852 (also called National Safety)
Equitable Life Assurance Society of the United States	1859 N.Y.	1859–1900	1874–1900	1874–1900	
Equitable Life Insurance Company	1885 D.C.				
Equitable Life Insurance Company	1867 Ia.	1868–1900			
Equity Life Insurance Company of Virginia	1888 Va.				Failed, 1889

Appendix Table Bl. (Continued).

Company	Incor-porated	Assets, Income	Mort-gages	Real Estate	Comments
Excelsior Life Insurance Company	1867 N.Y.	1867-1872			Reinsured in National Life Insurance Company of U.S.A., 1873 (Capital, $125,000)
Farmers and Mechanics Life Insurance Company	1869 N.Y.	1869-1870			Failed, 1871 (Capital, $100,000)
Farmers Life and Trust Company	1822 N.Y.				Retired, 1843
Federal Life Insurance Company	1899 Ill.	1900			
Fidelity Mutual Life Insurance Company	1878 Pa.	1879-1900		1879-1900	
Franklin Life Insurance Company	1884 Ill.	1884-1900			
Franklin Life Insurance Company	1866 Ind.	1867-1881			Retired, 1882
General Life and Accident Mutual Life Insurance Company	1865 N.J.				Failed, 1869

Appendix Table B1. (Continued).

Company	Incor-porated	Assets, Income	Mort-gages	Real Estate	Comments
Georgia Mutual Life Insurance Company					Reinsured in Cotton States Life Insurance Company
Germania Life Insurance Company	1860 N.Y.	1860-1900	1874-1900	1874-1900	
German Mutual Life Insurance Company	1853 Mo.	1858-1900	1874-1900		
Girard Life Insurance and Annuity Company	1836 Pa.	1843-1899			Reinsured in Equitable Life, 1900 (also other similar names)
Globe Life Insurance and Trust Company	1837 Pa.				Failed, 1857
Globe Mutual Life Insurance Company	1864 N.Y.	1864-1878			Failed, 1879 (Capital, $100,000)
Government Security Life Insurance Company	1870 N.Y.	1870-1873			Reinsured in North America Life Insurance Company (N.Y.), 1874 (Capital, $100,000)
Grangers Life and Health Insurance Company	1874 Ala.				

Appendix Table B1. (Continued).

Company	Incorporated	Assets, Income	Mortgages	Real Estate	Comments
Great Western Life Insurance Company	Ill.				Reinsured in Republic Life Insurance Company, 1869
Great Western Mutual Life Insurance Company	1865 N.Y.	1866–1870			Failed, 1870 (Capital, $100,000)
Greenborough Mutual Life Insurance Company	1853 N.C.				Failed, 1865
Guardian Life Insurance Company	1859 N.Y.	1859–1873			Failed, 1873 (Capital, $100,000)
Hahneman Life Insurance Company	1865 O.	1860–1871			Reinsured in Republic Life Insurance Company, 1872 (Capital, $200,000)
Hand-In-Hand Mutual Life Insurance Company	1867 Pa.	1868–1874			Failed, 1874
Hand-In-Hand Mutual Insurance Company	1858 N.H.	1859–1863			Failed, 1864
Hartford Life Insurance Company	1866 Conn.	1867–1900	1874–1900	1874–1900	Also called Hartford Life Insurance and Annuity Company

Appendix Table B1. (Continued).

Company	Incorporated	Assets, Income	Mortgages	Real Estate	Comments
Hartford Life in Health Insurance Company	1848 Conn.	1848–1854			Retired, 1855
Hercules Mutual Life Assurance Society of the United States	1869 N.Y.	1869–1872			Failed, 1873 (Capital, $150,000)
Home Life Insurance Company	1860 N.Y.	1860–1900	1874–1900	1874–1900	
Home Life Insurance Company of America	1899 Del.	1899–1900			
Home Life Insurance Company	Ut.				Retired, 1892
Home Life Mutual Life Insurance Company	O.				Failed, 1871
Homeopathic Mutual Life Insurance Company	1868 N.Y.	1868–1885	1874–1885	1874–1885	Failed, 1888 (became inactive in 1887)
Homestead Bank and Loan Company	1868 Pa.	1868–1879			Failed, 1880
Homestead Building and Loan Company	Ind.				Retired, 1890

Appendix Table Bl. (Continued).

Company	Incorporated	Assets, Income	Mortgages	Real Estate	Comments
Homestead Life Insurance Company	O.				Failed, 1880 (Capital, $100,000)
Hope Mutual Life Insurance Company	1846 Conn.	1846–1852			Failed, 1853
Hope Mutual Life Insurance Company	1869 N.Y.	1869–1871			Reinsured in New Jersey Mutual Life Insurance Company, 1872 (Capital, $215,500)
Howard Life Insurance Company	1852 N.Y.	1852–1855			Reinsured in United States Life Insurance Company, 1856
Illinois Life Insurance Company	1899 Ill.	1899–1900			
Immediate Benefit Life Insurance Company	1897 Md.	1897–1900			
Imperial Life Insurance Company	1886	1886–			Reinsured in National Life and Trust (Conn.), 1892 (Capital, $118,000)
Indiana Life Insurance Company	1899 Ind.				Consolidated with American Central Life (Ind.), 1899 (Capital, $100,000)

Appendix Table B1. (Continued).

Company	Incor-porated	Assets, Income	Mort-gages	Real Estate	Comments
Industrial Life and Accident Company	Md.				Retired, 1888
Industrial Life Insurance Company	Ala.				Retired, 1888
Industrial Mutual Life Insurance Company	Minn.				Retired, 1894
Insurance Company of North America	1794 Pa.				Withdrew, 1798 (estab-lished in 1772)
Insurance Company of the State of Pennsylvania	1794 Pa				Withdrew, 1798
International Life and Trust Company	1868 N.J.	1869-1871			Reinsured in United States Life Insurance Company, 1872 (Capital, $166,000)
International Life Insurance Company	1868 Ill.	1869-1872			Reinsured in Universal Life Insurance Company, 1873
Inter-State Life Insurance Company	1899 Ill.	1899-1900			
Iowa Life Insurance Company	1893 Ia.	1893-1899			Consolidated with National Life of U.S.A. (see Life Indemnity, also (Capital, $100,000)

Appendix Table B1. (Continued).

Company	Incorporated	Assets, Income	Mortgages	Real Estate	Comments
Iowa Mutual Life Insurance Company	1884 Ia.	1886-1888			Retired, 1889
Iron City Mutual Life Insurance Company	1869 Pa.	1869-1874			Retired, 1875
Jefferson Life Insurance Company	1850 O.				Reinsured in Ohio Life and Trust Company, 1857
John Hancock Mutual Life Insurance Company	1862 Mass.	1863-1900	1874-1900	1874-1900	
Kansas City Life Insurance Company	1895 Mo.				
Kansas Mutual Life Insurance Company	1882 Kan.	1891-1900			Assessment business only before 1891
Kentucky Mutual Life Insurance Company	1850 Ky.	1850-1866			Failed, 1867 (located in Covington)
Kentucky Mutual Life Insurance Company	1855 Ky.				Failed, 1856 (located in Louisville)
Keystone Mutual Life Insurance Company	1850 Pa.				Failed, 1870
Knickerbocker Life Insurance Company	1853 N.Y.	1859-1881			Failed, 1882 (Capital, $100,000)

Appendix Table B1. (Continued).

Company	Incorporated	Assets, Income	Mortgages	Real Estate	Comments
Laboringmans Life Insurance Company					Failed, 1870 (located in Kewanee)
Lawrenceberg Insurance Company	1832 Ind.				Retired, 1836
Life Association of America	1868 Mo.	1869-1877			Failed, 1878
Life Indemnity and Investment Company	1881 Ia.	1886-1892			Name changed to Iowa Life Insurance Company, 1893
Life Insurance Clearing Company	1891 Minn.	1892-1897			Reinsured in Security Trust and Life Insurance Company, 1899 (Capital, $100,000)
Life Insurance Company of Virginia	1871 Va.	1879-1900			
Lincoln Life Insurance Company	1869 Ill.				Withdrew, 1869
Louisiana Equitable Life Insurance Company	1869 La.				Retired, 1881 (known to have done no business since 1878)
Manhattan Life Insurance Company	1850 N.Y.	1850-1900	1874-1900	1874-1900	

Appendix Table B1. (Continued).

Company	Incor-porated	Assets, Income	Mort-gages	Real Estate	Comments
Maryland Life Insurance Company	1864 Md.	1866-1900			
Massachusetts Hospital Life Insurance Company	1818 Mass.	1843-1872			Withdrew, 1878 (Had been nearly inactive for several years)
Massachusetts Mutual Life Insurance Company	1851 Mass.	1852-1900	1874-1900	1874-1900	
Masonic Orphans Home					Reinsured in Nashville Life Insurance Company, 1869
Merchants and Planters Insurance Company	La.				Failed, 1854
Merchants Life Insurance Company	1870 N.Y.	1870-1874			Reinsured in Globe Mutual Life Insurance Company, 1875
Meridian Life Insurance Company	1897 Ind.	1898-1900			
Metropolitan Life Insurance Company	1866 N.Y.	1867-1900		1874-1900	
Michigan Mutual Life Insurance Company	1867 Mich.	1868-1900	1874-1900	1874-1900	

Appendix Table B1. (Continued).

Company	Incor-porated	Assets, Income	Mort-gages	Real Estate	Comments
Miners Life Insurance and Trust Company	1862 Pa.				Known to be retired by 1873
Minnesota Mutual Life Insurance Company	1870 Minn.	1873			Reinsured in Northeastern Mutual Life Insurance Company, 1875
Mississippi Insurance Company	1833 Miss.				Retired, 1837
Mississippi Valley Insurance Company	1866 Ky.	1866-1871			Reinsured in St. Louis Mutual Life Insurance Company, 1872
Missouri Life and Trust Company	1837 Mo.				Retired, 1841
Missouri Mutual Life Insurance Company	1837 Mo.				Withdrew, 1840
Missouri Mutual Life Insurance Company	1867 Mo.	1867-1873			Reinsured in Mound City Life Insurance Company, 1874.
Missouri State Life Insurance Company	1892 Mo.				
Missouri Valley Life Insurance Company	1867 Kan.	1867-1880			Retired, 1880 (Capital, $100,000)

Appendix Table B1. (Continued).

Company	Incor- porated	Assets, Income	Mort- gages	Real Estate	Comments
Mobile Life Insurance Company	1871 Ala.	1872- 1888			Failed, 1889
Morris County Life and Fire Insurance Company	1849 N.J.				Withdrew, 1852
Mount City Life Insurance Company	1868 Mo.	1868- 1872			Name changed to St. Louis Life Insurance Company, 1873
Mutual Benefit Life Insurance Company	1849 La.				Failed, 1873
Mutual Benefit Life Insurance Company	1845 N.J.	1845- 1900	1874- 1900	1874- 1900	
Mutual Life and Accident Insurance Company	Pa.				Failed, 1876
Mutual Life and Trust Company	1900 Ia.	1900			
Mutual Life Insurance Company of Baltimore	1870 Md.	1871- 1900			
Mutual Life Insurance Company	1865 Ill.	1866- 1875			Failed, 1876
Mutual Life Insurance Company	1882 Ind.	1882- 1896			Reinsured, 1897

Appendix Tabel Bl. (Continued)

Company	Incor-porated	Assets, Income	Mort-gages	Real Estate	Comments
Mutual Life Insurance Company	1872 Pa.	1873			Failed, 1873
Mutual of Baltimore Life Insurance Company	1845 Md.				Reinsured in Mutual Life Insurance Co. of Baltimore, 1857
Mutual Life Insurance Company of Kentucky	1890 Ky.	1890-1900			Called Southern Mutual Life Insurance Co. before 1890 (Capital, $100,000)
Mutual Life Insurance Company of New York	1842 N.Y.	1843-1900		1874-1900	
Mutual Protection Life Assurance Company	1868 N.Y.	1868-1870			Name changed to Reserve Life Insurance Co., 1871 (Capital, $100,000)
Mutual Protection Life Insurance Company	1870 Pa.	1871-1874			Failed, 1875
Mutual Reserve Life Insurance Company	1881 N.Y.	1881-1900			Assessment insurance sold as Mutual Reserve fund Life Association
Nashville Life Insurance Company	1867 Tenn.	1867-1875			Reinsured in Globe Mutual Life Insurance Co., 1876
Nashville Mutual Protection Company	1851 Tenn.				Failed, 1955

Appendix Table B1. (Continued).

Company	Incorporated	Assets, Income	Mortgages	Real Estate	Comments
National Capitol Life Insurance Company	1867 D.C.	1868-1872			Reinsured in Penn Mutual Life Insurance Co., 1873 (Capital, $150,000)
National Life and Health Insurance Company	1865 Mich.				Failed, 1866
National Life and Travelers' Insurance Company	1863 N.Y.	1865-1866			
National Life and Trust Company	1892 Conn.				Failed, 1896 (Capital, $100,000)
National Life and Trust	1899 Ia.	1899-1900			
National Life Insurance Company	1865 Ill.	1868-1874			Failed, 1874
National Life Insurance Company	N.J.				Failed, 1872
National Life Insurance Company	1863 N.Y.	1865-1872			Failed, 1873 (National Life and Limb Insurance Co.) (Capital, $150,000)
National Life Insurance Company	1848 Vt.	1850-1900	1874-1900	1892-1900	

Appendix Table B1. (Continued).

Company	Incor-porated	Assets, Income	Mort-gages	Real Estate	Comments
National Life Insurance Company of the U.S.A.	1868 D.C.	1868-1900	1874-1900	1879-1900	Principal office located in Chicago during later years.
National Safety and Trust Company	1841 Pa.				Reinsured in Aetna, 1852 (Equitable Life and Trust)
National Union Life and Limb Insurance Company	1863 N.Y.	1864			Named National Life Insurance Co. (N.Y.), 1865
Natural Premium Life Society	La.				Failed, 1890 (No information, an Assessment Co.?)
New England Mutual Life Insurance Company	1835	1844-	1874-	1874-	Not active until 1843
New Hampshire Life Insurance Company	1883 N.H.				
New Jersey Mutual Life Insurance Company	1863 N.J.	1865-1875			Failed, 1877 (Capital, $100,000)
New York Insurance Company	1798 N.Y.				Withdrew 1803
New York Life Insurance and Trust Company	1830 N.Y.	1843-1874			Withdrew, 1874 (previously inactive for several years)

Appendix Table B1. (Continued).

Company	Incor-porated	Assets, Income	Mort-gages	Real Estate	Comments
New York Life Insurance Company	1841 N.Y.	1845–1900	1874–1900	1874–1900	
New York Mechanics Life Insurance Company	1812 N.Y.				Failed, 1813
New York State Life Insurance Company	1866 N.Y.	1866–1871			Reinsured in Guardian Life Insurance Co., 1872 (Capital, $120,000)
North America Life Insurance Company	1862 N.Y.	1862–			Failed, 1875
North America Life Insurance Company	1860 Pa.	1869–1875			Reinsured in Penn Mutual Life Insurance, Co., 1875
North American Mutual Life and Health Insurance Company	1849 Pa.				Also called Spring Garden Life Insurance Co.
North Carolina Mutual Life Insurance Company	1849 N.C.				Failed, 1862
North Carolina State Life Insurance Company	1872 N.C.	1873–1881			Reinsured in Life Insurance Co. of Virginia, 1882
Northeastern Life Insurance Company	1892 N.H.	1892–1893			Retired, 1894 (Capital, $25,000)

Appendix Table B1. (Continued).

Company	Incorporated	Assets, Income	Mortgages	Real Estate	Comments
North Pacific Mutual Life Association	1874 Ore.				
Northern Central Life Insurance Company	1899 O.	1900			Commenced business, 1900
Northwestern Life and Savings Company	1896 Ia.	1896-1900			(Capital, $100,000)
Northwestern Mutual Life Insurance Company	Ill.				Failed, 1865
Northwestern Mutual Life Insurance Company	1857 Wis.	1859-1900	1874-1900	1874-1900	
Ocean Mutual Marine and Life Insurance Company	1835 La.				Withdrew, 1840
Odd Fellows Life and Trust Company	1840 Pa.				Failed, 1857
Ohio Life and Trust Company	1834 O.				Failed, 1857
Ohio Life Insurance Company	1874 O.	1874			Failed, 1875
Pacific Mutual Life Company	1867 Cal.	1868-1900			

Appendix Table B1. (Continued).

Company	Incorporated	Assets, Income	Mortgages	Real Estate	Comments
Peabody Life Insurance Company	N.Y.				Reinsured in Farmers and Mechanics Life, 1872
Penninsular Mutual Life Insurance Company	1862 Mich.				Failed, 1866
Penn Mutual Life Insurance Company	1847 Pa.	1848-1900	1874-1900	1874-1900	
Pennsylvania Company for Insurance on Lives	1812 Pa.	1843-1900			Inactive in obtaining new business after 1872
Pennsylvania Life Insurance Company	1848 Pa.				Failed, 1850
Peoples Industrial Insurance Company	1887 Conn.	1888-1892			Reinsured in Metropolitan Life Insurance Co., 1893 (Capital, $100,000)
Peoples Life Insurance Company	1895 N.Y.				Voluntary liquidation, 1895 (No policies ever issued)
Philadelphia Life Insurance Company	1848 Pa.				Retired, 1852
Phoenix Life Insurance Company	1849 No.				Reinsured in New York Life Insurance Co., 1895

Appendix Table B1. (Continued).

Company	Incorporated	Assets, Income	Mortgages 1874–1900	Real Estate 1874–1900	Comments
Phoenix Mutual Life Insurance Company	1851 Conn.	1852–1900	1874–1900	1874–1900	First called American Temperance Life Insurance Company
Piedmont and Arlington Life Insurance Company	1862 Va.	1862–1879			Failed, 1880 (Capital, $200,000)
Policyholders' Life and Tontine Insurance Company	S.C.				Reinsured in Life Association of America, 1873
Pottsville Life and Trust Company	1863				Retired, 1870
Presbyterian Ministers Fund	1759 Pa.	1875–1900			Called Presbyterian Annuity, 1877–1892 (assets small)
Protection Life Insurance Company	1867 Ill.	1871–1876			Failed, 1877 (Commenced business, 1871)
Protection Insurance Company	1833 Miss.				Retired, 1835
Providence Life Insurance Company	1889	1899–1900			Industrial business only, prior to 1899
Provident Fund and Life Insurance Company	1867 N.Y.	1867			Retired, 1868 (Capital, 1867)

Appendix Table B1. (Continued).

Company	Incorporated	Assets, Income	Mortgages	Real Estate	Comments
Provident Life and Investment Company	1865 Ill.				Reinsured in Eagle Life Insurance Co. (Ill.), 1867
Provident Life and Trust Company	1865 Pa.	1865-1900	1874-1900	1874-1900	
Provident Life Insurance Company	Minn.				Retired, 1887
Provident Life Insurance Company	1889 W.Va.	1889-1899			
Provident Mutual Life Insurance Company	S.C.				Failed, 1870
Provident Savings Life Assurance Society of N.Y.	1875 N.Y.	1875-1900	1875-1900	1875-1900	
Prudential Insurance Company of America	1877 N.J.	1876-1900	1874-1900	1874-1900	Widows and Orphans Friendly Society, 1873 Prudential Friendly Society, 1875
Putnam Life Insurance Company	1871 Conn.	1871			Withdrew, 1872
Railway Passengers Assurance Company	1865 Conn.				Not included; a casualty insurance company

Appendix Table B1. (Continued).

Company	Incorporated	Assets, Income	Mortgages	Real Estate	Comments
Register Life and Annuity Insurance Company	1889 Ia.	1889-1900			
Republic Life Insurance Company	1869 Ill.	1870-1874			Failed, 1875 (Capital, $947,000)
Reserve Life Insurance Company	1871 N.Y.	1871			Reinsured in Guardian 1872; Mutual Protection to 1868 (Capital $136,260)
Reserve Loan Company	1897 Ind.				Assessment only, before 1900
Royal Union Life Insurance Company	1886 Ia.	1886-1900			
Safety Deposit Life Insurance Company	1869 Ill.	1870-1874			Reinsured in Mutual Life Insurance Co. (Ill.), 1879
St. Louis Life Insurance Company	1873 Mo.	1873-1874			Reinsured in Columbia, 1875 (Was Mound City Life to 1873)
St. Louis Mutual Life Insurance Company	1857 Mo.				Data appears as German Mutual (1853, Mo.)
St. Louis Mutual Life Insurance Company	1868 MO.	1869-1872			Reinsured in Mound City Life Insurance Co., 1873

Appendix Table Bl. (Continued).

Company	Incorporated	Assets, Income	Mortgages	Real Estate	Comments
Security Life Insurance and Annuity Company	1862 N.Y.	1862-1875			Failed, 1876 (Capital, $110,000)
Security Mutual Life Insurance Company	Neb.				
Security Mutual Life Insurance Company	1886 N.Y.	1887-1900		1887-1900	Mostly assessment business prior to 1899
Security Trust and Life Insurance Company	1871 Pa.	1895-1900			Commenced business, 1895
South Atlantic Life Insurance Company	1900 Va.	1900			
Southern Industrial Insurance Company	La.				Amalgomated with American Life and Accident (above), 1895 (Capital, $100,000)
Southern Life and Trust Company	1836 Ala.				Retired, 1841
Southern Life Insurance Company	1866 Tenn.				Failed, 1876
Southern Mutual Life and Trust Company	Ala.				Reinsured in New York Life Insurance Co., 1869

Appendix Table B1. (Continued).

Company	Incor-porated	Assets, Income	Mort-gages	Real Estate	Comments
Southern Mutual Life Insurance Company	1847 Ga.				Reinsured in Southern Mutual Life (S.C.), 1856
Southern Mutual Life Insurance Company	1866 Ky.	1866-1890			Name changed to Mutual of Kentucky (above), 1890
Southern Mutual Life Insurance Company	1850 La.				Reinsured in United States Life and Trust Co., 1853
Southern Mutual Life Insurance Company	1854 S.C.				Failed, 1868
Southwestern Life Insurance Company	1875 Tex.				
Southwestern Mutual Life Insurance Company	1a.	1897	1897		
Spring Garden Life Insurance Company	1849 Pa.				Reinsured in New York Life, 1853 (see N. America)
Standard Life and Accident Insurance Company	1884 Va.				No record of Life policies issued prior to 1901
Standard Life Insurance Company	1867 N.Y.	1867-1870			Reinsured in Gov't Security Life Insurance Co., 1871 (Capital, $125,000)

Appendix Table B1 (Continued).

Company	Incorporated	Assets, Income	Mortgages	Real Estate	Comments
Star Life Insurance Company	W.Va.				Reinsured in Provident Life Insurance Co., 1899
State Life Insurance Company	1894 Ind.	1897-1900			Assessment company; reincorporated "Legal Reserve" 1897.
State Life Insurance Company	1860 Pa.	1895			Withdrew (Life), 1896 (commenced Life business, 1895) (Capital, $100,000)
State Mutual Life Insurance Company	1844 Mass.	1846-1900	1874-1900	1874-1900	
Sun Life Insurance Company of America	1890 Ky.	1890-1900			
Sun of America Life Insurance Company	1900 Ind.	1900			
Susquehanna Mutual Life Insurance Company	1854 Pa.				Reinsured in American Life Insurance Co. (Pa.) 1856
Teutonia Life Insurance Company	1869 Ill.	1870-1875			Failed, 1876 (Capital, $200,000)
Texas Life Insurance Company	1896 Tex.				

Appendix Table B1. (Continued).

Company	Incorporated	Assets, Income	Mortgages	Real Estate	Comments
Texas Mutual Life Insurance Company	1870 Tex.				Reinsured in Alabama Gold Life Insurance Co., 1875
Toledo Mutual Life Insurance Company	1872 O.	1873-1882			Retired, 1883 (Capital, $120,000)
Travelers Insurance Co.	1863 Conn.	1866-1900	1874-1900	1874-1900	Commenced Life business 1866
Trenton Mutual Life Insurance Company	1847 N.J.	1849-1850			Failed, 1852
Union Assurance Company	1818 N.Y.				Failed, 1840
Union Central Life Insurance Company	1867 O.	1867-1900	1874-1900	1874-1900	
Union Life Insurance Company	1885 Neb.	1891-1898			Reinsured in Royal Union 1899 (Assessment, 1885-1890
Union Mutual Life Insurance Company	1848 Me.	1850-1900	1874-1900	1874-1900	Commenced business, 1849
United Fire, Life and Marines Insurance Company	Ky.				Failed, 1870
United Insurance Company	1798 N.Y.				Retired, 1801

Appendix Table Bl. (Continued).

Company	Incor- porated	Assets, Income	Mort- gages	Real Estate	Comments
United Security Life Insurance and Trust Co.	1868 Oa.	1868– 1870			Reinsured in Penn Mutual Life Insurance Co., 1871 (Capital, $100,000)
United States Annuity and Life Insurance Company	1850 Conn.				Failed, 1851
United States Industrial Insurance Company	1888 N.J.	1888– 1896			Risks reinsured in Metro- politan Life Insurance Co., 1897
United States Life and Trust Company	1850 Pa.	1850– 1861			Failed, 1862
United States Life Insurance Company					Failed, 1888
United States Life Insurance Company	1850 N.Y.	1850– 1900	1874– 1900	1874– 1900	
United States Mutual Life Casualty Company	N.J.				Failed, 1869
Universal Life Insurance Company	1863 N.Y.	1864– 1876			Failed, 1877 (Capital, $200,000)
Vermont Life Insurance Company	1868 Vt.	1868– 1899			Reinsured in Metropoli- tan Life Insurance Co., 1900 (Capital, $100,000)

Appendix Table B1. (Continued).

Company	Incorporated	Assets, Income	Mortgages	Real Estate	Comments
Washington Life Insurance Company	1860 N.Y.	1860-1900	1874-1900	1874-1900	
Western and Southern Life Insurance Company	1888 O.	1888-1900			
Western Life Insurance Company	O.				Reinsured in Cincinnati Mutual Life Insurance Co., 1869
Western Mutual Life Insurance Company	Mo.				Reinsured in Commonwealth Life Insurance, 1869
Western Mutual Life Insurance Company	1879 N.Y.	1879			Failed, 1881 (Capital, $125,000)
Western New York Life Insurance Company	1868 N.Y.	1868-1878			Name changed to Western Mutual Life Insurance Co., 1879
Widows and Orphans Benefit Life Insurance Co.	1864 N.Y.	1864-1871			Reinsured in Mutual Protection Life Assurance Co., 1871 (Capital, $200,000)
Widows and Orphans Fund Life Insurance Company	1867 Tenn.	1868-1873			Failed, 1876 (No record of new business after 1873)

385

Appendix Table B1. (Continued).

Company	Incor-porated	Assets, Income	Mort-gages	Real Estate	Comments
Widows and Orphans Life Insurance Company	Mo.				Reinsured in Life Association of America, 1868
Wilmington Life Insurance Company	Del.				Reinsured in Life Insurance Company of Virginia, 1868
Wisconsin Life Insurance Company	1895 Wis.				
Wisconsin Mutual Life Insurance Company	1862 Wis.				
World Mutual Life Insurance Company	1866 N.Y.	1866–1873			Failed, 1873

APPENDIX C

LEGAL REQUIREMENTS

APPENDIX C

LEGAL REQUIREMENTS

Presented in this section are specific legal requirements
made of the Life Insurance Industry during the period being
considered. In many cases these have been mentioned only
generally in the text of the study. They are collected
here for purposes of more specific reference. Some requirements cited as they appeared in the original documents.
Many others were taken from digests of the law and are
presented only in part to reduce the use of the lengthy
rhetoric of many legal provisions.

Extracts from general laws of the states are presented
first, than the extracts from the charters of some of the
major companies.

General Laws

Since 1900 the states, companies, and insurance industry organizations have made progress toward eliminating some of the worrisome, and essentially useless, differences between the regulations of the various states. However, anyone surveying the following sections completely may be inclined to a moment of sympathy for the thought expressed before the Armstrong Committee by John F. Dryden, President of Prudential:

> "...one of the great evils of the business today is the multiplicity of laws; Massachusetts has one set; New York has another set; New Jersey has a different set; California has still another set, and Louisiana a different one from any of them; and the result of it is that the companies do not know and cannot know from time to time what requirements are expected of them, or with what rules and regulations and laws they must comply. We have in a very recent date noted litigation in one of our States upon the interpretation of a statute which had been in force I think for twenty-five years, certainly for a long time, and upon which a certain interpretation had been given and followed. But a new commissioner comes into office; he reads that law differently, and he puts a new interpretation upon that law, and he requires the company to comply with his interpretation. The result of it is the companies, at great expense and trouble, must go to the Courts for the interpretation of a law which has been upon the statute books for many years...."(1)

Many of the provisions of the laws of the various states have been extracted hereafter with the hope of presenting a brief sketch of the major provisions and changes in the investment and tax laws of each as related to life insurance. No note has been made if a provision, previously mentioned, persists in succeeding years without significant change. Many extracts will be cited as having come from official publi-

---

(1) New York State, Armstrong Report..., VI, 4995-4996.

cations.   Other have come from digests in the <u>Spectator</u>.(2)

---

(2) The Spectator Company, <u>Insurance Yearbook</u> (New York: The
Spectator Company, 1874-1900, yearly editions).

Alabama

"...The company (shall)...be possessed of at least one Hundred
Thousand dollars of actual capital, invested in stock of at least par
value, or in bonds or mortgages of real estate worth double the amount
for which the same is mortgaged.... The gross amount of premiums...
received shall be subject, in every county in which...an agent is established, to a tax of one per centum...."(3)

"Every life insurance company shall file with the Auditor...a statement...showing the gross amount of premiums received in this State...and
the amount invested in this State.... Also a reciprocal provision in
relation to taxes...."(4)

"...A tax of two percent per annum (on gross premiums)."(5)

"...A tax of one percent is imposed upon the amount of gross
premiums."(6)

Arizona

"Agents must submit a report of premium receipts...(and pay a tax of)
one and one-half percent on premium receipts."(7)

---

(3) Letter of M.A. Chisholm, Comptroller of Public Accounts, to the
New York Insurance Department, Montgomery, Alabama, September 27, 1867.

(4) Spectator, 1874, p. 178.

(5) Spectator, 1881, p. 65.

(6) Spectator, 1890, p. 34.

(7) Spectator, 1890, p. 34.

Arkansas

"...No laws in this State upon this instant save one act regarded and acted upon as obsolete..."(8)

"Every company shall make a report to the commissioner...showing the entire amount of premiums received in this state during the year...and pay ...a tax of 3 per centum upon such premiums..."(9)

"...A tax of 2-1/2 percent...."(10)

"...companies must have a subscribed capital of $100,000."(11)

California

"...Companies shall pay a 1 percent tax on gross premiums..."(12)

"...All taxes are collected under the reciprocal provisions of the statute..."(13)

"...Companies are required to have a cash capital of $200,000..."(14)

"...Reciprocal provisions ruled unconstitional..."(15)

---

(8) Letter of Robert White, Secretary of State of Arkansas, to the New York Insurance Department, June 15, 1867.

(9) Spectator, 1874, p. 180.

(10) Spectator, 1879, p. 60.

(11) Spectator, 1881, p. 65.

(12) State of California, Act of April 15, 1862.

(13) Spectator, 1874, p. 182.

(14) Spectator, 1881, p. 65.

(15) Spectator, 1890, p. 38.

Colorado

"...1 percent tax on gross receipts."(16)

"No joint stock life insurance company shall be permitted to do any business in this State unless it is possessed of an actual paid-up cash capital of not less than two Hundred Thousand dollars...(and pay a) 2 percent tax on the excess of premiums received over losses and ordinary expenses."(17)

Connecticut

"Whenever...any of the United States...taxes, (requires) deposits... statements, licenses, attorneys or other obligations...the same...shall be imposed upon all similar insurance companies doing business in this State... incorporated by...such other State..."

"Every agent shall make a return...of the gross amount of premiums... and the amount of tax due thereon under the provisions of the reciprocal law (2 percent of gross premiums), and shall pay the same...to the State Treasurer."(19)

"No loan or investment shall be made by any life insurance company of this state without the unanimous approval of its finance or executive committee, or the approval of a majority of the directors of such company present at any meeting of such directors, and the name of every director

---

(16) Spectator, 1879, p. 60.

(17) Spectator, 18885, pp. 31-32.

(18) New York State, "Insurance Laws of other States" (Albany: Scrapbook Kept by the New York Insurance Department, 1868).

(19) Spectator, 1874, p. 185.

approving or disapproving any loan or investment so made shall be entered upon the records of the company."(20)

"No portion of the capital, assets, or income of any life insurance company of this State shall be used in the purchase of the stocks or bonds of any mining or manufacturing company in any event, nor in the purchase of the stocks or bonds of any other private corporation upon which last-mentioned stocks a regular dividend shall have been passed or upon which last-mentioned bonds a regular interest payment shall have been defaulted at any time within three years prior to such investment; provided, that no investment shall be made by said companies in any of the stocks or bonds last above referred to, which have not been issued for the space of three years prior to such investment, or which have not a market value equal to the par value thereof, unless the written approval by the Insurance Commissioner of such investment shall first have been obtained. And no loan shall be made by any such company upon the security of the stock of any mining company. And no loan shall be made by any such company upon the security of the stock of any manufacturing company unless the same shall be accompanied by the individual guarantee of some responsible party or parties, or by other collateral security of equal value to the amount of the sum loaned."(21)

Delaware

"We have no special enactment in this state in relation to insurance

---

(20) State of Connecticut, "An Act Relating To Insurance Companies", Article III, Passed, January, 1879.

(21) State of Connecticut, Acts of 1881, Chap. 17, Sec. 2.

companies except the acts incorporating such specific company..."(22)

"Every agent...shall furnish the State Treasurer a statement under oath, showing the amount of premiums received...within the State...and shall pay a tax of 2-1/2 percent upon the amount of such premiums...."(23)

"Companies must have $150,000 capital over all liabilities....and must pay a tax of 3-1/2 percent on gross premiums..."(24)

"A tax of 2-1/2 percent is imposed upon gross premiums..."(25)

"Companies are required to pay a tax of 1-1/2 percent on gross premiums ...."(26)

District of Columbia

"A tax of 1 percent upon gross receipts...."(27)

"...No company...shall transact the business of insurance...unless the whole capital of such company be not less than $100,000."(28)

Florida

"Every company must possess one Hundred Thousand dollars in United States bonds, or other bankable interest-bearing stocks of the United States

---

(22) Letter of State of Delaware Executive Department to the New York Insurance Department, Dover, Delaware, March 14, 1868.

(23) Spectator, 1874, p. 185.

(24) Spectator, 1881, p. 65.

(25) Spectator, 1886, p. 35.

(26) Spectator, 1900, p. 40.

(27) Spectator, 1879, p. 60.

(28) Spectator, 1890, p. 43.

at their market value, or in mortgages on unencumbered real estate worth

double the amount loaned thereon..."(29)

"A State tax is imposed of $200 on each company..."(30)

"Each company is required to pay an annual tax of two percent on gross

premiums..."(31)

Georgia

"Every company...must make a written return...to the Comptroller

General...showing the total amount of premiums received in the State, and

pay...a tax of 1 percent thereon. Also reciprocal provision in reference

to taxes."(32)

"A minimum capital and deposit of $100,000 is required...."(33)

"Life companies must have $100,000 invested in bonds and stocks, or

in mortgages, worth twice the amount loaned..."(34)

Idaho

"...A company must possess actual assets of at least $100,000 properly

invested...and deposited."(35)

Illinois

"Every company...must show an actual capital of at least $100,000

invested in stocks, bonds, and mortgages...worth double the amount loaned

---

(29) Spectator, 1874, p. 186.

(30) Spectator, 1882, p. 67.

(31) Spectator, 1900, p. 41.

(32) Spectator, 1874, p. 187.

(33) Spectator, 1880, p. 66.

(34) Spectator, 1882, p. 67.

(35) Spectator, 1892, p. 41.

thereon... Every agent... shall return to the Assessor of the county...the amount of gross receipts of such agency, which shall be entered on the tax list of the proper county, and subject to the same rate of taxation..."(36)

"...A reciprocal provision in reference to taxes...."(37)

Indiana

"...No company incorporated by any other state...shall transact any business of insurance in this State, unless such company is possessed of at least $100,000 of actual capital, invested in the stocks and bonds of some one or more of the States of this Union, or of the United States...or in bonds or mortgages of real estate worth double the amount for which the same is mortgaged, and free from any prior encumberance..."(38)

"Every company shall...report to the Auditor...the gross amount of premiums received in the State and shall...pay the State Treasurer the sum of $3,000 for every one hundred dollars of such premiums, less losses actually paid within the State."(39)

"Each company must possess an actual cash capital of not less than $200,000 invested in United States or State securities, or in mortgages on unencumbered real estate worth twice the amount loaned thereon."(40)

"No company organized under the provision of this act shall invest its funds in any other manner than as follows: In bonds of the United

---

(36) Letter of O.H. Miner, Auditor of Public Accounts, to the New York Insurance Department, Springfield, Illinois, August 21, 1865.

(37) *Spectator*, 1874, p. 190.

(38) State of Indiana, "An Act Regulating Foreign Insurance Companies," Approved, December 21, 1865.

(39) *Spectator*, 1874, p. 191.

(40) *Spectator*, 1885, p. 39.

States; in bonds of this State or of any other State, if at or above par; in bonds and mortgages on unincumbered real estate within this State, or any other State in which said company is transacting an insurance business, worth at least double the amount loaned thereon, and the value of such real estate shall be determined by a valuation made under oath by two freeholders of the county where the real estate is located (if buildings are considered as part of the value of such real estate, they must be insured for the benefit of the mortgagee); in bonds or other evidence of indebtedness, bearing interest, of any county, incorporated city, town or school district, within this State, or any other State in which said company is transacting an insurance business, where such bonds or other evidences of indebtedness are issued by authority of law, and upon which interest has never been defaulted; in loans upon the pledge of stick, bonds or mortgages of par value, if the current value of such stock, bonds or mortgages is at least twenty-five percent more than the amount loaned thereon; and in loans upon its own policies, provided that the amount so loaned shall not exceed the reserve against said policy at the time such loan is made."

"No company organized under this act shall be permitted to purchase, hold, or convey real estate, except for the purpose and in the manner herein set forth:

1. For the erection and maintenance of buildings at least ample and adequate for the transaction of its own business.

2. Such as shall have been mortgaged to it in good faith by way of security loans, for money due; or

3. Such as shall have been conveyed to it in satisfaction of debts previously contracted in the course of its dealings; or

4. Such as shall have been purchased at sales upon judgments, decrees, or mortgages obtained or made for such debts, and no company incorporated as aforesaid shall purchase, hold, or convey real estate in any other cases or for any other purposes.(41)

Iowa

"(The company must possess)...an actual capital stock of at least one hundred thousand dollars, invested in stocks of at least par value, or in bonds on mortgages on real estate, worth double the amount for which the same is mortgaged...Stocks in bonds or other corporations shall be proven by the certificate of a Commissioner of the State of Iowa...."(42)

"A tax of 2-1/2 percent on gross premiums..."(43)

Kansas

"It shall not be lawful for any life insurance company organized or incorporated under the laws of the United States, or of any other state of the United States, to transact in this state any business unless $100,000 of the capital or assets of such company be invested in treasury notes or stocks of the United States, or in bonds of the State of Kansas, or of the state under the laws of which such company is incorporated, or loaned on notes or bonds secured by mortgages or deeds of trust on unincumbered real estate worth at least double the amount loaned thereon; nor unless securities of the kind or kinds aforesaid, to the actual value of $100,000, shall have

---

(41)   State of Indiana, "Engrossed Senate Act No. 33, Sec. 22, Approved, February 10, 1899.

(42) Letter of J.A. Elliott, State Auditor of Iowa, to the New York Insurance Department, Des Moines, Iowa, April 15, 1868.

(43) Spectator, 1879, p. 60.

been deposited for the security of its policy-holders with the superintendent or commissioner of insurance, or chief financial officer of the state,
and under or by the laws of the state in which such company is incorporated;
of if such company is incorporated under the laws of the United States,
with some financial officer of the United States: Provided, That any
such company not having such deposit made in the state in which it is
organized, or with some officer of the United States, may make such deposit in this state in the manner and subject to the provisions set forth
in the forty-ninth section of this act."

"No insurance company of any kind, organized under the laws of this
state, shall directly or indirectly deal or trade in any goods, wares,
merchandise or other commodities whatsoever, except as provided in this
act."

"No life insurance company organized under the laws of this state
shall be permitted to purchase, hold or convey real estate, excepting for
the purposes and in the manner herein set forth, to wit:

1. Such as shall be requisite and convenient for its accommodation
in the transaction of its business; or,

2. Such as shall have been mortgaged in good faith by way of security
for loans previously contracted for moneys due; or,

3. Such as shall have been conveyed to it in satisfaction of debts
previously contracted in the course of its dealings; or

4. Such as shall have been purchased at sales upon the judgments,
decrees or mortgages obtained or made for such debts."(44)

----

(44) State of Kansas, Insurance Laws of Kansas, 1874 (Topeka: State
Printer, 1874), Sections 61, 70, 71.

Kentucky

"...Companies must possess...and deposit...an actual capital of at least one hundred and fifty thousand dollars....A tax of five dollars upon each one hundred dollars of the premiums received or agreed to be received within the State...."(45)

"Every company must possess well-invested assets to the amount of one hundred thousand dollars...The State agent or manager of every life company...shall...return to the Auditor a correct statement under oath of all premiums received...in this state...(and) pay into the State treasury... a tax of $2.50 upon all such premiums received in cash."(46)

Louisiana

"...From...every insurance company incorporated by the laws of this State...$500 shall be collected as license...from...every insurance company not incorporated by the laws of this State...$1,000...."(47)

"Every company shall pay...an annual tax of 1 percent upon the gross amount of premiums earned each year from policies issued through agencies in this state.(48)

"Graduated tax scale based upon amounts of premiums...."(49)

---

(45) Letter of William T. Samuels, State Auditor of Kentucky, to the New York Insurance Department, Frankfort, Kentucky, March 3, 1865.

(46) Spectator, 1874, pp. 198-99.

(47) Letter of J.H. Hardy, Secretary of State of Louisiana, to the New York Insurance Department, New Orleans, September 1, 1867.

(48) Spectator, 1874, p. 200.

(49) Spectator, 1887, p. 45.

Maine

"...Annual filing of the condition of business (is required)...."(50)

"No insurance company shall be incorporated in this state with a capital of less than $100,000 to be paid in at periods and in the proportions required by the charter.."

"The capital and other assets of insurance companies incorporated in this state, except such as may be needed for immediate use, shall be invested in the funded debt or bonds of the United States, or any of the New England States, or in the bonds or securities of county, city or other municipal corporations of said New England States, or in the purchase of real estate in fee, or loans on mortgage of real estate, or deposit in savings banks in said states, or in the bonds or stocks of incorporated companies of said states of an undoubted character for credit, insurance company stock or bonds excepted, and in no case shall any such funds be loaned on the security of names alone. (Amd. 1873)"(51)

"Every life insurance company or association, organized under the laws of the state, in lieu of all other taxation, shall be taxed as follows: First, its real estate shall be taxed by the municipality in which such real estate is situated, in the same manner as other real estate is taxed therein. Second, it shall pay a tax of 2 percent upon all premiums, whether in cash or notes absolutely payable, received from residents of this state during the year preceding the assessment, as hereinafter provided, first deducting therefrom all dividends paid to policy holders in this

---

(50) State of Maine, Insurance Law of 1859, Chapter 67, Sec. 1.

(51) State of Maine, Revised Statutes of the State of Maine, 1880, Chapter 49, Sec. 7.

state on account of said premiums. Third, it shall pay a tax of 1/2 of 1 percent per annum on its surplus, computed according to the laws of this state, after deducting the value of its real estate in this state, as fixed in determining such surplus, said surplus to be determined by the insurance commissioner, and his certificate therof to the state treasurer to be final."(52)

"The capital and other assets of stock insurance companies, incorporated in this state, except such as may be needed for immediate use, shall be invested in such manner and in such funds, stocks and bonds, as it is provided savings banks of this state may invest in, as provided in chapter 47, Section 100, of the revised statues of this state and acts additional and amendatory thereto, and said insurance companies shall be restricted in their investments in the same manner as are the savings banks of this state."(53)

Maryland

"Every company...must file an annual statement..."(54)

"Every company must possess well-invested assets to the amount of $100,000...The agents of every company are required to report under oath the amounts of gross premiums received in the State each license year, and, if a tax of 1-1/2 percent upon such premiums exceeds the amount of

---

(52) State of Maine, "An Act Providing For Taxation of Life Insurance Companies", Approved March 5, 1885.

(53) State of Maine, An Act to Ammend Chapter 49 of the Revised Statutes", Public Laws Relating to Insurance, Chapter 187, Sec. 8.

(54) State of Maryland, Code of Public General Laws, "Domestic Insurance Company", Passed, 1868.

the license tax, such excess shall be paid into the State Treasury....
Reciprocal provision in reference to taxes..."(55)

Massachusetts

"Acts 1836, c.207: An Act relating to Insurance Companies. Authorizing
Companies to invest such part of their capital as may be for their interest,
in the stock of any corporation established in this State, whose corporate
property consists entirely of real estate, or in the funded debt of any
city or town in this State."

"Acts 1847, c. 192: An Act to cause the several Insurance Companies
to make Annual Returns. Under the provisions of this act each Insurance
Company having a specific capital was required to make annual returns to
the Secretary of the Commonwealth, instead of the Treasurer as before..."

"Acts 1838, c. 35: An Act concerning Insurance Companies. Under
the provisions of this act Insurance Companies were permitted to invest
one-third of their capital in the stocks of railroad companies incorporated
within this Commonwealth, but not more than one-fifth of said capital in
the stock of any one railroad corporation, other conditions of such investment substantially corresponding with those now in force."

"Acts 1845, c. 55: An Act concerning Insurance Companies. Any
Insurance Company is authorized by this act to invest one-third of its
capital in the stock of railroad corporations incorporated in this Commonwealth..."

"Under the provisions of chapter 231 of the Acts of 1852, the
Secretary, Treasurer and Auditor of the Commonwealth were constituted a
Board of Insurance Commissioners, and were charged with the performance

---

(55) Spectator, 1874, p. 203.

of certain limited duties. The codified statute of 1854, chapter 453, already referred to, continued the same Board with substantially the same official service; but the Act of 1855,...abolished that Board, and provided for the appointment of a new board of three Commissioners, delegating to them the administration of a regularly organized Insurance Department. The last-named Act was approved March 31, 1855..."

"Acts 1864, c. 29: An Act relating to the Investment of the Capital and Funds of Insurance Companies. Authorizing investments in the stock of banking-houses organized under acts of the United States."(56)

"Every company must possess available cash funds to the amount of $100,000....Life companies are taxed 2-1/2 percent under provisions of reciprocal statute.(57)

Michigan

"...All companies doing business in this State...must state...the amount of premiums received...and pay...a specific tax of 1 percent on the gross amount of all premiums...(Companies must have)...invested in stocks of some one or more of the States of this Union or of the United States, the amount of $100,000...."(58)

"Every company...shall file a statement of the gross amount of premiums received in this State, during the proceding year, with the State treasury, and shall pay a tax of 3 percent thereon..."(59)

---

(56) Clarke, pp. 19-55.

(57) Spectator, 1874, p. 206.

(58) State of Michigan, The Laws of 1867, Act #54, Sec. 9.

(59) Spectator, 1874, p. 209.

Minnesota

"...Life insurance companies organized under the laws of any other State shall (be possessed of) $100,000 in United States or State bonds or other bankable, interest-bearing stocks of the United States...or in mortgages on unencumbered real estate worth double the amount loaned thereon ...."(60)

"...A tax of 2 percent upon all premiums collected within the State during the year...Reciprocal provisions..."(61)

Mississippi

"...(Provided) the company is possessed of at least one hundred fifty thousand dollars of actual capital, invested in stocks of at least par value, or in bonds or mortgages of real estate worth double the amount for which the same is mortgaged..."(62)

"...A tax on privileges shall be levied as follows, to wit: in each insurance company doing business in this State, $1,000..."(63)

Missouri

"Every company must have on deposit with the proper officer of the State where it is incorporated, $100,000 in stocks and bonds of the

---

(60) State of Minnesota, "Laws of the State of Minnesota Regulating Foreign and Domestic Insurance Companies", Approved, January 31, 1867, Sec. 2.

(61) Spectator, 1874, p. 211.

(62) Letter of Thomas T. Swann, Auditor of the State of Mississippi, to the New York Insurance Department, Jackson, Mississippi, November 13, 1865.

(63) Spectator, 1874, p. 213.

United States, or of the State where it is incorporated, or of this State,
or loaned on bonds or notes secured by mortgages of unemcumbered real
estate, worth double the amount loaned..."(64)

"A sworn return of premiums must be made to Superintendent....upon
deducting losses 1 percent tax must be paid...Reciprocial Legislation.."(65)

Montana

"Each insurance company transacting business in the Territory shall
be taxed upon the excess of premiums received over losses and ordinary
expenses incurred within the territory...at the same rate that all other
personal property is taxed..."(66)

"...Each company must possess not less than $200,000 capital.."(67)

Nebraska

"...(Insurance companies of other States must be) possessed of at
least $100,000 of actual capital, invested in stocks of at least par value,
or in bonds or mortgages on real estate worth double the amount for which
the same is mortgaged...(The company shall) file a statement...showing the
amount of premiums received in this State...and shall deposit in this
State, in such manners as the Auditor of the State shall dictate, 5 percent
of the amount received in money...."(68)

---

(64) Spectator, 1874, p. 214.

(65) Spectator, 1882, p. 70.

(66) Spectator, 1885, p. 54.

(67) Spectator, 1890, p. 65.

(68) Letter of John Gillespie, State Auditor of the State of Nebraska,
to the New York Insurance Department, 1868.

"Receipts on net premiums are taxed at the same rate as other property. Reciprocal legislation..."(69)

Nevada

"...The agent shall pay to the Treasury of the county or city and county in which his agency is located a tax...1 percent on the amount of premiums collected from life risks.."(70)

"Companies of other States...are required to have a paid-up capital of not less than $200,000...Mutual life companies possessing $1,000,000 or more assets, are exempt from the requirements regarding capital."(71)

New Hampshire

"Every insurance company organized under the laws of any other State.. shall be subject, in this State to the same taxes, fines, penalties, deposits of money or securities...as are in such other State imposed on any insurance company organized under the laws of this State..."(72)

"Every company shall possess assets to the amount of $100,000.... Every company shall...make to the commissioner a statement...showing the gross amount of premiums received in the State...(and pay) a tax of one per cent upon such premiums..."(73)

"Each company must have available assets valued at not less than $200,000..."(74)

----

(69) Spectator, 1879, p. 60.

(70) Spectator, 1874, p. 219.

(71) Spectator, 1882, p. 70

(72) Letter of J.D. Lyman, Secretary of State of New Hampshire, to the New York Insurance Department, Concord, New Hampshire, December 27, 1867.

(73) Spectator, 1874, p. 220.

(74) Spectator, 1885, p. 57.

New Jersey

"A tax, for the use of this State at 3 percent upon the gross amount that shall be received...for premiums...(1846)."

"...All life insurance companies organized under the laws of other States or foreign governments...(shall) deposit with the Secretary of State of this State the sum of $50,000...in public stocks of the United States of this State, or stocks or bonds of the incorporated cities of this State...or in bonds and mortgages on unencumbered, improved real estate within this State, and worth at least 50 percent more than the amount of the mortgage thereon...(1852)."

"...Companies of those states imposing larger taxe_ or assessments than the foregoing...shall pay...a tax of 2 percentum per annum on the whole amount of premiums taken or received...during the yrar..."(75)

New Mexico

"Each company must possess a paid-up capital of not less than $300,000, exclusive of any deposits made in other States or Territories.... Every insurance company...shall be taxed upon the excess of premiums received over losses and ordinary expense incurred...at the same rate that all other personal property is taxed...Reciprocal legislation..."(76)

New York

"Life insurance companies of other States making such applications must be possessed of an actual capital of $100,000, being the amount of

---

(75) Letter of Whitfield S. Johnson, Secretary of State of New Jersey, to the New York Insurance Department, Trenton, New Jersey, January 4, 1866.

(76) Spectator, 1885, p. 58.

capital required of similar companies in this State formed under the provisions of the general Act, passed June 24, 1853, entitled "An Act for
the Incorporation of Life and Health Insurance Companies, and in relation to
Agencies of such Companies;" and such capital must be deposited with the
Auditor, Comptroller, or chief financial officer of the State by whose
laws the Company is incorporated; and the Superintendent must be furnished
with the Certificate of such officer, under his hand and official seal,
stating that he, as such officer, holds in trust and on deposit for the
benefit of all the policyholders of such Company the security before
mentioned, giving the items thereof, and stating that he is satisfied
that they are worth $100,000. (See N.Y. Insurance Laws, pp. 84, 78, 79.)

Approved forms for this Certificate will be furnished by the
Department. The above capital should be invested in, and the deposit
with the Auditor, Comptroller or chief financial officer can be made only
in the following four classes of securities:

1. United States stocks or Treasury notes;
2. New York State stocks or Treasury notes;
3. The State stocks of the State in which the Company is located;
4. In bonds and mortgages on improved unincumbered real estate,
   situated within the State where the Company is located,
   worth 75 percent more than the amount loaned thereon, and
   good therefore for not more than 4/7 of the valuation,--

Or in such stocks and securities as now are, or hereafter may be,
receivable by the Bank Department of this State; this provision does not
under existing laws enlarge the above four classes."

"Accumulated funds of New York Companies can only be invested in or
loaned upon: (1) United States stocks or Treasury notes; (2) New York State
Stocks; (3) Bonds and Mortgages on unincumbered real estate in this
State for 2/3 its value; (4) Stocks of any incorporated city of this

State; and (5) Real estate under certain limitation."(77)

"Deposit of securities.--Every deposit made with the superintendent of insurance by any domestic or foreign insurance corporation, shall be in the stocks or bonds of the United States or of this state, not estimated above their current market value, or in the bonds of a county or incorporated city in this state, authorized to be issued by the legislature, not estimated above their par value nor their current market value, or in bonds and mortgages on improved, unincumbered real property in this state, worth fifty percentum more than the amount loaned thereon. If the value of such real property consists in part of buildings thereon, such buildings shall be kept insured for the benefit of the mortgagee in such sum as the superintendent of insurance shall approve. No one bond or mortgage so deposited shall be for a less sum than $5,000. The cash capital of every domestic insurance corporation required to have a capital, to the extent of the minimum capital required by law, shall be invested and kept invested in the kinds of securities in which deposits with the superintendent of insurance are required by this chapter to be made. The residue of the capital and the surplus money and funds of every domestic insurance corporation over and above its capital, and the deposit that it may be required to make with the superintendent, may be invested in or loaned on the pledge of any of the securities in which deposits are required to be invested or in the public stocks or bonds of any one of the United States, or except as herein provided, in the stocks, bonds or other

---

(77) New York State, <u>Annual Report</u>...(1865), pp. 604-605.

evidence of indebtedness of any solvent institution incorporated under the
laws of the United States or of any state thereof, or in such real estate
as it is authroized by this chapter to hold; but no such funds shall be
invested in or loaned on its own stock or the stock of any other insurance
corporation carrying on the same kind of insurance business. Any domestic
insurance corporation may, by the direction and consent of 2/3 of its
Board of Directors, managers or finance committee, invest, by loan or otherwise, any such surplus moneys or funds in the bonds issued by any city,
county, town, village or school district of this State, pursuant to any
law of this State. Any corporation organized under the ninth subdivision
of Section 70 of the insurance law, for guaranteeing the validity and
legality of bonds issued by any State, or by any city, county, town,
village, school district, municipality or other civil division of any
State, may invest by loan or otherwise any of such surplus moneys or funds
in the bonds which they are authorized to guarantee. Every such domestic
corporation doing business in other states of the United States or in
foreign countries, may invest the funds required to meet its obligation
incurred in such other states or foreign countries and in conformity to
the laws thereof, in the same kind of securities in such other states or
foreign countries that such corporation is by law allowed to invest in,
in this state. Any life insurance company may lend a sum not exceeding
the lawful reserve which it holds upon any policy, on the pledge to it of
such policy and its accumulations as collateral security. But nothing in
this section shall be held to authorize one insurance corporation to obtain
by purchase or otherwise, the control of any other insurance company."

"Reciprocal requirements.--If, by the existing or future laws of any state, an insurance corporation of this state having agencies in such other state or the agents thereof, shall be required to make any deposit of securities in such other state for the protection of policy holders or otherwise, or to make payment for taxes, fines, penalties, certificates of authority, license fees or otherwise, greater than the amount required by this chapter from similar corporations of such other state by the then existing laws of this state, then and in every case, all insurance corporations of such state, established or heretofore having established an agency or agencies in this state shall be and they are hereby required to make the like deposit for the like purposes in the insurance department of this state, and to pay the superintendent of insurance for taxes, fines, penalties, certificates of authority, license fees and otherwise, an amount equal to the amount of such charges and payments imposed by the laws of such other state upon the insurance corporations of this state and the agents thereof."(78)

North Carolina

"All insurance companies may carry on business in this State...upon paying...1 percent of their gross receipts, including premium notes...."(79)

"...Two percent on gross receipts...."(80)

---

(78) Andrew Hamilton, Statutory Revision of the Laws of New York Affecting Insurance Companies (Albany: Banksand Co., 1903), pp. 8-13

(79) Letter of K.T. Battle, Treasurer of the State of North Carolina, to the New York Insurance Department, Raleigh, North Carolina, June 12, 1867.

(80) Spectator, 1879, p. 60.

"...the agent...must make a sworn statement...giving amount of premiums received in this State...and pay a tax of 2 percent on such premiums...but if the company shall invest in mortgages of property situation in the State, to an amount equal to 1/2 of gross receipts, such tax shall be only 1 percent...."(81)

"General agents shall...make a sworn statement of the gross receipts obtained by them from residents of the State...and shall...pay to the Insurance Commissioner a tax of 2 percent upon such gross receipts. If, however, the agent can show that the company has invested in State, City, and county bonds, or property situated and taxed in the State in a sum equal to 1/4 of entire assets, then the tax shall be but 1 percent on such gross receipts; if 3/4, then 1/4 of 1 percent."(82)

North Dakota

"Each company...must have on deposit with the proper officer...$25,000... (and) pay a tax...of 1 percentum on all premiums received."(83)

"The company must possess available cash funds of not less than $200,000...At the time of filing the annual statement the company must pay to the Commissioner of Insurance a tax of 5 percent on the gross premiums received in the State during the year 1897 and 2-1/2 percent in subsequent years."(84)

Ohio

"...(The company) must show that the company is possessed of an available capital in money and securities...of not less than $150,000....(1866)."

---

(81) Spectator, 1882, p. 72.

(82) Spectator, 1900, p. 64.

(83) Spectator, 1886, p. 34.

(84) Spectator, 1890, p. 65.

"It shall be...lawful for any company organized under this act to invest its funds or accumulations in bonds and mortgages on unencumbered real estate within the State of Ohio, worth fifty percent more than the sum so loaned...or in stocks of national banks incorporated in the State of Ohio...or in stocks or treasury notes of the United States, stocks of this State, or bonds on any incorporated city of this State and to loan upon the same...or in railroads...."(85)

"The agent of every insurance company shall return...a statement of the gross amount of premiums received by him, which shall be entered on the tax list of the county, and be subject to the same rate of taxation as personal property...Reciprocal provision...."(86)

Oregon

"All companies...shall pay...$100...."(87)

"The company must possess $50,000 in United States or State bonds..."(88)

"The company must possess, paid up, unimpaired cash capital of at least $200,000...pay a tax of 2 percent upon gross receipts...and a statement showing receipts of premiums must be filed..."(89)

Pennsylvania

"...Any life insurance company...incorporated by any other State of

---

(85) Letter of James H. Godman, Auditor of the State of Ohio, to the New York Insurance Department, Columbus, Ohio, May 7, 1866.

(86) *Spectator*, 1874, p. 228.

(87) *Spectator*, 1874, p. 229.

(88) *Spectator*, 1880, p. 66.

(89) *Spectator*, 1900, p. 68.

the United States....(must be) possessed of cash assets, safely invested,
amounting to at least $200,000...Every insurance company licensed under...
this act, shall retain (and pay)...a sum equal to a tax of 3 percentum upon
the entire amount of...premiums or commissions...in money or notes...
Reciprocal legislation...."(90)

Rhode Island

"...(The Company shall) pay a tax of 2 percent on the amount of...
premiums and assessments...."(91)

"Every company must possess $100,000 dollars in good and safe stocks
or securities...Every agent shall...make return...of the amount of premiums
received and assessments collected during the same period, and shall at
the same time pay to the general treasurer a tax of 2 percent on the
amount of such....Reciprocal provision..."(92)

South Carolina

"Each company must deposit with the Comptroller General $50,000
par value of the bonds or stocks of this State, of the United States...
Each agent shall...return to the Auditor of the county...a sworn statement
of the gross receipts of such agency...and shall be charged with taxes on
the amount at the same rate as other property...."(93)

---

(90) State of Pennsylvania, "An act to Revise, Amend and Consolidate
the Several Laws Regulating Insurance Companies", Approved, April, 1868.

(91) State of Rhode Island, Revised Statutes of the State of Rhode
Island (1859), Chapter. 129, Sec. 12.

(92) Spectator, 1874, p. 232.

(93) Spectator, 1874, p. 234.

South Dakota

"Every insurance company...shall...pay into the State treasury, as taxes, 2-1/2 percent of the gross amount of premiums received....
Reciprocal legislation...."(94)

Tennessee

"...The company (must be possessed) of at least $100,000 of actual capital invested in stocks or at least par value, or in bonds or mortgages of real estate worth double the amount for which the same is mortgaged..."(95)

"A tax of 1-1/2 percent on gross premium receipts...Reciprocal Legislation..."(96)

"...2-1/2 percent..."(97)

Texas

"...We have no laws in this State relating...to insurance companies..."(98)

"Every life insurance company shall pay an annual tax of $500..."(99)

"...Life companies must have $100,000 of actual assets invested in any satisfactory securityies of the market value of $100,000...Life insurance companies must pay an annual tax of $300 and $10 in every county

(94) *Spectator*, 1890, p. 83.

(95) State of Tennessee, *Code of Tennessee*, Chapter III, Sec. 1498.

(96) *Spectator*, 1879, p. 60.

(97) *Spectator*, 1890, p. 83.

(98) Letter from the Office of the Secretary of State of Texas to the New York Insurance Department, Austin, Texas, June 23, 1867.

(99) *Spectator*, 1874, p. 236.

in which it has transactions...."(100)

"the company must possess at least $100,000, invested in State securities... deposited with the proper officer...Companies are required to pay a tax of 2 percent on gross premiums collected within the State..."(101)

Utah

"No specific life laws...."(102)

"Life companies are required to have a paid-up capital of not less than $100,000...."(103)

"...(A company must have) paid-up capital of not less than $200,000 except fraternal or mutual companies...(and pay a tax of) 1-1/2 percent on gross premiums collected..."(104)

Vermont

"...The company (must have) $100,000 actually paid in and invested... Reciprocal provision...."(105)

"Every company must possess at least $100,000 and in addition, assets equal to its liabilities...Reciprocal provision....ä tax of 2 percent upon

---

(100) Spectator, 1882, p. 74.

(101) Spectator, 1900, p. 75.

(102) Spectator, 1885, p. 69.

(103) Spectator, 1890, 86.

(104) Spectator, 1900, p. 75.

(105) State of Vermont, The Insurance Law of the State of Vermont (Montpelier: Printed at the Freeman Printing Establishment, 1868), Sec. 12.

premiums received in the State...."(106)

Virginia

"Every company shall certify...the gross amount of all premiums collected in this state, and shall immediately pay into the treasury of the state a tax of 1-1/2 percent thereon....Reciprocal provisions...."(107)

Washington

"A company....(must) make a deposit...of not less than $200,000 in the bonds of the United States, the bonds of this state, or the bonds of the state of New York or Massachusetts...."

"No company...shall purchase, hold or convey real estate except... first, such as shall be requisite for its convenient accommodation in the transaction of its business; or second, such as shall have been Mortgaged to it in good faith as security for loans previously contracted, or for money due, or, third, such as shall have been conveyed to it in satisfaction of debts previously contracted in its legitimate business; or, fourth, such as shall have been or may be purchased at sales upon judgements, decrees or mortgage foreclosures obtained or made for such debts...."(108)

"Every company doing business in the State must pay an annual tax of 2 percent on the gross amount of premiums collected...."(109)

---

(106) Spectator, 1900, p. 76.

(107) Spectator, 1874, p. 238.

(108) State of Washington, Annual Report of the Commisional of Insurance, 1890 (Seattle: State Printer, 1891), pp. 6, 9.

(109) Spectator, 1890, p. 88.

West Virginia

"Every company doing business in this state shall...pay...a tax of
3 percentum upon the gross amount of premiums collected in this State...
Every life insurance company which shall invest in this state the whole
amount of its net receipts from its business therein, shall pay only 1/3
of such tax...Reciprocal provisions...."(110)

Wisconsin

"The company (must be) possessed of at least $150,000 in value of
actual capital in cash, or invested in stocks or bonds, or mortgages on
real estate worth double the amount for which the same is mortgaged...(a
tax of)...3 percent upon the gross amount received in the State of
Wisconsin for premiums and interest...shall be paid...."(111)

"Every company must possess $100,000 invested in safe securities...
Reciprocal provisions for taxation...."(112)

Wyoming

"Each company must have a capital of not less than $300,000 fully
paid-up and properly invested....The excess of premiums collected in the
State over losses and ordinary expenses is liable to be taxed the same
as other property....(113)

"A tax of 2 percent upon gross premiums is exacted, and a report
of premiums collected must accompany the annual report...."(114)

---

(110) Spectator, 1874, p. 239.

(111) State of Wisconsin, "An Act to Regulate Insurance Companies Not
Incxorporated by the State of Wisconsin," April 16, 1867, Sec. 1, 5.

(112) Spectator, 1874, p. 240.

(113) Spectator, 1885, p. 73.

(114) Spectator, 1900, p. 79.

Charter Requirements

Upon making a thorough review of the codified insurance laws of the several states one might be inclined to think that he had obtained an understanding of the legal climate within which the various companies functioned. For many states this thought would be correct. For most companies chartered after the formation of distinct insurance departments within their parent state this would also be true. But, for numbers of the major companies of early origin, the thought would be decidedly incorrect.

Many companies of the class just mentioned were chartered by special acts of their respective legislatures. Many times the chartering acts contained specific provisions regarding investment policy, reporting, or other phases of the company's business which were taken to have precedence over some of the regulatory provisions later made generally binding upon all other companies by general statute.

For example, the New York Life Insurance and Trust Company, by virtue of the requirements of its 1831 charter provisions, continued to file annual statements and reports which were different from those required generally by the New York Insurance department for virtually every year through 1874. In that year it stopped reporting because of its inactivity. Its charter had specified the form of the firm's report and the agent to whom such report was to be made, and the formation of the Insurance Department in 1859 notwithstanding, the company continued to report as it had always done.

The American Life Insurance Company, or Pennsylvania, provides another illustration. The company was originally incorporated by

special legislative act April 9, 1850. The original act was relatively
restrictive in providing investment opportunities. Subsequent statutes
also made various provisions for the regulation of investment by life
insurance companies. But when the company, having a capital stock of
$1,000,000 and a large number of policies outstanding, failed because
of insolvency in 1873, the regulatory officials were reminded once
again of the matter of charter provisions. It seems that the company
had applied for relief from the provisions of the original charter and
had obtained a supplemental act. This act, approved in April of 1857
had virtually removed the company officers from regulation in the
matter of investments.

> "It shall be lawful for said company to invest any part of their
> capital stock, money, funds or other property in any public
> stocks, or any funded debt created or to be created, by or
> under any laws of this or any other state, or of the United
> States; the same to sell, transfer or exchange at pleasure,
> and again to invest the same, or any part thereof, in such stocks
> or funds or otherwise, whenever and as often as said company may
> deem it expedient; or they may loan the same to individuals
> or corporations, on real or personal security, or deposit
> the same with any banking or savings institution, with or
> without interest, for such time and on such terms and under
> such restrictions as the directors of said company, for the
> time being, shall deem most expedient."[1]

The foregoing examples are only a few of many that could be
extracted from the early charter provisions and given individual treatment. While such an approach might prove to be quite entertaining
it could also be inordinately lengthy. Alternatively, extracts have

---

[1] American Life Insurance Company, The, "Charter" (Philadelphia:
The American Life Insurance Company, 1850).

been drawn from many of the original and ammended charters of the
early companies and will be quoted here directly but without individual
comment. It is hoped that this procedure will permit various special
provisions related to investment regulation to be presented as compactly
as possible.

For convenience, other charter provisions which may have materially
altered the character of a company's business are also included.

Most of the Charters cited herein may be found in the Spectator
compilation. Earlier versions, together with by-laws, are compiled in
the New York Insurance Report, 1868.

Aetna:[2]

"...are empowered to purchase,...lands, tenements, rents, hereditaments, goods, chattels, and effects of every kind, and nature; as
also United States stocks, and bank stock of the United States Bank,
or any bank in the United States,...". (p. 5, Sec .1, approved May 5, 1819)

"Upon the petition of the Aetna Insurance Company, praying for
such an alteration of its charter as will constitute the shareholders
of the annuity fund of said company,...a distinct corporation for the
purpose of life insurance, and the assumption of life risks, as per
memorial on file dated May 9th, A.D. 1853,..." (approved May 28, 1853)

Bankers Life Insurance Company of the City of New York:

"shall have power to invest all surplus funds of the company in
such securities, mortgages, or other investments, as, in its discretion,
it may deem proper." (By-Laws Sec. 12, March 24, 1864)

Berkshire Life Insurance Company:

"The funds of the said corporation shall be invested in such
purchases and loans as are permitted to savings banks, in the seventy-
eighth and seventy-ninth sections of the thirty-sixth chapter of the
Revised Statutes, and in the forty-fourth chapter of the Acts of the
year one thousand eight hundred and forty-one. The said company may
hold real estate to the amount of ten thousand dollars, for the purpose
of securing suitable offices for the institution." (Sec. 5, 1851)

---

[2] Spectator Company, The, Charters of American Life Insurance
Companies charters (New York: The Spectator Company, 1906), P. 5. The remaining
is of from pp. 10-366.

The Berkshire Life Insurance Company is hereby authorized to purchase and hold real estate to an amount not exceeding seventy-five thousand dollars; provided, that no part of said amount shall be invested in real estate except in the purchase of a suitable site and the erection or preparation of suitable buildings to be used wholly or in part for the purpose of said company; and all income, if any, arising from such real estate, shall be devoted exclusively to the interests of said company. (ammendment, 1866)

Connecticut General Life Insurance Company:

"...are empowered to purchase, have, hold and enjoy lands, tenements, hereditaments, chattels, stocks, choses in act on, and effects of every kind, and the same to sell, grant, demise, alien and convey,..." (1865)

"The capital stock, acquired moneys and personal estate of said corporation may be invested at the discretion of the directors in loans upon real estate on bonds and mortgages, and loans upon or purchase of United States note and bonds, bank stocks or bonds issued by States or by municipal or other corporations, or may be loaned upon endorsed promisory notes not having more than twelve months to run; and the same may be called in and reinvested under the provisions of this act..." (Sec. 11, 1865)

The Connecticut Mutual Life Insurance Company:

"...to purchase, hold and convey any estate, real or personal, for the use of said corporation; ... provided, the real estate so holden be only such as shall be necessary for the purpose of erecting buildings thereon, in which to meet and transact the business of said corporation, or such as shall have been bonafide mortgaged to it by way of security, or conveyed in satisfaction of debts contracted in the course of its business, or taken in execution on judgements or decrees, which shall have been obtained for such debts or for other cause." (Sec. 7, 1846)

"...That it shall be lawful for said corporation to loan their funds and moneys, or any part thereof, upon bond and mortgage of encumbered real estate (but the same at the time shall be worth at least double the amount loaned thereon), and upon State stocks and bank stocks (such stocks to be worth twenty-five per cent above the amount loaned thereon), and upon State stocks and bank stocks (such stocks to be worth twenty-five per cent above the amount loaned thereon at the time,) and may call in and reinvest the same at pleasure, under the provisions of this section." (Sec. 7, 1846)

"That the corporation may take the promissory notes or other obligations of the insured in part or for the whole of the premium of insurance at the discretion of said company. (Sec. 9, 1846)

"That the company may receive notes or other securities for premiums in advance from persons intending to receive its policies, for which such persons may be allowed a sum not exceeding six per cent per annum..." (Sec. 13, 1846)

"...It is the business of said company to invest said funds as allowed by law, and to hold all real estate, wherever situate, which shall have been, or shall hereafter be, obtained in compliance with the provisions of the first section of the charter of said company; and all such investments in and acquisitions of real estate are declared to be necessary, suitable, and proper for carrying forward the chartered purposes of said corporation." (ammendment, 1881)

"That the Connecticut Mutual Life Insurance Company shall have the power to invest, in addition to the powers of investment in real estate granted in their charter and ammendments, a sum not exceeding five per centum of their assets in productive real estate outside of this State." (ammendment, 1881)

Des Moines Life Insurance Company:

"All funds of the company which may be invested shall stand in the name of the Des Moines Life Insurance Company in such investments as are permitted by the law of the State of Iowa, and no investment shall be taken in the name of any individual as an officer of the company. (Sec. 1, 1900)

Equitable Life Insurance Company of Iowa:

"The funds of the corporation, however arising shall be invested as directed by the board of trustees, subject, however, to the limitations and provisions of the laws of the State of Iowa." (art. 11, 1867)

Federal Life Insurance Company:

"The real estate which it shall be lawful for this company to purchase, hold and convey, shall be: 1. Such as shall be necessary for its accomodation in the convenient transaction of its business. 2. Such as shall have been mortgaged to it in good faith by way of security for loans previously contracted, or for money due. 3. Such as shall have been conveyed to it in satisfaction, either in whole or in part, of debts previously contracted in the regular course of business. 4. Such as shall have been purchased at sales upon judgments, decrees or mortgages obtained or made for such debts." (1900)

The Hartford Life Insurance Company:

"Said company may from time to time invest, collect and reinvest the whole or any portion of its capital and assets, in any bonds or stocks of the United States, or of any of the States of the United States, or of any corporations which are or may be created under authority of the United States or of any of said States; or in notes or bonds, secured by mortgage or real estate or otherwise; as shall be approved by the directors and in conformity with the Charter and by-laws of said company." (Sec. 5, 1867)

The Life Insurance Company of Virginia:

"That it shall be lawful for said corporation to purchase, hold and convey real estate as follows:
First. Such as shall be requisite for its immediate accomodation in the convenient transaction of its business; or, Second. Such as shall have been mortgaged to it in good faith, by way of security, for loans previously contracted, for moneys due; or, Third. Such as shall have been purchased at sales upon judgements, degrees, or mortgages, obtained or made for such debt; or, Fourth. Such as shall have been conveyed to it in satisfaction of debts previously contracted in the course of its dealings..." (Sec. 8, 1871)

"...the premium reserve or reinsurance fund shall be invested in or loaned out upon the following securities and no other: First. The real estate as herein described. Second. Bonds or negotiable paper, secured by mortgage or deeds of trust on unencumbered real estate, worth, in each case, at least double the amount loaned. Third. Stocks of the United States of America. Fourth. Stocks of the several States, and of incorporated cities therein. Fifth. Bonds of any incorporated company." (Sec. 9, 1871)

"...And it shall also be lawful for said company to improve, exchange for other property real or personal or otherwise use or dispose of said real estate, or any part or parcels thereof, and all such real estate as shall not be necessary for the accommodation of said company in the convenient transaction of its business shall be sold and disposed of within twenty years after the said company shall have acquired title to the same, and it shall not be lawful for the said company to hold such real estate for a longer period than that above mentioned... Obligations secured by his company's policy contracts in force (may also be held)." (Sec. 8, ammendments, 1894)

Maryland Life Insurance Company of Baltimore:

"...and be it enacted, That the said guarantee capital stock shall be invested in the securities of the United States, the State of Maryland, or of the city of Baltimore, either one or all of said securities, and the same deposited with the treasurer of this State as a guarantee for the payment of the policies of insurance issued by said company. And the said company, from time to time as they shall deem proper, may sell and dispose of said securities, and exchange and re-deposit the same with the said treasurer under such rules and regulations for said exchange and redeposit as said treasurer shall direct, the said company confining the said business of sale disposition and exchange of said securities to either or all of said securities, above named in this section, the interest and profits accruing and made on said securities, and the sale or exchange thereof, to be collected by and paid over to said company." (Sec. 4, 1864)

Massachusetts Mutual Life Insurance Company:

"The funds of the said corporation shall be invested in such

purchases and loans as are permitted to savings banks, in the seventy-
eighth and seventy-ninth sections of the thirty-sixth chapter of the
revised statutes, and in the forty-fourth chapter of the acts of the
year one thousand eight hundred and forty-one. The said company may
hold real estate to an amount not exceeding ten thousand dollars,
for the purpose of securing suitable offices for the institution.
(Sec. 5, 1851)

"The Massachusetts Mutual Life Insurance Company is hereby authorized to hold real estate in the city of Springfield, to an amount not
exceeding in cost forty thousand dollars, in addition to the amount of
the thousand dollars now authorized to be held by them." (Sec. 1, 1864)

"...It may make,...investments in bonds, stocks, mortgages, and
other securities, and it may sell,... (Sec. 13, ammendment, 1866)

Mutual Benefit Life Insurance Company:

"...Mutual Benefit Life Insurance Company, shall be in law capable
of purchasing, holding and conveying any estate, real or personal for
the use of said corporation; provided, the lands, tenements, and
hereditaments, which it shall be lawful for the said corporation to hold,
be only such as shall be requisite for the purpose of erecting buildings
thereon, in which to meet and transact the business of the corporation,
or such as shall have been bonafide mortgaged to it by way of security,
or conveyed to it in satisfaction of debts previously contracted in the
course of its business, or purchased as sales on judgements or decrees,
which shall have obtained for such debts;..." (1845)

Mutual Life Insurance Company in New York:

"The real estate which it shall be lawful for the said corporation
to purchase, hold and convey, shall be: 1. Such as shall be requisite
for its immediate accommodation in the convenient transaction of its
business; or, 2. Such as shall have been mortgaged to it in good faith
by way of security for loans previously contracted, or for moneys due;
or, 3. Such as shall have been conveyed to it in satisfaction of debts
previously contracted in the course of its dealings; or, 4. Such as
shall have been purchased at sales upon judgements, decrees or mortgages
obtained or made for such debts.
The said corporations shall not purchase, hold or convey real
estate in any other case, or for any other purpose, ..." (Sec. 2, 1842)

"The whole of the premium received for insurance by said corporation,
except as provided for in the following sections, shall be invested in
bonds and mortgages on unincumbered real estate within the State of
New York; the real property to secure such investment of capital shall,
in every case, be worth twice the amount loaned thereon." (Sec. 10,
1842)

"The trustees shall have power to invest a certain portion of the
premiums received, not to exceed one half thereof, in public stocks of
the United States or of this state, or of any incorporated city in this
State." (p. 176, Sec. 11, 1842)

National Life Insurance Company:

"All the funds, capital or stock of the said corporation, not
required for immediate use in the payment of losses and contingent
expenses, shall be safely and permanently invested, either in the
stock of the United States, or in the public State stocks of any State
of the union, or in bonds and mortgages of improved and unencumbered
real estate within the State of Vermont, or the value of fifty percent
more than the sum invested or loaned or for which stock shall be issued
in exchange." (Sec. 6, 1848)

"...in addition to the securities in which they are now allowed to
invest the assets of said company, shall be allowed to invest said
assets in city stocks, or bonds, and mortgages on unencumbered real
estate beyond the limits of this State, worth fifty per cent more than
the sums loaned; and said assets except real estate, shall not be liable
to taxation so long as the known and contingent liabilities of said
company shall exceed its assets." (ammendment, 1852)

New York Life Insurance Company:

"The company shall be authorized to make loans and investments
as provided by the insurance law and by the statutes of the State of
New York now in force or hereafter passed, and may also loan all
premiums received and invest the same in bonds and mortgages or unencumbered real estate within the State of New York worth fifty percent
more than the sum charged thereon, and in all stocks created by or
under the laws of this State or of the United States. (art. 7, Sec. 1,
ammendment, 1893)

The Northwestern Mutual Life Insurance Company:

"...The real estate which it shall be lawful for this corporation
to purchase, hold, possess and convey shall be: 1. Such as shall be
requisite for its immediate accommodation in the convenient transaction
of its business. 2. Such as shall have been mortgaged to it in good
faith, by way of security, for loans previously contracted, or for money
due. 3. Such as shall have been conveyed to it, in satisfaction of
debts previously contracted in the course of its dealings. 4. Such
as shall have been purchased at sales upon judgements, decrees or
mortgages obtained or made for such debts."
    "The said corporation shall not purchase, hold or convey real
estate in any other case,..." (Sec. 3, 1857)

It shall be lawful for siad corporation to invest the said premiums
in the securities designated in the two following sections... Sec. 10.
Real Estate Investments. The whole of the premiums received for
insurance by said corporation, except as provided for in the following
section, shall be invested in bonds secured by mortgages, or unencumbered
real estate within this State. The real estate or other property to
secure such investment of capital, shall in every case, be worth twice
the amount loaned thereon." (Sec. 9, 1857)

"The trustee shall have power to invest a certain portion of the premiums received not to exceed one half thereof in public stocks of the United States, or of this State, or of any incorporated city of this State." (p. 219, Sec. 11, 1857)

"...the said act is hereby so ammended as to read as follows, vis.: "Sec. 10. The whole of the premiums received for insurance by said corporation, except as provided for in the following section, shall be invested in bonds secured by mortgages on unencumbered real estates. The real estate or property to secure such investment or capital, shall in every case be worth twice the amount loaned thereon." (Sec. 10, ammendment, 1863)

"...said act is hereby so ammended as to read as follows, viz., Sec. 11. The trustees shall have power to invest a certain portion of the premiums received, not to exceed one-half thereof, in public stocks of the United States or of any incorporated city of this State, and the company may loan to policyholders in said company, from time to time, sums not exceeding one-half of the annual premiums on their policies, upon notes to be secured by the policy of the person to whom the loans may be made." (Sec. 4, ammendment, 1863)

"Unless said corporation shall procure a certificate from the Commissioner of Insurance of this State that it will suffer materially from a forced sale thereof, in which event the sale may be postponed for such period as such Commissioner may therein directly provide, that whenever any real estate occupied by said corporation in the transaction of its business shall no longer be required for that purpose, by reason of the occupation of other real estate for the same purpose, or for any other cause, such real estate shall be sold within ten years after the time it shall cease to be so occupied,..." (ammendment, 1885)

The Penn Mutual Life Insurance Company:

(Real Estate provisions as above for Northwestern except Sec. 4 reads:) "Such as shall be purchased at sales upon judgements, decrees or mortgages obtained or made for debts due said company or for debts due other persons where said company have liens or encumbrances on the same and the purchase is deemed necessary to save the company from loss on the liens or encumbrances held by it. The said corporation shall not purchase, receive, hold or convey real estate in any other case..." (Sec. 3, 1847)

"It shall also be lawful for the said corporation to loan or invest, not exceeding twenty-five per cent of their funds, in loans or stocks of any incorporated city or borough or other good securities and the same to sell..." (Sec. 12, 1847)

"It shall be lawful for the said corporation to invest their premiums, profits and capital in bonds and mortgages, ground rents, stocks and loans of the United States and State of Pennsylvania and to sell, transfer and change the same, and reinvest the funds of the said corporation, when the trustees shall deem it expedient." (Sec. 11, 1847)

"That it shall be lawful for the said corporation to invest their
premiums, profits and capital in bonds and mortgages, ground rents, stocks
and loans of the United States and State of Pennsylvania, and also in
all stocks created by or under the laws of the United States or of this
State or of any of the other States of the Union, and to lend the
same upon the security of such stocks and to sell, transfer and change
the same and to invest the funds of said corporation when the trustees
shall deem the same expedient." (Sec. 3, ammendment, 1851)

"That it shall also be lawful for the said corporation to lend
or invest not exceeding fifty per cent of their funds in loans or
stocks of an incorporated city, district or borough or other good
securities and the same to sell,..." (Sec. 4, ammendment, 1851)

Phoenix Mutual Life Insurance Company: (American Temperance Life Insurance Company):

"That the capital stock of said corporation shall be invested
either in loans upon bond and mortgages upon real estate, or in United
States stocks, or any sound stocks created by any State of this Union,
or any incorporated city of this State; provided, that said corporation
may loan or invest twenty-five per cent of its capital upon and in
endorsed promisory notes, not having more than twelve months to run."
(Sec. 13, 1851)

"...to invest its funds as allowed by law, and to hold all
real estate wherever situate, shich shall have been, or shall hereinafter be, obtained in compliance with the provisions of its charter,
and all such investments in and acquisitions or real estate are
declared to be necessary, suitable, and proper for carrying forward the
chartered purposes of said corporation." (Sec. 13, 1851)

Presbyterian Ministers Fund:

"...to take, have, hold, receive and enjoy, and to transmit to their
successors, lands, tenements, rents and hereditaments to the value of
one thousand pounds sterling..." (1759)

(1759, called: "The corporation for Relief or Poor and Distressed
Presbyterian Ministers and of the Poor and Distressed Widows and
Children of Presbyterian Ministers," in 1856, changed to: "The
Presbyterian Annuity Company" in 1875 changed to"The presbyterian Annuity
and Life Insurance Company," in 1889 changed to: "Presbyterian
Ministers Fund.")

Provident Life and Trust Company of Philadelphia:

"That it shall and may be lawful for said companies to employ
and invest their capital stock and other moneys of said companies in
bonds and mortgages on real estate, in respondentia or bottomry bonds,
ground rents, stocks or loans of the United States and State of
Pennsylvania, and in stocks or loans of any borough, city or institution
incorporated by the laws of this State, and in other good securities,

and to sell and transfer the same, and to reinvest the proceeds of such
sale or transfer in other such loans, stocks or securities; and the
real estate which it shall be lawful for said company to purchase,
receive, hold and convey, shall be

1. Such as shall be requisite for its immediate accommodation in
the convenient transaction of business.

2. Such as shall have been mortgaged to it in good faith, by way
of security for loans previously contracted, or for moneys due.

3. Such as shall have been conveyed to it in satisfaction of
debts previously contracted in the course of its dealings.

4. Such as shall be purchased at sales upon judgments, decrees or
mortgages obtained or made for debts due said company, or for debts
due other persons where said company may have liens or incumbrances
on the same, and the purchase is deemed necessary to save the company
from loss; provided, that no real estate acquired by the coproration,
except that necessary for the transaction of business, shall be
retained by said corporation for a longer period than five years."
(Sec. 9, 1865)

Prudential Insurance Company of America (The "Widow's and Orphan's
Friendly Society," To 1875; the "Prudential Friendly Society, to
1877):

"It shall and may be lawful for the said corporation to purchase
and hold such real estate as may be necessary and convenient for the
transaction of its lawful business, and also to take and hold any
real estate or securities, mortgages or pledges to said company, either
at law or in equity, and also to purchase at sales made under judgments
or decrees at law or in equity, or in any other legal proceedings or
otherwise; to take and receive any real or personal estate in payment
or toward satisfaction of any debt previously contracted and due the
said company and to hold the same until it can be conveniently sold or
converted into money, and for the purposes of investing any part of
their capital stock, funds, or money. The said company may purchase and
hold, sell and convey, any bonds or public stock issued or created by
this State, or by any of the incorporated cities or townships of this
State, or by the United States, or by the States of New York, Massachusetts or Connecticut, or may invest the same in bonds secured by mortgages on unincumbered real estate within this State, worth double the
sum invested or loaned." (Sec. 8, 1877)

State Mutual Life Insurance (Assurance) Company:

"The funds of the said company shall be invested in the stocks of
the United States, of the State of Massachusetts, of the city of Boston,
and in notes secured by bond and mortgage of unincumbered real estate
in Massachusetts, worth three times the amount loaned thereon. The said
company may hold real estate to an amount not exceeding ten thousand
dollars, for the purpose of securing suitable offices for the
institution." (Sec. 4, 1844)

"The State Mutual Life Assurance Company of Worcester may invest their funds in such purchases and loans as are permitted to savings banks in the seventy-eighth and seventy-ninth sections of the thirty-sixth chapter of the revised statutes and in the forty-fourth chapter of the acts of the year eighteen hundred and forty-one." (ammendment, 1846)

"The State Mutual Life Assurance Company in the city of Worcester is hereby authorized to purchase and hold real estate in said city, to an amount not exceeding fifty thousand dollars; provided, that no part of said amount shall be invested in real estate, except in the purchase of a suitable site, and the erection or preparation of suitable buildings, to be used, wholly or in part, for the purposes of said company; and all income, if any, arising from such real estate shall be devoted exclusively to the interests of said company."
(Sec. 1, ammendment, 1866)

Travelers Insurance Company:

"The capital stock, moneys and personal estate of said corporation may be invested, at the discretion of the directors, either in loans upon bonds and mortgages upon real estate, or in United States stocks, bank stocks, or stocks or bonds created by any State, or of corporations created by this State; and the same may be called in and reinvested at pleasure, under the provisions of this act;..." (Sec. 10, 1863)

"Said company shall have power to invest, in addition to the powers of investment in real estate granted in its charter and amendments, a sum not exceeding five per centum of its assets in productive real estate outside of this State." (ammendment, 1887)

Union Mutual Life Insurance Company:

"The directors shall at all times superintend the affairs, and manage the funds, property, and estate of the company; and shall invest the funds of the company in the name of the company; or they may invest them in the name of trustees, whenever they deem it necessary to do so in order to preserve and protect the interests of the company, and to secure a perfect title to property held as investments or as security for investments. But it shall not be lawful for them to loan any sum of money to any director or other officer of the company upon any security whatever." (Sec. 7, ammended, 1889)

Other companies whose charters were reviewed but found to be
without provisions of the sort noted above included:

    Equitable Life Assurance Society of the United States, The
    Fideltiy Mutual Life Insurance Company, The
    Franklin Life Insurance Company
    Germania Life Insurance Company, The
    Home Life Insurance Company
    Interstate Life Assurance Company of Indianapolis
    John Hancock Mutual Life Insurance Company
    Manhattan Life Insurance Company
    Metropolitan Life Insurance Company, The
    Michigan Mutual Life Insurance Company
    Minnesota Mutual Life Insurance Company
    National Life Insurance Company of the United States of America
    New England Mutual Life Insurance Company
    Pacific Mutual Insurance Company of California, The
    Provident Savings Life Assurance Society of New York
    Reliance Life Insurance Company of Pittsburg
    Security Mutual Life Insurance Company
    Security Trust and Life Insurance Company (Name as of 1896.
        Originally called: Germantown Deposit, Trust and Insurance
        Company; from 1889 to 1896 the company's name was: The
        Security Trust Company.)
    State Life Insurance Company of Indianapolis
    Union Central Life Insurance Company, The
    United States Life Insurance Company, The
    Washington Life Insurance Company, The
    Wisconsin Life Insurance Company

VITA

Bruce Michael Pritchett was born in American Fork, Utah on November 3, 1940, to Melrose Jed and Lois Watson Pritchett. He is a citizen of the United States. In May, 1959, he graduated from American Fork High School, American Fork, Utah. He married Patricia Louise Sunderland, daughter of Jarold Louis and Marvel Davis Sunderland, June 19, 1964. They have three children, Bruce Michael Junior, Laura, and Steven Louis. His undergraduate education was taken at Brigham Young University, Provo, Utah. He graduated in June, 1965, with a B.S. degree in economics. He received the M.S. and Ph.D. degrees in economics from Purdue University January 1 of 1967 and 1970 respectively.

Dr. Pritchett is currently employed by Brigham Young University as an Assistant Professor of Economics. During his last year as an undergraduate, Dr. Pritchett was a teaching assistant in basic economics. He also taught basic economics and macroeconomics, at the intermediate level, while a graduate instructor at Purdue University.

Dissertations in American Economic History

An Arno Press Collection

1977 Publications

Ankli, Robert Eugene. **Gross Farm Revenue in Pre-Civil War Illinois.** (Doctoral Dissertation, University of Illinois, 1969). 1977

Asher, Ephraim. **Relative Productivity, Factor-Intensity and Technology in the Manufacturing Sectors of the U.S. and the U.K. During the Nineteenth Century.** (Doctoral Dissertation, University of Rochester, 1969). 1977

Campbell, Carl. **Economic Growth, Capital Gains, and Income Distribution: 1897-1956.** (Doctoral Dissertation, University of California at Berkeley, 1964). 1977

Cederberg, Herbert R. **An Economic Analysis of English Settlement in North America, 1583-1635.** (Doctoral Dissertation, University of California at Berkeley, 1968). 1977

Dente, Leonard A. **Veblen's Theory of Social Change.** (Doctoral Dissertation, New York University, 1974). 1977

Dickey, George Edward. **Money, Prices and Growth;** The American Experience, 1869-1896. (Doctoral Dissertation, Northwestern University, 1968). 1977

Douty, Christopher Morris. **The Economics of Localized Disasters:** The 1906 San Francisco Catastrophe. (Doctoral Dissertation, Stanford University, 1969). 1977

Harper, Ann K. **The Location of the United States Steel Industry, 1879-1919.** (Doctoral Dissertation, Johns Hopkins University, 1976). 1977

Holt, Charles Frank. **The Role of State Government in the Nineteenth-Century American Economy, 1820-1902:** A Quantitative Study. (Doctoral Dissertation, Purdue University, 1970). 1977

Katz, Harold. **The Decline of Competition in the Automobile Industry, 1920-1940.** (Doctoral Dissertation, Columbia University, 1970). 1977

Lee, Susan Previant. **The Westward Movement of the Cotton Economy, 1840-1860:** Perceived Interests and Economic Realities. (Doctoral Dissertation, Columbia University, 1975). 1977

Legler, John Baxter. **Regional Distribution of Federal Receipts and Expenditures in the Nineteenth Century:** A Quantitative Study. (Doctoral Dissertation, Purdue University, 1967). 1977

Lightner, David L. **Labor on the Illinois Central Railroad, 1852-1900:** The Evolution of an Industrial Environment. (Doctoral Dissertation, Cornell University, 1969). 1977

MacMurray, Robert R. **Technological Change in the American Cotton Spinning Industry, 1790 to 1836.** (Doctoral Dissertation, University of Pennsylvania, 1970). 1977

Netschert, Bruce Carlton. **The Mineral Foreign Trade of the United States in the Twentieth Century:** A Study in Mineral Economics. (Doctoral Dissertation, Cornell University, 1949). 1977

Otenasek, Mildred. **Alexander Hamilton's Financial Policies.** (Doctoral Dissertation, Johns Hopkins University, 1939). 1977

Parks, Robert James. **European Origins of the Economic Ideas of Alexander Hamilton.** (M. A. Thesis, Michigan State University, 1963). 1977

Parsons, Burke Adrian. **British Trade Cycles and American Bank Credit:** Some Aspects of Economic Fluctuations in the United States, 1815-1840. (Doctoral Dissertation, University of Texas, 1958). 1977

Primack, Martin L. **Farm Formed Capital in American Agriculture, 1850-1910.** (Doctoral Dissertation, University of North Carolina, 1963). 1977

Pritchett, Bruce Michael. **A Study of Capital Mobilization, The Life Insurance Industry of the Nineteenth Century.** (Doctoral Dissertation, Purdue University, 1970). Revised Edition. 1977

Prosper, Peter A., Jr. **Concentration and the Rate of Change of Wages in the United States, 1950-1962.** (Doctoral Dissertation, Cornell University 1970). 1977

Schachter, Joseph. **Capital Value and Relative Wage Effects of Immigration into the United States, 1870-1930.** (Doctoral Dissertation, City University of New York, 1969). 1977

Schaefer, Donald Fred. **A Quantitative Description and Analysis of the Growth of the Pennsylvania Anthracite Coal Industry, 1820 to 1865.** (Doctoral Dissertation, University of North Carolina, 1967). 1977

Schmitz, Mark. **Economic Analysis of Antebellum Sugar Plantations in Louisiana.** (Doctoral Dissertation, University of North Carolina, 1974). 1977

Sharpless, John Burk, II. **City Growth in the United States, England and Wales, 1820-1861:** The Effects of Location, Size and Economic Structure on Inter-urban Variations in Demographic Growth. (Doctoral Dissertation, University of Michigan, 1975). 1977

Shields, Roger Elwood. **Economic Growth with Price Deflation, 1873-1896.** (Doctoral Dissertation, University of Virginia, 1969). 1977

Stettler, Henry Louis, III. **Growth and Fluctuations in the Ante-Bellum Textile Industry.** (Doctoral Dissertation, Purdue University, 1970). 1977

Sturm, James Lester. **Investing in the United States, 1798-1893:** Upper Wealth-Holders in a Market Economy. (Doctoral Dissertation, University of Wisconsin, 1969). 1977

Tenenbaum, Marcel. **(A Demographic Analysis of Interstate Labor Growth Rate Differentials;** United States, 1890-1900 to 1940-50. (Doctoral Dissertation, Columbia University, 1969). 1977

Thomas, Robert Paul. **An Analysis of the Pattern of Growth of the Automobile Industry:** 1895-1929. (Doctoral Dissertation, Northwestern University, 1965). 1977

Vickery, William Edward. **The Economics of the Negro Migration 1900-1960.** (Doctoral Dissertation, University of Chicago, 1969). 1977

Waters, Joseph Paul. **Technological Acceleration and the Great Depression.** (Doctoral Dissertation, Cornell University, 1971). 1977

Whartenby, Franklee Gilbert. **Land and Labor Productivity in United States Cotton Production, 1800-1840.** (Doctoral Dissertation, University of North Carolina, 1963). 1977

1975 Publications

Adams, Donald R., Jr. **Wage Rates in Philadelphia, 1790-1830.** (Doctoral Dissertation, University of Pennsylvania, 1967). 1975

Aldrich, Terry Mark. **Rates of Return on Investment in Technical Education in the Ante-Bellum American Economy.** (Doctoral Dissertation, The University of Texas at Austin, 1969). 1975

Anderson, Terry Lee. **The Economic Growth of Seventeenth Century New England:** A Measurement of Regional Income. (Doctoral Dissertation, University of Washington, 1972). 1975

Bean, Richard Nelson. **The British Trans-Atlantic Slave Trade, 1650-1775.** (Doctoral Dissertation, University of Washington, 1971). 1975

Brock, Leslie V. **The Currency of the American Colonies, 1700-1764:** A Study in Colonial Finance and Imperial Relations. (Doctoral Dissertation University of Michigan, 1941). 1975

Ellsworth, Lucius F. **Craft to National Industry in the Nineteenth Century:** A Case Study of the Transformation of the New York State Tanning Industry. (Doctoral Dissertation, University of Delaware, 1971). 1975

Fleisig, Heywood W. **Long Term Capital Flows and the Great Depression:** The Role of the United States, 1927-1933. (Doctoral Dissertation, Yale University, 1969). 1975

Foust, James D. **The Yeoman Farmer and Westward Expansion of U.S. Cotton Production.** (Doctoral Dissertation, University of North Carolina at Chapel Hill, 1968). 1975

Golden, James Reed. **Investment Behavior By United States Railroads, 1870-1914.** (Doctoral Thesis, Harvard University, 1971). 1975

Hill, Peter Jensen. **The Economic Impact of Immigration into the United States.** (Doctoral Dissertation, The University of Chicago, 1970). 1975

Klingaman, David C. **Colonial Virginia's Coastwise and Grain Trade.** (Doctoral Dissertation, University of Virginia, 1967). 1975

Lang, Edith Mae. **The Effects of Net Interregional Migration on Agricultural Income Growth:** The United States, 1850-1860. (Doctoral Thesis, The University of Rochester, 1971). 1975

Lindley, Lester G. **The Constitution Faces Technology:** The Relationship of the National Government to the Telegraph, 1866-1884. (Doctoral Thesis, Rice University, 1971). 1975

Lorant, John H[erman]. **The Role of Capital-Improving Innovations in American Manufacturing During the 1920's.** (Doctoral Thesis, Columbia University, 1966). 1975

Mishkin, David Joel. **The American Colonial Wine Industry:** An Economic Interpretation, Volumes I and II. (Doctoral Thesis, University of Illinois, 1966). 1975

Winkler, Donald R. **The Production of Human Capital:** A Study of Minority Achievement. (Doctoral Dissertation, University of California at Berkeley, 1972). 1977

Oates, Mary J. **The Role of the Cotton Textile Industry in the Economic Development of the American Southeast:** 1900-1940. (Doctoral Dissertation, Yale University, 1969). 1975

Passell, Peter. **Essays in the Economics of Nineteenth Century American Land Policy.** (Doctoral Dissertation, Yale University, 1970). 1975

Pope, Clayne L. **The Impact of the Ante-Bellum Tariff on Income Distribution.** (Doctoral Dissertation, The University of Chicago, 1972). 1975

Poulson, Barry Warren. **Value Added in Manufacturing, Mining, and Agriculture in the American Economy From 1809 To 1839.** (Doctoral Dissertation, The Ohio State University, 1965). 1975

Rockoff, Hugh. **The Free Banking Era: A Re-Examination.** (Doctoral Dissertation, The University of Chicago, 1972). 1975

Schumacher, Max George. **The Northern Farmer and His Markets During the Late Colonial Period.** (Doctoral Dissertation, University of California at Berkeley, 1948). 1975

Seagrave, Charles Edwin. **The Southern Negro Agricultural Worker:** 1850-1870. (Doctoral Dissertation, Stanford University, 1971). 1975

Solmon, Lewis C. **Capital Formation by Expenditures on Formal Education, 1880 and 1890.** (Doctoral Dissertation, The University of Chicago, 1968). 1975

Swan, Dale Evans. **The Structure and Profitability of the Antebellum Rice Industry:** 1859. (Doctoral Dissertation, University of North Carolina at Chapel Hill, 1972). 1975

Sylla, Richard Eugene. **The American Capital Market, 1846-1914:** A Study of the Effects of Public Policy on Economic Development. (Doctoral Thesis, Harvard University, 1968). 1975

Uselding, Paul John. **Studies in the Technological Development of the American Economy During the First Half of the Nineteenth Century.** (Doctoral Dissertation, Northwestern University, 1970). 1975

Walsh, William D[avid]. **The Diffusion of Technological Change in the Pennsylvania Pig Iron Industry, 1850-1870.** (Doctoral Dissertation, Yale University, 1967). 1975

Weiss, Thomas Joseph. **The Service Sector in the United States, 1839 Through 1899.** (Doctoral Thesis, University of North Carolina at Chapel Hill, 1967). 1975

Zevin, Robert Brooke. **The Growth of Manufacturing in Early Nineteenth Century New England.** 1975